AMERICAN ARTS AND CRAFTS TEXTILES

AMERICAN ARTS AND CRAFTS TEXTILES

Dianne Ayres Timothy Hansen Beth Ann McPherson Tommy Arthur McPherson II

Harry N. Abrams, Inc., Publishers

Editor: Elisa Urbanelli
Designer: Joseph Cho / Stefanie Lew, Binocular, New York

Library of Congress Cataloging-in-Publication Data
American arts and crafts textiles / Dianne Ayres . . . [et al.].
p. cm.
Includes index.
ISBN 0–8109–0434–9
1. Textile fabrics—United States—History. 2. Arts and crafts movement—United States—History. I. Ayres, Dianne.
NK8812.A47 2002
746'.0973'09034—dc21
2001006012

Published in 2002 by Harry N. Abrams, Incorporated, New York

Printed and bound in Italy
10 9 8 7 6 5 4 3 2 1

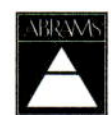

Harry N. Abrams, Inc.
100 Fifth Avenue
New York, N.Y. 10011
www.abramsbooks.com

Abrams is a subsidiary of

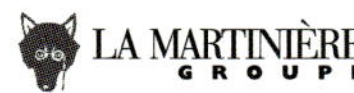

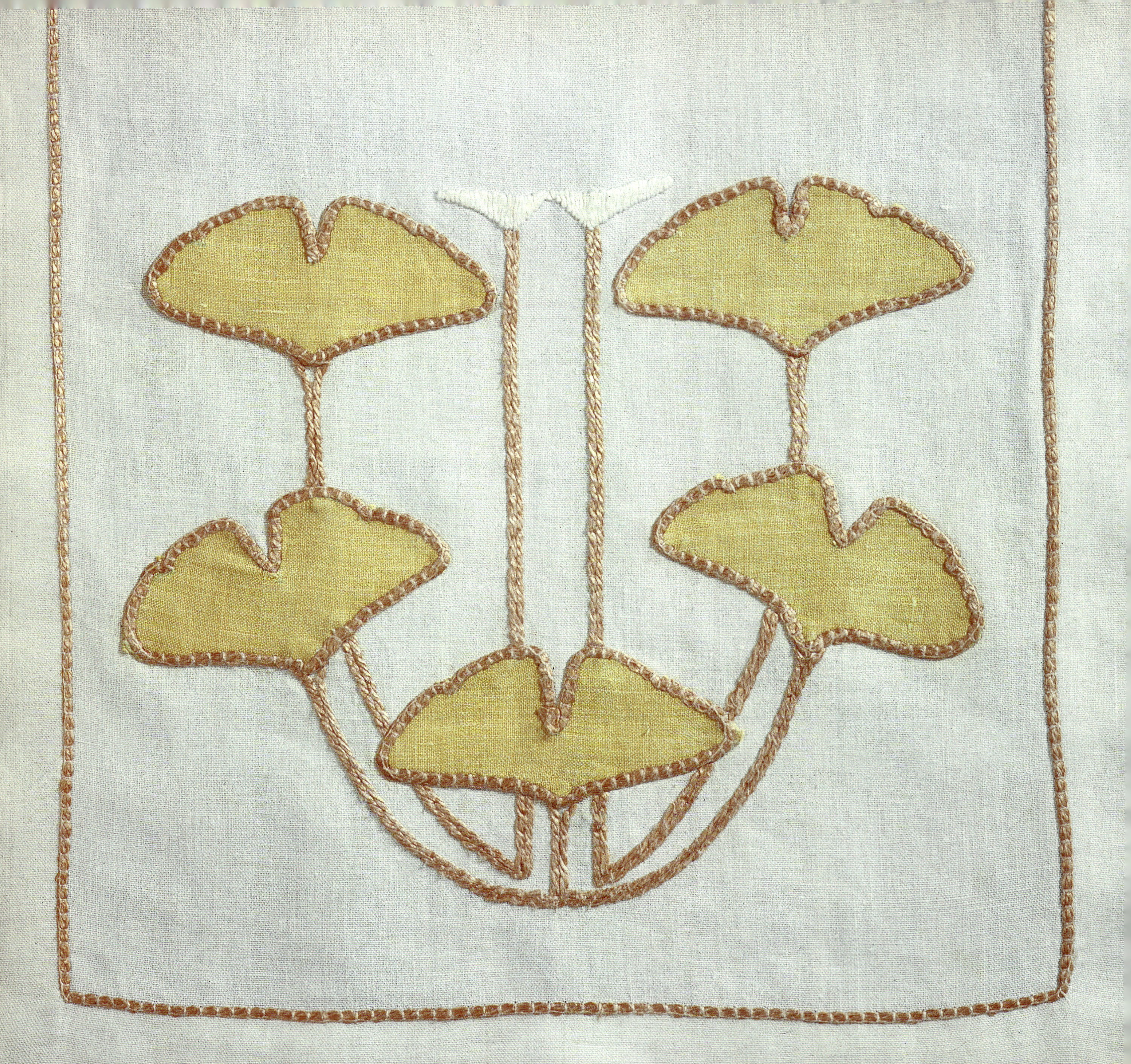

1 Inspiration and Evolution: The Development of American Arts and Crafts Textiles

Textiles embody the diversity, simplicity, and sometimes complexity of the Arts and Crafts lifestyle more clearly than any other material or medium. Art historians have long recognized that textiles convey developments and trends in style or ideology faster than any medium, excepting silver.[1] Throughout history textiles have been symbols of wealth and status, and the colors and motifs ornamenting them have often conveyed clear messages regarding the owner's social class, religious persuasion, or economic station. These messages are often easily understood and sometimes require little context to interpret.

Reflecting the progressive philosophies of the late nineteenth and early twentieth centuries, textiles were used by all social classes, and they incorporate a wide panoply of styles, techniques and materials. Worldwide mass production of goods in the nineteenth century made household wares available to more people than ever before. Machines made it easier to produce goods inexpensively, which lowered the prices and made products more attainable to the average consumer.

Nineteenth- and twentieth-century reformers who championed the cause of preserving handicraft skills because industrialization was rapidly diminishing the ranks of professional potters, silversmiths, and furniture craftsman faced an altogether different set of concerns when they contemplated the state of textile arts. The hundreds of thousands of women who made clothing, embroidered table linens, darned socks, and quilted or tatted for household needs were not all prepared to be receptive to the social reformers' suggestions that there was value inherent in

▶
Ann Macbeth. Fireplace screen. Date unknown. Natural linen embroidered with silk threads, fabric panel: 21¾ × 17¾" (54.8 × 44.7 cm). Collection Ann and Andre Chaves

their labor and that approaching textiles as art would better their lives. Nor were Arts and Crafts reformers always comfortable with the quality and design of the typical household productions.

The prevalence of preexisting textile skills among the public meant that the use of elaborately crafted textiles in the home could transcend traditional economic boundaries. The skills necessary to produce a beautiful Arts and Crafts style pillow cover from a prefabricated kit were prevalent. Nineteenth-century English philosophers John Ruskin and William Morris viewed art as the creator's expression of joy in his work. By this definition an art object might be defined by the process of handicraft and/or the motivations of the maker—quite independent of style. The writings and teachings of Ruskin and Morris influenced nineteenth- and twentieth-century culture in Europe and America, encouraging consumers to think about the meaning and aesthetic value of the goods with which they surrounded themselves: the aims were to seek truth and beauty, and to surround oneself at home with nothing that one does not know to be useful or believe to be beautiful.

Arts and Crafts reformers looked to the medieval guilds, which stressed the importance of artisans in society and the melding of skill and practicality. Gothic revivalist A.W. Pugin and other nineteenth-century architects and interior designers wrote about designing to a purpose. Ruskin continued with these ideas, popularizing them in his 1849 work *The Seven Lamps of Architecture*. He added strength to the movement by trying to offer simpler designs, which physically indicated they were handmade, at more affordable prices.

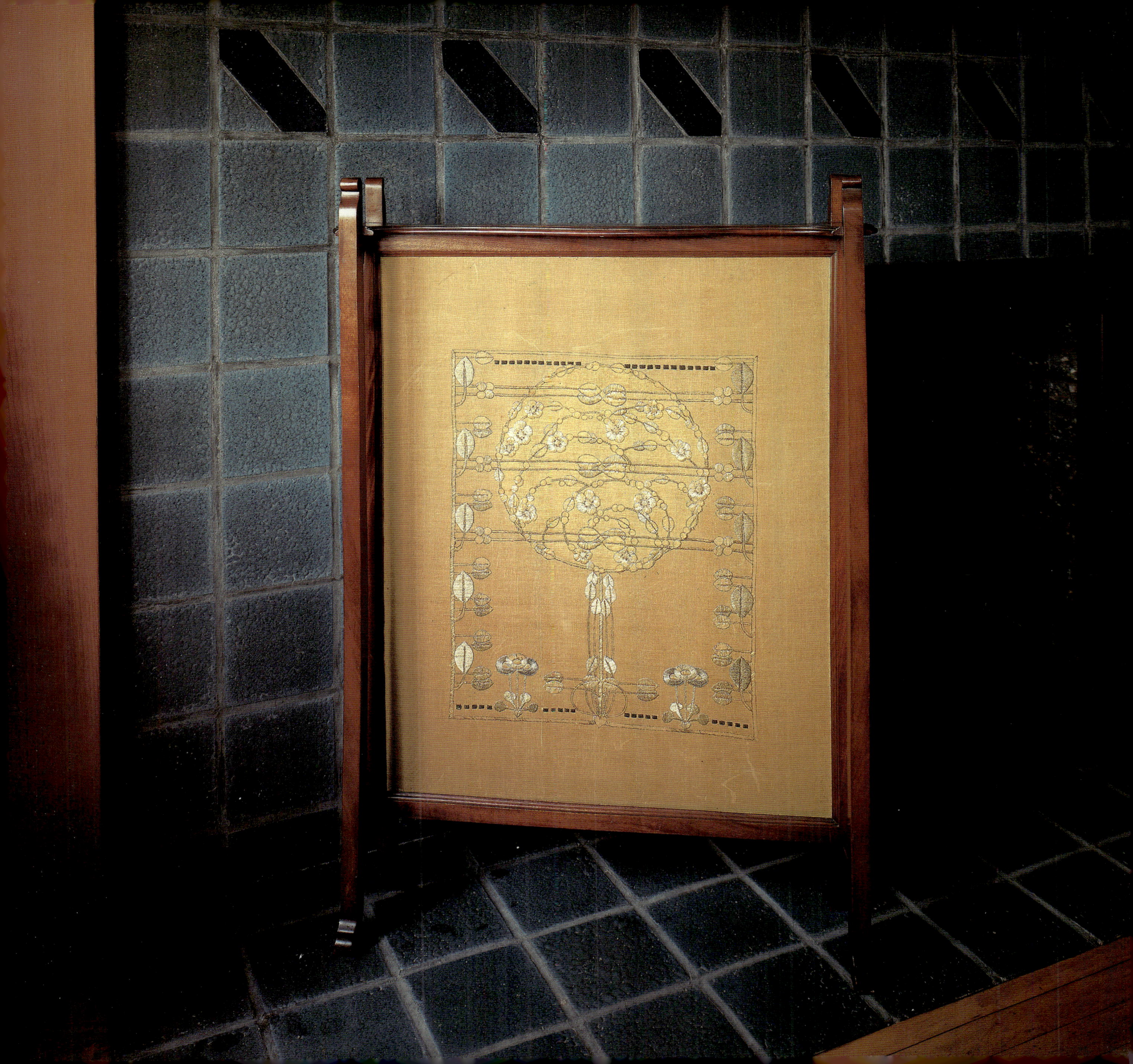

▶
Louis Comfort Tiffany. Doorway and drapery. Illustrated in Constance Cary Harrison's *Woman's Handiwork in Modern Homes*. 1881
Interior decorating books such as Harrison's inspired the use of textiles in homes across the country.

Morris practiced his philosophy in a commercial sense, opening a design firm that produced textiles, wallpaper, and carpets. Heavily influenced by English history and the contemporary Pre-Raphaelite movement with its allegorical allusions and interest in nature's forms, Morris created intricate patterns of stylized motifs. Like many European reformers, Morris involved his family in his business. His wife Jane and daughter May both embroidered. May later worked within Morris's needlework business, became a known designer, and authored *Decorative Needlework* (1893). Through his polemical writings and the success of his business, Morris became a public figure, inspiring the formation of guilds and other organizations seeking to encourage women to sew for a living.

The Aesthetic movement of the late nineteenth century continued to spawn interest in textiles in Europe and America. These objects were strongly inspired by Japanese design, as well as historic precedents and exotic textiles of the world.

Despite the European focus on good design, American critics did not take up the cause of good American design for industry and the preservation of historic craft until the Philadelphia Centennial Exposition of 1876. The Centennial was one of many expositions across the country that helped spread international ideas about art and industry. It included displays of handicraft, antique furniture, and the art of needlework thriving in Europe. The well known Royal School of Art Needlework, which began in 1872 as an occupation for the nobility to produce finished pieces and to repair historic pieces needing work, exhibited the designs of Walter Crane and William Morris to highly receptive audiences. Despite class issues stemming from differing backgrounds,

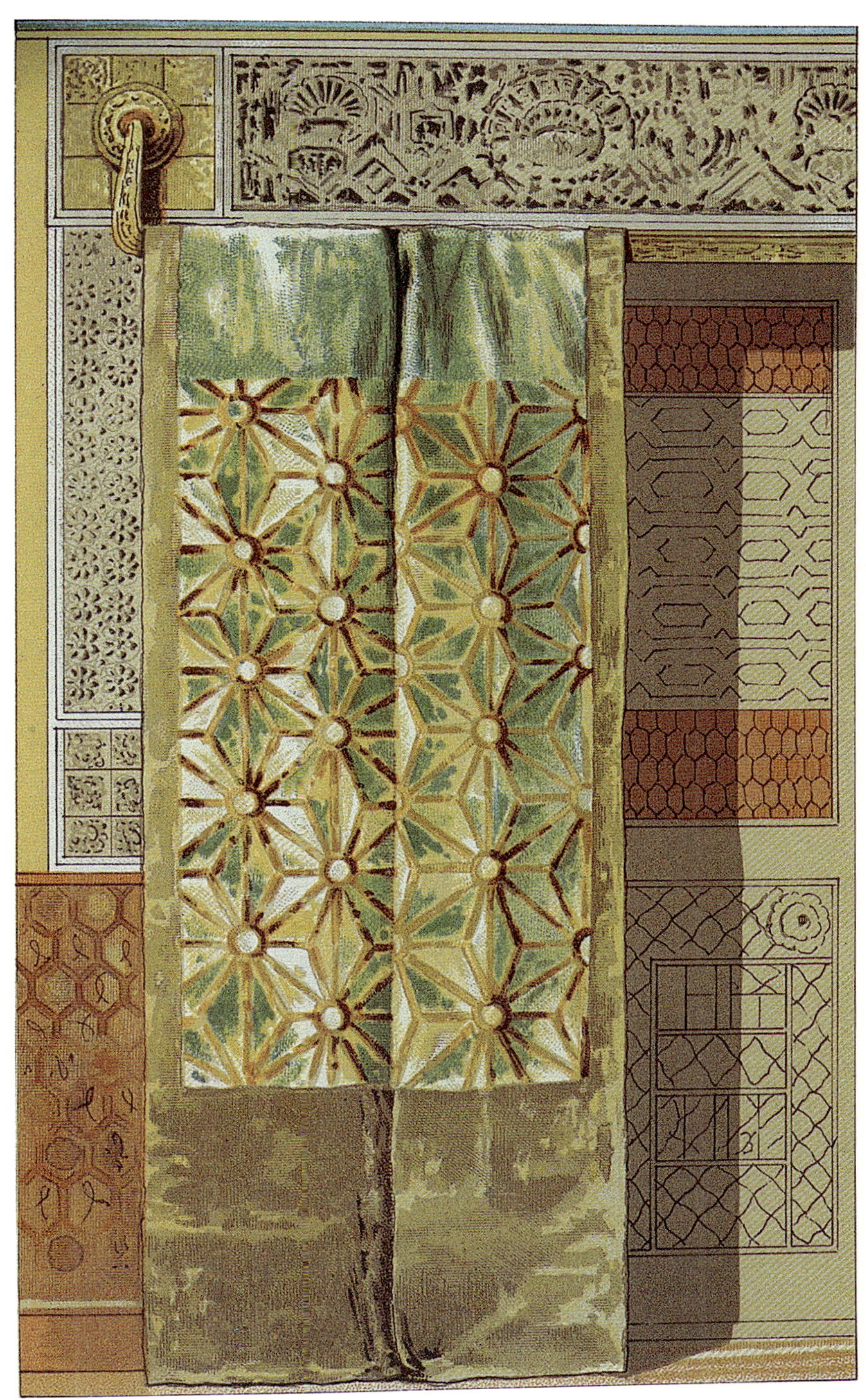

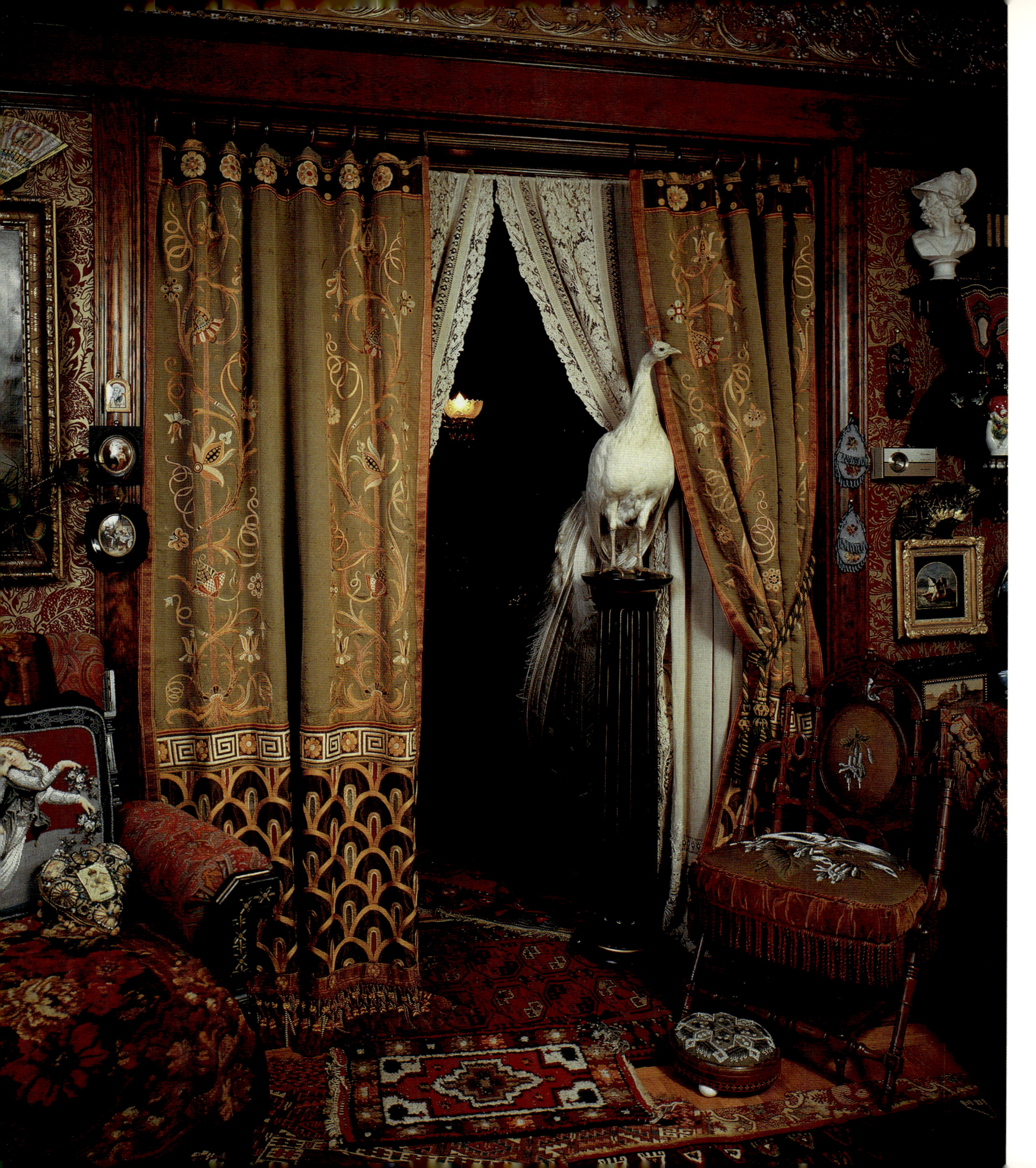

◀
Sir Lawrence Alma-Tadema. Portieres. Collection Brian Coleman
Sir Lawrence Alma-Tadema designed portieres for the Greek Revival parlor of Henry Marquand's mansion, designed by Richard Morris Hunt, on Madison Avenue and 68th Street in New York. Furniture in the parlor had mother-of-pearl inlay in the same pattern as in the portieres.

the School was very successful in its efforts to promote the flexibility and ease needlework offered women as a profession.

The Centennial Exposition exposed Americans to the monumental tapestries and embroideries being produced in Europe. Ultimately their inclusion called attention to the fact that in a nation of stitchers there simply were no similar products available. Nonetheless, as America responded to contemporary aesthetic dictates, the demand for goods to decorate the new "house beautiful"[2] rose. Historically, textiles were the largest commodity imported into the American colonies in the seventeenth and eighteenth centuries,[3] and in the late nineteenth century the tradition continued. The Aesthetic movement's exotic goods were often imported from around the world. The avant-garde in America was aware of the development of the Arts and Crafts movement in Europe, and many either ordered or commissioned goods from William Morris and other companies praised by Sir Charles Eastlake and other authors. Morris' textiles were imported into the United States from 1871 on by J. M. Bumstead and Co. of Boston and others. This included stamped and unstamped velvets, curtain stuffs, carpets, and laces.

As the new style in Europe continued to develop, leading practitioners helped spread their approach to Arts and Crafts design across the continent. Needlework offered an opportunity for women from country to country to participate in the movement. Jesse Newberry, a teacher at the leading Glasgow School of Art in Scotland, put forth that good design ensured that quality needlework could be produced by needleworkers of all skills and levels. She encouraged the use of

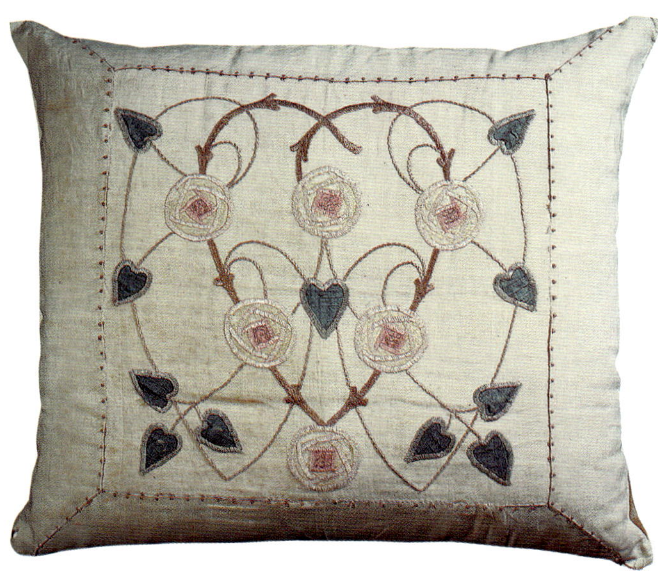

◀
Jessie King. Pillow. c.1900. Linen, cotton, and silk embroidery thread. 22 × 25" (56 × 63.5 cm). Collection Crab Tree Farm
Trained at the Glasgow School of Art, Jessie King designed embroidery, batiks, and woven and printed fabrics, and was particularly noted for the clothes she designed. This pillow illustrates colors and designs typical of the Scottish Arts and Crafts movement.

inexpensive, accessible fabrics as well as simple stitches. Her own designs often incorporated strong linear elements, a characteristic embroidered lettering of mottoes, and extensive use of appliqué. Her work, along with that of her most prolific student, Ann Macbeth, was often included in expositions and published in *The Studio* magazine.

Glasgow designers adopted a color scheme utilizing primarily pink, lavender, white, and black, and their needlework included abstract natural forms. The Glasgow rose is the most internationally recognized symbol of the Scottish. Charles Rennie Mackintosh, the most celebrated designer of the Glasgow School, worked with the Macdonald sisters and other Glasgow based needleworkers. His fame helped bring awareness to their work as well.[4]

In Vienna, the Secession movement formed in the 1890s as a reaction to the academic art movement, the Kunstlerhaus. Artists such as Gustav Klimt and others blended eastern influences, such as Byzantine mosaics, with the stylized forms of Art Nouveau. Designers Josef Hoffmann and Koloman Moser took leading roles in perpetuating the Secession's motto, stated in their magazine *Ver Sacrum*, "We recognize no difference between the high art and the low art." The Wiener Werkstätte was founded to produce furniture, graphic arts and books, housewares, and textiles. The textile department produced fabric designs, some so successful that they are still in production by Baukhausen, which has been producing them since 1900.

The craze for Japonisme that swept America after Japanese goods were exhibited at the Centennial provided a link between the Aesthetic movement and the evolution of the Arts and

▼

Minnie Dow instructing an Ipswich Summer School weaving class, Ipswich Massachusetts. c. 1903. Courtesy of the Ipswich Historical Society

Summer schools offered students the opportunity to pursue crafts, including weaving, spinning, and embroidery.

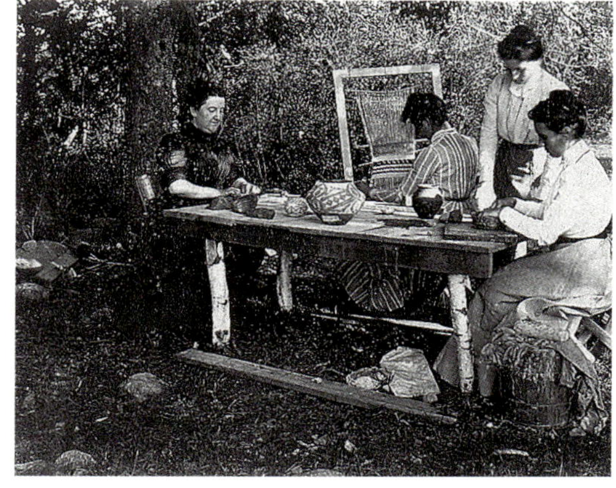

Crafts style in this country The exotic beauty of the simple handcrafted textiles, woodblock prints, and furniture that were imported from Japan captured the nation by storm. In the 1860s and 1870s Japan began producing goods for export to the western market and soon after American retailers began producing goods "à la Japonese" for the American public. Japanese theories of design, education, and lifestyle, which were ultimately integrated into the American aesthetic through the work of Arthur Wesley Dow, Gustav Stickley, Frank Lloyd Wright, and Greene and Greene, give the American Arts and Crafts style many of its unique qualities.

Importing goods became more expensive as time went on. Stiff import taxes were in place about 1890 and from then on one can document the beginnings of America's evolution from its role as a consumer of European Arts and Crafts goods and ideas to that of a producer, developing a distinctive American Arts and Crafts belief and aesthetic system.

The importance of the Centennial Exposition was recognized within decades of the event. Irene Sargent, acting editor of *The Craftsman*, noted in her address at the 1903 United Crafts exhibition that the Centennial of 1876 gave to "thousands among the less cultured middle classes of our country their first ideas of the paramount part which must be played by beauty in every well-ordered and harmonious life, irrespective of wealth and social position. It afforded the untraveled manufacturer and artisan glimpses of the possibilities which lay before them. And if a period of ugliness ensued, in all that pertains to the fine and the lesser arts, it was but transitional, like that awkward, unlovely, but happily short, period of life bridging together childhood and developed youth."[5]

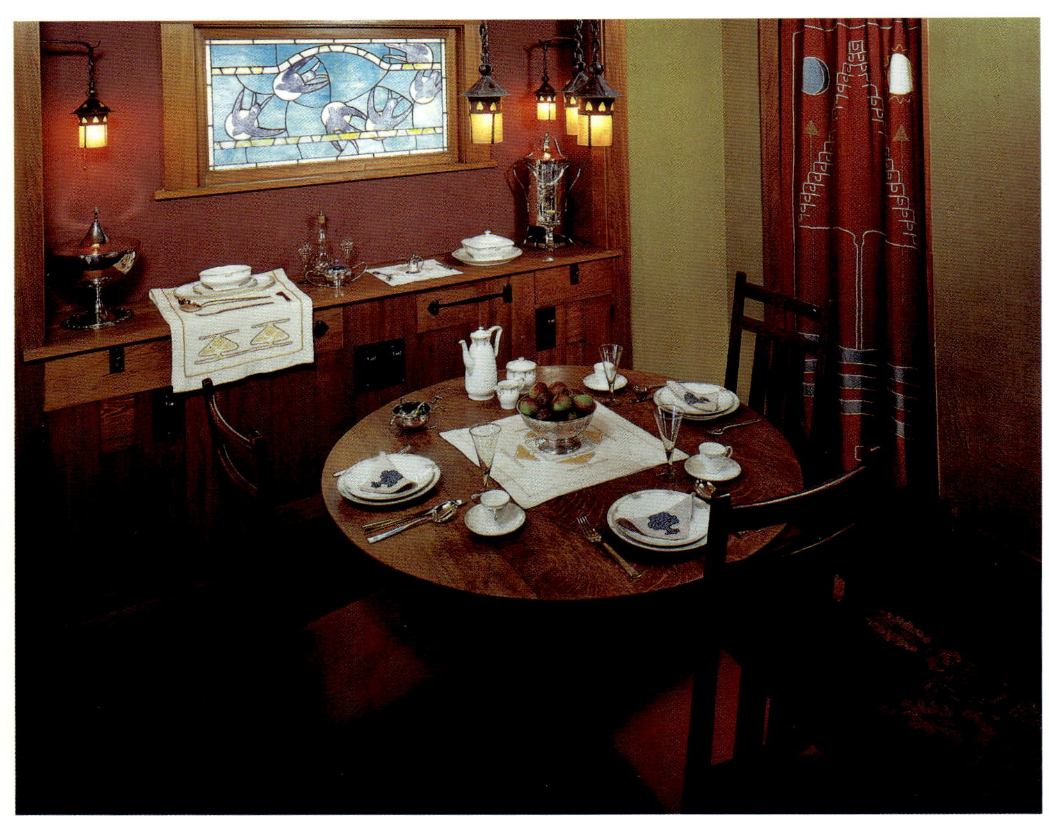

◀
Harvey Ellis. Craftsman-designed dining room. Collection Crab Tree Farm
Dining textiles were sold in both kit and completed form. The Craftsman company offered several options. This interior features Craftsman Workshops' teazle pattern runner and luncheon squares, c. 1905, and a pine-tree portiere reproduced from a design published in *The Craftsman*, November 1903.

The "Craftsman ideal" began to develop rapidly in America in response to these ideas. The philosophy popularized in this country sought to end the division between the creativity of spirit and the reality of the material world. The definition of art was expanded beyond the fine arts of painting, sculpture, and architecture to include decorative arts. The ideology surrounding the Craftsman ideal offered an alternate set of symbol systems, social values, and behavior patterns that represented a simpler, virtuous, natural way of life that its adherents wanted saved.

The Craftsman movement in America based its definition of art on that promoted by Ruskin and Morris, who viewed art as the creator's expression of joy in his work. Ruskin and Morris dedicated themselves to reuniting art and craft/labor by reintroducing "art" into everyday life through handicraft production. This principle found its expression in the ceramics, copperwork, and furniture of countless craftsmen, whose decorative objects came to symbolize the middle class. As the product of such a class searching for its identity and autonomy, the Arts and Crafts movement was full of contradictions. It was both functional and romantic, traditional and innovative, communal and individualistic, international and American. This apparent confusion con-

▼
Dora Wheeler, Associated Artists. *Aphrodite.* 1883. Needlewoven tapestry, illustrated in Candace Wheeler's *The Development of Embroidery in America*
In the European tradition, American designers in the 1880s began producing their own monumental artistic pieces.

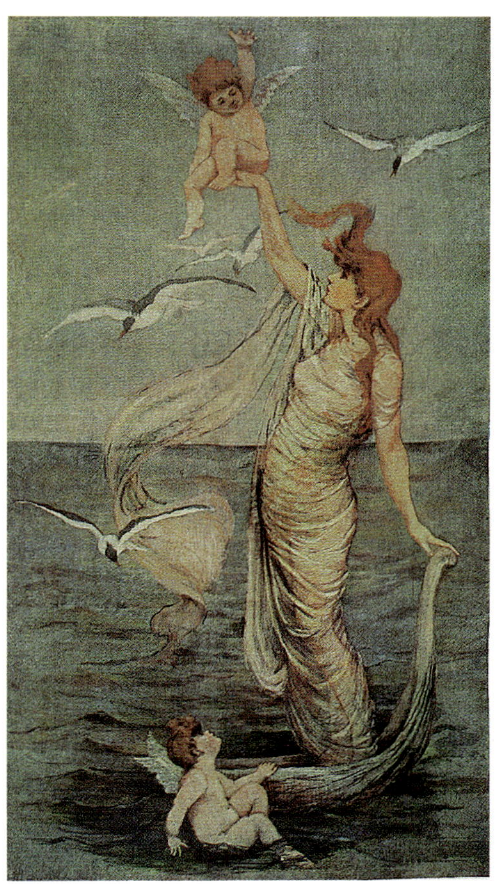

cisely reflects the nature of a generation that looked back to a comfortable past as it created a very new world.

The earliest American Arts and Crafts textiles date from the late nineteenth century, when Candace Wheeler and other designers and decorators for the elite thrived. Many of these textiles were inspired by Japanese examples, some by historic textiles in the collections of European museums and others by the imported productions of William Morris and his European peers. To the extent that decorators of the period filled their clients' homes with elaborately tucked and patterned drapes and upholsteries, their work is distinctly Victorian. However, by incorporating handcrafted, hand woven, or simple Japanese and indigenous artifacts into homes they represented the earliest significant American manifestations of Arts and Crafts ideas conveyed through objects.

Textiles at the turn of the century are not characterized by developments in techniques; rather, they are significant for developments in design. Artisans and craftspeople were well aware of international style as seen through periodicals, exhibitions, and, most importantly, importation, and they were certainly influenced by their surroundings. Furniture, metal, and pottery could be prohibitively expensive, but textiles were indispensable in the home and, therefore, most likely to bear new design motifs into the homes of the masses. Thus, by the twentieth century, textiles became a major medium for spreading Arts and Crafts ideas.

Candace Wheeler, a prominent New York City stockbroker's wife, turned to the arts in her later years. In 1876, at the Centennial Exposition, forty-nine year old Wheeler was inspired by the

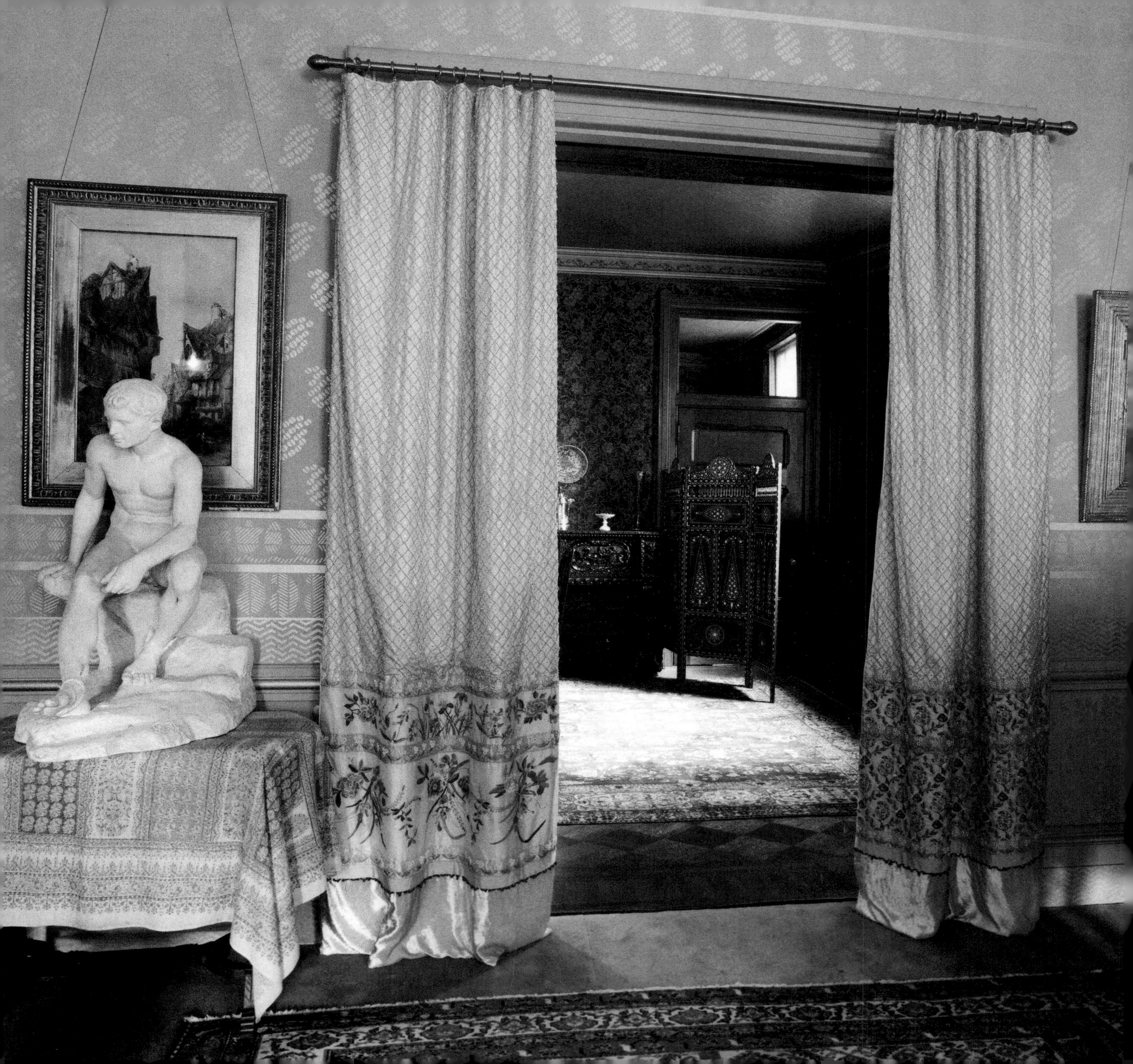

◄
Associated Artists. The Mark Twain House drawing-room portieres. c. 1886. Silk sari, silk embroidery thread, pearls, sequins. Collection The Mark Twain House, Hartford, Connecticut
Textiles in Aesthetic movement interiors contributed to the harmonious design of the room by tying together the overall color scheme.

concept behind the Royal Society's art needlework. Long a proponent of the importance of the home environment, in 1877 she joined forces with other New York matrons to help found the New York Society of Decorative Art, an organization that intended to "encourage profitable industries among women who possess artistic talent, and to furnish a standard of excellence for their work." Wheeler helped organize the Women's Exchange to help women in need sell their wares.[6]

Wheeler was an inspiring figure, writing and lecturing nationally, and setting an example as an American businesswoman specializing in home decoration textiles. She joined forces with Louis Comfort Tiffany, Lockwood de Forest, and Samuel Colman to form Associated Artists in 1879. During the period at Associated Artists Wheeler's work was heavily influenced by British and American nineteenth-century art needlework. As head of Associated Artists' embroidery and tapestry division, she participated in the interior projects at the White House and at the Mark Twain House in Hartford, Connecticut (see page 18). When the partnership dissolved in 1883, Wheeler took over Associated Artists with her daughter Dora, and the firm continued with an even greater emphasis on textiles. Candace traveled the world, bringing back antique and exotic textiles for her workshops to transform into useable wonders for her clients' homes.

Products by Wheeler and Associated Artists followed the most basic tenets of Arts and Crafts interior decoration: color, harmony, and balance. The Mark Twain House interior reflects Wheeler's synthesis of these principles. Wheeler and Associated Artists, second incarnation, redid the drawing room in 1886. Curtains in the room were a light Indian muslin with a delicate

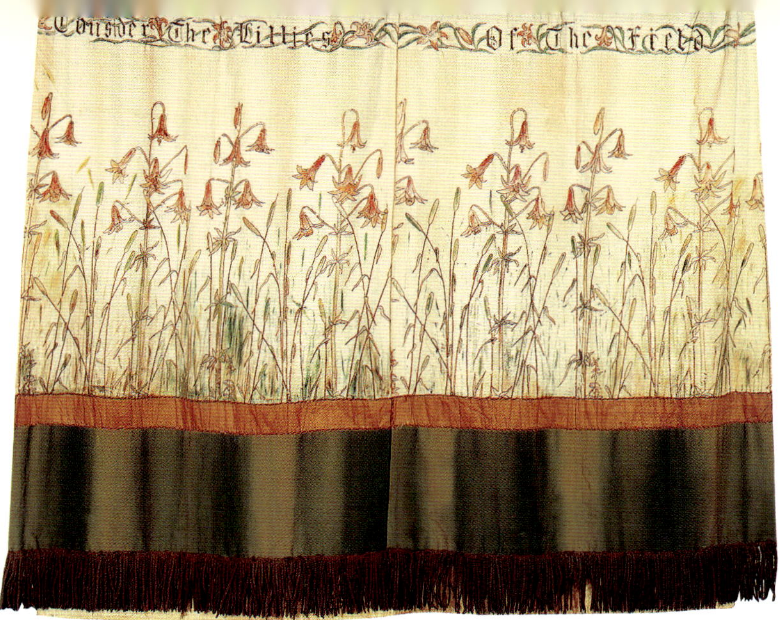

embroidered pattern, allowing light to shine into the room. The portieres designed for the space were made from an Indian silk sari, with a piece of oriental embroidery tacked on one end to balance the length and design. Each panel was stitched with thousands of pearls and sequins to decorate it and reflect the gas light. These key textiles, although not Arts and Crafts in the style[7] we expect, embodied Arts and Crafts principles.

Wheeler authored *Principles of Home Decoration with Practical Examples* (1903) and several other books that brought her ideas about interior decoration into American homes. Her books and articles emphasized the ways that anyone could use common household materials to beautify their house. Wheeler followed these principles in her own home, and she gathered scrap materials including denims, cottons, silks, and pieces of her own fabrics to be worked into rugs, awnings, and curtains.

For Candace Wheeler home decoration was a way to unite domestic science and aesthetics for both the upper class and the middle class in the "house beautiful." She noted in 1894 that "a perfectly furnished house is a crystallization of the culture, the habits, the taste of the family and not only expresses but makes character."[8]

In other ways Wheeler was influential. She employed young women in her workrooms, offering them job opportunities. In 1918 she reminded women: "In the life in which I grew up, there were no girls of fortune. . . . The career of a powerful and competent woman, as we know today, was an unheralded dream." In true Arts and Crafts fashion, Wheeler also founded a summer artist's

◀

Candace Wheeler. "Consider the Lilies of the Field" portieres. 1879. Embroidered, painted, cotton, serge, and wool. Collection The Mark Twain House, Hartford, Connecticut
This example of Wheeler's Aesthetic work illustrates the Arts and Crafts principles of organic design, color, harmony, and balance.

colony in Onteora, New York. Her interest in the American past and in creating an American style led her to also establish a rag rug industry near her home in the Catskills. She was comfortable with mass production and designed for a number of commercial firms, including Cheney Brothers Silks, and partnered with several other firms to create mass-produced fabric and wallpapers. The important thing for her was to bring beautiful things into the home.

Wheeler's public approach to her work helped popularize her ideas about textiles and the home. Art needlework continued to grow in popularity through the 1880s. Schools such as that at the Museum of Fine Arts, Boston, established classes, and similar groups sprouted up across the country. As Director of Applied Arts and Color for the Women's Building at the 1893 Chicago World's Fair, Wheeler had the opportunity to promote and encourage developments in American needlecraft and textile design. Many early figures were influenced by aesthetic ideals that they carried through to the Arts and Crafts era, and Wheeler is one such example. She helped women to state that they had not only revived lost handicrafts but had managed to apply new rules to "indigenous motifs."[9]

Art and women's clubs as well as museum schools across the country fanned the flames. Women's clubs, popular in America in the nineteenth century, concentrated on self improvement. With the growth of the middle class, more and more women had leisure time to pursue activities. China painting, drawing, needlework, and textiles were popular club activities. They offered women two options: to develop skills and use them in a commercial venture or to simply use the skills to fill a creative void in their lives. Wheeler encouraged women to explore their role in the

▶
Deerfield Society of Blue and White Needlework. Bedding-head curtain "Pomegranates." c. 1900. Embroidered linen on linen, 76½ × 62" (194.3 × 157.5 cm). Memorial Hall Museum Collection, Deerfield, Massachusetts. Gift of Mrs. (Metcalf) Green, Holyoke, 1956
This piece won the silver medal for color and design at the 1901 Pan-American Exposition in Buffalo, New York.

decorative arts "not indeed to prevent starvation of the body, but to comfort souls . . . who pined for independence."[10] These groups naturally evolved into Arts and Crafts societies and clubs that centered around the arts, literature, and philosophy.

During this period a Needlework & Textile Guild was set up at the Art Institute of Chicago, and the Museum of Fine Arts, Boston established a School of Needlework. Clubs were organized by regions. For example, Emily Noyes Vanderpool organized a needlework display for the local historical society, encouraging the study of old stitches in Litchfield, Connecticut.[11]

The women's club movement was equally active in the South. The General Federation of Women's Clubs identified manual training as a state concern. Tallulah Falls School was founded to educate the youth of this former resort community. The campus craft shop served as an outlet for the students' work. The school emphasized the philosophy of the Arts and Crafts movement, stressing "a full life, thus emphasis is placed upon creative development in handwoven textiles."[12]

The figures who worked to preserve traditional craft techniques and indigenous productions were equally influential during the Arts and Crafts movement. Today, colonial style handcrafted blue and white, drawn work and stump work textiles are still produced, especially in New England. Also, there are thriving craft traditions among the nation's quilters, basketmakers, and weavers in the Appalachians, the Adirondacks, New Mexico, Arizona, Maine, and elsewhere. These traditions survive because Arts and Crafts reformers called attention to these continuing traditions,

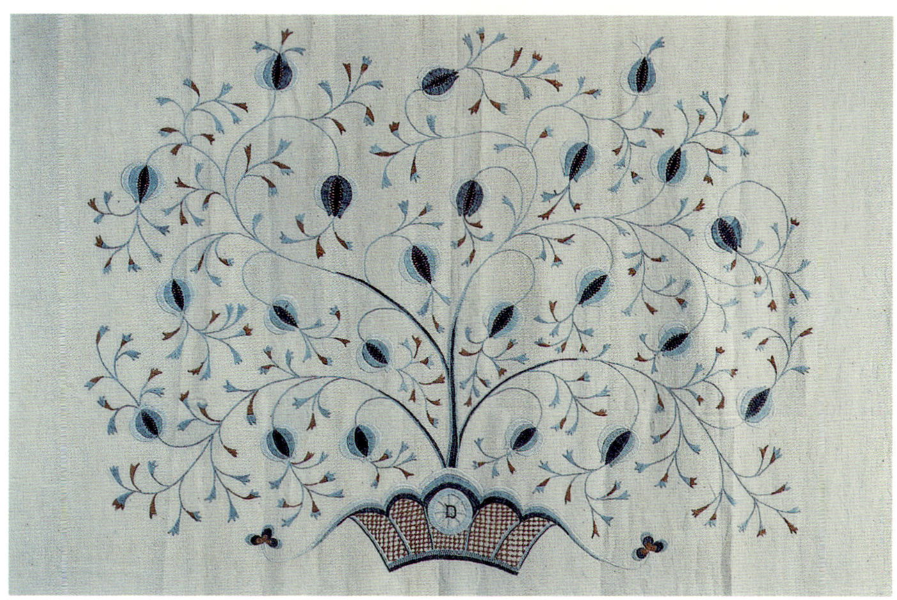

marketed products to national and international audiences, and encouraged those interested in the Arts and Crafts movement to include locally produced craft products in their interiors.

Much of New England's interest in textiles stemmed from wanting to preserve its colonial past. The Arts and Crafts reformers' interest in handcrafted textiles rose rapidly as the textile mills in Lowell, Massachusetts, and elsewhere forced small cottage industries out of business. New England Arts and Crafts textile makers were influenced by the modern designs seen in the magazine *International Studio*, the colonial artifacts around them, and the handicraft ethic as interpreted in the pages of *The Craftsman*. *The Craftsman* published articles on the handicrafts of Greece, Sweden, Germany, Italy, and other nations. The European peasant became romanticized and, as *The Craftsman* reported in the case of Russian needlework, "symbolizes the primitive society . . . when there was neither nobleman or serf, but simply 'the lords of their own hands.'"[13]

The Society of Arts and Crafts, Boston, reminded members to look around themselves for inspiration. "We have examples of Greek, Gothic, Renaissance, Chinese, Persian, Japanese, and Moorish craftsmen all around us, in our museums and collections, our homes, in books and photographs, to inspire and guide the worker."[14] The Museum of Fine Arts offered a Textile Study Room, established in 1898, which was designed to assist students and the local community to find inspiration from the museum's collection.

The Deerfield Society of Blue and White Needlework in Deerfield, Massachusetts, was one of the best known regional textile ventures. Deerfield was typical of many small New England villages

▼
Frances and Mary Allen. Blue and White Society embroiderers. c. 1903. Platinum print, 7 × 5" (17.8 × 12.6 cm). Memorial Hall Museum Collection, Deerfield, Massachusetts
Historical pieces in museum collections across the nation inspired women to restore and create period pieces.

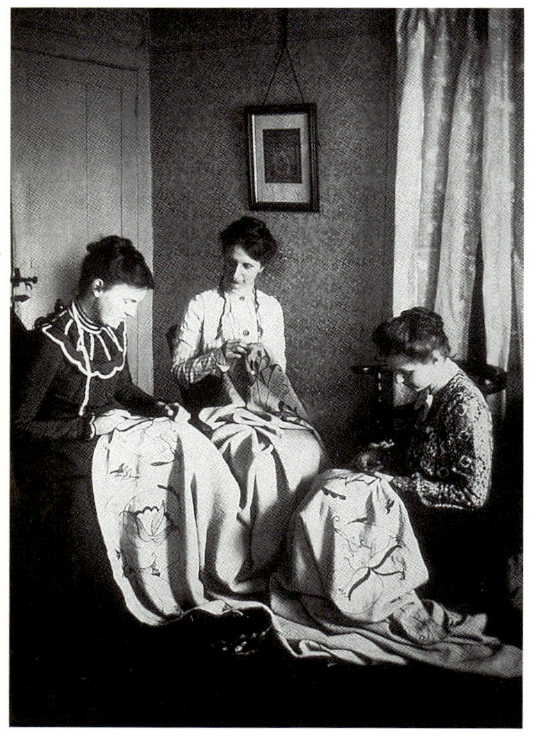

in the nineteenth century; amid a degrading economy, the past was venerated. In the 1890s Margaret Whiting and Ellen Miller, former National Academy of Design students, revived the art of Blue and White crewel embroidery in an effort to preserve period pieces in its local museum. The group created its own patterns, and more than thirty women made testers, coverlets, and tea sets, which were marketed nationally. The linen materials for their products came from Berea College in Kentucky and McCutcheon's in New York City, and yarns were imported from Scotland.[15]

The Deerfield Society treated the intellectual work of design and the manual skill of stitching as equally important. They kept records of the time involved in the projects, and product stability led to an increased ability to provide a handcrafted but more predictable product. This became more and more of a challenge as the interest in and demand for their products grew.[16] Although traditional, historical designs were most popular, the group began developing designs incorporating more modern Arts and Crafts design ideas. Deerfield work was available locally, by mail order, and in retail shops, including the Society of Arts and Crafts, Boston, gallery.[17]

The Society was the impetus for the Arts and Crafts movement's growth in Deerfield. By 1899 the women were participating in a village improvement society and women's club and were holding arts and crafts exhibitions in town. Products included furniture, andirons, jewelry, netting, baskets, and rugs. By 1907 a third of the town's women were participating in the organized crafts group.

The women shared their work through interviews and articles in *The Ladies' Home Journal.* In October 1901 Mary Allen authored an article on "A Village Remembered," sharing news on how

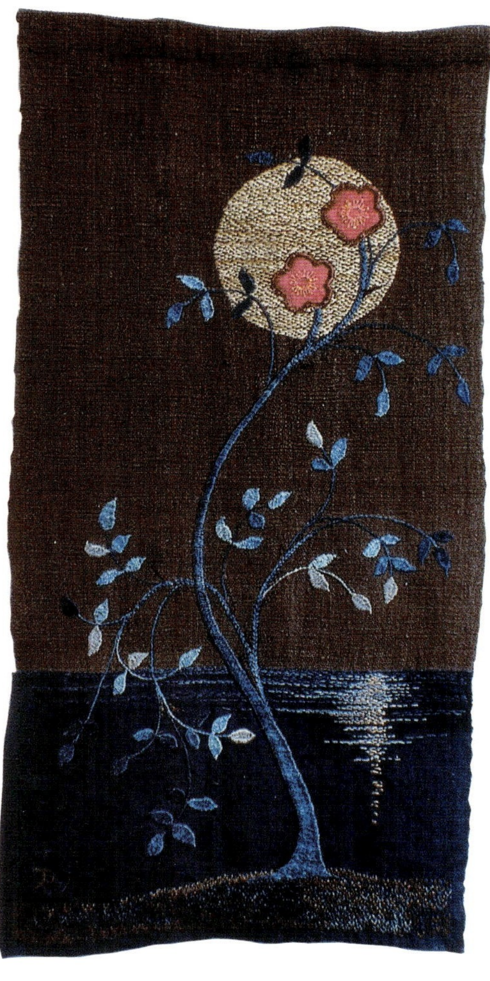

◀
Deerfield Society of Blue and White Needlework. *Two Red Roses Across the Moon*. c. 1919. Appliqué and embroidery on linen, 31½ × 14½" (80 × 36.8 cm). Memorial Hall Museum Collection, Deerfield, Massachusetts
This work was inspired by a William Morris poem of the same title. Note the Deerfield Society "D" emblem at bottom left.

Deerfield's craft community was faring. The group had local exhibitions in the community center.

> Once a year it is filled for three days with an exhibition of handicraft for which the village is becoming famous. This "Arts and Crafts" movement has no connection with the Village room beyond occupying it for this exhibit but it shows the same spirit of cooperation and enterprise developed still further and calls for a brief mention. Its most conspicuous success is the blue and white needlework which now has a national reputation. This is wrought by 25 or 30 women in their own homes under the guidance of Miss Whiting and Miss Miller the leaders of the craft.

The article goes on to discuss other crafts, including other textiles, in practice in Deerfield such as rug making and basket making. "The really remarkable exhibition draws hundreds of interested visitors. It brings honor to the town, and a substantial sum of money as well. The proceeds of the sales go directly to the exhibitors. The entrance fees are added to the Village room fund."[18]

With such well publicized success stories, other women were encouraged to contemplate similar ventures. It is important to note, however, that these women were proving independence and providing income, but within an acceptable set of parameters. Working with textiles, a women's art, the women were seen by society to work "as leisure permits, without interrupting the family life."[19] They did also incur great criticism. Frederic Allen Whiting of the Boston Society of Arts and Crafts attacked some of the small groups forming women's exchanges to sell their wares, stating that "The Arts and Crafts movement. . . . is certainly not an endeavor to supplant the old time sewing circle "[20] The critics voiced a concern that bad craft negatively influenced

▼
Mable Tuke Priestman. "Pratt Point—An Evolution of Old Italian Point Lace." Illustration from *Handicrafts in the Home*. 1910

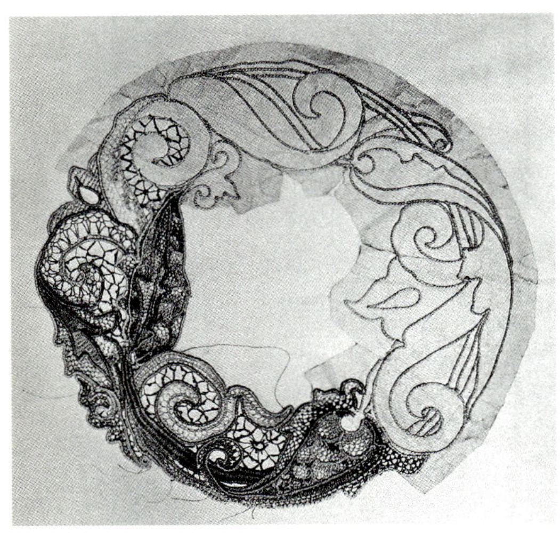

the ability to elevate the crafts to art or present them as alternate choices in home furnishings. Nonetheless, across the nation women's groups persevered in selling crafts, reveling in a new found economic freedom that did not entail working in a factory.

Boston's Women's Educational and Industrial Union, founded in 1877 by Dr. Harriet Clisby, an early female physician, and other prominent Bostonians was established to help immigrant women to secure advancement. One of the skills emphasized was textiles.[21] These women were particularly interested in seventeenth- and eighteenth-century needlework and colonial patterns.

Other colonial crafts became popular. Lacemaking underwent a revival on the East Coast as part of the Arts and Crafts movement. Boston and New York served as centers for the revival. In Europe, the lacemaking revival had a slight negative connotation, as it was spearheaded by upper-class women who "assisted" peasant women as part of their charitable responsibility. The South End House and the Boston Society of Arts and Crafts sponsored a project that worked with Irish girls to produce Italian lace. Interest in Boston stemmed from collectors, such as Florence Weber, who collected lace and needed to repair their pieces. Weber publicized her work in *The Craftsman* and developed a following. In New York, Greenwich Shop worked with lace, and Katherine Davis opened the Handicrafts Shop for Italian Needlecraft in Philadelphia.[22]

In New England, as in other parts of the country, the growing immigrant population had a rising social, economic, and political impact. Vida Scudder, a Wellesley professor who worked with Boston's Denison House immigrants learning to turn lacemaking into a form of income,

▶
B. E. M. Howard. Nims Parlor of Deerfield Society of Blue and White Needlework exhibit. 1915. Hand-colored photograph, 7⅞ × 9¾" (20 × 24.8 cm). Memorial Hall Museum Collection, Deerfield, Massachusetts. Gift of Margery B. Howe, Northfield, Massachusetts

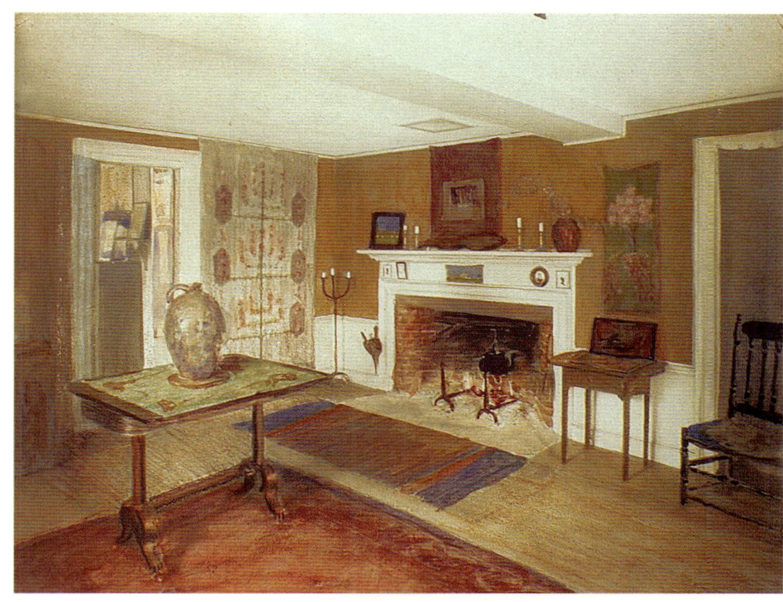

stated: "Few people realize the rising importance of the Italians in Boston as a political factor They now number over 60,000 and they are beginning to waken to their political power. . . . Let us all—we Americans who are trying to look ahead to guard against the 'melting-pot' melting out the best and leaving the dregs to be fused into our national character—let us help to save as much as possible of this quality by actively interesting ourselves in this Arts and Crafts movement."[23]

Interest in the Arts and Crafts movement and in the American past encouraged a widespread national rag rug revival. Rag rugs were usually woven out of scraps, sometimes dyed before the rug was produced and sometimes after. Almost any material could be used. If the scraps were made of different fibers, the dye hues would take differently to each material. Aniline-based dyes were usually used in coloring the pieces. The scraps were woven into both geometric patterns and outlines of natural shapes, such as leaves or pine trees. Small industries sprang up, and rugs were produced by Abnakee Rugs from Pequaket, New Hampshire[24]; Sabatos and Cranberry Island Rugs from Maine; Subbekashe Rugs[25]; Lucy D. Thomson in Belchertown, Massachusetts; Pilgrim Rugs of Pittsfield, Massachusetts; and the Society of Arts and Crafts, Hingham. Deerfield's Madeline Yale Wynne carefully marketed her rugs as artwork, stating: "The rug of pleasing colors and good weave bears the same relation to the weaver that the picture does to the artist."[26]

The South and West played a significant role in the preservation and documentation of historic craft traditions. The products of Southern artisans were distributed and consumed by knowledgeable Arts and Crafts movement figures nationwide. In 1937 Allen Eaton published the

Handicrafts of the Southern Highlands, which surveyed many of the south's continuing traditions and paid tribute to the Arts and Crafts ideology. Eaton wrote: "I do not know of any one who has written more clearly of art and its relation to life than William Morris of England who said, 'Art is the Expression of Man's Joy in Work.' He spoke as an artist and craftsman and I doubt if from the worker's standpoint anything better will ever be said." Because or their traditional nature, the handicraft traditions that Eaton chronicled in the South have been interpreted as continuing traditions, as folk art, as Arts and Crafts, and as transitional craft. Nevertheless, whatever their style or the intent of their maker, the survival of the objects is among the most enduring legacies of the Arts and Crafts movement.

The textile world is also a transient one, and many women were able to put their skills to use in more than one location as they moved either of their own accord or following their spouses. Frances L. Goodrich was a driving force in reviving traditional Appalachian weaving in the 1890s. Goodrich began her work in New England, believing textiles to be a "natural" choice for women. In 1897, Goodrich moved to Allanstand, North Carolina, and continued working with coverlets. Women were paid to produce set designs at home. The work was marketed throughout the North as "folk" products.

A graduate of the Yale School of Fine Arts, Goodrich worked in the Presbyterian ministry in North Carolina. She founded Allanstand Cottage Industries in 1902 in Madison County, North Carolina, to preserve old weaving patterns and techniques and to market them to the tourist trade. Goodrich contacted Gustav Stickley about 1903, and shortly thereafter Allanstand and Berea Industries of Kentucky were included on the selection list for the Arts and Crafts exhibit in Rochester, New York.[27] In 1908 she opened a shop in the resort town of Asheville, North Carolina, catering to the Arts and Crafts consumers frequenting Grove Park Inn.

Edith Vanderbilt was equally aware of Arts and Crafts philosophy. In 1905 she founded the Biltmore Homespun shop at the Vanderbilt estate in Asheville. She began by marketing hand-loomed woolen cloth and in 1906, she added all-woolen dress goods. Homespun was woven by estate residents on home looms and natural dyes were used in coloring the wool. Eventually, Biltmore Industries produced its own yarn and provided looms. The textiles were advertised in national magazines and marketed through the mail as well as in shops.[28] Although reflective of Arts and Crafts ideals, these textiles, particularly when used in back-country bungalows, were marketed nationally as indigenous or "folk" craft.

The Spinning Wheel in Asheville was founded by Clementine Douglas, a Pratt Institute graduate. Inspired by a lecture from Helen Dingman, who worked for the Presbyterian Home Missions, Douglas volunteered to join the Presbyterian Mission board in Smith, Kentucky. She taught in the South in the summer and spent her winters teaching at the Finch School in New York, and also worked at the Pine Mountain Settlement School, Berea College, and the Weave Shop. While at the Spinning Wheel from 1925 to 1945, Douglas hired local weavers to train in the heritage crafts. Ettamae Deweese and Margaret and Myrtle Jump were such weavers. Douglas

▶
Rustic interior. Illustrated in Richardson Wright's *Inside the House of Good Taste.* 1918
The 1918 caption for this illustration noted: "For a country bungalow this furniture is eminently fitting. The sturdy dining-room chairs are covered with hide upon which the hair remains, a touch which shows the careful carrying out of a single scheme of fitness." Native American textiles such as the rugs on the floor provided a perfect accent.

saw her shop as a way to offer them the opportunity for creativity and independence. The women also learned from her teachings about international weaving. According to one of the weavers: "Seems to me if you were to learn all there is to know about weaving, you'd pretty nigh know all there is to know."[29]

Wilmer Stone Viner, another influential leader in the Southern textile community, worked at the Pine Settlement School before World War I. Viner moved to Saluda, North Carolina, in 1923, founding the Weave Shop. Viner was known for creating vegetable dyed pieces of exquisite beauty. The Weave Shop produced wall hangings and table linens using both natural and stylistic designs.[30]

Pi Beta Phi's Arrowcraft Shop in Gatlinburg, Tennessee, kept the coverlet tradition alive. Wingone Redding, a Canadian native educated in Boston, worked there from 1925 to 1929. Redding both taught local women and girls and collected samples of weaving. The shop supplied materials and instructions, and Redding created the designs for the pieces with a well-educated awareness of her markets.

Many organizations merged to form a group known as the Southern Highland Handicraft Guild, based on the Allanstand Cottage Industries. Incorporated in 1917, its stated aim was "to help the people of the Southern Highlands to produce and to market handiwork, especially hand-woven articles, basketry and woodwork, and by so doing, to bring money into communities far from markets, and to give paying work to members of such communities; to give to the workers the interest of producing beautiful things, the delight of the skilled worker and artist; to save

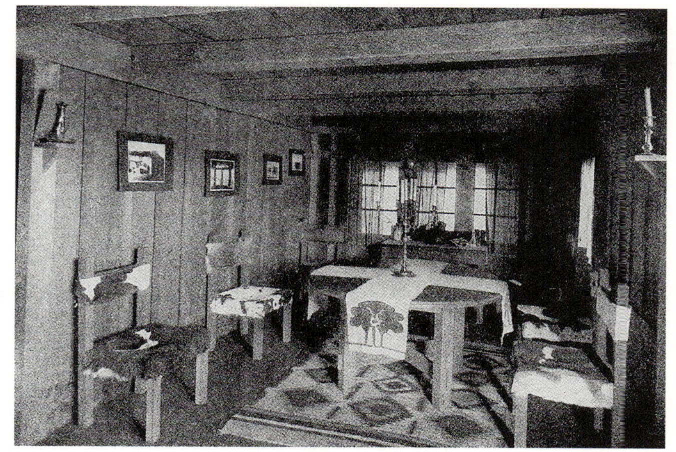

from extinction and to develop the old-time crafts of the mountains."[31] In 1931, Goodrich gave Allanstand to the Guild, cementing its position in the craft community.

The indigenous textiles of the Southwest have been collected and coveted by crafts enthusiasts since the West became settled. Native American textiles and weaving techniques have been extensively explored. At the height of the Arts and Crafts movement both *House and Garden* and *The Craftsman* proposed that Native American blankets and rugs could be used in the home.

With the development of the National Park system and the growth of the railways, collectors brought numerous souvenirs back from the West. Tourists who visited the Grand Canyon, Mesa Verde and the Pueblos could witness the weaving of Native-American textiles and be inspired by sites, such as the 1905 Hopi House designed by Arts and Crafts architect Mary Colter.

Those inspired by the west who could not visit or tourists who returned home wishing they had purchased more found Navajo blankets available through several nationally distributed catalogs focusing on authentic and Native American–inspired textiles. John B. Moore, a licensed Indian trader in New Mexico, issued catalogs from 1903 to1911. The Hudson Bay Company advertised fur rugs from Alaska. The well-known Pendleton Woolen mills sold "Indian design" blankets, throw rugs, robes, and couch covers. The first catalog came out in 1915, but the company may have been selling the material before that date. Francis E. Lester Company in Mesilla advertised in *The Craftsman* that it provided "Indian blankets direct from the Indian weaver to the customer. . . . The blankets I sell are entirely hand-woven by the best Navajo and Pueblo Indian weavers of

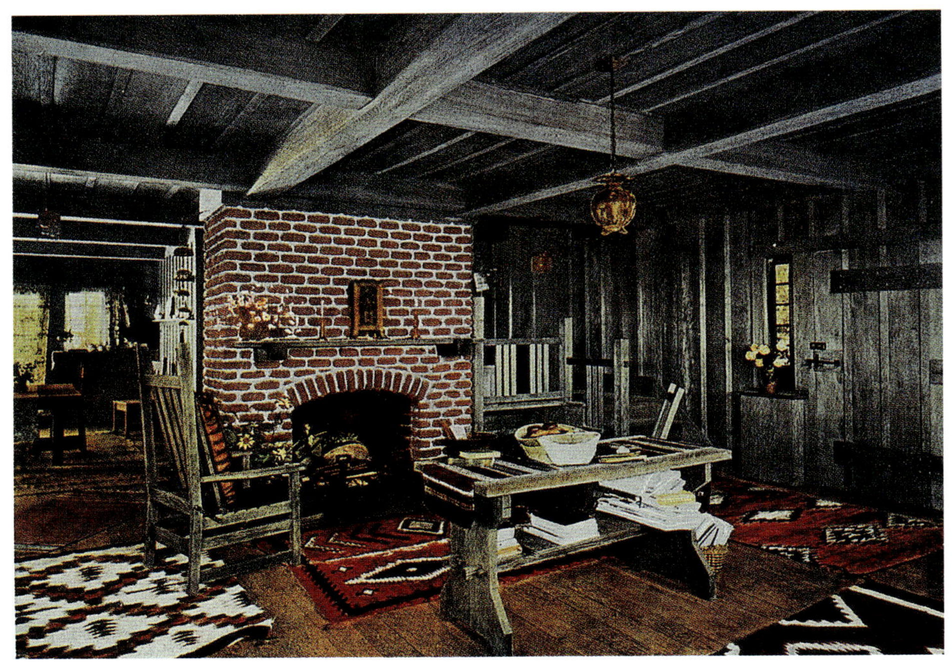

◀
National Lead Company. Bungalow. Illustrated in *Artistic Interiors for Homes*. 1909
The exotic influences so popular during the Aesthetic movement were augmented during the Arts and Crafts period with the beauty of America's own Native American textiles.

their tribes, from pure native wool handclipped by the Indians from their own sheep and entirely handspun. . . . It is woven under my personal supervision and every strand of it is pure native handspun wool. . . . The weave is close and heavy, just right for floor use and the rug will literally last a lifetime."[32] Collectors who wanted older, rare, or even better-made examples often made their purchases directly or hired traders to get exactly what they desired.

The Craftsman published numerous articles on Native American–inspired pieces. In 1903 an article on "Three Craftsman Canvas Pillows" with Native American–inspired motifs such as a "pine-tree motif, deer motif, and a bear motif" ran in the magazine. Native motifs were presented in designs for "Nursery Wall Coverings." These native North American motifs were seen as having an educational and artistic purpose, similar to what Celtic motifs had for the English people. Many of these designs were inspired by the Hopi Indians of northern Arizona.[33]

There were multiple sources of inspiration that defined the evolution and continuing development of textiles in America at the end of the nineteenth century. International expositions, exhibitions, and leading designers shared new and innovative ideas with American artisans, manufacturers, and consumers at the turn of the century. These venues stressed the importance and

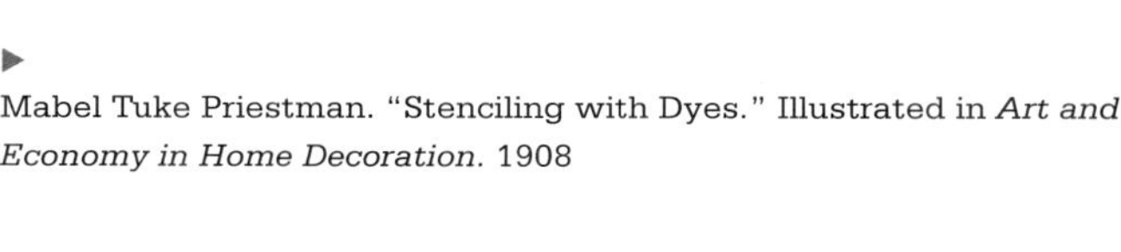

▶
Mabel Tuke Priestman. "Stenciling with Dyes." Illustrated in *Art and Economy in Home Decoration*. 1908

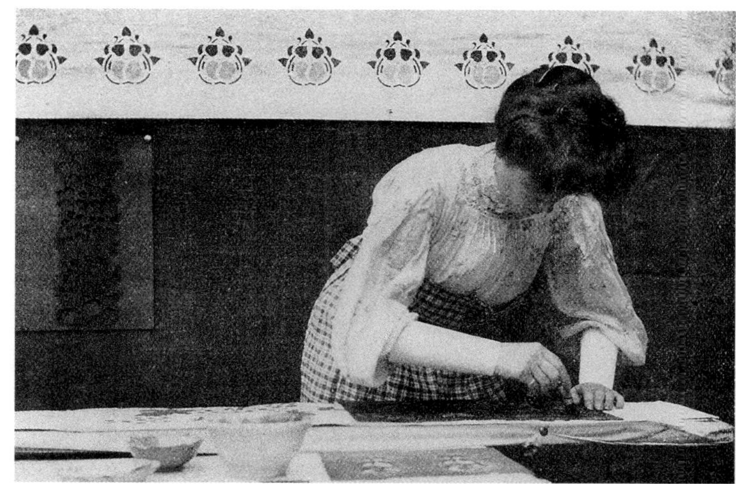

beauty of handcraftsmanship as well as the preservation of the craft tradition. Women, coming into their own as a result of the suffragette movement and other factors, sought work through craft. Textile production came to serve as a tool for women in the late nineteenth century to better their lives, either through beautifying their homes or economically caring for themselves. Regional influences and lifeways came to bear on the textiles produced—New England showing a strong interest in the colonial era, the West in Native American material, and the South in continuing craft traditions. Each assisted in laying the groundwork for textiles to continue to develop as the Arts and Crafts movement gained momentum in the early decades of the twentieth century. ❖

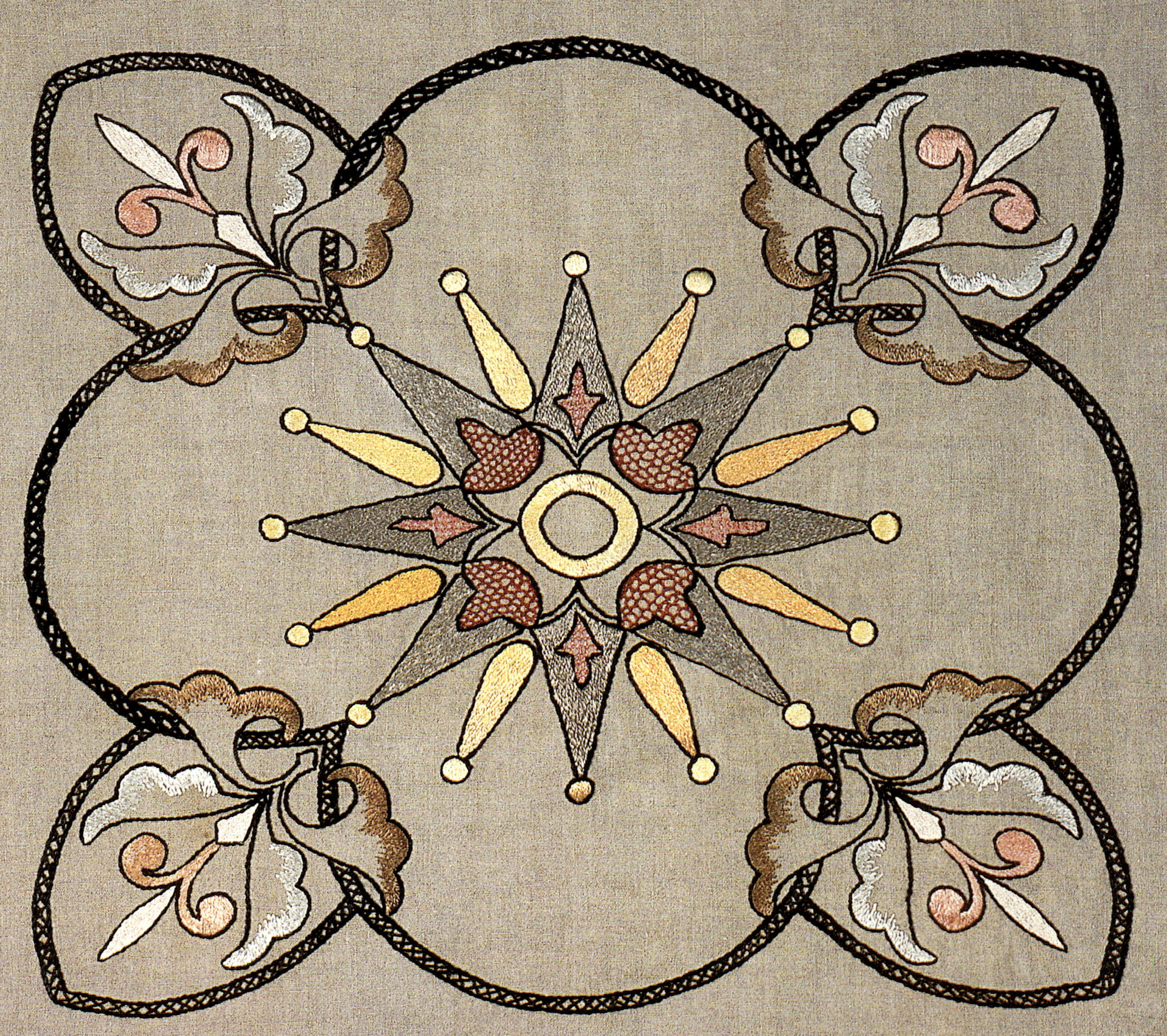

2 Art and Utility: Design Principles of the Arts and Crafts Movement

Rooted in the nineteenth century, the American Arts and Crafts movement was philosophically dependent upon the writings of William Morris, John Ruskin, Thomas Carlisle, and others. The movement influenced domestic and artistic textile production in America from the 1870s onward. Numerous Americans experienced Morris's textiles in Europe, while others encountered them in elite domestic environments or at exhibitions and expositions around the country. Nevertheless, today American art needlework of the period from 1870 to 1900 is seldom encountered, and it is usually interpreted as Aesthetic or Victorian in style rather than Arts and Crafts.

Design and *style* are words which are frequently bantered about among artists, historians, curators, and laymen with no clear consensual definition providing touchstones to our understanding of their use. Perhaps this is the reason that when collectors, scholars, antiques dealers, and artists congregate to discuss Arts and Crafts objects there are frequently strong disagreements about particular artifacts. A scholar or collector might consider a pot or a textile from the 1870s or 1880s to reflect the Arts and Crafts styles; an equally knowledgeable colleague might insist that it is Victorian, Aesthetic, Gothic Revival, Eclectic or Proto–Arts and Crafts.

Contemporary scholars seldom argue that the Arts and Crafts movement is defined by style. Few, if any, of the most respected exhibitions of Arts and Crafts material have been limited to artifacts considered Arts and Crafts on the basis of style alone. *The Art that is Life* (1987), *Living the Good Life* (1993), *Southern Arts and Crafts* (1996) and *Inspiring Reform* (1997) have all been both praised and criticized for the inclusion of objects in the Aesthetic, Japanese, Romantic Revival,

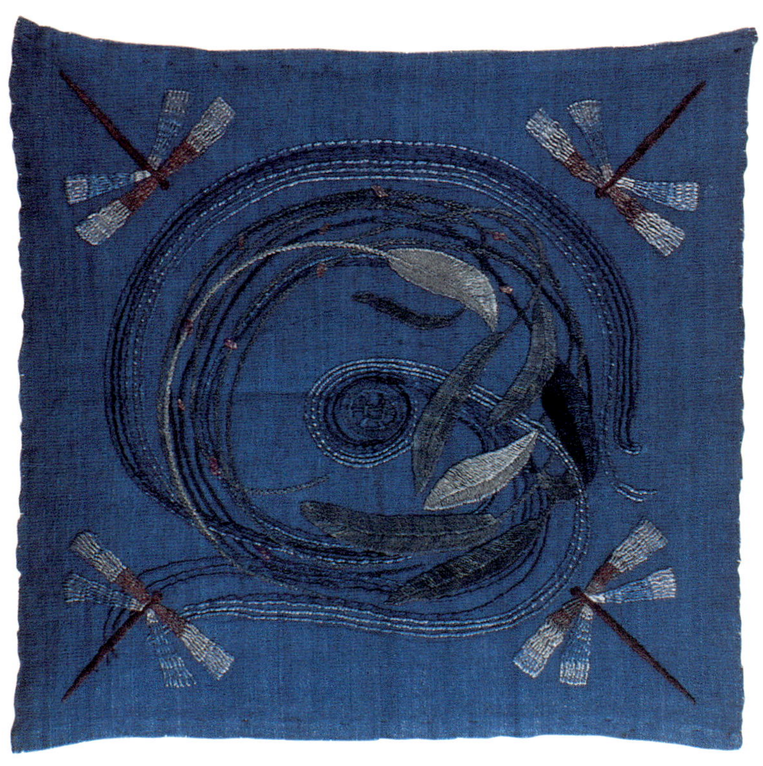

◀
Deerfield Society of Blue and White Needlework. Table square "Seaweed and Dragon Flies." 1905–15. Embroidered linen on linen, 15½ × 15" (39.4 × 38.1 cm). Memorial Hall Museum Collection, Deerfield, Massachusetts

Folk, and Colonial Revival styles. Yet each of these exhibitions has carefully documented the relationship of the items to William Morris, John Ruskin, Gustav Stickley, and Arthur Dow, as well as to the various manifestations of social liberalism, manual art education, and handicraft revivals as they were encountered across America.

Artists and designers approach design as a creative process rather than as a completed product in a particular style. For those who design things, *design* is a verb. This is why it is important for us to consider the relationship of designers working in Aesthetic, Gothic Revival, Victorian, and Romantic styles to the Arts and Crafts movement. An artist inspired by Morris and Ruskin may execute artistic objects for the home, and thus create important Arts and Crafts designs that bear no clear relationship to public taste at the turn of the twentieth century or today. Examined today, these objects are bound to generate debate (page 50 bottom).

The relationship between the American Arts and Crafts movement and what we now recognize to be the American Arts and Crafts style will perhaps always be debated. The appliquéd and embroidered textiles produced in Gustav Stickley's Craftsman Workshops or at Newcomb College

▶
Christopher Dresser. "Sharp, Angular, or Spiny Forms Suggesting Excitement." Illustration from *Principles of Decorative Design*. 1873
Different lines and shapes give rise to different emotions. This illustration, solely by means of its lines, is intended to illicit in the viewer a sense of excitement.

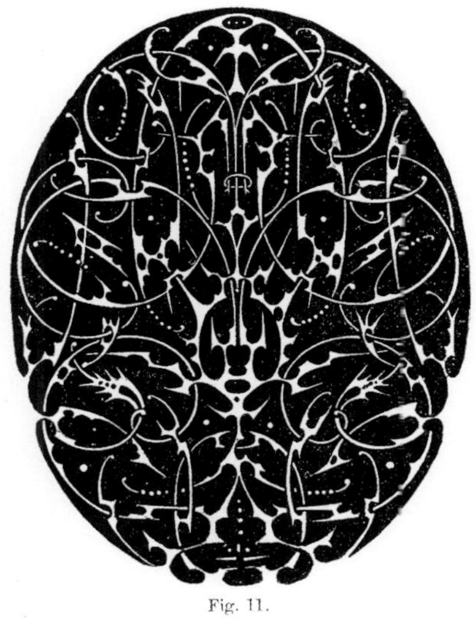

Fig. 11.

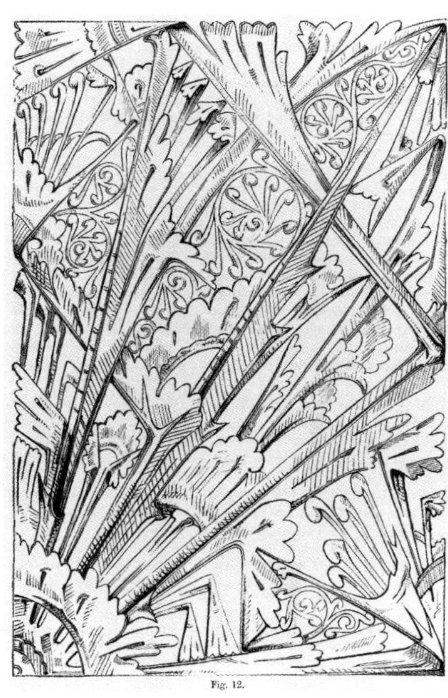

Fig. 12.

▲
Christopher Dresser. "Lines Suggesting Power, Energy, Force or Vigor." Illustration from *Principles of Decorative Design*. 1873

are broadly recognized icons of Arts and Crafts textile design. However, the lace produced under the direction of the Society of Arts and Crafts, Boston, and the portieres, runners, and rugs woven in the Emerson House at Arthur Wesley Dow's Ipswich Summer School of Art have not been collected, curated, or exhibited as Arts and Crafts objects since the early twentieth century.

The embroidered exhibition work done by the women involved with the Deerfield Society of Blue and White Needlework has only begun to be sorted into two bodies of material, one reflecting primarily an Arts and Crafts aesthetic and the other the Colonial Revival style.[1] Some consider almost any embroidered, stenciled, darned, or block-printed textile worked on brown, tan, ecru, or green linen, hemp, or burlap to represent the Arts and Crafts style. Others would restrict the style to those examples dating from about 1906 to about 1915 that display abstract stylized pattern and bold outline drawing.

Prevailing opinion among scholars has approached the Arts and Crafts movement as a body of loosely knit ideas. Arts and Crafts reformers were concerned with the improvement of public taste, the incorporation of art into daily life for all classes of people, the preservation of handicraft technologies, and the development of a simple, natural, and functional aesthetic. Iconic designs of the Arts and Crafts style are broadly perceived to reject unnecessary ornament, to rely upon function to determine form, and to solicit nature for inspiration regarding color and texture.

So, simply defined, perhaps the purest of Arts and Crafts style textiles are naturalistically colored handwoven linens, burlaps, or cottons bereft of embroidery or stenciled pattern but with

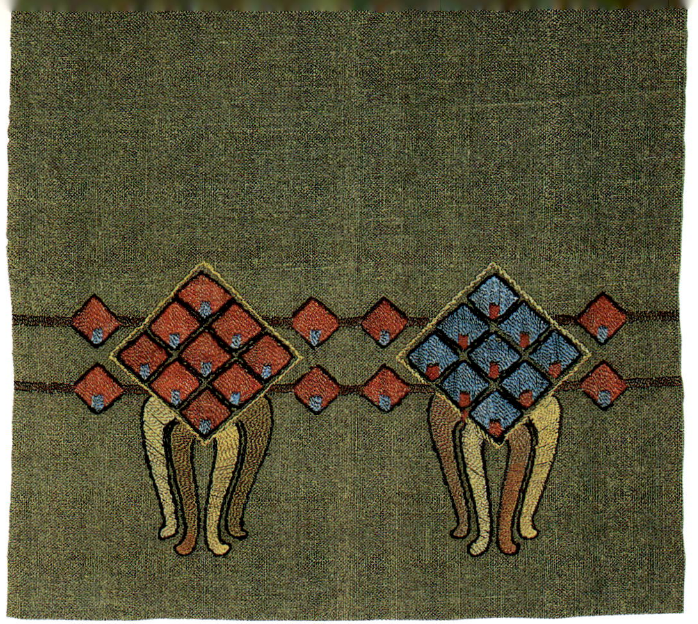

◀
Anonymous. Library table scarf with stylized floral design. c. 1914. Flax and jute fabric with rayon and metallic embroidery, 20 × 56" (51 × 142 cm). Collection Timothy Hansen and Dianne Ayres

positive spaces relieved by carefully executed drawn-work patterns that emphasize the structure of the fabric. Few textiles are recognized as such, and naturally dyed woven portieres, runners, and rugs fitting this description have never been exhibited as icons of the Arts and Crafts style. Yet, examples of plain textiles playing an important decorative role in period interior designs can be seen in the *Craftsman Homes* color plate showing plain corn-yellow linen scrims (see page 68), or in the L & JG interior showing copper-colored scrims (see page 106). Numerous mass-produced pillows and table scarves with stylized embroidery have been exhibited in major exhibitions as examples of the Arts and Crafts style. In addition, the rare but meticulously crafted and extensively ornamented needlework projects done at Newcomb, in Deerfield, and by famous artists are exhibited as representative of the style (pages 25, 36).

The inclusion of mass-produced patterns in most major museum collections and the elevation of ornamented textiles to iconic symbols are curious given the movement's initial preoccupation with handicraft and the democratization of art. It seems clear that museums and collectors have reached the unspoken consensus that ornament, rather than process, defines the style—at least in regard to decorative items like textiles. It is equally clear that flat, stylized ornament applied to naturalistically colored fabrics is greatly preferred to more naturalistic embroidery on a white background. Similarly, embroidered, block-printed and appliquéd work is greatly preferred to drawn, crocheted, or woven work.

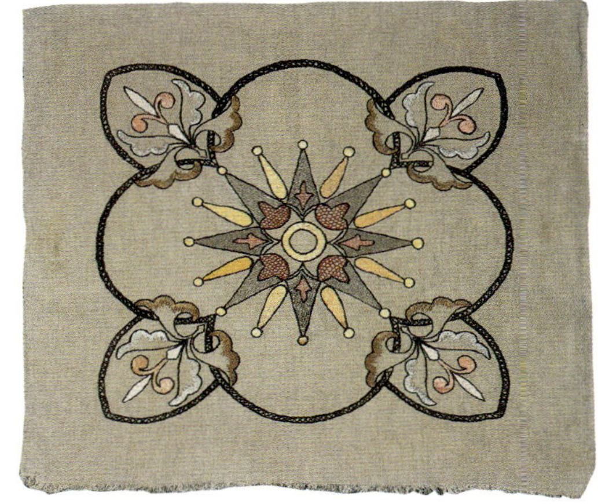

▶
Brainerd & Armstrong Company. Sofa cushion. "Star Design 478A." 1900. Cotton and silk embroidery on linen, 23 × 44" (58 × 112 cm)

▼
M. H. Birge & Sons Company. "Mission Interior Suggesting a Comfortable, Friendly, Cheerful Environment." Illustration from *Decoration of the School and Home*. 1916
The broad beams and simple lines are soothing, and the bold forms add interest without compromising the restfulness of the room.

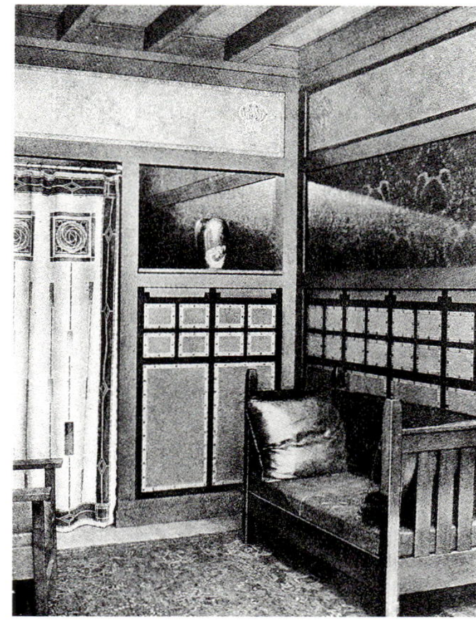

The Arts and Crafts Movement's Beginnings as a Revival of Craft

Shortly after the 1876 Centennial Exposition, Candace Wheeler and others established the New York Society of Decorative Art. Immensely successful, the group served as a model for many similar institutions throughout the country. One important function of these groups was the gathering and display of historical objects as examples of technique and as a resource for good design. One such exhibit was held by the Ithaca Branch of the New York Society of Decorative Art[2] in 1879. The exhibit contained more than fourteen hundred items for artistic inspiration, including embroidery and needlework (157 items), laces (114 items), bric-a-brac (331 items), furniture (18 items), and many other artifacts from all over the world. The exhibit also showed sixty-nine new pieces by Society members. Of these, twenty were embroideries. These twenty embroideries are not likely to be identified as Arts and Crafts unless the society member's intellectual relationship to the Arts and Crafts movement is known.

Candace Wheeler's textiles are among the earliest of American textiles that can be intellectually associated with the ideals of the Arts and Crafts movement. The elaborate pearl-laden portieres produced for The Mark Twain House in Hartford and the "Consider the Lilies of the Field" portieres (page 20) now in the collection of the Twain House embody the movement's principles; they are physical evidence of the impetus to elevate handicraft and beautify the home with art objects, albeit with objects that are conspicuously precious and, like Morris's own designs, inaccessible to all but the wealthiest consumers.

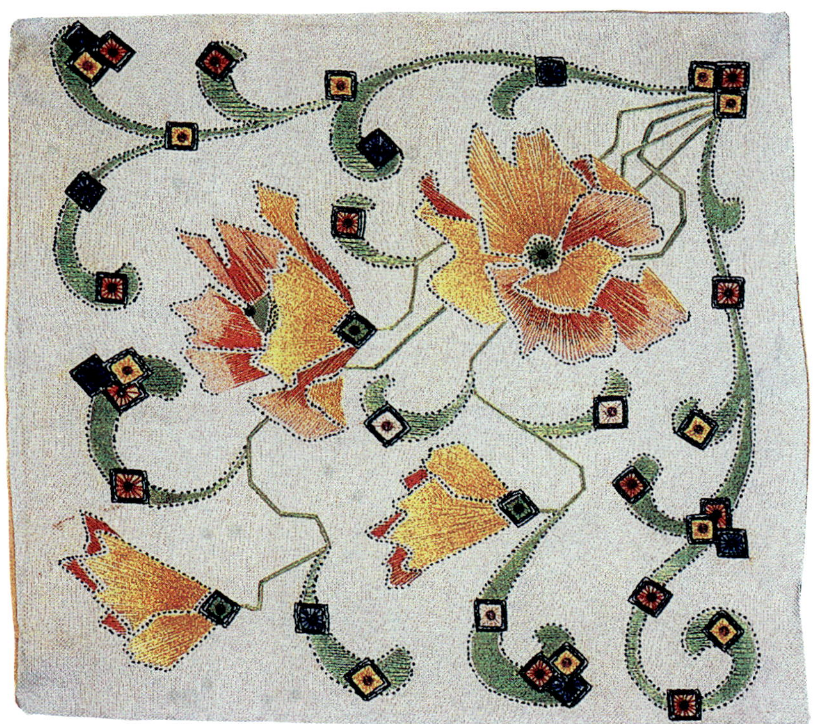

◀
Anonymous. Pillow with conventionalized poppy design. c. 1906. Silk embroidery over stenciling with glass beads on cotton monk's cloth, 20 × 18½" (51 × 47 cm). Collection Timothy Hansen and Dianne Ayres
The design radiates out from the lower left, getting lighter as it goes. This draws the eye up and to the right, which is more instinctive than drawing the eye in other directions.

From the beginning of the movement's influence on textiles in this country, their design was essentially determined by the source of inspiration and by the utilitarian role the artifact enjoyed in the home. American reformers and embroiderers were clearly aware of the artistic needlework movement in Europe through books, periodicals, and exhibitions. However, very few large tapestries, pictorial embroideries, and other monumental textiles were produced for American homes.

It is important to remember that the vast majority of the textiles encountered today were designed for middle-class homes. Amateur embroiderers desired home-based projects that could be completed rather quickly by individuals with moderate skill. Numerous design manuals and magazines provided direction to the women and men who designed the pillows, curtains, and runners that are identified as Arts and Crafts today. For those who found a prefabricated pattern just what they were looking for, or considered designing their own pattern too challenging, numerous ready-made kits including the pattern, fabric, and thread were available.

Both Arts and Crafts design (as a process or idea) and the Arts and Crafts style have their roots in nineteenth-century art practitioners' handbooks and manuals. Professional designers

▼

Charles G. Leland. "Teaching Aid Illustrating the Dyce Outline Method of Design." Illustration from *Drawing and Designing*. 1889
The student is urged to spend ninety percent of his time refining the construction lines, as in the top illustration, and then, at the end, adding the leaves or flowers, as shown in the bottom illustration.

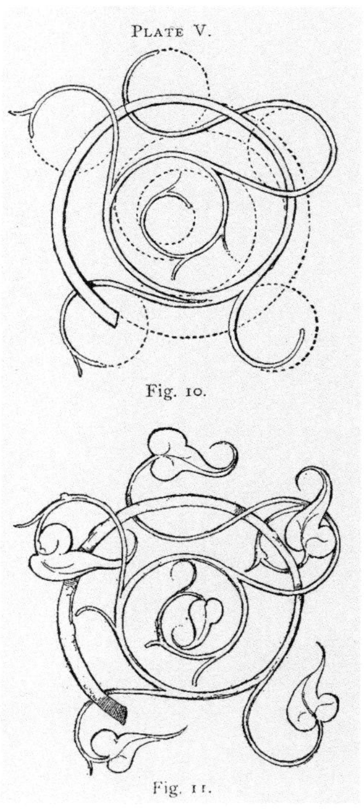

began publishing art-education texts that focused on the design process long before the Arts and Crafts period, yet these publications continued to influence artists long past the time when their initial audiences set them aside. William Dyce wrote and illustrated *Drawing Book*, a design text produced for English schools, in 1842. Although it is unlikely that American textile workers had ever even heard of William Dyce, they were familiar with his ideas through the work of Charles Leland and others. Textile pillows and curtains decorated in the Dyce "outline method" are encountered throughout the Arts and Crafts period and into the 1920s. The method was probably not taught in American schools much after 1900, replaced by teachings influenced by Arthur Wesley Dow and Denman Ross.

Charles Leland's *Drawing and Designing* was published in 1889 and was a standard American text at the time.[3] Leland stressed constructing an outline to which the leaves, flowers or details were then attached (left). Leland's faith in his students' abilities to create art must have endeared him to numerous students. He claimed that the study of these two plates prepared one to do anything author and designer Edward Hulme could do.[4] The flower-based design manuals generated by Leland, Hulme, and others proved inspirational to numerous textile workers, and close analysis of the stylization of flowers found in their work demonstrates that numerous American amateur and professional designers were aware of them.[5]

Christopher Dresser published his important text the *The Principles of Decorative Design* in 1873; three years later he visited New York, Philadelphia, and San Francisco during the

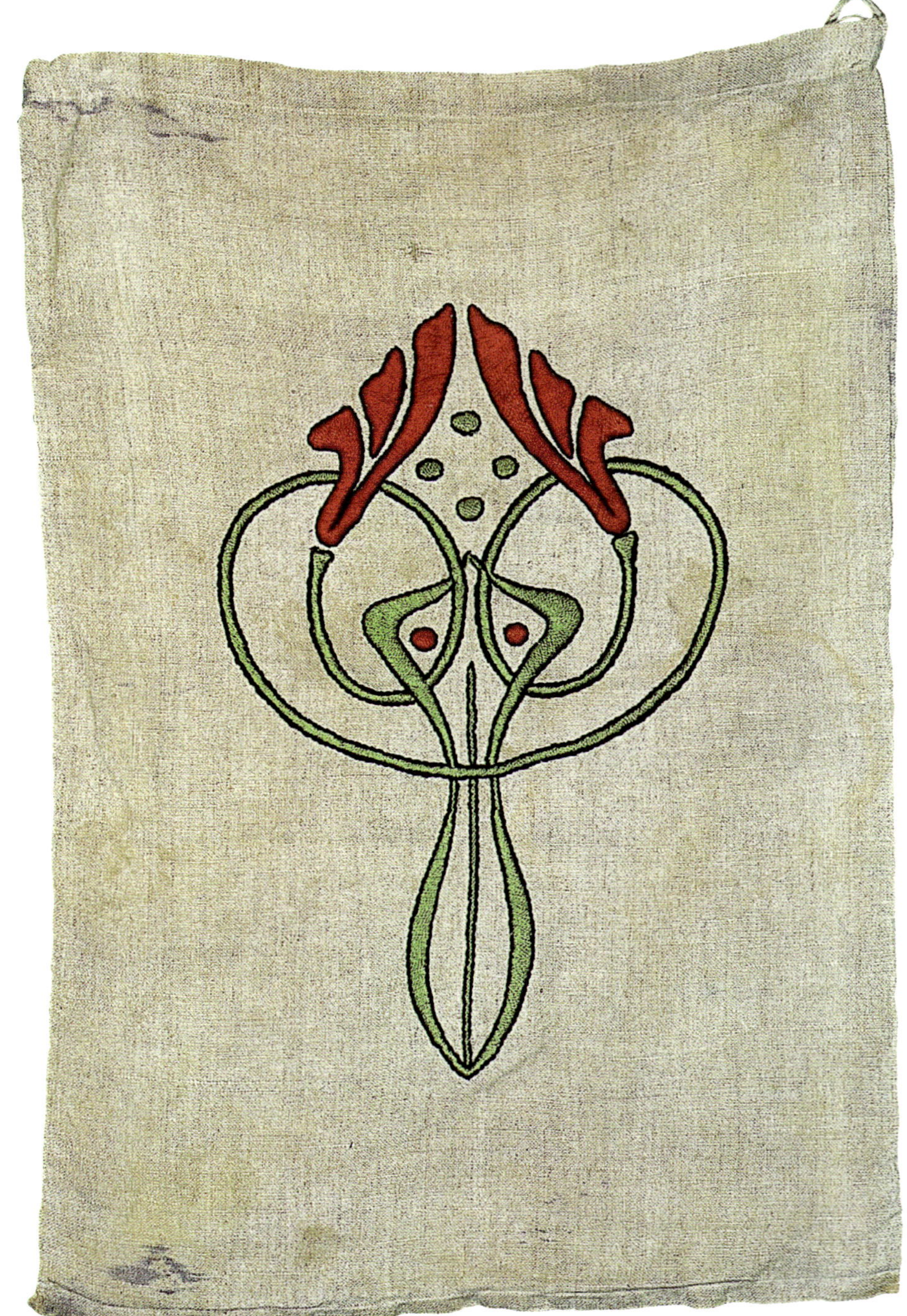

▶
Anonymous. Laundry bag with abstract design. c. 1909. Cotton embroidery on linen, 24 × 16" (61 × 41 cm). Collection Timothy Hansen and Dianne Ayres
This design can be seen as a conventionalized flower, but it also can be interpreted as an abstracted face. One way to determine if a design contains a face is to look for elements that can serve as the eyes. Once eyes are located a face will become apparent.

▶

Arthur Wesley Dow. "Schemes of Dark and Light in Two Values Using Flowers of Different Shapes." Illustration from *Composition*. 1913
Dow is credited with changing the emphasis in design teaching from construction lines to shapes and their tones. This change helped open up the way for conventionalized designs.

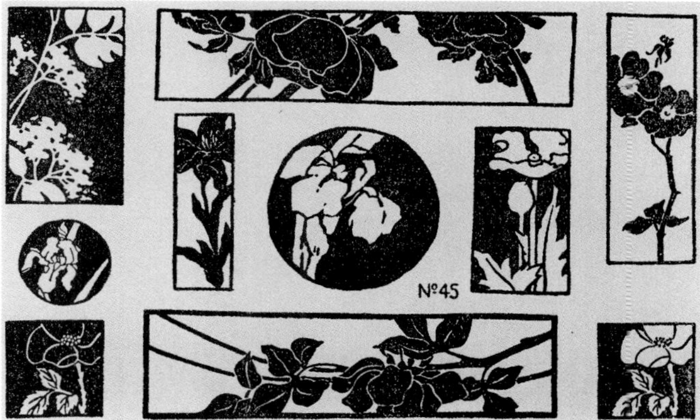

Philadelphia Centennial, spreading his ideas. Dresser and his work were widely admired in this country, and his book is a treasure of design information. His work illuminates the ability of designers, through the choice of lines and shapes, to give rise to feelings of harmony and repose or of energy and excitement. During this period the fashion was for designs that showed a lot of "excitement." In the illustration on page 37 (top) Dresser demonstrates how sharp, angular, or spiny forms could be more or less exciting. He also states that bold and broad forms are soothing, or tend to give repose. Such forms, identified with the Mission style, would become the fashion thirty years later. The illustration on page 37 (bottom), also by Dresser, conveys a sense of power, energy, force, and vigor. According to the text, he took his inspiration from bird bones (associated with the organs of flight), fish fins, and bursting buds in spring.

There is another kind of strength shown in the illustration on page 39 (bottom), suggested by the massive size of the beams and the solid woodwork, that conveys comfort and a sense of security. The text associated with the illustration explains:

> The proper balance between decorated and undecorated surfaces will result in a general effect of simplicity and restfulness, and yet there will be no lack of interest. . . . The wall has been broken into pleasing spaces by well-related panels, the general character of which is carried out in the design of door hanging. The more elaborate enrichment of the curtain is justified as it relieves the severity of the mission furniture and wall treatment.[6]

It is clear that the new style did not reject ornament; rather, it simply embraced a new kind of

▼
Maude Lawrence and Caroline Sheldon. Illustration from Teachers' Edition, *The Use of the Plant in Decorative Design*. 1912
The column of designs on the right are conventionalized from the naturalistic drawing on the left. Some of the designs are cross-sections focusing only on a small part of the plant. Color is changed to meet the needs of the design.

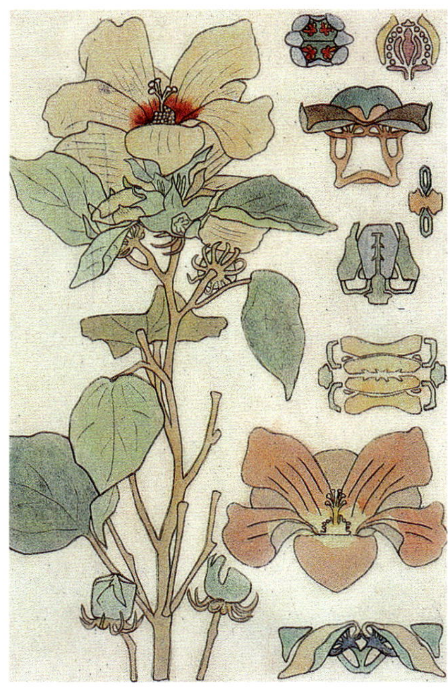

ornament that jettisoned the excitement of the earlier period and embraced the simple, cheerful, comfortable look that had become fashionable.

Textiles ornamented in a distinct Arts and Crafts style do not appear until the turn of the twentieth century. From about 1900 abstract stylized forms were used to ornament Gustav Stickley's Craftsman line. Shortly thereafter, women at the Newcomb College Embroidery began producing runners and decorative objects incorporating Arthur Wesley Dow's design principles. By 1906 and 1907 mass-produced patterns and kits for pillows, table scarves, laundry bags, and a limitless variety of forms were available through the mail to the readers of decorating and ladies' magazines.

With the emerging new style came a need for new methods of teaching design. The essence of the Arts and Crafts style as we understand it today can be gleaned from a basic study of Dow's influential book *Composition* (1899), Ernest Batchelder's books *The Principles of Design* (1904) and *Design in Theory and Practice* (1912), and Denman Ross's *Theory of Pure Design, Harmony, Balance and Rhythm* (1907). Dow is perhaps most responsible for the development of the American Arts and Crafts style. His interest in Japanese art, especially woodblock prints and textiles, led him, after his studies in France, to Boston. At the Museum of Fine Arts, Boston, he and Ernest Fenollosa, the noted connoisseur of Japanese art, developed a system of art that intended to synthesize Eastern and Western aesthetics. Their "synthetic system" became the basis of art education programs in the United States and Japan. From 1891 the system was taught at the Ipswich Summer School of Art, where prominent female designers and educators from Newcomb College were

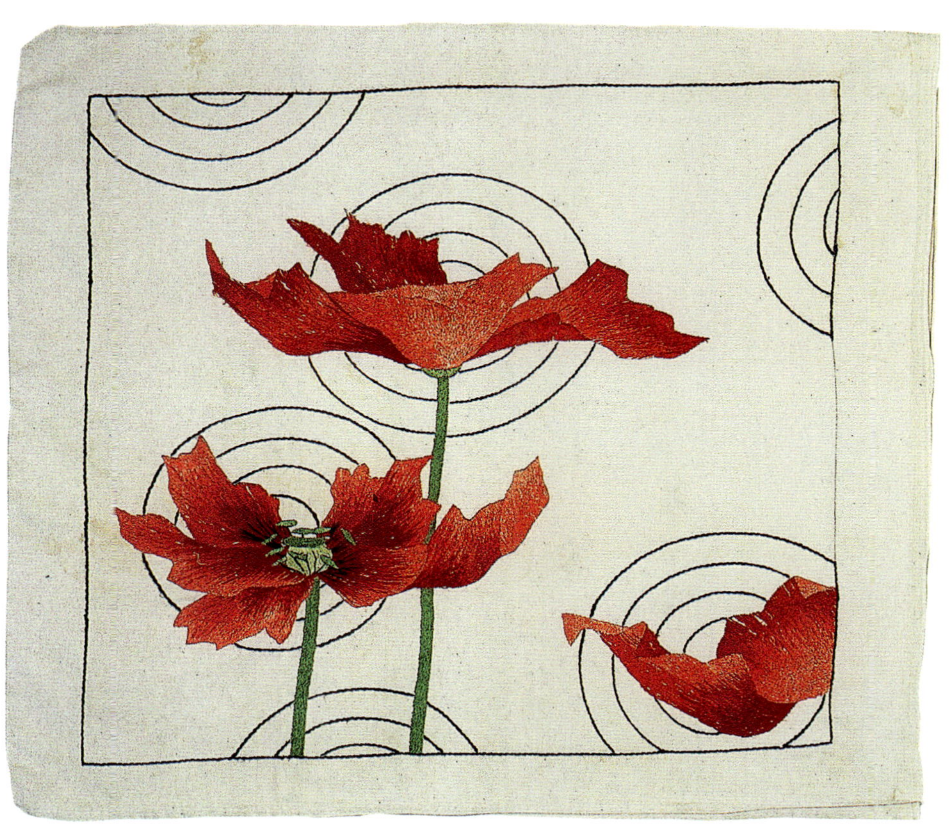

▶
Attributed to Belding Brothers. Pillow with stylized poppies and circles. c. 1903. Silk embroidery on cotton fabric, 19½ × 22" (49.5 × 56 cm). Collection Timothy Hansen and Dianne Ayres
The circles are used to draw the eye to the poppies and to create balance. The stylistic rendering of the flower in contrast to the geometric circles adds a considerable amount of interest.

among the noteworthy students. In 1895 Dow's system began reaching even larger audiences when he assumed a teaching post at Pratt Institute in Brooklyn, New York; in 1904, he left Pratt to direct the Teachers College of Fine Art at Columbia University.

Dow's influence on Arts and Crafts and American design is incalculable. He identified line, Notan (darks and lights in harmonic relations), and color as the three critical concerns of the artist. His suggestion that artists begin with bold outline drawing and then pursue sophisticated shade and color studies provided an ideal starting point for painters, woodblock printers, textile designers,

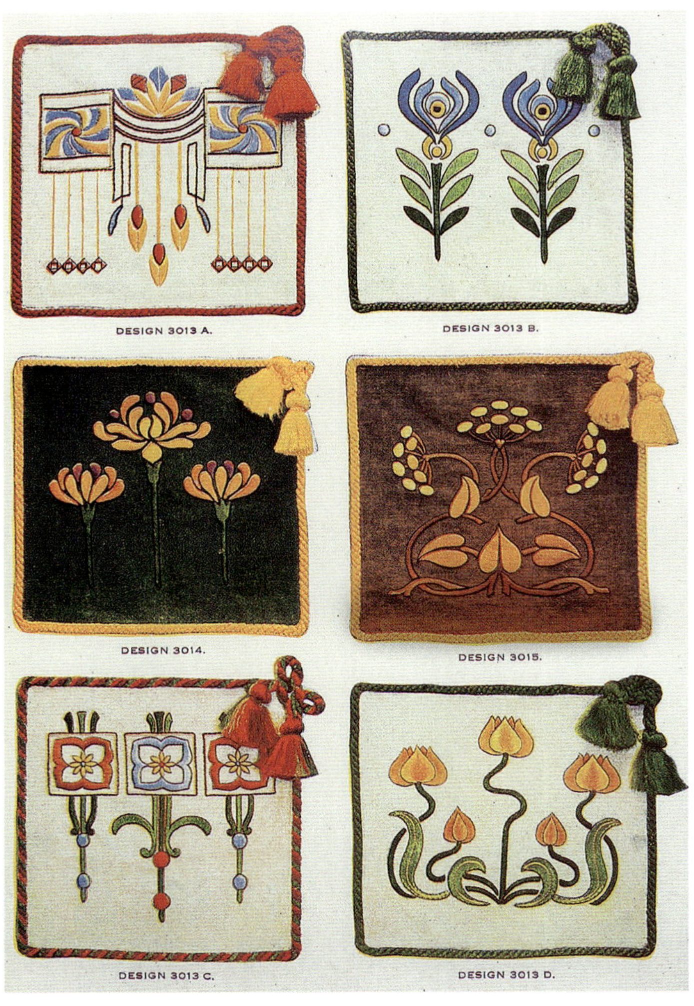

◄
Brainerd & Armstrong Company. "Six sofa cushions of conventional design." Illustration from *Embroidery Lessons With Colored Studies*. 1911
It is likely the artist derived these designs by using his or her general knowledge of plant forms, rather than basing them on specific plants.

►
Pedro de Lemos. "The Four Divisions of Design." Illustration from *Applied Art*. 1920
The terms used to describe different designs changed over time. Here the term stylized has been dropped, perhaps because it could be seen as a degree of conventionalization, or because it was associated with the Dyce Outline Method of designing, which had completely fallen out of favor among educators many years earlier.

and china painters (see page 43). Textiles produced in Gustav Stickley's Craftsman Workshops, in the Newcomb College embroidery guild, by the H. E. Verran Company, and by others all reveal the bold outline drawing and flat stylized patterns inspired by Dow and woodblock prints.

The Dow/Fenollosa system was first published in 1899 in *Composition*, a book that went through twenty editions over the next four decades. The choice of illustrations—including images of pottery, basketwork, tiles, and graphics—was markedly different from that found in other contemporary design manuals. The implied message was clear: artists should approach the decorative arts with the same exercise of aesthetic and compositional values as they approach painting. Likewise, painters could learn much about compositional balance and harmony from the study of the decorative arts.

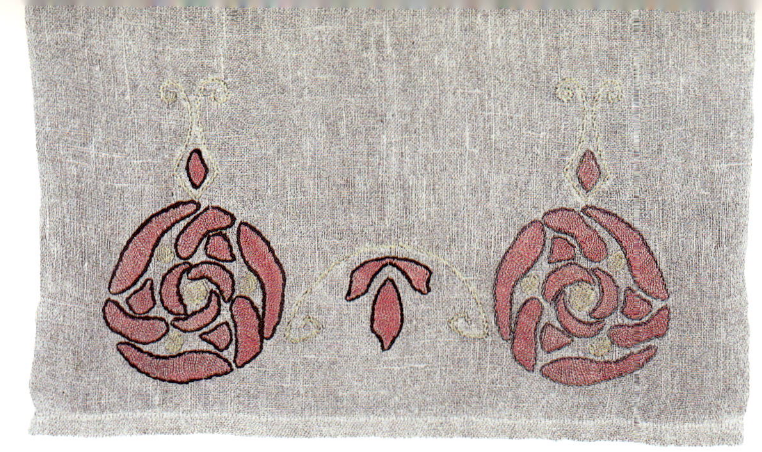

▶
Anonymous. Table scarf with conventionalized rose design. c. 1909. Cotton embroidery on linen fabric, 16 × 41" (41 × 104 cm). Collection Timothy Hansen and Dianne Ayres
Outlining an area with black or with the area's complementary color generally makes that area appear brighter. Here, the pink thread of both conventionalized flowers is the same, but the eye sees the flower outlined in black as brighter.

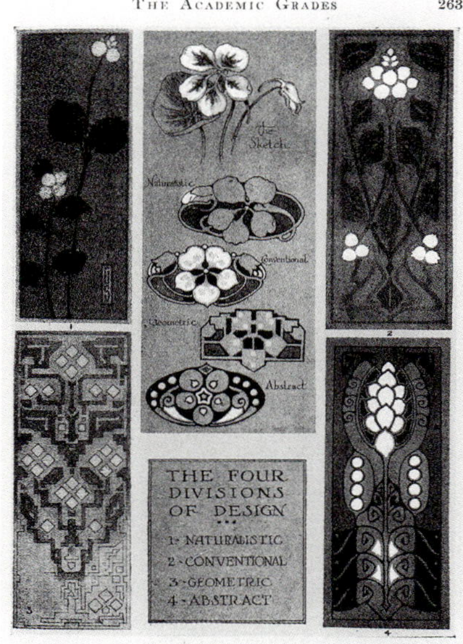

Denman Waldo Ross (1853–1935) received his PhD from Harvard in medieval studies in 1880. In 1907 he published the widely influential *A Theory of Pure Design, Harmony, Balance and Rhythm*. Ostensibly aiming his method toward painters and sketchers, Ross used abstract principles to explain the fundamental basis of design. He wrote, "in the practice of Art . . . we use certain terms and practice certain principles. . . . They are, so to speak, the form of the language . . . I propose to explain, not the artist, but the mode of expression which the artist uses. My purpose, in scientific language, is to define, classify, and explain the phenomena of Design."[7] Ross's work was used as a design textbook at Harvard and in many of the nation's most prominent art schools at the graduate level.

Ernest Batchelder, with his book *The Principles of Design* (1904), made some of the theories of Denman Ross accessible at the high school and undergraduate levels. Batchelder had studied with Ross at the Harvard Summer School of Design in 1901.[8] By stressing rhythm, balance, and harmony, the text had a profound effect on the design of the period. The emphasis on rhythm is perhaps the most significant contribution to Arts and Crafts design made by Ross and Batchelder. Rhythm in a design can be achieved by the regular repetition of a shape, as in the table scarves on page 49, or by the interrelationship of lines without repetition, as in the example on page 50 (top).

Batchelder's second book, *Theory and Practice of Design* (1907), breaks new ground in many areas. In addition to his significant discussion of the play impulse, his in-depth treatment of conventionalizing form is unsurpassed. He suggests that there are two main ways to derive conventionalized designs. One can start with a particular plant and abstract from it a design (page 44), or

◀
Charles Kelley and William Mowll. "Spot Composition in a Field." Illustration from *A Text-Book of Design*. 1912
This teaching aid shows how pleasing designs can be made through the repetition of elements.

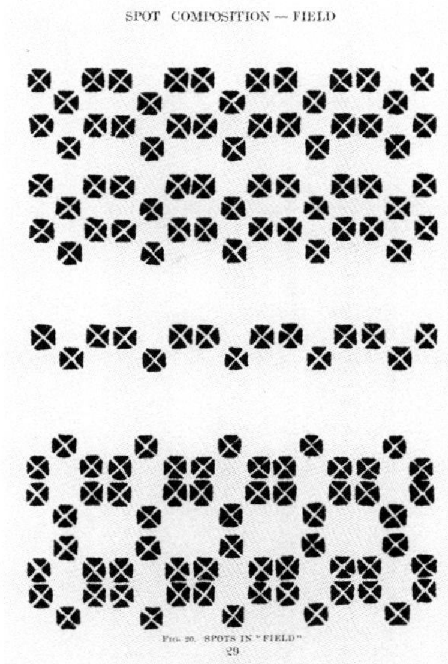

one can start from an abstract pattern and work one's knowledge of general plant forms into the design (page 46). In the first method it would be possible, given enough information, to determine what plant the design is derived from. In the second method there is no natural plant or flower to trace the design back to; thus, the question of what plant a particular design represents is meaningless.

It is often noted that poppy and rose motifs are very common in Arts and Crafts design. This is because they lend themselves easily to conventionalization. A period textbook explains:

> Every plant is just as worthy of study as the nasturtium, though some lend themselves more readily than others to application in decorative design. These, therefore, are more frequently seen in design. The most prominent in these characteristics is the rose, both the single wild rose and the double or cultivated rose. The former of these is easy to draw, exceedingly adaptable to any kind of decorative treatment, and is therefore more prominent than any other floral form in our modern decorative motives. The poppy seems to be next in favor, and this admits of even a wider diversity of treatment than does the rose, owing to the greater variety in the form of the leaf and the flower, but it is more difficult to draw and therefore does not find so much favor with the unskilled. But the iris, peony, thistle, daffodil, hollyhock, and numerous other bold, striking flowers are frequently seen in modern decorative designs and lend themselves readily to decorative treatment.[9]

Also, the designer was free to choose any color for conventionalized forms.[10]

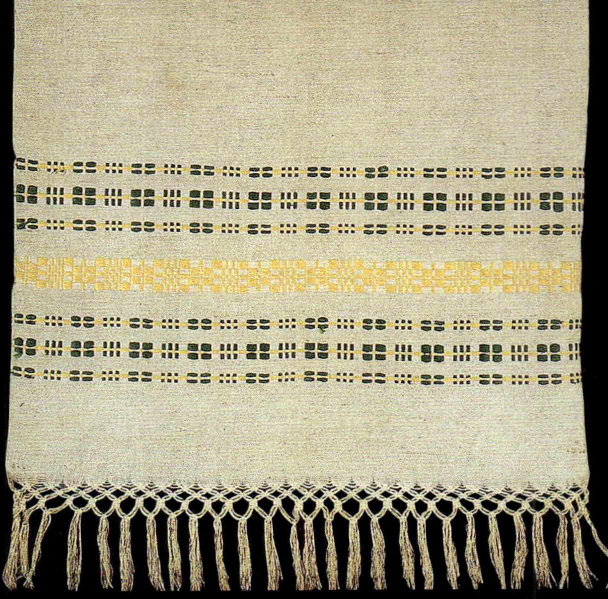

◀
Anonymous. Table scarf with spot composition ornament. c. 1912. Cotton embroidery on cotton and flax fabric, 20 × 62" (51 x157.5 cm). Collection Timothy Hansen and Dianne Ayres

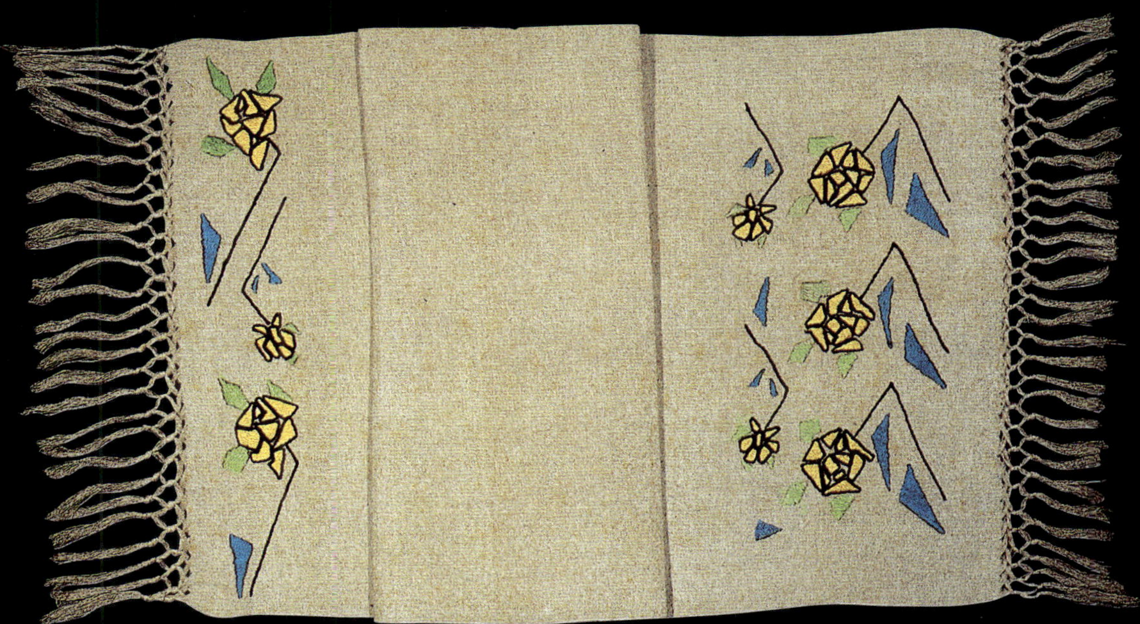

▶
Anonymous. Table scarf with conventionalized rose. Date unknown. Cotton embroidery on linen fabric, 17 × 51" (43 × 129.5 cm). Collection Timothy Hansen and Dianne Ayres
This design shows strong rhythm primarily through the repetition and direction of the bent stems and pointed leaves of the roses.

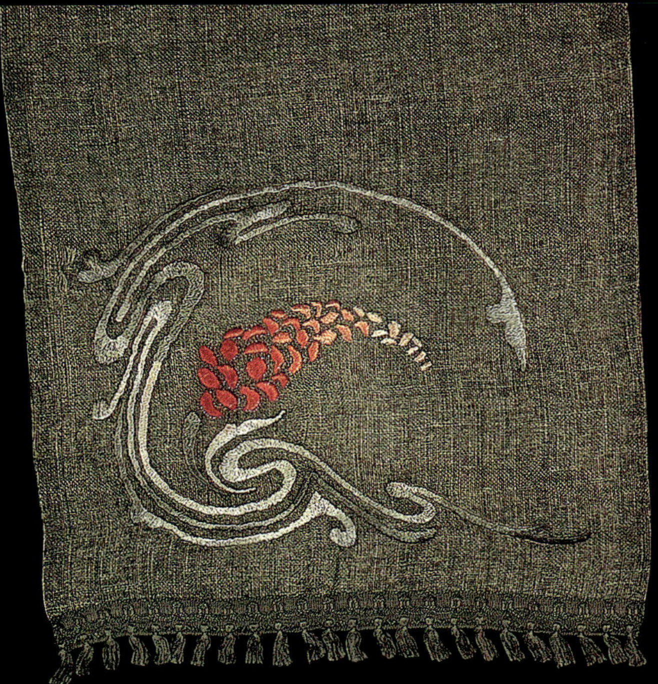

▲

Anonymous. Library table scarf with stylized floral design. c. 1914. Flax and jute fabric with rayon and metallic embroidery, 20 × 56" (51 × 142 cm). Collection Timothy Hansen and Dianne Ayres

The eye generally looks in the direction of converging lines. Here the eye is pulled in a clockwise direction.

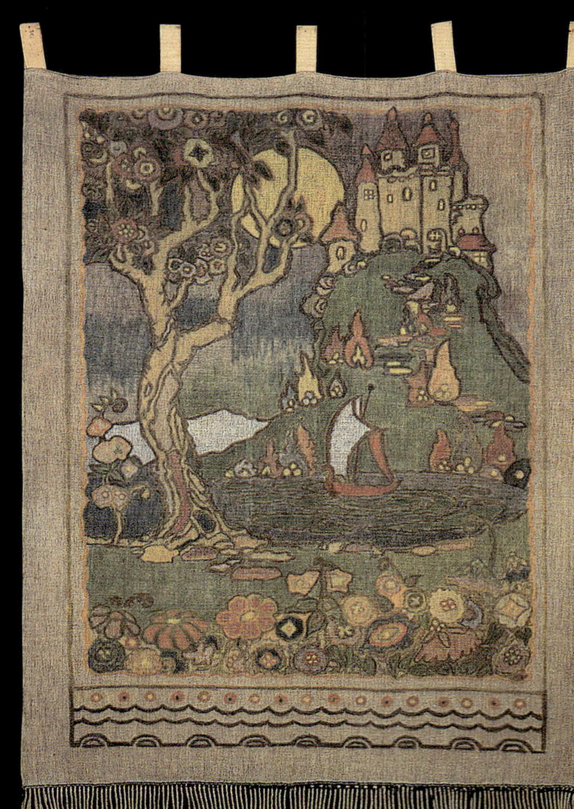

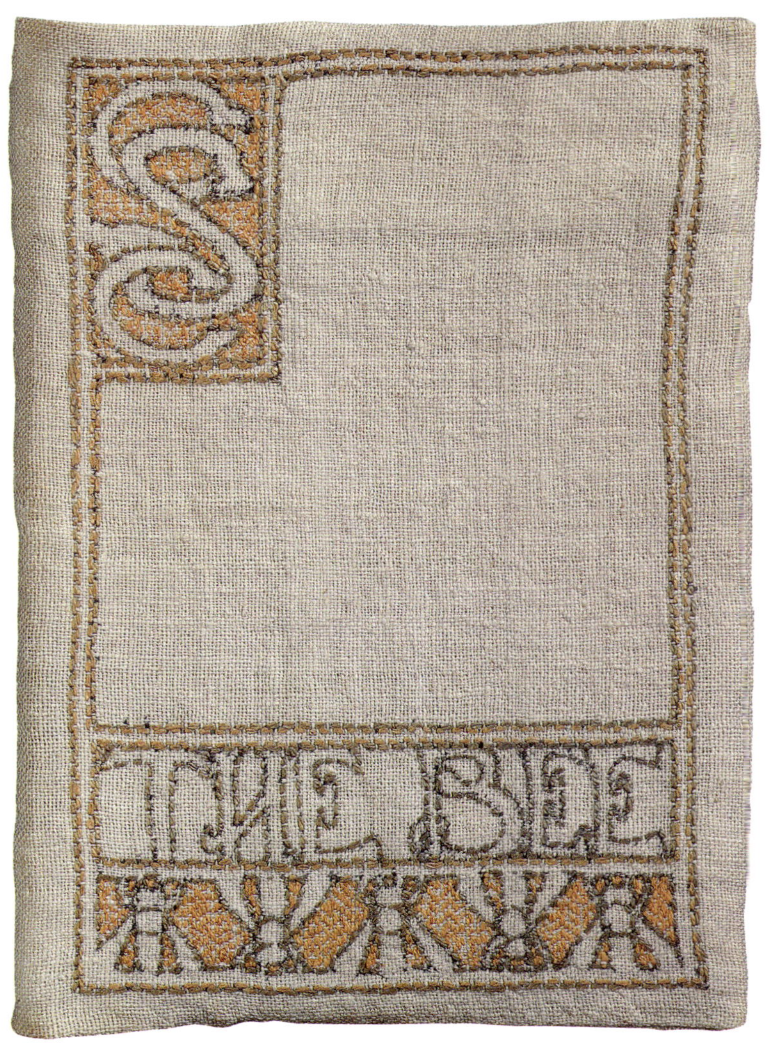

◀
Newcomb College. Book cover, *The Bee*. 1902–17. Linen and silk embroidery thread, 7½ × 9¾" (19 × 25 cm) . Collection Crab Tree Farm
Book covers were one of the forms produced within the Newcomb College curriculum. Labeled "The Bee," this book cover may have been designed for a favorite copy of Edward Maeterlinck's poplar work of that title.

The design manuals published by Dow and his contemporaries encouraged artists and craftsmen to break away from naturalistic representation and to explore a new set of conventionalized and abstract forms to express ideas. They also suggested that artists consider balance, proportion, simplicity, fitness to purpose, and truthfulness to materials as important guiding principles. To many Arts and Crafts designers and theorists, a successful design had to be not only handcrafted and appropriately ornamented but also of the correct scale, color, texture, and material for the room, placement, and purpose it was to serve. ❖

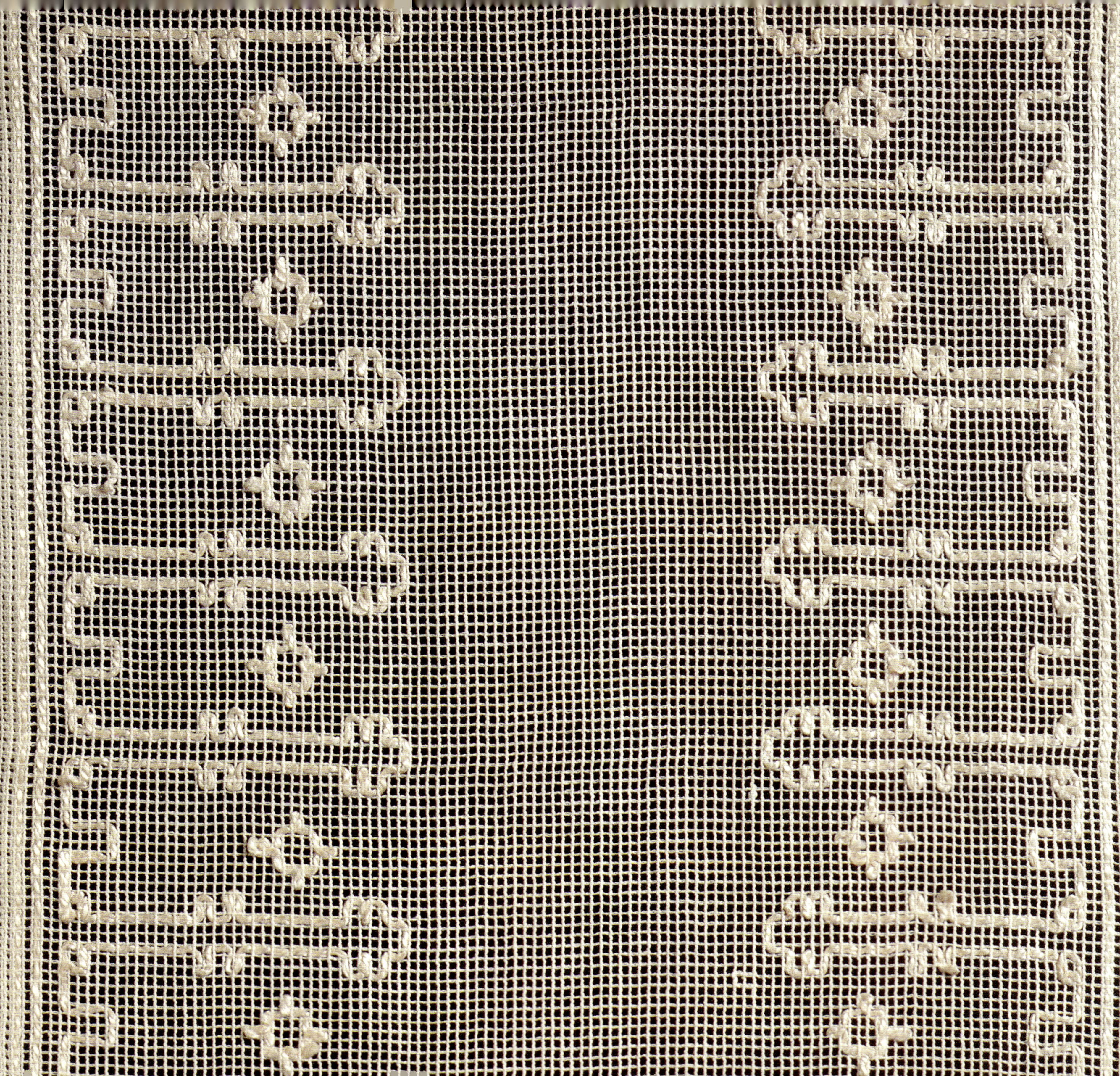

3 Coast to Coast: Dissemination of Ideas

> Democratic nations will therefore cultivate the arts that serve to render life easy in preference to those whose object is to adorn it. They will habitually prefer the useful to the beautiful and they will require that the beautiful should be useful.[1]
>
> — Alexis de Tocqueville

From the eighteenth century forward, writers such as Alexis de Toqueville popularized the idea of the simple life. Early twentieth-century designers and theorists recognized that to spread the ideas of the simple life of the Arts and Crafts movement they needed to reach the public through books, magazines, advertising, and schools.

The education and refinement of homeowners was critical. Nationwide, many families were able to own houses for the first time in their lives. Social theorists of the day recognized that the home played a critical role in human beings' individual, social, and cultural lives. Theorists decided to assist in the decorative process, producing hundreds of magazine articles and books on interior decoration.

During the Arts and Crafts period the majority of women did not go to college. Many encountered Arts and Crafts philosophy and design principles through magazines, lectures and women's clubs. In the late nineteenth century the circulation of home magazines grew across the country, aided by inexpensive printing techniques. Founded in 1896, *House Beautiful* reached a circulation of forty thousand by 1906. The much larger *Ladies' Home Journal*, which reached a circulation of one million readers, included designs for houses and interiors by noted Arts and Crafts designers

"How Other Women Live." Cover of *The Ladies' Home Journal*. February 15, 1911
Edward Bok, editor of *The Ladies' Home Journal* from 1889 to 1919, held tremendous sway with the opinions of American women. The series "Inside of 100 Homes" was responsible for helping the magazine to become the first to reach a circulation of one million. It could be relied upon for advice not only on home decoration but nearly any aspect of life that concerned women.

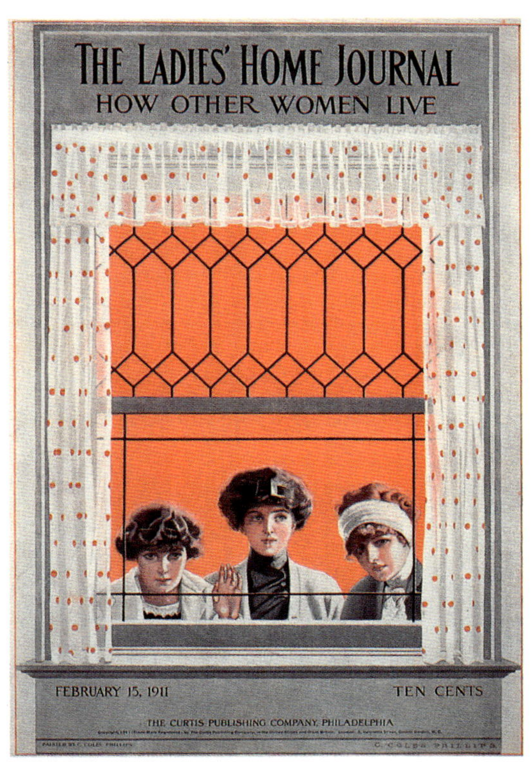

Will Bradley and Frank Lloyd Wright. *American Homes and Gardens, Good Housekeeping, The Delineator,* and *Harper's Bazaar* all carried articles on the home. These magazines thrived because thousands of middle-class Americans in the growing economy developed the means to fulfill the "American Dream" of owning a home.

Gustav Stickley established *The Craftsman* magazine in 1900 to share Arts and Crafts principles and philosophies for a simple life with this burgeoning group of new homeowners. *The Craftsman* was more philosophically oriented than its competitors but it reached a small dedicated audience. Like the larger shelter magazines, it offered practical designs for home furnishing, emphasizing simplification in both decoration and lifestyle and encouraging pleasure in handiwork.

Textiles were used in every room of the turn-of-the-century house. For Stickley and other proponents of the Arts and Crafts lifestyle, the continuing development of textiles as a home art furthered the development of the middle-class home as a place of repose, beauty, and artfulness. The generation of Americans who purchased and built the majority of Arts and Crafts homes were first-time home buyers, particularly receptive to decorating with objects and furnishings appropriate to the style of architecture. The majority of linens and accessories used in these homes were made by the homemaker, her daughters, or her female friends.

Numerous high-end architects included textiles as part of the complete interiors their clients requested. Early Frank Lloyd Wright, George Maher, and Greene and Greene interiors incorporated stenciled, appliquéd, woven, and embroidered textile pieces. However, the philosophical

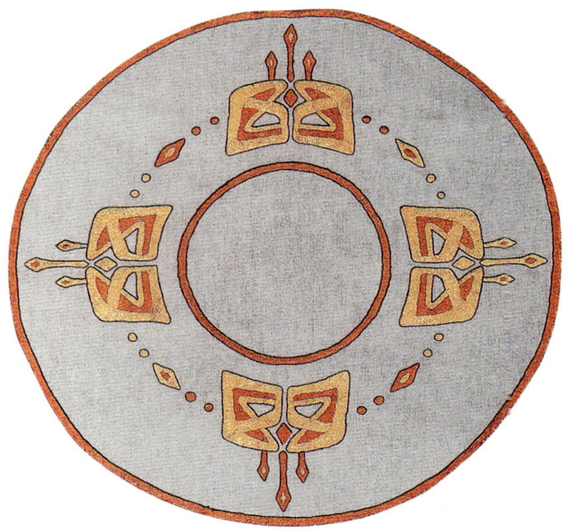

▶
The Home Pattern Company. Round table linen. c. 1912. Linen with silk hand embroidery, 21" (53.34 cm) diam. Collection Chris Walther and Susan Stockton
The Home Pattern Company was the *The Ladies' Home Journal*'s branch for marketing textile kits and patterns. This design was said to be of German origin although it has strong Celtic lines.

approach of many of these leaders differed from that of the practitioners and proponents who supplied material to the magazines. Knowing their work was unattainable to the American masses, they sought to fulfill the Arts and Crafts edicts of excellent craftsmanship and design. But the role of disseminating the political and social ideas of the movement and specifying objects that reflected the sentiment of the craftsperson was filled by the influential writers who published articles offering how-to advice on techniques, do-it-yourself projects, and lessons in design. Through this popularization of the Arts and Crafts movement, more affordable, albeit sometimes lesser quality, items were produced.

Specialized needlework magazines such as *The Modern Priscilla*, *Home Needlework Magazine*, and *Needlecraft* all published techniques, designs, and methods for home textile projects. In 1911 *The Modern Priscilla* had a circulation of more than three hundred thousand copies and by 1914 it had increased to four hundred thousand.[2] *Keramic Studio* carved a unique role for itself by cross-marketing to both specialized china-painting and textile enthusiasts. The editor's awareness that two-dimensional patterns for china were applicable to textiles, pottery, and woodblock prints helped boost circulation.

The articles and advertisements in the shelter and needlework magazines shared three themes: beautifying the American home, illustrating new production techniques, and creating one's own gifts. Textiles one might make for gifts included towels, ornamental storage bags for laundry, collar and cuff sets, and tie racks. Natural motifs were encouraged, such as using pine

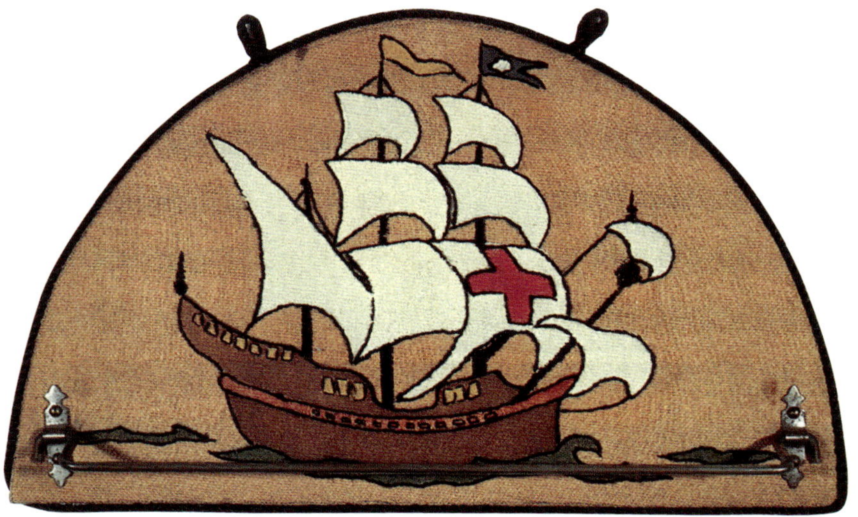

◀
Anonymous. Ship tie rack made from a kit. c. 1906–15. Stenciled and hand embroidered linen on cardboard, 8 × 13" (20.3 × 33 cm). Collection Tommy and Beth Ann McPherson

cones as a decorative element on pine-needle-filled pillows. In July 1905, the Craftsman Workshops ran an ad that read: "What better way to spend the leisure hours of vacation time than with some of the Craftsman needlework. It is not tedious and is just the thing to take with you to the country or the seaside. It may be there is need for a pillow in your window seat; a pair of portieres for the winter home; a luncheon set as a Christmas gift. Any of these we will be glad to send you stamped, with all materials, ready for working."[3]

The Ladies' Home Journal and *Harper's Bazaar* introduced textile contests that encouraged their readership to utilize Arts and Crafts ideals by crafting objects. Projects included pillows, runners, and other home goods, and both men and women participated in these contests. Sometimes competition exhibitions were open to the public; *Harper's Bazaar*'s exhibitions sometimes attracted upwards of twenty thousand visitors.[4] Periodicals played a key role in demonstrating how Arts and Crafts style textiles could be used in decorating in the modern-day home. Without their influence, few people would have been aware of the new design trend.

John Dewey and other progressive educational philosophers of the era emphasized the importance of integrating activities of the mind and body. Schools instructed women in both textiles and

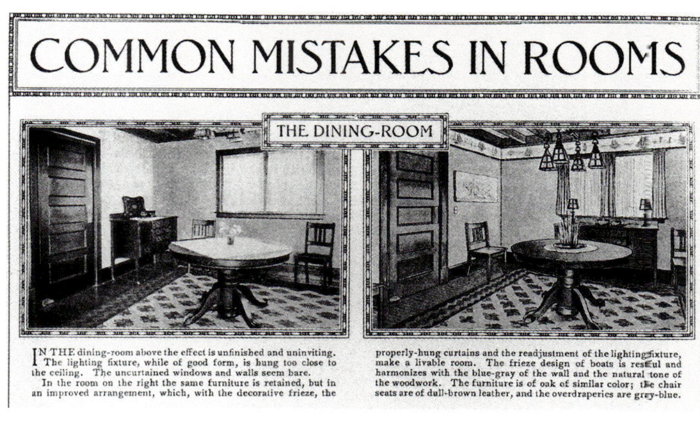

COMMON MISTAKES IN ROOMS

THE DINING-ROOM

IN THE dining-room above the effect is unfinished and uninviting. The lighting fixture, while of good form, is hung too close to the ceiling. The uncurtained windows and walls seem bare.

In the room on the right the same furniture is retained, but in an improved arrangement, which, with the decorative frieze, the properly-hung curtains and the readjustment of the lighting fixture, make a livable room. The frieze design of boats is restful and harmonizes with the blue-gray of the wall and the natural tone of the woodwork. The furniture is of oak of similar color; the chair seats are of dull-brown leather, and the overdraperies are gray-blue.

▲

"Common Mistakes in Rooms." *The Ladies' Home Journal*. October 1909

design because art was one of few acceptable forms of education for women. During the late nineteenth and early twentieth centuries art education came into its own, teaching future female teachers the importance of art education in teaching basic principles of good design. Design manuals, art education programs, and women's organizations emerged to support these ideas, and even child development theories began to emphasize children's natural tendencies toward art.

During the 1890s widespread popular interest in decorative arts, including American needlework, and in the ideals of the Arts and Crafts movement converged. Over a period of less than ten years the demand for design manuals presenting a codified aesthetic system and the related school programming required to train artists and teachers evolved. The new methods reached the masses quickly, as the new style was taught in almost all academic programs and included in popular journals concerned with modern decorative arts and interior design. The suitability of textiles as a medium for utilizing new design principles was emphasized.

Arthur Wesley Dow is perhaps most responsible for the development of the Arts and Crafts style. His interest in Japanese art, especially woodblock prints and textiles, led him from his studies in France to Boston, where he and Ernest Fenollosa developed a system of art that intended to integrate Eastern and Western aesthetics and made it the basis of art-education programs in the United States and Japan. Their theories found practical application through Dow's publication *Composition* (1899), and by about 1900 their concepts were being taught at Pratt Institute and Columbia University.

▼

"Embroidered Accessories." *Home Needlework Magazine*. December 1906

Myriad items were available for the home needleworker: desk blotters, pen wipers, cravat holders, collar bags, work bags, calendars, cases for rolling other embroidered linens, laundry bags, toilet aprons for the traveler, and match scratchers.

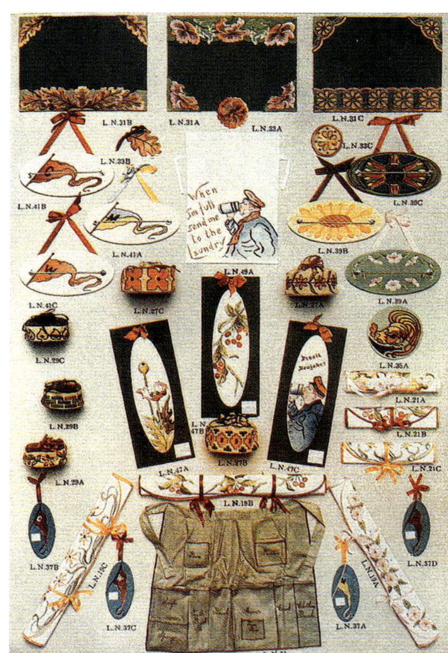

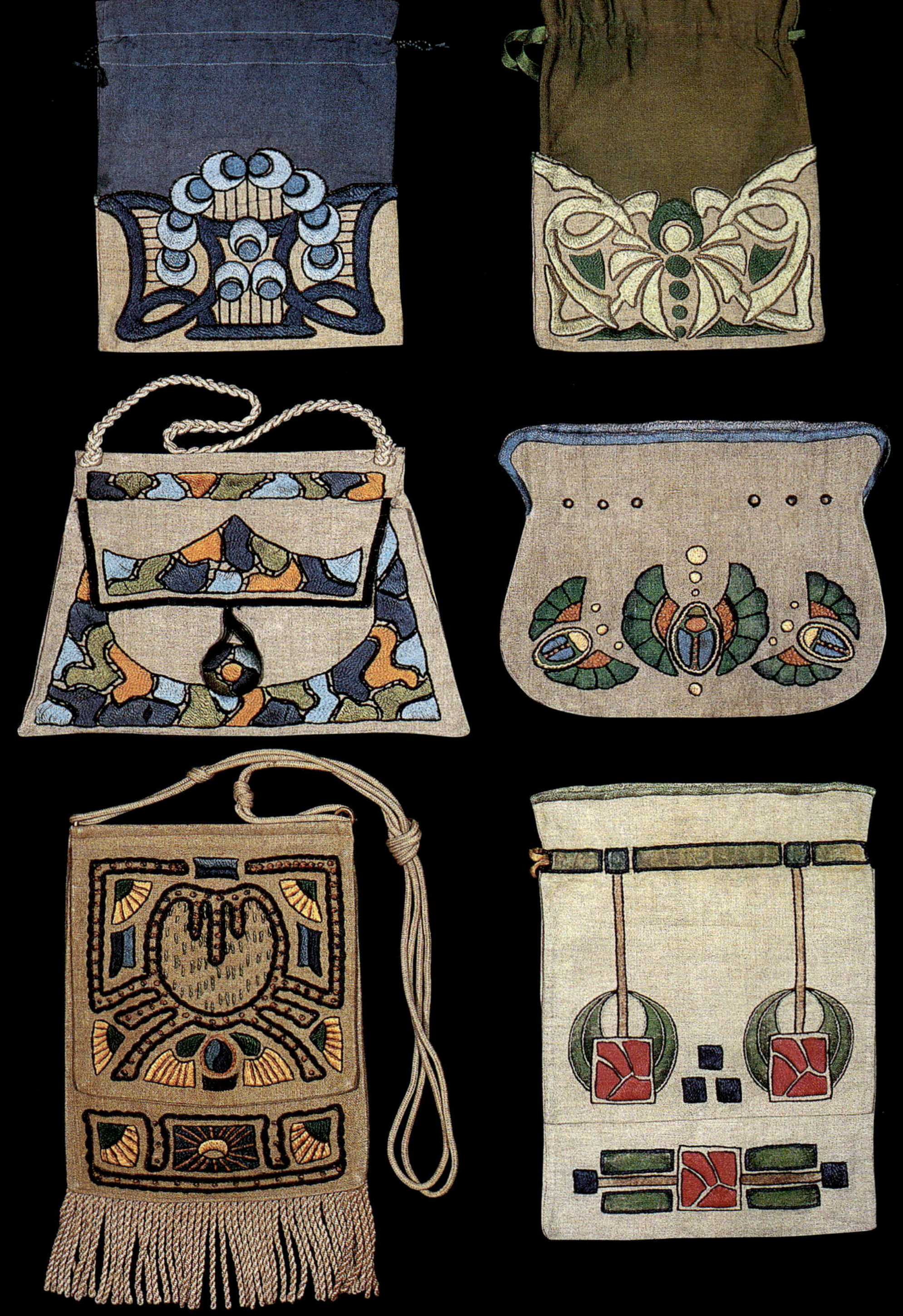

◀
H. E. Verran Company (bottom four) and others. Group of embroidered bags. c. 1912. Linen with hand embroidery. Collection Chris Walther and Susan Stockton
Bags were made for a variety of purposes. The top two and center right are work bags for taking one's needlework project along on a trip. The bottom right is a double work bag, having a second smaller pocket on front for supplies. The center and lower left are hand bags; kits for these included the bone stays and handles.

Dow was far from a lone practitioner in the development of the new style. Denman Ross, Ernest Batchelder, Pedro de Lemos, and numerous others included and emphasized historic and Far Eastern textiles and crafts in their manuals and design courses taught throughout the country. Nationally available textbooks at the primary and secondary levels, such as the Prang series, helped to spread the principles of Arts and Crafts design. Working from Dow's system of composition, the textbooks emphasized balance, harmony, and rhythm and utilized drawing to explain the basic principles of design. These ideas were transferred to various craft techniques and interpreted in different mediums.

One principle advised taking advantage of nature's tendencies toward subtle colors and rhythm rather than discord. Students were encouraged to keep notes on nature's colors and to render natural objects in a realistic or naturalistic way before learning to draw in a stylized or conventionalized manner.

Art educators included interior decoration in their curricula even for their young students. Bonnie Snow and Hugo Froehlick's Industrial Art Textbooks taught youth the inherent value of color, art, costume, and interior decoration. Prang and the A. S. Barnes Company published school workbooks that conveyed Arts and Crafts ideas to children from coast to coast, who could manufacture miniature room settings and learn the principles of interior color harmony. Chapters on domestic art demonstrated the importance of textiles in the home: "There is no more vital or practical medium for the expression of design than a needle and thread."

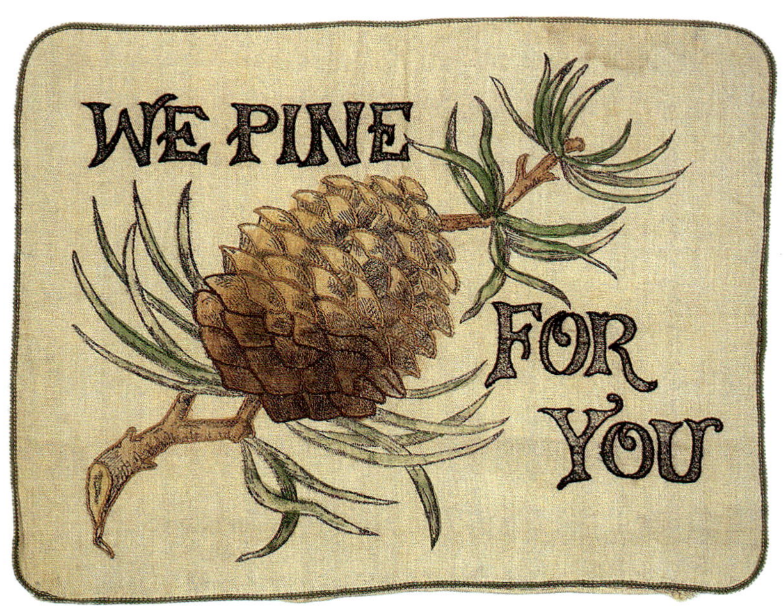

◄
Anonymous. "We Pine for You" pillow. c. 1905–15. Linen with stencil and cotton embroidery, 11½ × 15" (29.2 × 38.1 cm). Collection Tommy and Beth Ann McPherson

Several university-level schools sponsored exhibitions of Arts and Crafts materials. The gallery at Pratt Institute, for example, hosted numerous shows of Grueby pottery, Tiffany glass, and Japanese and Persian textiles. Museums also supported Arts and Crafts textile enthusiasts. A Needlework & Textile Guild was set up at the Art Institute of Chicago and the Museum of Fine Arts, Boston, established a School of Needlework.

The majority of the education programs and manuals focused upon the process of design. However, they seldom lost sight of the fact that their mission was to develop consumers as well as artisans. By 1900 the majority of educators realized "most of our pupils will be the purchasing public of the future, and it is of as much importance for them to buy intelligently as for the designer and craftsman to create intelligently."[5] It was believed that if people were given knowledge of form, color, and composition they would become both better artists and better consumers. The textiles and crafts produced for home use were primary vehicles through which the principles of fitness of design could be introduced into the typical American living room.

Design reformers working with the ideas of Arthur Wesley Dow as presented in *Composition* and Denman Ross as presented in *A Theory of Pure Design, Harmony, Balance and Rhythm* (1907) saw textiles as a means to reach large numbers of people across economic boundaries. Part of the attraction to these new design principles was their flexible application to any type of art or object; however, the designs were easiest to achieve in flat mediums, such as textiles. Artisans and craftspeople producing commissioned work for patrons or juried exhibitions worked in a style

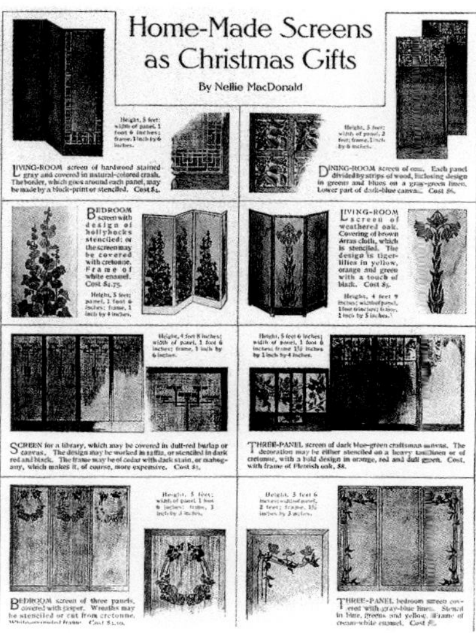

Home-Made Screens as Christmas Gifts

By Nellie MacDonald

LIVING-ROOM screen of hardwood stained gray and covered in natural-colored crash. The border, which goes around each panel, may be made by a block-print or stenciled. Cost $4.

Height, 5 feet; width of panel, 1 foot 6 inches; frame, 1 inch by 6 inches.

DINING-ROOM screen of oak. Each panel divided by strips of wood, inclosing design in greens and blues on a gray-green linen. Lower part of dark-blue canvas. Cost $6.

Height, 5 feet; width of panel, 2 feet; frame, 1 inch by 6 inches.

BEDROOM screen with design of hollyhocks stenciled; or the screen may be covered with cretonne. Frame of white enamel. Cost $4.75.

Height, 5 feet; panel, 1 foot 6 inches; frame, 1 inch by 4 inches.

LIVING-ROOM screen of weathered oak. Covering of brown Arras cloth, which is stenciled. The design is tiger-lilies in yellow, orange and green with a touch of black. Cost $5.

Height, 4 feet 9 inches; width of panel, 1 foot 6 inches; frame, 1 inch by 5 inches.

Height, 4 feet 8 inches; width of panel, 1 foot 6 inches; frame, 1 inch by 6 inches.

SCREEN for a library, which may be covered in dull-red burlap or canvas. The design may be worked in raffia, or stenciled in dark red and black. The frame may be of cedar with dark stain, or mahogany, which makes it, of course, more expensive. Cost $3.

Height, 5 feet 6 inches; width of panel, 1 foot 6 inches; frame 1½ inches by 1 inch by 4 inches.

THREE-PANEL screen of dark blue-green craftsman canvas. The decoration may be either stenciled on a heavy tan linen or of cretonne, with a bold design in orange, red and dull green. Cost, with frame of Flemish oak, $8.

▶
Nellie MacDonald. "Home-Made Screens as Christmas Gifts." *The Ladies' Home Journal.* October 1909

that could be replicated or copied by almost any needleworker. The simplicity of design and the dissemination of Arts and Crafts ideals through inexpensive manuals and exhibitions made high-style textile design accessible to middle-class consumers.

By the turn of the century many colleges and technical schools, such as the Massachusetts Normal School and Tallulah Falls Industrial School, began offering courses in textiles as part of their industrial arts programs. Newcomb College's craft program in New Orleans, Louisiana was established in 1886–87, one of the first of its kind; Gertrude Roberts Smith taught a course on textiles in 1902–03. By 1907–08 Smith was listed as a professor of watercolor painting and decoration of textiles. She supervised the production of embroideries, which grew to be as well known in their day as the school's line of pottery. Advertisements for Newcomb read "Newcomb Pottery & Embroidery—The Art Crafts of the South."

Materials commonly used at Newcomb consisted of heavy linen crash and silk threads. Designs were conventionalized motifs inspired by flora and fauna indigenous to the South. Outline stitches demarcated and emphasized form, while shades of color created appropriate shades of light and dark.

In 1904 spinning and weaving was added to the Newcomb curriculum, with some pieces being spun, woven, designed, and executed by one worker. *The Craftsman* of December 1903 extols their work: "The real artist delights to become the craftsman. The craftsman finds his keenest joy in work which appeals to the artist within him. . . . In their skilful [sic] hands, each

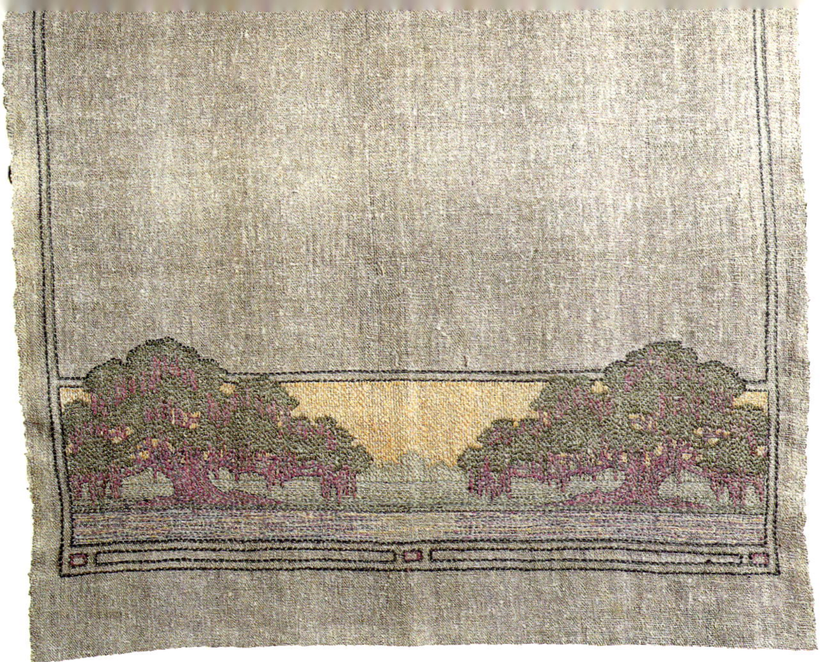

◀
Anna Francis Simpson. Newcomb table runner "Cypress Trees." c. 1902–15. Handwoven linen with hand embroidery in silk, 26 × 87" (66 × 221 cm.). Collection Crab Tree Farm
Newcomb textiles were sold at Newcomb College, in exhibitions, and at many shops throughout the United States that also sold Newcomb pottery, such as Paul Elder's Bookshop in San Francisco. This may be the piece listed in a special exhibition of the Art Association of New Orleans, May 1915, as "Runner, Cypress $30."

design becomes individual and unique. Planned for its best service, however simple, it is recognized as a creation; and the signature of the creator is stitched into the design, as well as the mark of the college approbation N.T.N."[6] (opposite).

Berea College in Kentucky developed an influential textile program in spinning and weaving. Founded on the democratic principles of education that Gustav Stickley and the editorial staff promoted through *The Craftsman*, the college stated in its 1893 catalog: "education cannot be gathered primarily from books . . . the hand must be trained to obey the mind, and the eye to distinguish between things which differ. . . . Every young person should be taught to enjoy doing manual work well, both as a preparation for real life, and as a development of character."[7] In 1902 Berea College president William Goodell Frost set up a textile workroom in a log cabin. The college sponsored homespun fairs to encourage the continuing development of this "fireside industry," and by 1903 Berea objects were included in exhibitions sponsored by *The Craftsman*. By 1911, Anna Ernberg, a Swedish weaver from New York City who taught at Pratt Institute and Teacher's College, Columbia University, joined the staff to continue to expand the program. The purchase of a Berea coverlet required a strong commitment to support Arts and Crafts movement ideals: Berea coverlets sold for six to eight dollars each, quite out of reach for most people.[8]

Lucy Calista Morgan, a former Berea student and a teacher at the Appalachian Industrial School for adults and children, founded the Department of Fireside Industries/Penland Weavers and Potters in Penland, North Carolina, to preserve local craft traditions. Her annual workshops

▼

Anna Francis Simpson. Mark on Newcomb table runner, "Cypress Trees" [detail]. Collection Crab Tree Farm

Newcomb textiles were judged by the Newcomb Art School Jury of Standards. Those deemed worthy received the "NC" mark. Early pieces (1902–04) may have been marked "NTN." Sometimes the artist's initials were hidden among the stitches or embroidered next to the Newcomb College mark.

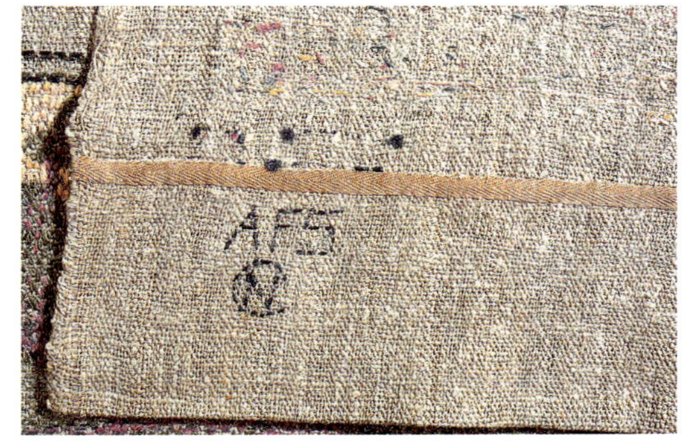

evolved into a weaving institute and today's Penland School of Handicraft.[9] Morgan understood the relationship between Arts and Crafts movement ideals and traditional Southern craft and she stated "The revival of colonial weaving . . . brings a new kind of industrial revolution. It makes possible for the people to stay in the mountain home with its high ideals and to do there a work which brings economic independence, at the same time satisfying a natural artistic taste and an inborn creative impulse."[10]

On the West Coast, Arts and Crafts programs also opened their doors to students interested in learning the applied and fine arts. In 1906, the Oregon School of Arts and Crafts was founded in Portland by Julia Horrman to teach seven disciplines in the applied arts. Classes were offered in bookplates, bindings, calligraphy, metalwork, ceramics, furniture, glass, embroidery, and rugs. In the following year, Frederick Henry Meyer founded the School of the California Guild of Arts and Crafts, later to become the California College of Arts and Crafts. The school initially offered primarily applied-arts coursework, including drawing, design, and composition. Further courses introduced students to jewelry making, woodcarving, pottery, and textile arts, including weaving and embroidery.

Many devotees of handicrafts could not afford a two- or four-year industrial arts program but instead chose to attend one of the countless summer schools offered from coast to coast. Summer schools devoted to art were popular in the nineteenth century, and in the last decade of the century applied arts were added to their curricula. In 1891 Arthur Wesley and Minnie Dow

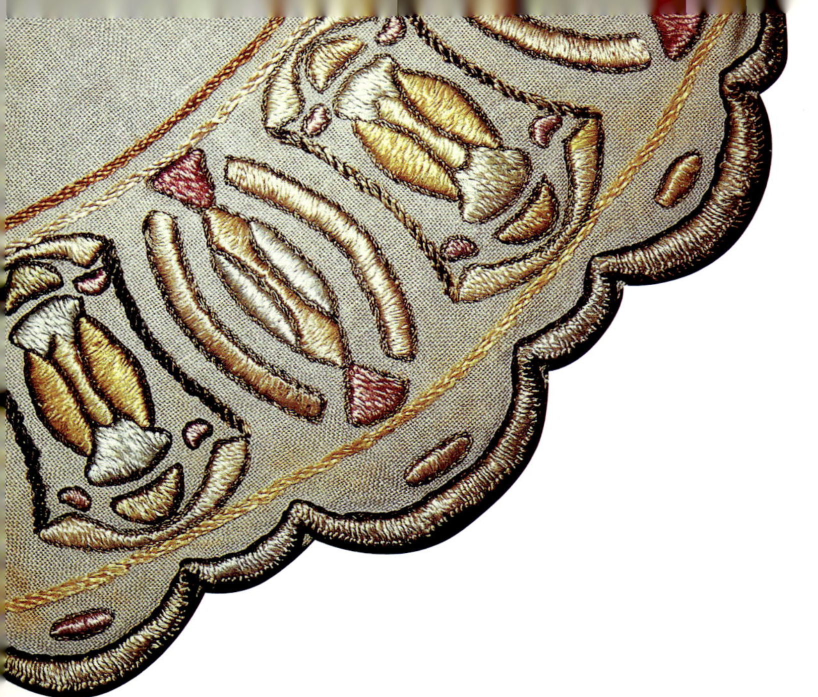

◀
Lamont Warner Estate. Table round made from a kit. c. 1902–15. Hand embroidered on linen, 28" (71 cm) diam. Collection Tim Gleason
Even designers enjoyed the benefit of the kit industry. This table round descended from Lamont Warner, a designer for Stickley's Workshops, and is remembered as decorating his dining-room table.

opened a summer school in Ipswich, Massachusetts. The students were exposed to Dow's principles of composition and design while taking classes on pottery, weaving, lacemaking, woodblock printmaking, binding, tinpunching, and hooked-rug making. The Ipswich summer school was highly regarded, attracting both established artists, such as photographer Alvin Langdon Coburn, and emerging artisans, such as Newcomb College's annual scholarship recipients from New Orleans, Louisiana.

Many of the summer schools advertised in the pages of *Keramic Studio, The Craftsman*, *Home Needlework, House Beautiful*, and *International Studio*. Specialized schools focused on a particular medium, such as the Four Winds summer school in Syracuse, New York, that taught ceramics. However, programs devoted solely to textiles are not documented.

Mary Crovatt Hambridge, a native of Georgia, was a textile designer who trained in Georgia, worked in New York City, and moved back to Georgia in 1927. Although late in terms of the traditional definition of Arts and Crafts, Hambridge embodied and executed all its principles. She executed textiles utilizing the principles of dynamic symmetry as taught by her husband, Edward Jay Hambridge. Based on the natural growth patterns of humans and plants, dynamic symmetry symbolizes the genetic forces within an organism that produce a proportional relationship of the part to the whole. Inspired in part by a trip to Greece, Hambridge interpreted these principles through weaving. Her color choices were strongly influenced by the Blue Ridge mountain environment,[11] and she created a plain weave cloth whose silk warp thread allowed it great luminosity.

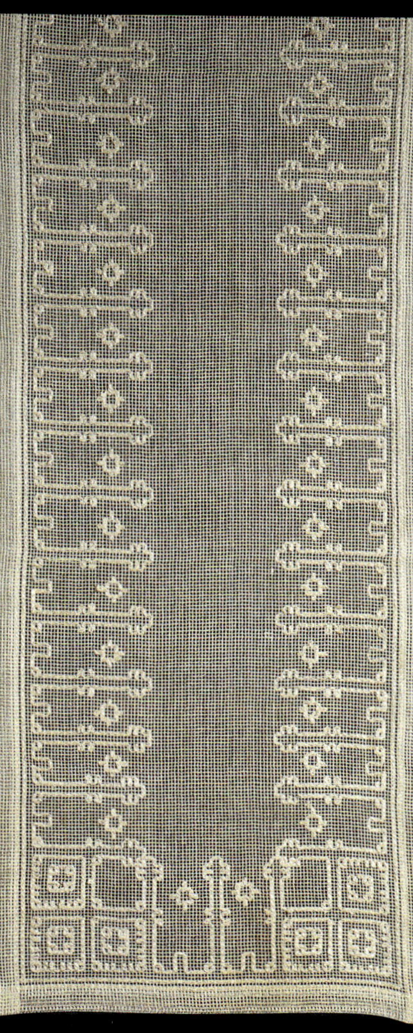

Craftsman Workshops. Filet net runner. 1904–16. Linen with hand embroidery, 12 × 54" (30 × 137 cm). Collection Crab Tree Farm
Filet net curtains and runners were a popular product sold through the Craftsman catalogs.

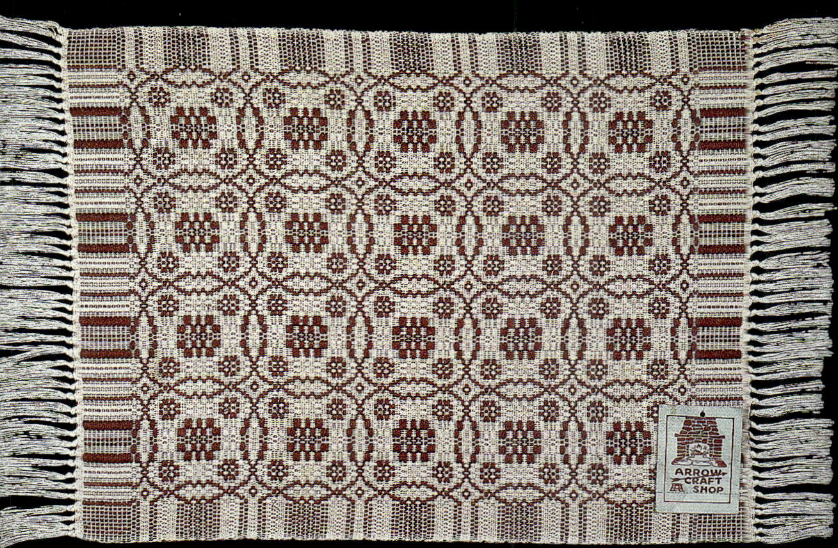

Arrowcraft Shop, Pi Beta Phi Settlement School. "Whig Rose" runner. Date unknown. Handwoven cotton, 11¾ × 18½" (29.8 × 47 cm). Collection Craig Kuhns

▶
California School of Arts and Crafts. "Work of the Students in Elementary Design." Illustration from *Catalogue A, Eighth Annual Sessions, California School of Arts and Crafts, Berkeley, California*. 1914

When Hambridge moved to Georgia in 1927 she began marketing her work through a retail outlet in New York City. She saw the value of the traditional Southern heritage: "Here was the true pioneer stock of America. They had kept their craft knowledge and their native integrity but their looms had been relegated to the attics, their spinning wheels are put away to be used only now and then to spin a little thread for their men's socks." After traveling back and forth to New York for years, in 1934 Mary Hambridge started "in the South a practical application of Mr. Hambridge's theories of design. She has established a home at Clayton and is training some of the folk of the Blue Ridge Mountains in art craft, applying Mr. Hambridge's theories of dynamic symmetry to the design for weaving knitting and other work—the first steps in the establishment of an art craft foundation which will mean fine development for the South."[12] Her 1936 exhibit, under the name of Rabun Studios, was described as "handmade textiles spun and woven by the peasants of America with original designs by Jay Hambridge, Discoverer of Dynamic Symmetry. These are the first textiles designed and dyed according to the principles of Dynamic Symmetry and Dynamic Color."[13] The group produced fabrics used in a variety of capacities. Color was an area of particular importance. The group's pieces were available in categories, with names such as earth harmonies, tree harmonies, sky harmonies, and other colors in nature.

Throughout the 1940s Rabun Studios continued to grow in popularity and eventually adopted the letterhead "Rabun Studios American Arts and Crafts" even in the 1950s. Hambridge's marketing was in the Arts and Crafts spirit, stating "the power of our shop is its smallness, unpretentiousness,

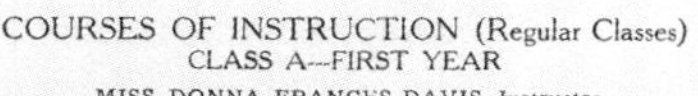

COURSES OF INSTRUCTION (Regular Classes)
CLASS A—FIRST YEAR

MISS DONNA FRANCES DAVIS, Instructor

Plant Analysis
Drawing of flowers, fruits and foliage in pencil, wash, or water-color; and conventionalization of the same, for use in designing.

Wash Drawing and Elementary Water-Color
Simple studies from nature of fruits, flowers, casts, drapery and still life.

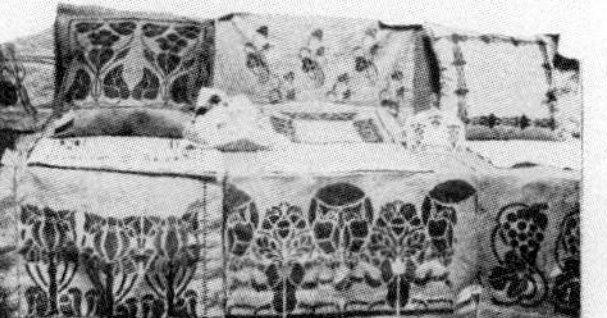

WORK OF STUDENTS IN ELEMENTARY DESIGN

Mrs. E. H. BRADLEY,
FALL TERM, 1914.
Mr. R. F. SCHAEFFER,
SPRING TERM, 1915.
Instructors

Elementary Design
Study of proportion as a fundamental principle of art; of fine relations of color and value; of flower and landscape composition; stenciling and wood-block printing.

Note: Elementary Design deals with decoration and the different methods of applying the same to flat surfaces.

MR. ALDICE DINSDALE, Instructor

Freehand Drawing
Drawing from simple objects in outline and light and shade. Type solids. Vases and jars. Subjects are drawn singly and in groups, in pencil, crayon and charcoal.

Instrumental Drawing
Practice in the use of instruments. Drawing of geometrical problems and designs. Lettering. Construction of Mathematical curves.

Note: Instrumental drawing is the work given in High Schools for matriculation to the Universities.

11

human quality which gives it individuality, which gives it warmth. . . . [O]ur kind of work can never compete with industry and mechanism."[14] She espoused "Since the domination of our present civilization by industry and the machine, the simple craft life of the people has been neglected. The absence of this cleansing power in the life of the people has resulted in neurotic diseases, unhealthy escapes, and an unbalanced education, as well as decadence and lack of vitalizing inspiration in the arts."[15]

Settlement houses sometimes established craft programs to provide morally and physically uplifting outlets for their occupants' energies and skills. Embroidery, weaving, and pottery were taught; many immigrant women honed their traditional skills of lace making and embroidery and learned to apply them to new materials and Arts and Crafts designs. Textiles were produced at Denison House and South End House in Boston, Greenwich House and Richmond Hill House in New York City, and Hull House in Chicago. Each settlement house had its own philosophical approach, some attempting to fully integrate the immigrant or destitute women into mainstream American culture while others sought to preserve the women's native values, techniques, and cultural traditions.

At the same time, Arts and Crafts societies sprang up across the nation. As outlets for the thousands of fledgling craftsmen some were new organizations and others evolved out of preexisting women's clubs. Many were modeled after the Arts and Crafts exhibition society in London and the Society of Arts and Crafts, Boston. The Societies' primary goals were to provide a forum

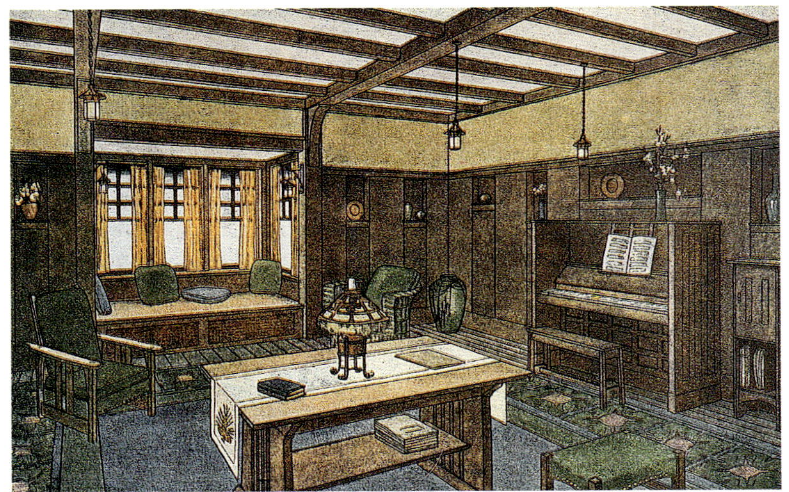

◀
Gustav Stickley. "Craftsman Living Room." Illustration from *Craftsman Homes.* 1905
Stickley's Craftsman Workshops began as a furniture company but soon developed lines of metalwork, lighting, and textiles, as well as a signature style of architecture and interior decoration. Window curtains were important in controlling the quality of light in the room. These "corn color" curtains were suggested for a room of browns and greens to give a warm, sunny effect. In the scheme, other fabrics were to form a background upon which decoration was used sparingly.

in which artists could exhibit their works and sometimes salesrooms for distribution, and to spread the mission through published journals and lectures. Through these methods of outreach the societies had their greatest impact, setting standards of a craftsmanship that began to be emulated by manufacturers and designers nationwide.

The museum setting offered the exciting opportunity for students to learn hands-on technical approaches by interacting with the collection and using it for study and inspiration. Many museums also sponsored exhibitions to display the work of their classes, guilds, and societies to the general public. New York City's Metropolitan Museum of Art mounted an annual exhibition of American industrial art inspired by objects in the museum's collection.

Designed to encourage craft and reach out to people, the Art Institute of Chicago began a well-attended series of Arts and Crafts exhibitions in 1898 that lasted until 1921. Chicago's Arts and Crafts Society was founded in 1907,[16] and Mrs. Bertha Honore Palmer Potter founded the Needlework and Textile Guild in Chicago.[17] Exhibitions by these organizations were national in their scope and outreach. Similarly, the Detroit and Cleveland Museums of Art also founded Arts and Crafts organizations but they remained somewhat local in focus.[18]

Arts and Crafts ideals continued to filter down to the middle classes. Gustav Stickley, a self-made man, assigned himself the role of representing the American middle class, "the greater middle classes, possessed of moderate material resources, modest in schemes and action, average in all but virtue. A simple democratic art should provide them with material surroundings conducive to plain living and high thinking, to the development of the sense of order, symmetry and proportion."[19] Through his Craftsman empire, Stickley influenced countless homes across America. As a leading proponent of the Arts and Crafts movement's philosophy and design, Stickley offered his line of Craftsman products in major cities across the United States through his own storefronts as well as regional furniture and department stores. The display of his goods introduced the general public to his product and showed how all the decorative elements were meant to work with one another to create a comprehensive scheme for the home.

Stickley's Craftsman empire claimed fifty retail outlets throughout the nation, including Washington, Boston, and New York City. In addition to impacting countless homes across America with articles in *The Craftsman* on the use of textiles in the home, beginning in 1903 Stickley began advertising his own textile line. The textile department included "Oriental rugs, India Druggets, Donegal Rugs to order, and Scotch rugs in a complete line of colors and sizes. In our Drapery Department, a full line of Portieres, Scarfs, Bedspreads, Pillows, etc. In all our Fabrics, also Laces in Made-Curtains and Nets, to be made up also Cretonnes, Block-Printed Linens, and Linens in all colorings, Scrims, Silks, and Canvas—Shades and Hangings, Curtain Poles, Rods and Fixtures."[20] Through *The Craftsman* one could purchase yard goods of simple materials, carpets, curtains, pillows, and kits to make the same, utilizing techniques such as stenciling patterns and stitching. The Craftsman Workshops line emphasized the value of rusticity and stressed the importance of the handworked appearance of the products, which was achieved

▶
Craftsman Workshops. Curtains and valance with pinecone design. 1904–16. Linen with hand embroidery, panels 17½ × 79" (44 × 201 cm) and valence 12 × 50" (30 × 127 cm). Collection Crab Tree Farm
Linen curtains were an alternative to the scrim and filet net window coverings offered by the Craftsman catalogs.

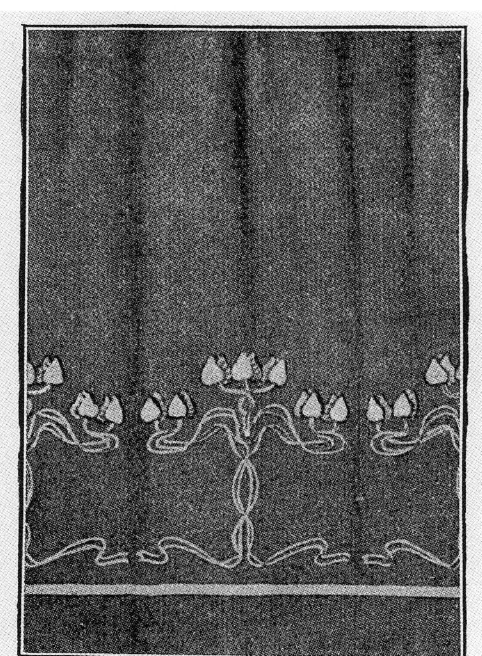
No. 11363.

No. 11363—Seed-pod design for appliqué. It is very effective and may be worked in a number of color combinations. The stems, branches and all the connecting lines should be couched with heavy floss. Perforated stamping pattern of this design, 18 inches wide by 21 inches high, including stamping preparation, 20 cents.

◀
"No. 11363 Seed-pod design for appliqué." Illustrated in *The Embroidery Catalog*. 1911–12
The borrowing of designs was very common in the early twentieth century. This seed-pod motif is a knock-off of a design by the same name from Craftsman Workshops.

by careful selection of the materials. The Craftsman Company offered a variety of fabrics in many different colors "so that the worker may use these fabrics in color schemes much as a painter composes upon his palette."[21] Custom fabrics were purchased from dealers across Manhattan in order to fill special orders. The bulk of the company's yardage was imported from Russia, Scandinavia, and other countries that produced inexpensive, plentiful, and rustic materials.

Stickley's textile department carefully chose its material and the Craftsman Workshop stocked over twenty-two different materials. Multiple variations of Craftsman canvas (similar to burlap), linen, velour, flax canvas in two weights, homespun linen, handwoven linen, Flemish linen, colored linens, bloom linen, block-printed designs and fabrics with woven designs, mandarin silk, madras, etamine, scrim, and crepe were available. They were all woven of natural fibers including linen, cotton, and silk and ranged in price from $.25 to $2.50 a yard.

Craftsman Workshops patronized The Linen Thread Company, purchasing mercerized linen floss in colors custom dyed to correspond to the Craftsman color scheme, such as gold, dark blue-green, and pale leather. The thread sold for five cents a skein. Craftsman products incorporated this thread in the finished product, emphasizing a select number of stitches: couching, buttonhole, outline, stem, satin, and French knots. The outline stitch, used to actually define the design, was the most extensively used stitch. Designs were stamped on the cloth, providing templates to be followed in the workshops or at home. Craft motifs included the seed pod, apple tree, gingko, pinecone, and tulip. Appliqué was another frequently employed method of decoration, cutting

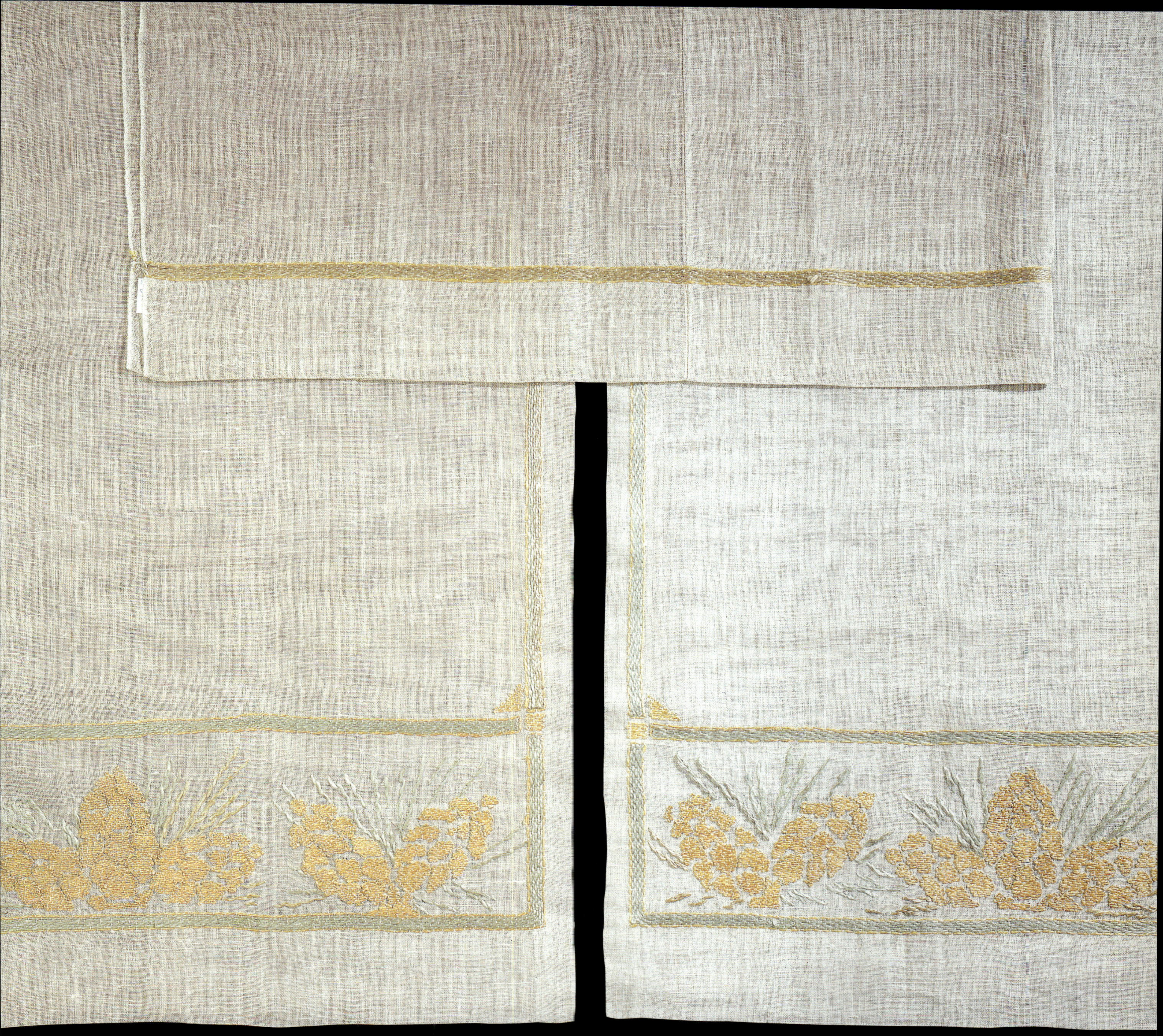

down on the amount of stitching necessary. Stenciling was frequently used in conjunction with rough and sheer fabrics, providing a decorative contrast.

Craftsman Workshop textiles are truly unique expressions of Arts and Crafts design. Patterns vary, suggesting the work of several designers within the department, such as Harvey Ellis and Lamont Warner among others. The designs were coordinated to complement the contemporary furniture Stickley's company was manufacturing. In general, Stickley's design team created compositions featuring broad masses of color and simple, abstract, natural forms that in their simplicity were both sophisticated and easy to reproduce. The catalog line names reflect this: horse chestnut, water lily, lotus, teazle, and gingko, to name a few. The simplicity in stitching and use of appliqué and stenciling reduced the cost of labor, thereby making the end product more affordable. However, though popular around the country, Stickley textiles were high-quality products and relatively costly for the time. Compared to $.50 to $1.00 for a typical kit square with materials, Stickley's kits cost $1.25 to $2.75, depending on size and material. Finished, the squares cost from $2.00 to $5.50, varying by design.

Several of the designs were modified over time to reflect the changing image of the Craftsman product. Despite these design changes, the product or catalog names frequently stayed the same. For example, the lotus portiere surfaces in a 1903–04 catalog and is then revised in later Craftsman catalogs. By 1911 some designs surfaced in the inventory listed as "old stock," including peacock, seedpod, gingko, pinecone, apple, tulip, checkerberry, cross stitch, plain hem, and

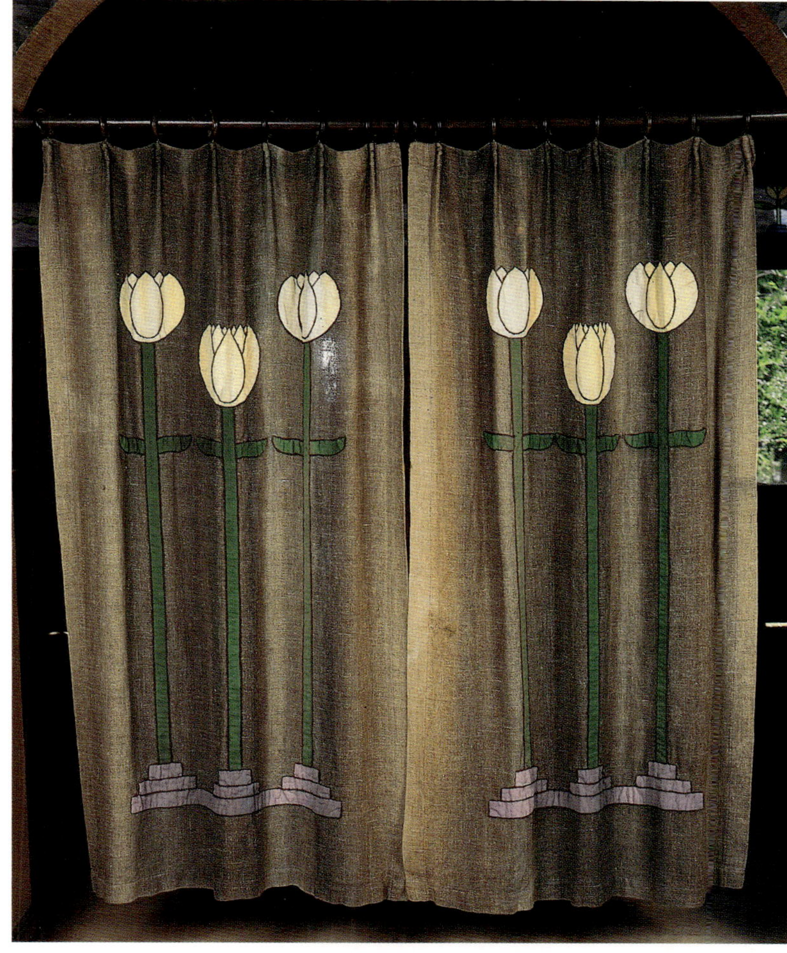

▶
Craftsman Workshops. Portieres with lotus design (reverse side of portieres shown on page 100) in the living room of the Michael J. Riordan House. c. 1904. Flax and jute "Craftsman canvas" with appliqué and hand embroidery. Collection Riordan Mansion State Park, Flagstaff, Arizona

stenciled textiles. According to the annual inventory, few finished products were kept in stock; most were custom made. The Native American–inspired designs seen in a 1903 article in *The Craftsman* disappeared; perhaps they were the work of Harvey Ellis, who died in 1904.

When textile designs were introduced in 1903, pieces were often sent out to be done by embroiderers working at home. Shop drawings were made for furniture and probably also for textiles. As the business grew, the factory in Syracuse, New York, expanded to include a fabric department, a pillow department, and an upholstery room. The fabric department employed eight to twelve women and the pillow department fifteen to nineteen.[22] Contemporary machinery such as single-needle Singer sewing machines as well as work tables and benches ensured the third-floor sewing department was necessarily equipped. The cushion room and the leather department

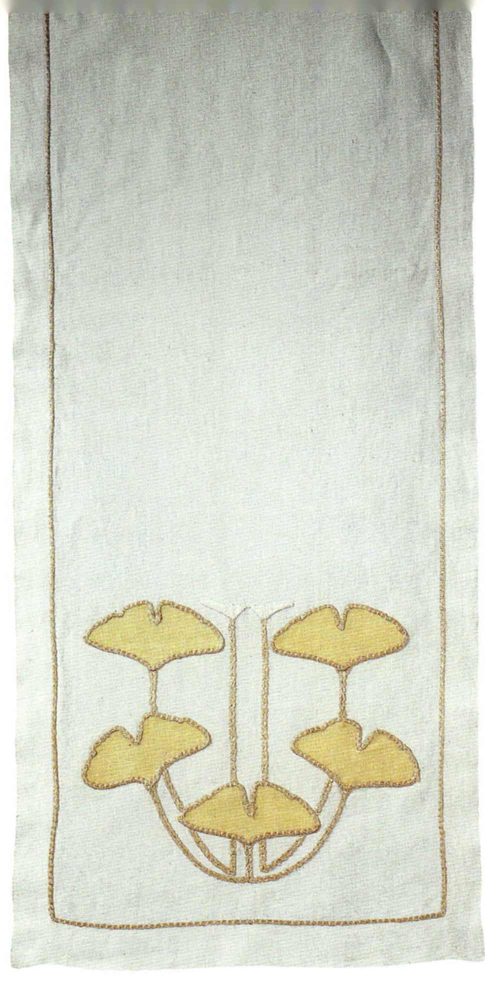

◀
Craftsman Workshops. Table scarf with ginkgo design. 1904–16. Linen with linen appliqué and hand embroidery, 15¼ × 91½" (39 × 232 cm). Collection Crab Tree Farm
Gustav Stickley's simple Craftsman designs influenced Arts and Crafts textiles nationwide.

were located on the third floor, and the fabric department on the second floor stocked many materials for both. By 1905, when Stickley opened his flagship Manhattan store, the business was supporting textile production enough to include a textile department in the store's design, on its upper levels. The textile room was well stocked, indicating the extent to which the department helped fill orders.

Few provenanced examples of Gustav Stickley textiles survive today. The Riordan house in Flagstaff, Arizona, is home to some of the few surviving portieres and possibly the only ones still in their original setting. Brothers Timothy and Michael Riordan and their wives built log houses joined by a common billiard room in 1903–04 with architect Charles Whittlesey (El Tovar in the Grand Canyon, 1905). Michael furnished with Craftsman furniture, primarily Harvey Ellis designs. Both brothers purchased Craftsman portieres for numerous doorways. Michael selected the Lotus design. The description in a circa 1904 catalog reads: "The Lotus portiere is carried out in blue-green canvas. All the appliqué is in 'Bloom linen,' changing from softest old rose to pale green. The outlining is done in floss of a dark blue color." The portieres are constructed with two faces; they were viewed from both sides. The pair retailed for $25.75. The existing portieres are somewhat different from the catalog description (see pages 73, 100). The appliqués are a twill weave of solid colors, and one side presents a pink lotus with a green stem and a gold ground. On the reverse the flowers are yellow, again with green stems, springing from a pink base. The outline stitching is a brown thread. The cloth is Stickley's "Craftsman canvas."

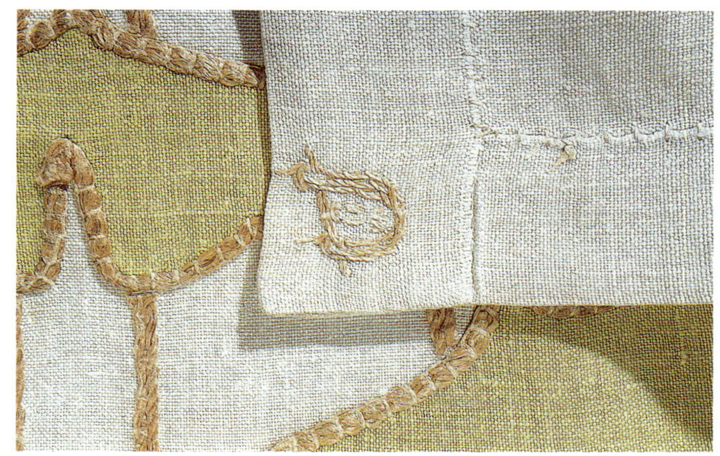

◀ **Craftsman Workshops. Detail of table scarf with ginkgo design. 1904–16. Linen with linen appliqué and hand embroidery, 15¼ × 91½" (39 × 232 cm). Collection Crab Tree Farm**
The ninety-inch "Ginkgo Table Scarf" was offered in Stickley's catalogs, either completed on Flemish linen for $4.50 or as a kit for $2.85. This is considerably more than the many other companies which offered kits for $.25 to $1.00.

Timothy's portieres are quite different (see page 118). They are of a basketweave linen fabric, possibly Stickley's "heavy flax canvas." The design is not a published Craftsman Workshops pattern, but can be attributed to them based on context and stylistic similarities. The appliquéd flowers are of a gold lamé fabric on one side and blue denim on the reverse on both the portieres and matching dining-room curtains.

Dard Hunter, a designer from the Roycroft community of craftspeople established in East Aurora, New York, influenced textiles as well. Hunter's graphic work was influenced by the Glasgow School and the Wiener Werkstätte and was picked up frequently by the popular press. However, the few known textiles produced within the Roycroft community were plain homespun linen with simple embroidery, and made for their personal use. Typical Roycroft community textiles are a far cry from the sophisticated design work Hunter inspired.

Despite efforts to keep prices low, products from the Roycrofters, Newcomb, and the Craftsman Workshops were out of reach of many Americans. But through the publicity efforts of many of the design reformers, the public was familiar with Arts and Crafts design and sought it from a source familiar to them, the embroidery companies. For decades, women had been buying embroidery kits and patterns from major distributors. Textile companies provided patterns, kits, and supplies in all types of conventional, historic, and Arts and Crafts designs. The thread and embroidery companies were a major source for disseminating Arts and Crafts textiles, for they reached beyond the homes of the elite into the workbaskets of stitchers everywhere.

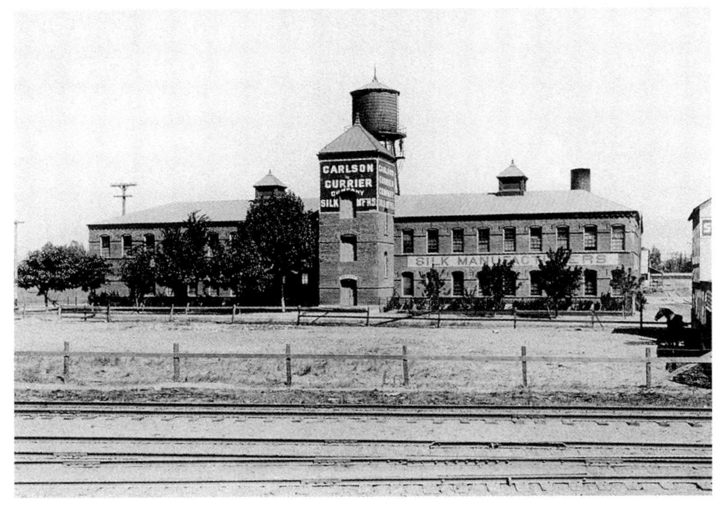

◀
Carlson Currier Silk Factory, Petaluma, California. Pre-1930 photograph. Collection Timothy Hansen and Dianne Ayres

The embroidery companies ranged from large corporations—mills whose primary business was the manufacturing of thread and cloth—to small, sometimes, one-person businesses. Many of the large companies had been in existence since the 1860s or before, offering kits for Victorian style work. The largest were Belding Brothers & Company, based in Northampton, Massachusetts, and the Nonotuck Silk Company, based in Florence, Massachusetts. Both had mills around the country and in Canada. While embroidery thread was only a small portion of their business, each devoted considerable marketing energy and advertising revenues to its promotion. Belding Brothers had sales offices in New York, Boston, Philadelphia, Baltimore, Chicago, Cincinnati, St. Louis, St. Paul, and San Francisco and had needlecraft departments in many major retail stores: "Demonstrator class-rooms became a feature of the leading departmental stores; here the socially-alert flocked, in search of the latest ideas."[23]

The embroidery companies developed a thorough marketing scheme as a vehicle to carry their products to the public. Kits consisted of the cloth with the design stamped or stenciled; the thread was either included or purchased separately. Simple iron on transfer patterns and more complicated paper and ink-stamping patterns were sold as well. Kits were often marked with the company name and kit or pattern number on the selvage (this was sometimes sewn into the hem). The thread companies produced needlework kits that were designed to be inexpensive, ranging between twenty-five cents and several dollars. Sometimes the patterns or stamped linens were even free, as an inducement to order the thread.

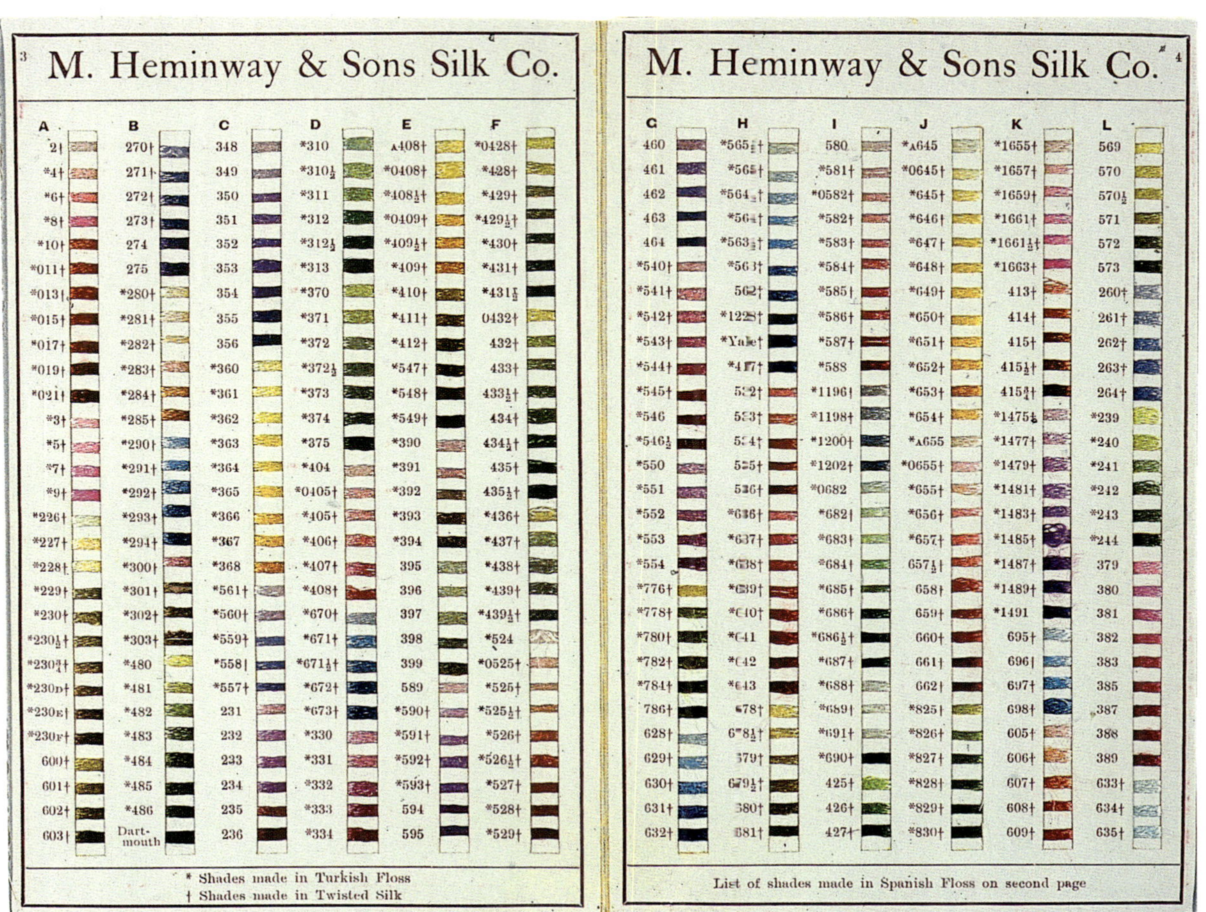

▲
M. Heminway & Sons Silk Company. Sample card of art needlework silks. c. 1900. Collection Timothy Hansen and Dianne Ayres

The kits did allow the needleworker room for creativity. A stitcher could participate in the process by executing part or all of the kit's design, changing the colors, and altering the stitches. Although companies offered different options, many pieces were on natural materials, particularly rough linen. Lighter fabrics were recommended for curtains, portieres, pillows, and runners and heavier ones, including canvas, taffetas, and goat hair fabrics, for wall hangings and coverings. The companies' simple designs captured the major tenets of the Arts and Crafts movement, introducing quality decorative objects into the home affordably. Economy and the appearance of simplicity encouraged the American public to produce the objects themselves.

Designs were often conventionalized versions of natural organic forms, sometimes geometric in execution and sometimes rendered in the flowing lines of Art Nouveau. The design to be worked

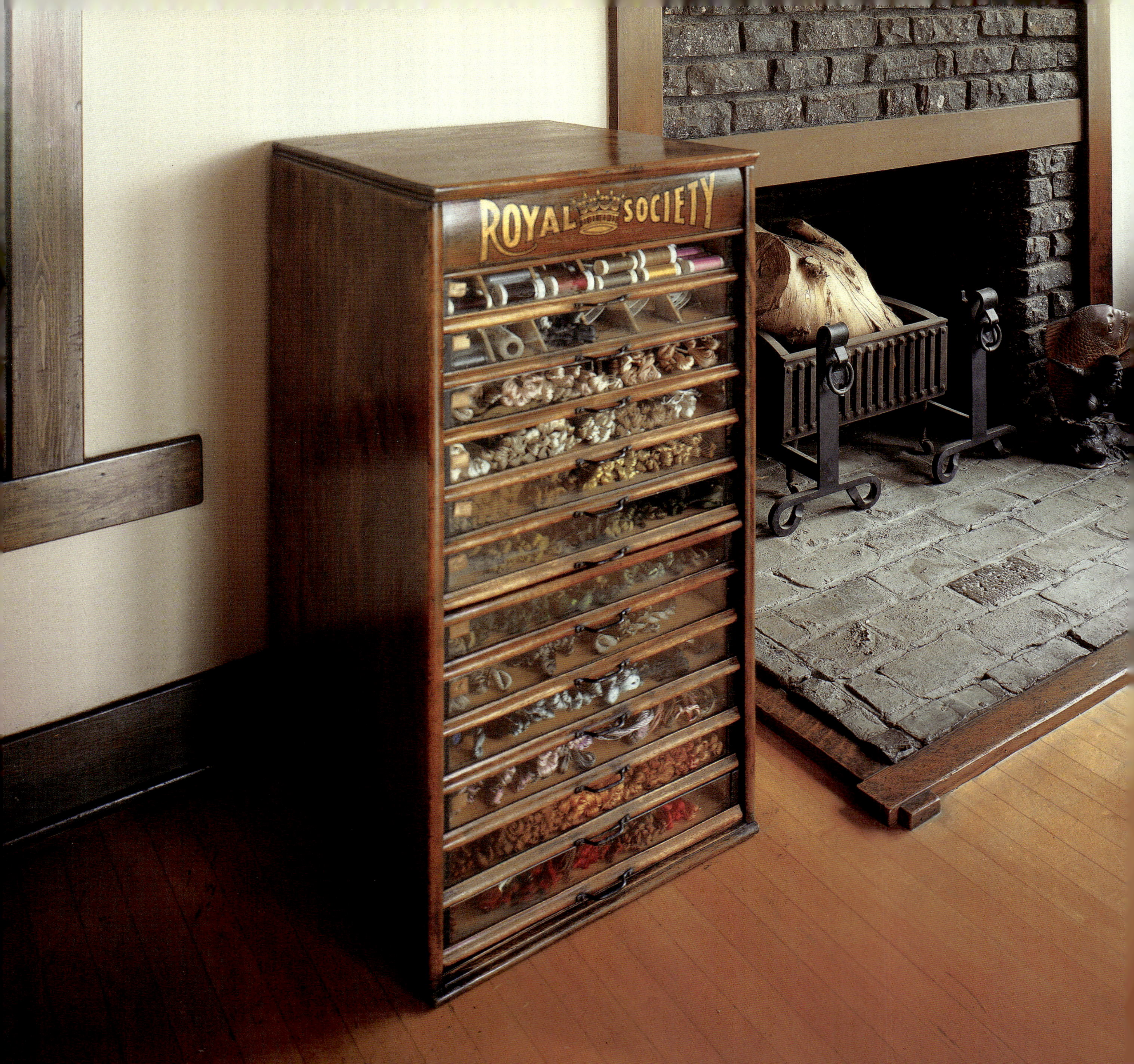
ROYAL SOCIETY

◀
Royal Society thread cabinet. Collection Ann and Andre Chaves

was printed and occasionally stenciled onto the fabric or included in the kit as a transfer print pattern. Similar to woodblock prints, many designs were outlined in black, emphasizing line. Pieces were executed in both vibrant and organic colors, depending on both the designer and the producer. Needlework, appliqué, and stenciling were the main techniques used in executing the kits. The emphasis was often on the speed with which a product could be achieved. On embroidered pieces, a variety of stitches were used including satin stitch, darning stitch, outline/stem stitch, and French knots. Pieces could be finished with special treatments, such as hem stitching, or edged with tatting, fringe, tassles, or other decorative elements. Ultimately how the piece was executed was up to the embroiderer, as one could modify all or part of the work based on one's own creativity.

Each manufacturing company developed its own catalogs and lesson books to entice people to their products. Beginning in 1887, Nonotuck published *Home Needlework*, a periodical offering lessons in embroidery and illustrating designs that could be purchased stamped on linen. Contributions were secured from Lillian Barton Wilson, Candace Wheeler, and other noted authorities on art needlework. Mostly known by their trade name, Corticelli, the Nonotuck Silk Company made advertising history in the early 1900s by mounting the first animated, lighted sign above Times Square. The Corticelli kitten, the company's logo, playfully unraveled a spool of silk to crowds of spectators below.

Raw silk was imported from the Far East; from the port in San Francisco the majority was sent by train to the industries on the East Coast, but some stayed in California to be processed by the

▶
Brainerd & Armstrong Company. Catalogs for the years 1899, 1901, 1902, 1904, 1905, 1906, 1907, 1910, 1911, 1912, 1913, 1914. Each approximately 9 × 6" (22.9 × 15.2 cm). Collection Timothy Hansen and Dianne Ayres
Vintage catalogs provide a window into the period and are a source for identifying patterns.

Carlson Currier Company in Petaluma into sewing, knitting and embroidery threads. Though listed by Corticelli as one of their mill sites, Carlson Currier was an independent company, offering its own lesson books, *Suggestions for Shadings*, and stamped linen designs (see page 76). The company manufactured 495 colors of embroidery silk. Of those, sixty-eight colors were designated for conventional designs: seven shades of bird blue; six shades each of old rose, terra cotta, new blue, old blue, old pink, bronze, tan, and olive; five shades of golden brown; and four shades each of blue-green and dove gray.

Belding Brothers also published a series of books entitled *Needle and Hook*, with embroidery instructions and linen designs, as did the M. Heminway & Sons Silk Company, based in Watertown, Connecticut, which issued *Treatise on Art Needlework* (page 77). Brainerd & Armstrong Company, based in New London, Connecticut, published an annual *Embroidery Lessons with Colored Studies*, which sold widely to a retail audience (opposite). The final edition, retitled *Embroidery Book for 1914*, lacks color illustrations. Since they were offered annually, Brainerd & Armstrong's books closely document the company's relationship to the Arts & Crafts movement.

From the mid-1890s until 1900 the designs are almost exclusively naturalistic renditions of flowers in the style termed "Art Needlework" (page 82). While very few designs are carried over from year to year, similar ones continue to be offered in declining numbers through 1913. In 1900, new trends began to appear. The "Star Design" (page 39 top) and two additional designs titled "conventional" were offered for sale in 1900.[24] Little fanfare surrounds the appearance of these

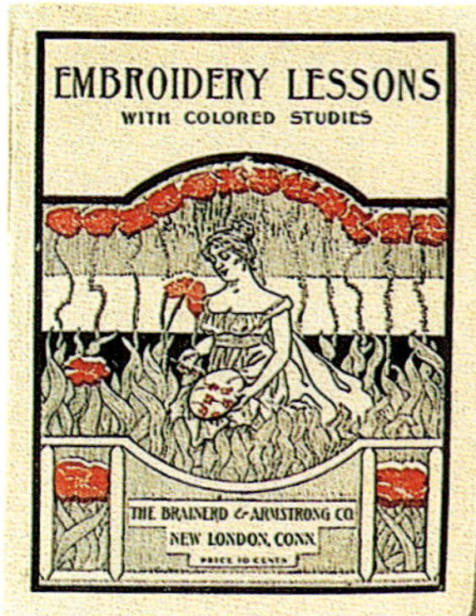
EMBROIDERY LESSONS
WITH COLORED STUDIES
THE BRAINERD & ARMSTRONG CO.
NEW LONDON, CONN.

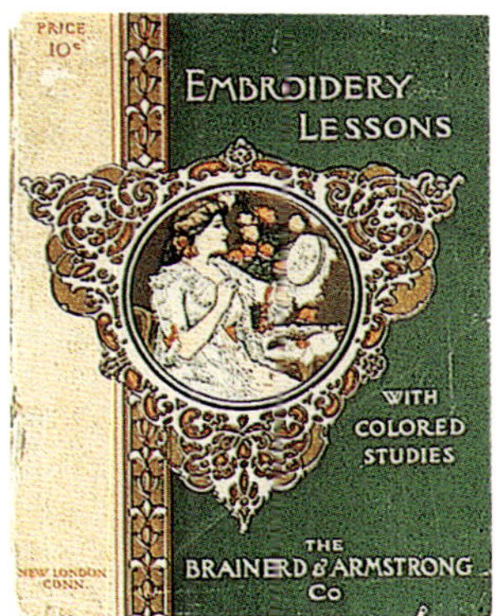
PRICE 10¢
EMBROIDERY LESSONS
WITH COLORED STUDIES
THE BRAINERD & ARMSTRONG Co
NEW LONDON CONN.

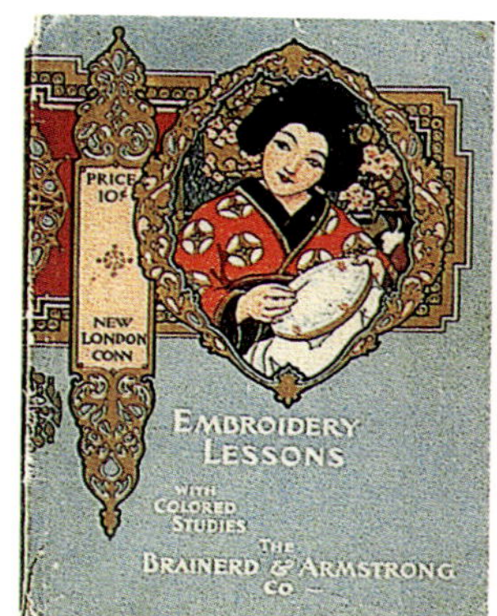
PRICE 10¢
NEW LONDON CONN
EMBROIDERY LESSONS
WITH COLORED STUDIES
THE BRAINERD & ARMSTRONG Co

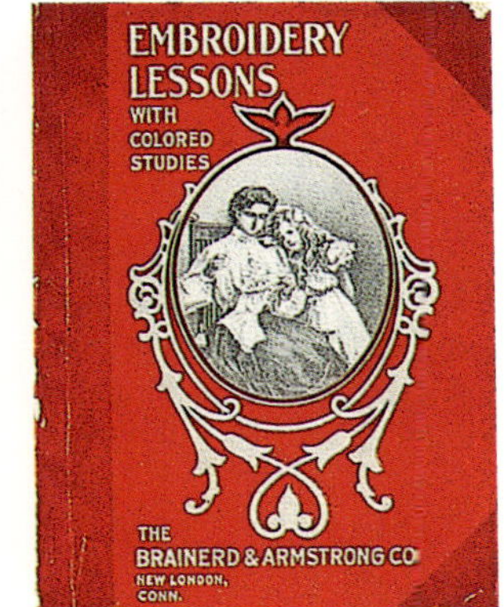
EMBROIDERY LESSONS
WITH COLORED STUDIES
THE BRAINERD & ARMSTRONG CO.
NEW LONDON, CONN.

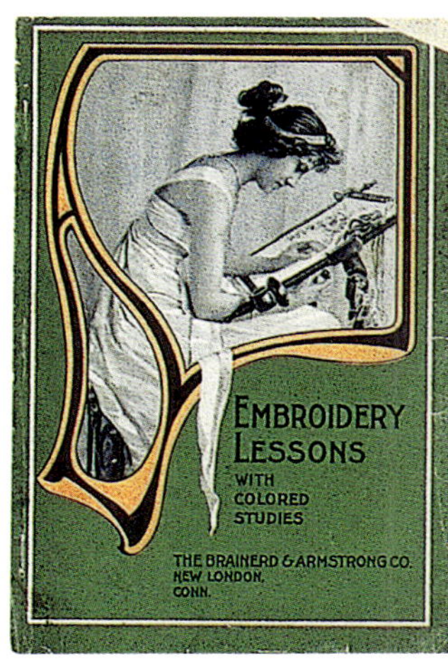
EMBROIDERY LESSONS
WITH COLORED STUDIES
THE BRAINERD & ARMSTRONG CO.
NEW LONDON, CONN.

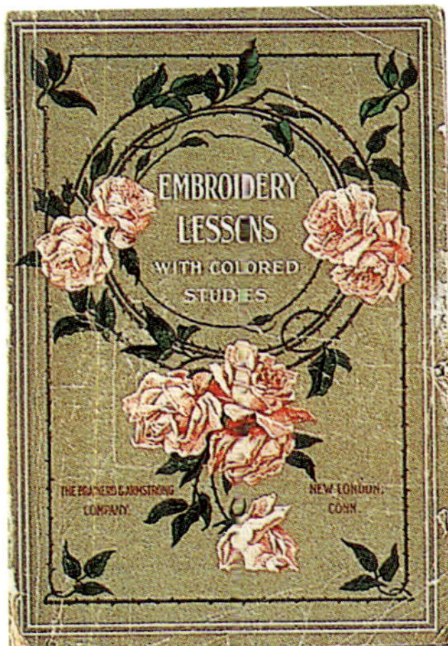
EMBROIDERY LESSONS
WITH COLORED STUDIES
THE BRAINERD & ARMSTRONG COMPANY
NEW LONDON, CONN.

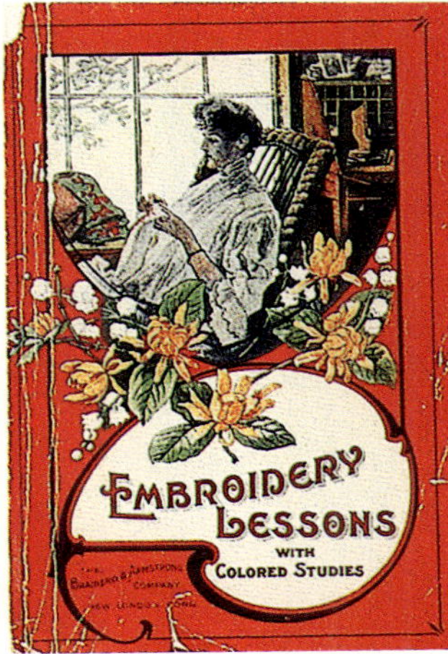
EMBROIDERY LESSONS
WITH COLORED STUDIES

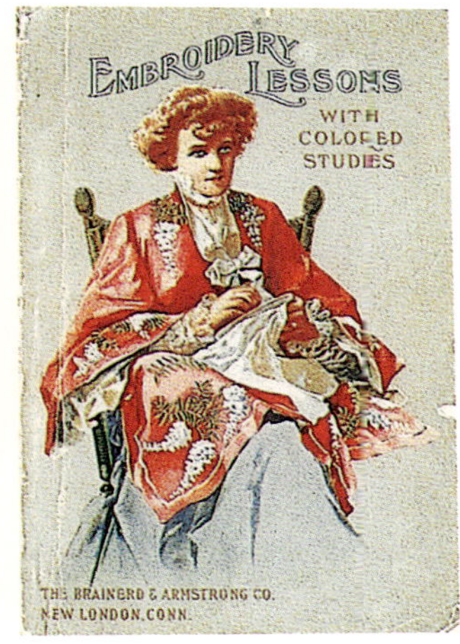
EMBROIDERY LESSONS
WITH COLORED STUDIES
THE BRAINERD & ARMSTRONG CO.
NEW LONDON, CONN.

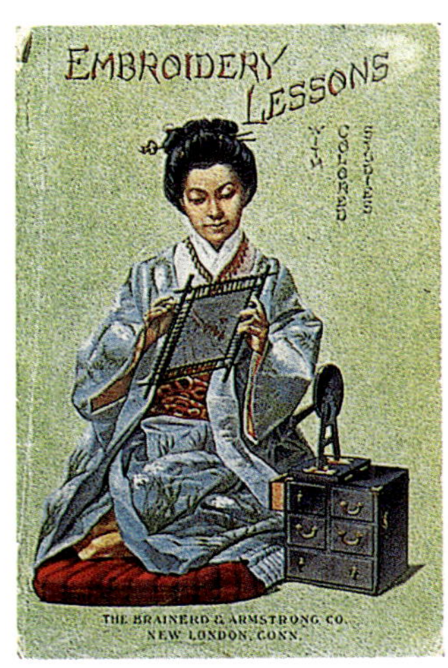
EMBROIDERY LESSONS
WITH COLORED STUDIES
THE BRAINERD & ARMSTRONG CO.
NEW LONDON, CONN.

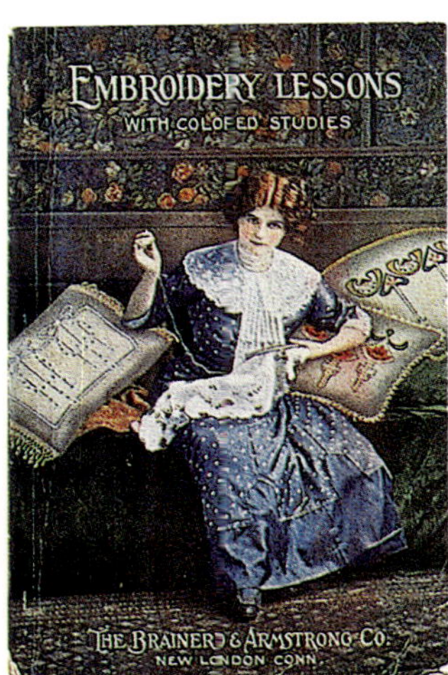
EMBROIDERY LESSONS
WITH COLORED STUDIES
THE BRAINERD & ARMSTRONG CO.
NEW LONDON CONN.

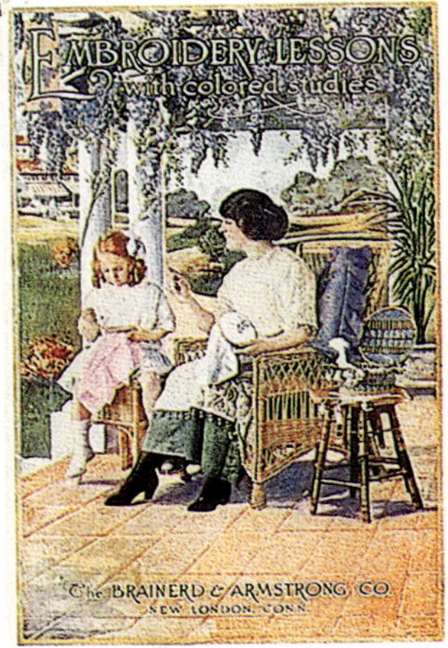
EMBROIDERY LESSONS
with colored studies
The BRAINERD & ARMSTRONG CO.
NEW LONDON CONN.

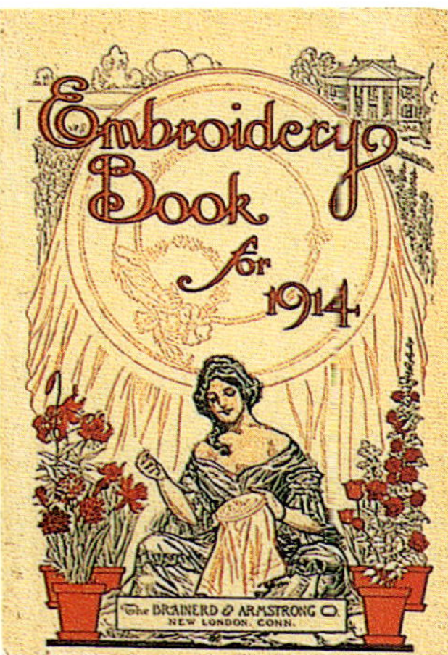
Embroidery Book for 1914
The BRAINERD & ARMSTRONG CO.
NEW LONDON, CONN.

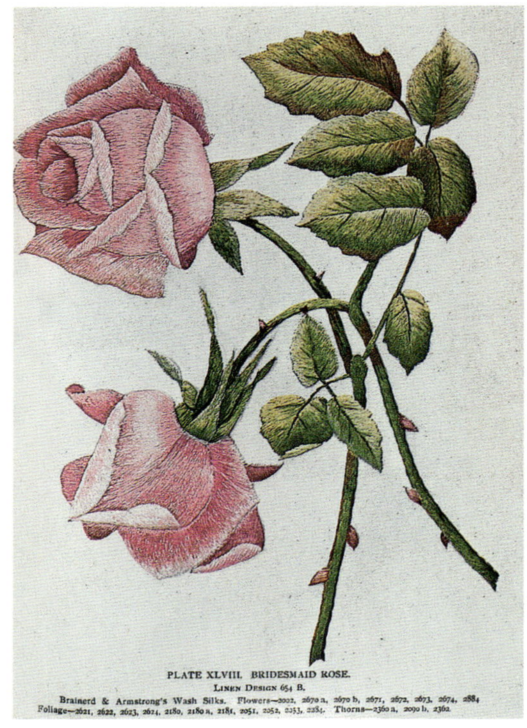

▼
Brainerd & Armstrong Company. Illustration from catalog. 1900
A typical "art needlework" style of design.

strikingly different designs among the sea of naturalistic flowers. A similar balance of Art Needlework and conventionalized designs continues in 1901 and 1902, with the naturalistic designs becoming bolder (page 84 left) and some Art Nouveau and Egyptian influences appearing (page 84 center). By 1904, more examples of the Art Nouveau style are evident in the catalogs (page 85 left) along with a greater number of conventional designs. Many of these, including the "Wild Rose" and the "Poppy" designs, exhibit a departure from Art Needlework by requiring only the edges of the flowers be worked in long and short stitch, leaving the "tinted" or stenciled linen at the base of the petals to show.

The illustrations from the 1905 Brainerd & Armstrong catalog (page 85 right) signal a bold new trend. The top figure is captioned: "This is something new in a very unique conventional design," while the bottom figure is identified as "Tinted Bulgarian." Brilliant colors outlined in black are typical of Bulgarian embroidery, but aside from the "Star" and "Kaleidoscopic" designs published in 1900 this introduces the outlining of all forms in black on conventionalized embroidery designs. The Bulgarian piece also represents "something new"—for a piece to be completed with such a minimal amount of labor. The needleworker was only to embroider the red and green outer squares in herringbone stitch and then outline all of the stenciled areas in black.

In 1906, conventionalized Art Nouveau designs are embraced even more. The offerings for the year show experimentation with many new types of embroidery. Design no. 8862 (page 86 top left group) is titled "Tinted Egyptian on Ecru Butter Cloth" and described as a "very oriental

▶

Brainerd & Armstrong Company. Illustrations from catalogs.1900

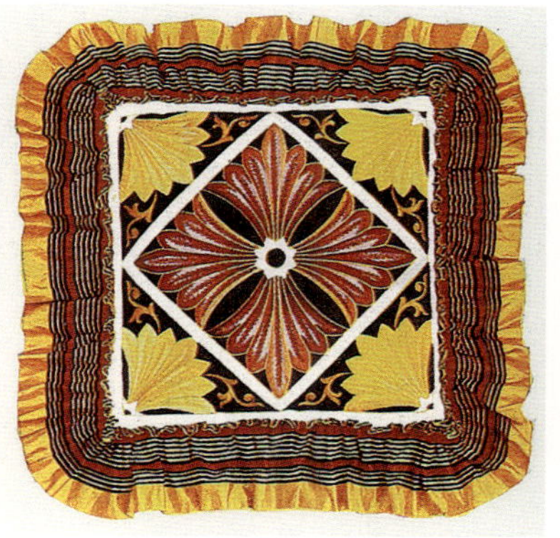

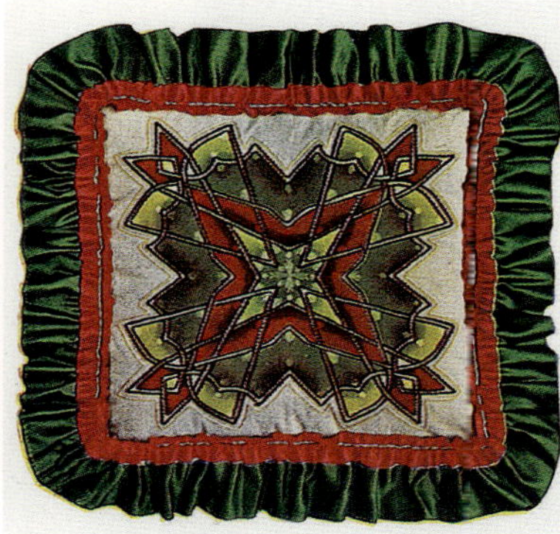

design . . . [which] is very easy to embroider, as the work consists of nothing more than heavily outlining all the tinted parts with black rope silk. The finished result is very rich and effective, and the embroiderers will be surprised that such an artistic cushion can be made at so little expense of time and money." But this impressive display marks the last year in which Brainerd & Armstrong featured Art Nouveau style designs.

The reliable dainty florals, Art Needlework, and eyelet designs continued in 1907; additional offerings included many pictorials and designs with a motto. Modifying some "Simple Conventional" designs from the previous year, a line called "Tinted Mission Designs for Embroidery" was introduced. "So popular has become the mission style of furniture, that now there is a real demand for such articles as centerpieces and sofa cushions in this same type of design." An example of Brainerd & Armstrong's "Mission Design" is shown in design no. 872 on page 86 (top right group). The "Mission" line includes one other sofa cushion and two table linens with similar designs worked in fancy herringbone stitch, satin stitch, and couching. One table linen, a square, is described in red, blue, and greens as cushion no. 872. The other cushion and a round table linen are described in greens, light and deep berry reds, black, yellow, copper, and light blue. One other "Mission Sofa Cushion on Ecru Ticking" is offered with a different style of design, featuring large conventional figures on long stems (page 91). The company was correct in its assessment that "This is a most characteristic Mission design and is sure to be a very popular one." This more conventionalized style of design became popular, not only with those who had Mission furniture, but a with wide

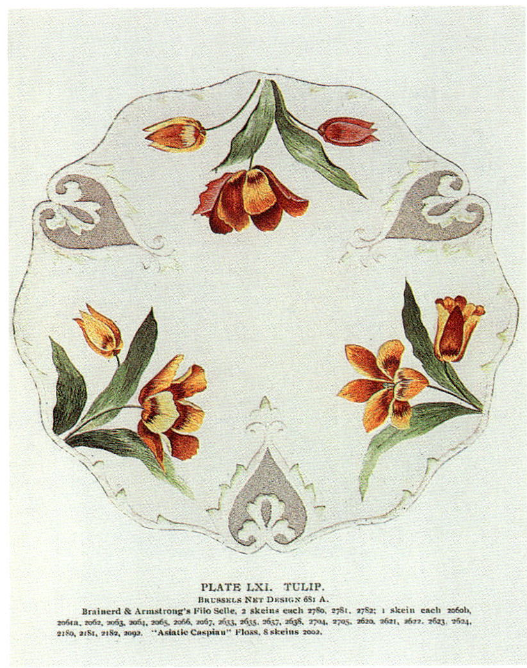

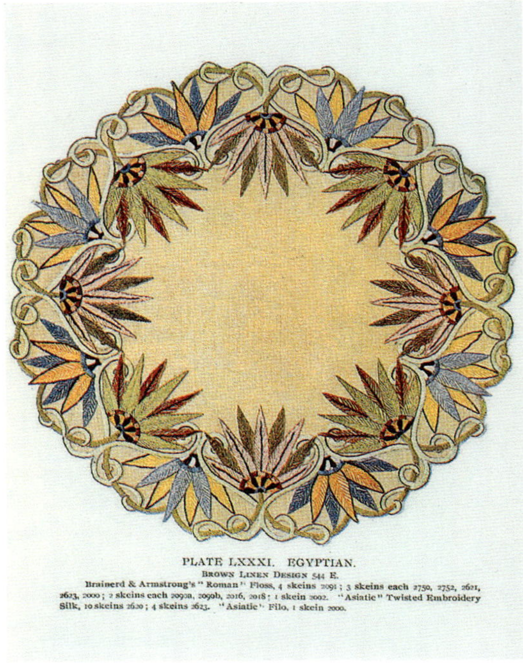

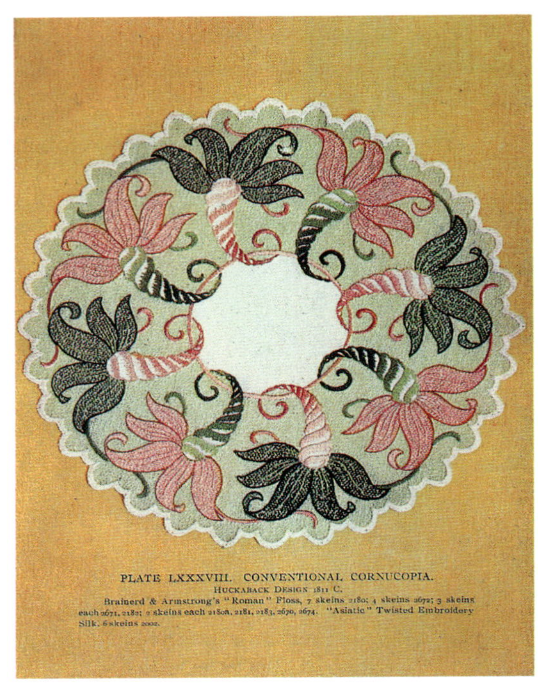

▲
Brainerd & Armstrong Company. Illustrations from catalogs. Left to right, 1901, 1902, 1903

spectrum of Arts & Crafts enthusiasts. In fact, subsequent offerings of "Mission"[25] style designs were not specifically designated "Mission" or even "Arts and Crafts," most likely because it was found that the market for these designs was broader than that designation would encourage.

The years 1908 and 1909 (page 86 bottom left and right groups) saw much experimentation with different styles of embroidery. In addition to Shadow and Montmellick Embroidery shown in previous years, designs in "Lazy Daisy," Eyelet, Coral Work (made up mostly of French Knots), Biedermaire, Wallachian, and the "New Simplex Stitch" embroidery were added during these years. Of these, Wallachian results in the most conventionalized designs, each form for a petal, leaf, or geometric element worked separately. While naturalistic floral designs predominate, a number of conventionalized designs were offered also, including, in 1908, the token Indian design for the year (design 422).

Beginning in 1910 and through the last *Embroidery Lessons with Colored Studies* issued for 1913, strong, conventionalized designs predominate Brainerd & Armstrong's offerings. These are mainly referred to as "stylish" and draw their inspiration from the same sources as designs offered by many other embroidery kit companies: roses, poppies, other flora, lotus, waterlily, pointsettia,

▶
Brainerd & Armstrong Company. Illustrations from catalogs. Left to right, 1904, 1905

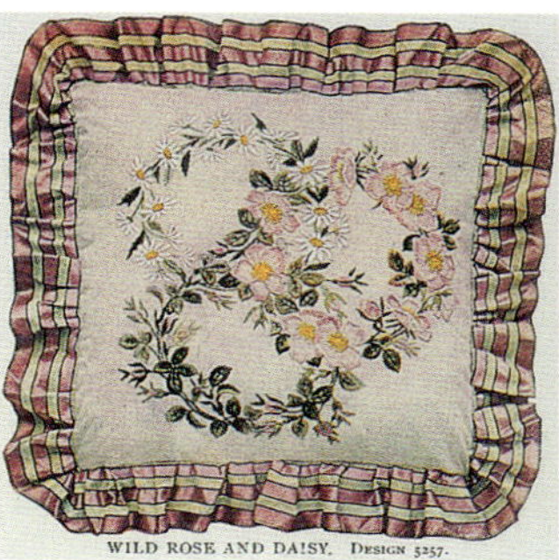

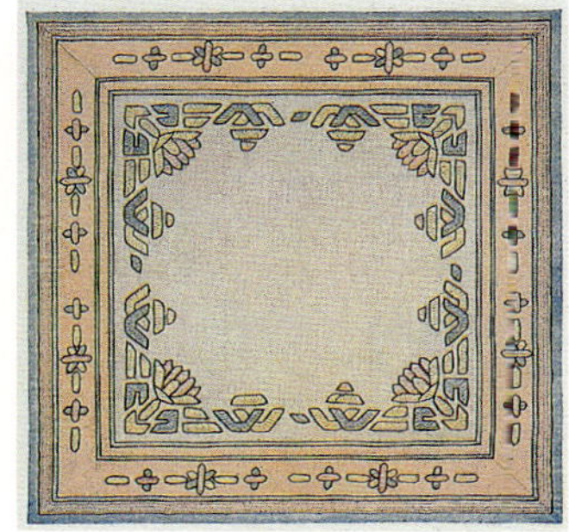

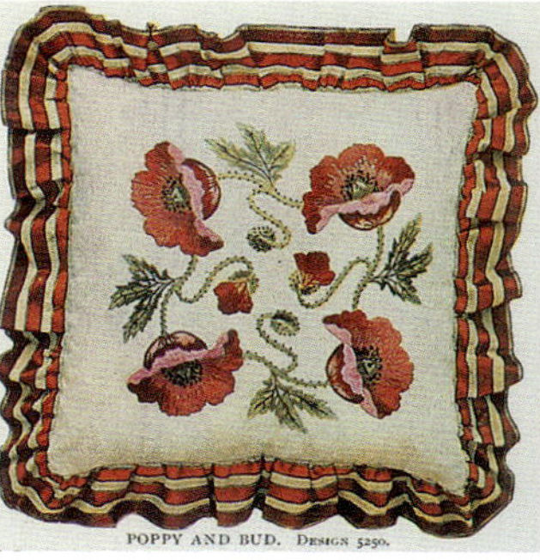

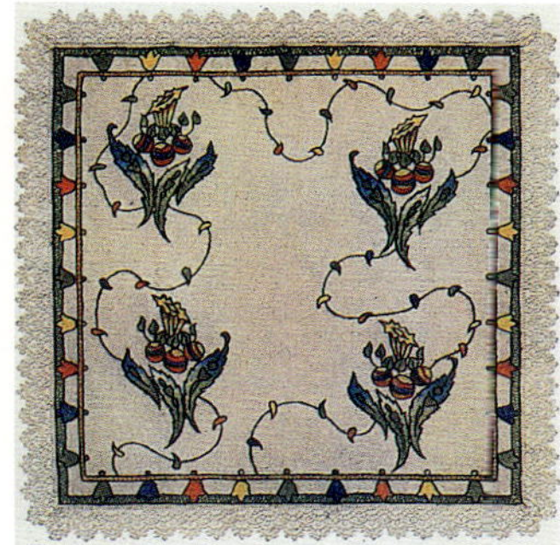

insects, and birds. The descriptions offered are unusually brief and deadpan for a company whose main selling point was the quality of their designs. Of design no. 911B (page 88 left) titled "Library Scarf on Dark Tan Linen" the description reads: "This is a very stylish scarf for use as a spread for the library table. The embroidered design is the same for both ends." The balance of the text describes the method of working, the round forms referred to as "jewels." Its Vienna Secessionist roots are not acknowledged. The table linen shown below it, no. 912G, is titled "Tinted Egyptian Oval Center on Dark Tan Linen" and described as "handsome." A coordinating sofa cushion is also offered.

While a few items were offered on colored fabrics in previous years, the 1911 catalog shows many items on green and brown burlap and crash (page 88 center). The term *conventional* is again used to designate most of these designs. In addition to the perennial warning to consumers to "Beware of Cheap Silks," another to "Avoid All Cotton Threads for Colored Embroidery" is added. Also, among the increasing number of advertisements is one for a self-published book *Silk, the Real Versus the Imitation*, signaling Brainerd & Armstrong's growing concern with their competition.

In 1912 the company tried a new marketing ploy illustrating "Brainerd & Armstrong's New Dye House" and promoting the permanence of the colors they are able to produce. "In the case of

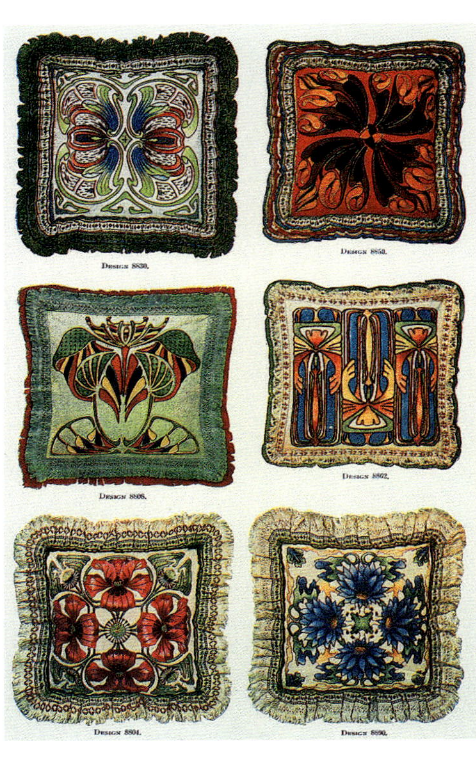
Design 8830.
Design 8850.
Design 8806.
Design 8862.
Design 8804.
Design 8890.

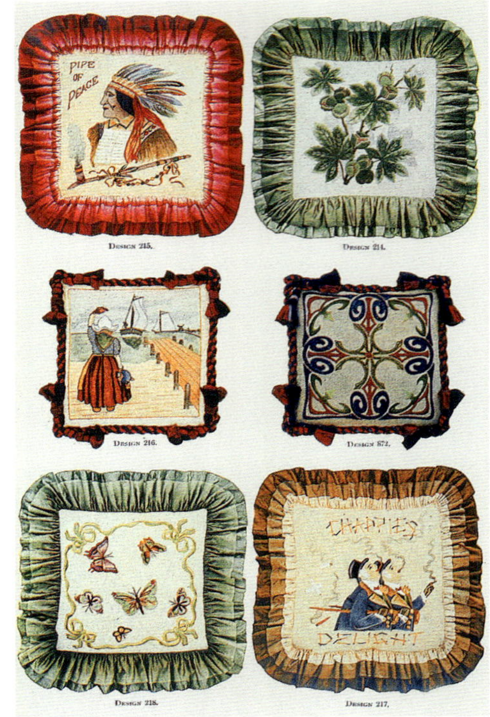
Pipe of Peace
Design 215.
Design 214.
Design 216.
Design 872.
Chappies
Delight
Design 218.
Design 217.

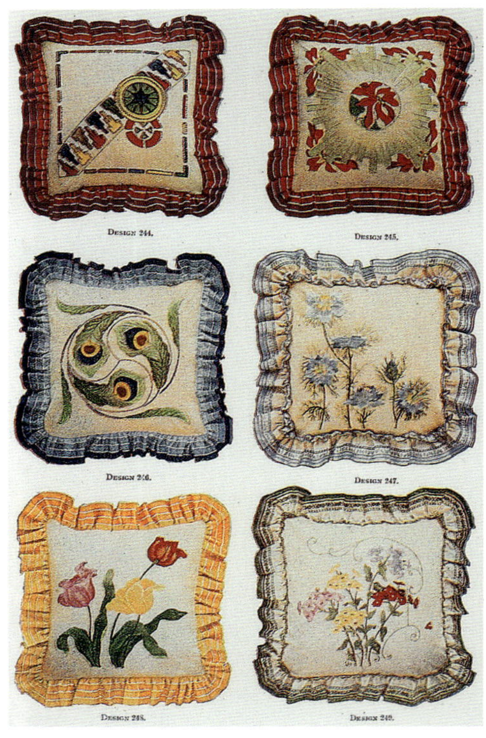
Design 244.
Design 245.
Design 246.
Design 247.
Design 248.
Design 249.

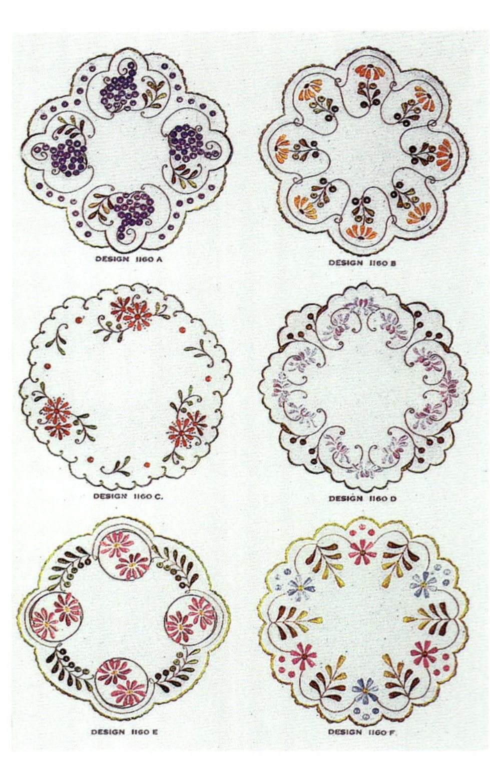
DESIGN 1160 A
DESIGN 1160 B
DESIGN 1160 C.
DESIGN 1160 D
DESIGN 1160 E
DESIGN 1160 F.

◀
Brainerd & Armstrong Company. Illustrations from catalogs. Clockwise from top left, 1906, 1907, 1909, 1908

the color that is probably more used than any other— Black—we claim that we dye the ONLY ABSOLUTELY FAST BLACK in the world. . . . We were the first to produce in this country fast color embroidery thread that could be washed without injury to the most delicate colors. We still maintain a masterly lead over all competitors in the production of these silks." Good, strong, Arts and Crafts style designs were offered in 1912 (page 88 right), along with a growing number of novelty items, such as "Dainty Pin Cushions" and "Shirt Waists and Underwear Sets." There is also more emphasis on coordinated sets of matching cushions and table linens.

This trend continued in 1913, with many designs offered as both a cushion and a table linen (page 89). Some patterns added a round centerpiece. Many of these designs were to be worked leaving much of the stenciling to show; the top and bottom designs require little more than the turned edges of the petals to be satin stitched and some outlining, and the center tulip design is mostly worked in scattered French knots. These kits required a substantial amount of time to prepare for a company whose primary business was silk manufacture. The company also began to offer in 1913 "Pillow Packets," "Scarf Packets," and "Centerpiece Packets"—linens with simplified designs, thread, and instructions for bargain prices.

Brainerd & Armstrong was not the first to develop Arts and Crafts designs for embroidery. Gustav Stickley's Craftsman Workshops needlework department had been operating since 1902, offering its unique style of design to accompany the Craftsman line of furniture. But Brainerd & Armstrong is to be credited with having creative, albeit anonymous, designers who produced

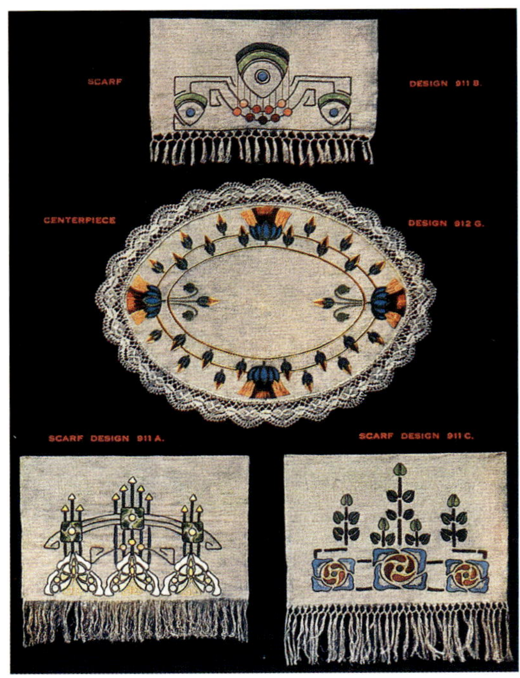

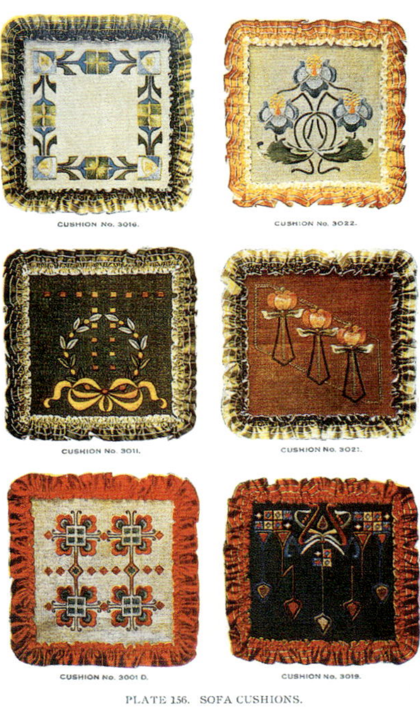

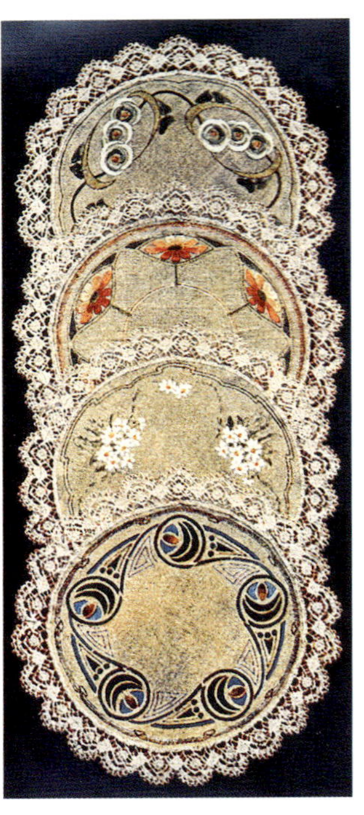

▲
Brainerd & Armstrong Company. Illustrations from catalogs. Left to right, 1910, 1911, 1912

some good Arts and Crafts designs. Nor were these the only companies to notice the trend toward Arts and Crafts design in the first decade of the twentieth century. The 1910 Richardson Silk Company catalog noted, "The gradual weakening of the Floral and the coming into favor of the Conventional and Arts and Crafts Embroidery is characteristic of the year. Our designs have been changed in accordance with this movement" (page 90). Richardson, based in Chicago, published its book of embroidery instructions titled *American Beauty Book*, as well as wholesale catalogs that went to embroidery shops. In addition to threads and kits, the catalogs offered display cabinets, needles, other supplies, and Electrotype advertisements that the merchants could run in their local papers. The company advertised in many national magazines, including *The Modern Priscilla* (page 92), *The Ladies' Home Journal*, and *The Delineator*. Promotions in these ads often offered a free pillow top stamped with a design when purchasing the thread to work it, or for sending in wrappers of embroidery silks the customer had already purchased. Retail catalogs also listed premium offers; a typical pillow top could be acquired for thirty cents or for sending in 120 tags. Richardson also promoted brand loyalty through the formation of Richardson's Art

▼

Brainerd & Armstrong Company. Illustration from catalog, 1913

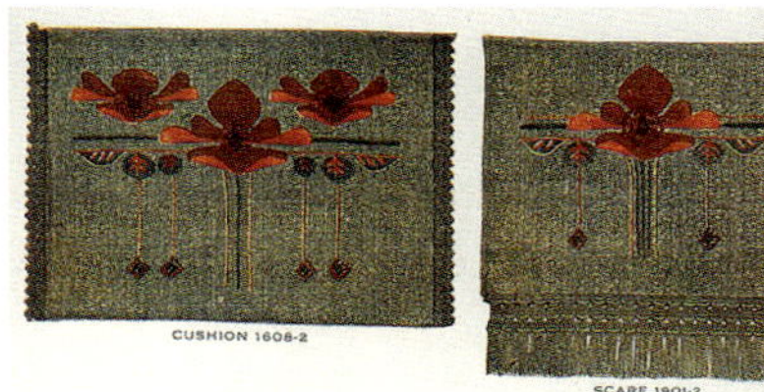

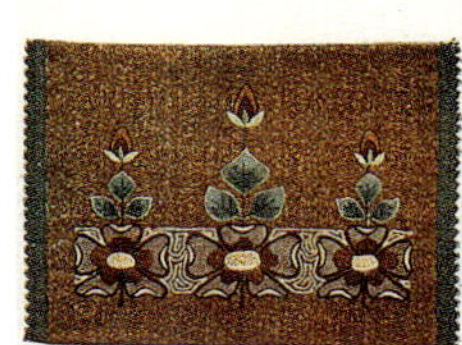

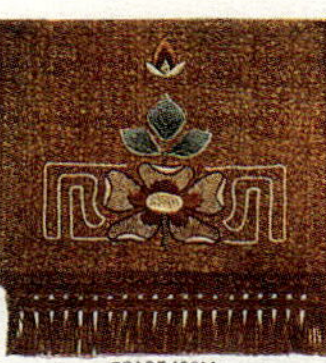

Embroidery Clubs (R.A.E.C.). The pamphlet (page 95), *How I became an Expert Embroideress, The Secret, R.A.E.C.,* describes:

> a national organization consisting of clubs formed by ladies who are interested in the Art of Embroidery. These ladies have pledged themselves to use only Richardson's Silks and Stamped Goods, so that they may receive our advice and assistance, our latest illustrated premium catalogs and all our special offers from time to time. . . .
>
> It costs nothing to become a member. There are no dues.
>
> Ten or more members constitute a club.
>
> WHY NOT JOIN?
>
> . . . A few advantages to be obtained by joining a club are:
>
> By uniting for the accomplishment of a common end, and
>
> By comparing work and assisting each other, and
>
> By making many new friends in a social way, and
>
> By sending to us for technical information, diagram lessons and color studies.

One wishing to be a club organizer was instructed to fill out a form and "send to us a statement from your merchant *showing that you and your members have each purchased one of our stamped designs (not smaller than a 22 inch Center Piece, or a pillow) and our silks to work same,* also a personally signed membership card from each club member." An individual could also apply to join an existing club or to have her name kept on file as a prospective R.A.E.C. member if a club

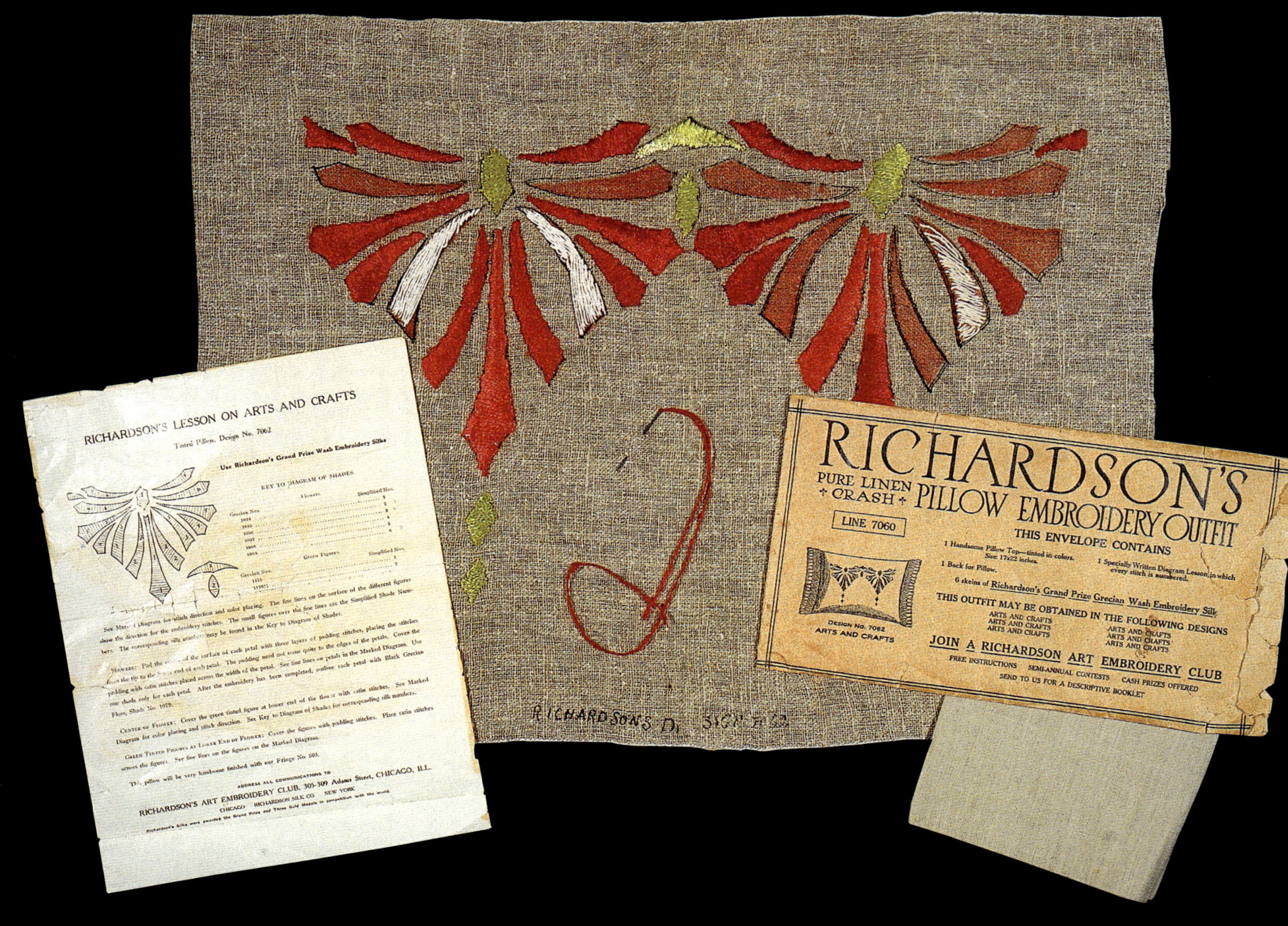

▲
Richardson Silk Company. Partially worked kit with its original packaging, instruction sheet, and backing fabric. 1911. Linen with silk hand embroidery, 17 × 22" (43.2 × 55.9 cm). Collection Timothy Hansen and Dianne Ayres

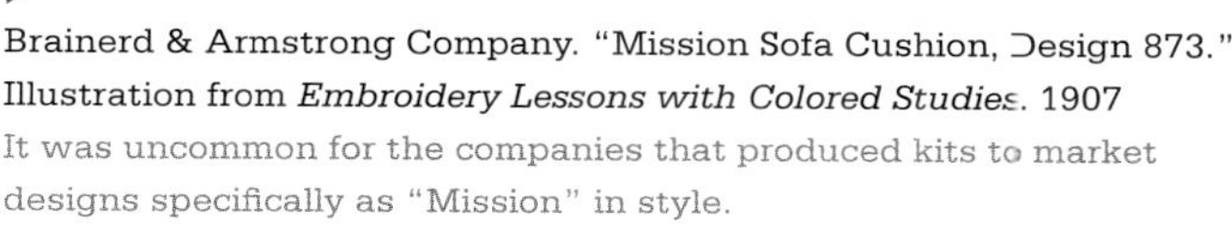

▶
Brainerd & Armstrong Company. "Mission Sofa Cushion, Design 873." Illustration from *Embroidery Lessons with Colored Studies*. 1907
It was uncommon for the companies that produced kits to market designs specifically as "Mission" in style.

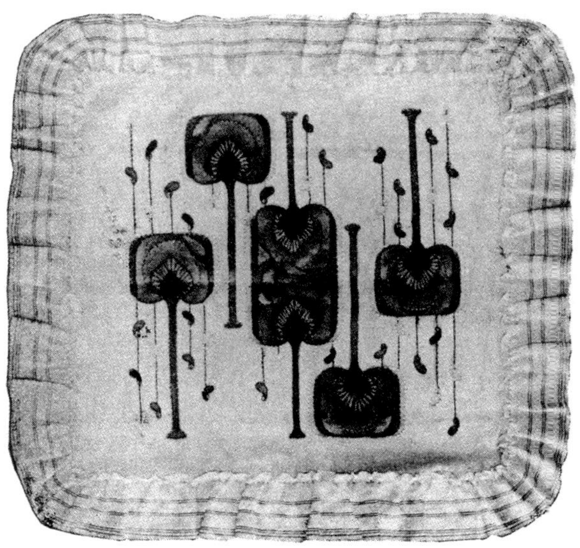

was not yet formed in her area. The club was to select a president, secretary, treasurer, and also a moderator, whose role was "to keep order at all meetings, and to confine members to one topic when discussing a subject." The members were also to wear the official pin and possess the R.A.E.C. pillow, both sporting their pansy logo. According to the company's literature, thousands of women joined. Embroidery teachers were also asked to contact the company for a "confidential proposition on 'How to Make More Money!'" Hundreds did.

In 1912, Richardson Silk Company introduced mercerized cotton floss in colors.[26] Cheaper to produce than silk, the product clearly caused alarm in the thread industry. Its development coincides with an increase in Brainerd & Armstrong's warnings against cotton embroidery threads and growing competition from new artificial silks, often a blend of rayon and other materials, which were coming onto the market. Cotton embroidery threads sold for about one-half the price of silk.

H. E. Verran Company of New York City produced kits, cotton embroidery threads, and crochet cottons under the trade name "Royal Society" (page 93 bottom). By 1913 it offered "Celesta," its trade name for an artificial silk, later known as rayon. The stamped linens and packaged kits sold well at retail shops. Other companies, such as Valley Supply Company of St. Louis, Missouri, also offered Royal Society items in their own wholesale catalogs, both as packaged kits and completed pieces that a retailer could show for display. Typical kit packages might note that they contain

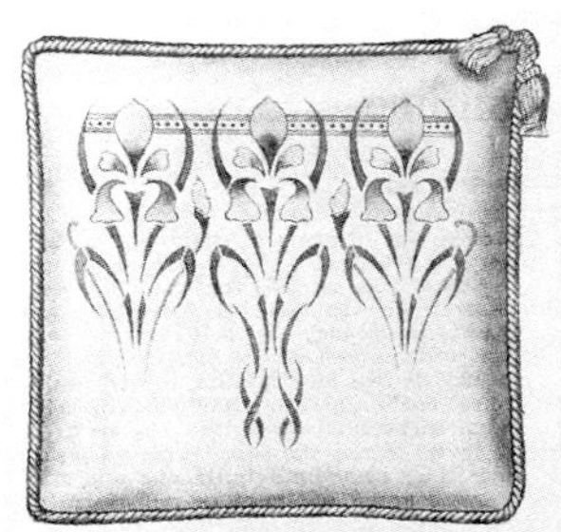

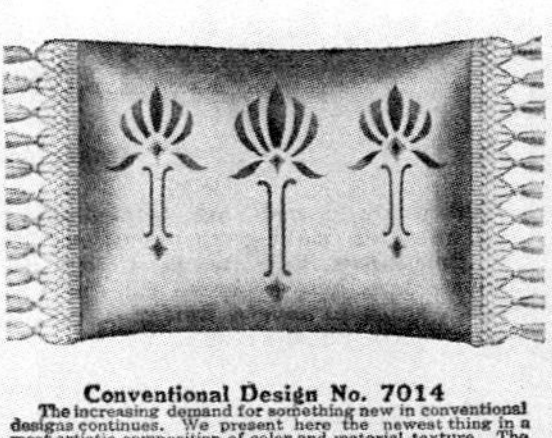

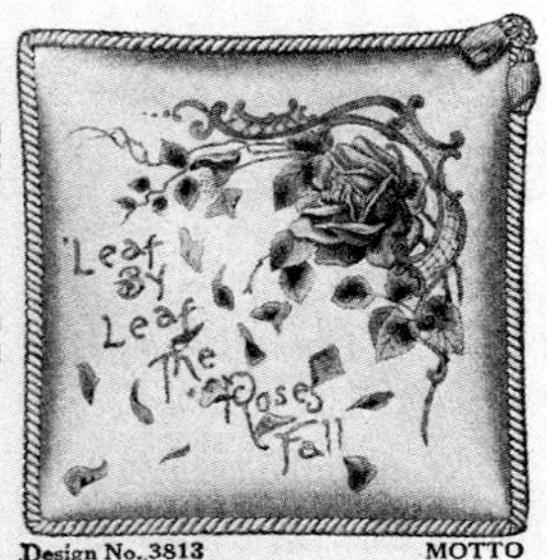

◀ Richardson Silk Company. Advertisement in *The Modern Priscilla*. November 1911

"embroidery floss to finish the article and instructions and materials as listed."[27] A kit for a typical handbag sold for fifty cents, with seven cents additional postage.

Numerous other companies advertised in the ladies' magazines and some published catalogs. Among them are: the Articraft Company, Springfield, Massachusetts; T. Buettner & Company, Chicago; Collingbourne's, Elgin, Illinois; Ladies' Art Company, St. Louis, Missouri; La Franc Company, Allegheny, Pennsylvania; E. D. Lorimer, Bentley-Franklin Company (trademark "Artamo"), and Meyer, Martin & Danda, all of New York City; and Walter P. Webber, Lynn, Massachusetts. Additionally, nearly every city had many businesses devoted to the embroidery trade, from those that purchased threads from the large mills, packaged it under their own label, and marketed their stamped designs on cloth, to individuals who offered their talents for embroidery.

Commercial mail-order houses, such as Sears Roebuck and Montgomery Ward offered kits. Of course, the magazine industry did not miss out on the opportunity to popularize needlework. *The Ladies' Home Journal, Harper's Bazaar, Home Needlework Magazine, The Modern Priscilla, The Pictorial Review,* and *The Delineator* maintained pattern departments. Some magazine pattern departments created their own works, while others retailed kits produced by Royal Society and others. Some, such as *Home Needlework Magazine*, sold thread also.

Not all of the Arts and Crafts kits were of American origin. DMC, a French-based company, participated in the American kit market and released at least six cross-stitch embroidery catalogs in the United States. These catalogs often reflected European Arts and Crafts design.

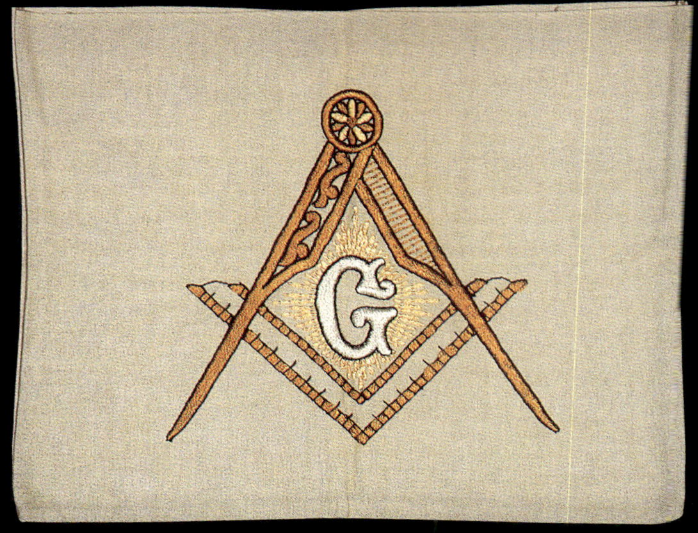

◀

Anonymous. Masonic pillow. c. 1912. Linen with hand embroidery, 16 × 21" (40.6 × 53.3 cm). Collection Tommy and Beth Ann McPherson
The 1913 catalog of Richardson Silk Company offered twenty-seven different "Society" and "Secret Order" pillow designs.

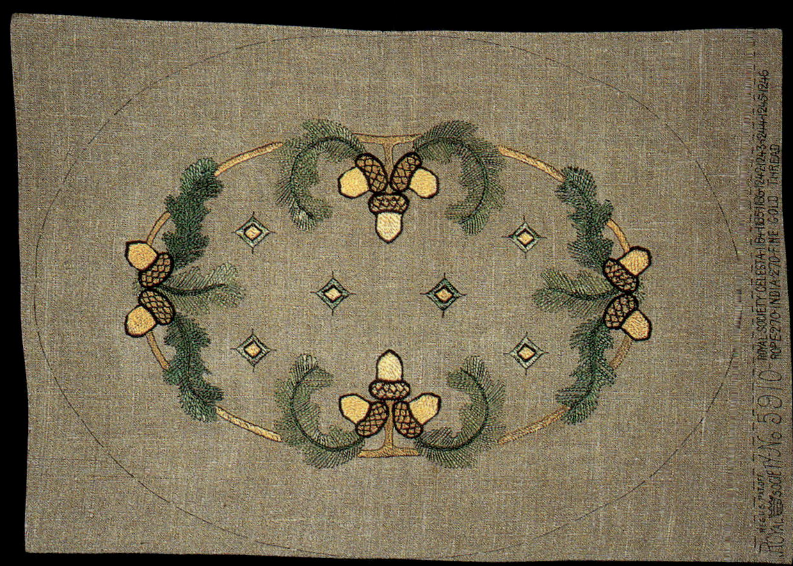

▶

H. E. Verran Company. "No. 5910, Royal Society" oak leaf and acorn mat. c. 1913. Linen with rayon and metallic embroidery, 17½ × 25" (44.5 × 63.5 cm). Collection Timothy Hansen and Dianne Ayres
Many table linens, when completed, had their identifying marks cut off.

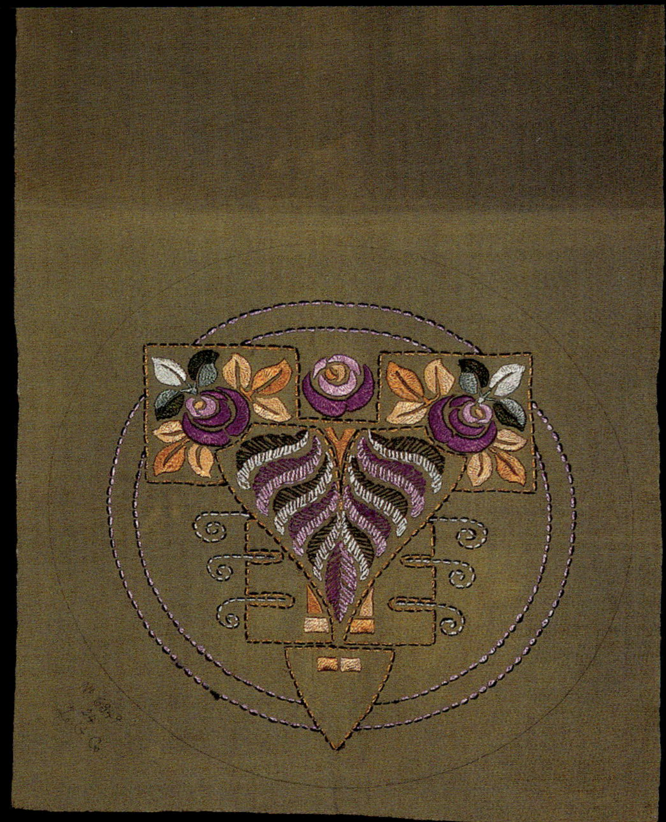

◀
I. G. Company. Pillow. c. 1912. Rayon with rayon embroidery, 23½ × 47" (59.7 × 119.4 cm). Collection Timothy Hansen and Dianne Ayres
This pillow was sold with the embroidery completed. The homemaker needed only to fold, sew, and fill it. The original price tag, reading "The Emporium $2.75," is stapled to the back.

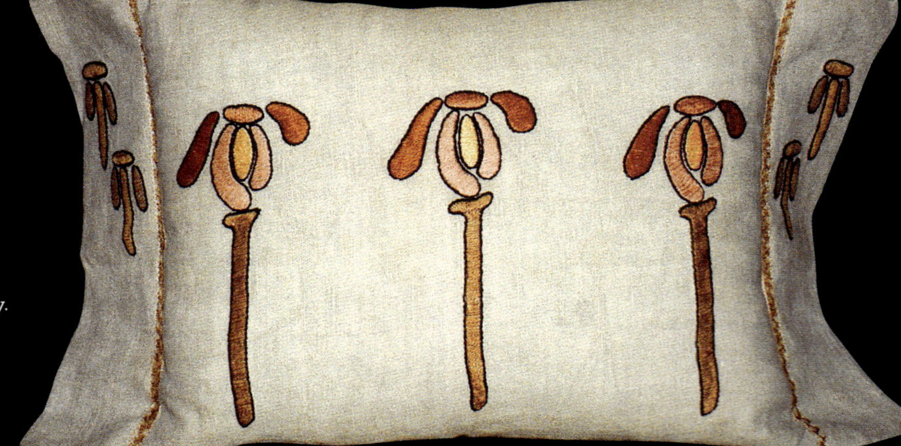

▶
Pacific Embroidery Company. Pillow. c. 1910. Linen with cotton embroidery. 15½ × 26" (39.4 × 66 cm). Collection Oakland Museum of California
Many of the Pacific Embroidery Company's textiles exhibit unusual colorings and designs.

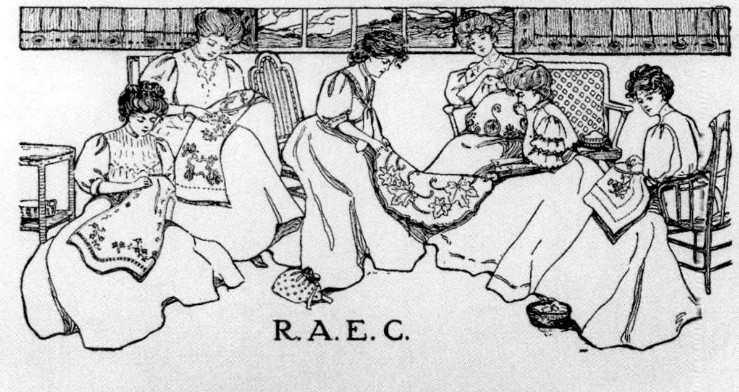

▶
Richardson Silk Company. "How I Became an Expert Embroideress, The Secret." Brochure of the R.A.E.C. (Richardson Art Embroidery Club). c. 1910

The majority of the creators of embroidery kit designs remain anonymous. Companies kept their own design staffs but also purchased patterns from independent designers. Belding Brothers claimed, "In addition to our own corps of artists, we have at all times the cordial assistance of other eminent Art Needlework authorities in the various metropolitan centers,"[28] but failed to give any names. *Home Needlework*, while under the direction of the Nonotuck Silk Company, did recognize some designers. Mrs. Isaac Miller Houck was one such designer who also published her own booklet, *A Treatise on Modern Drawn Work in Color.* From the alumni records of the California School of Arts and Crafts, the names of three designers for the Pacific Embroidery Company of San Francisco are known: Edith Anderson, Alma Vass, and Mary McCurdy; however, particular designs cannot be associated with them at this time. Nevertheless, companies offering embroidery kits gave many designers an opportunity to experiment with new concepts, and made it possible for the Arts and Crafts movement to reach a wide audience.

Arts and Crafts textiles represent one medium that actually attained the goals of the Arts and Crafts movement: to introduce and disseminate a new design aesthetic that was affordable, attainable, and of its time, and that emphasized an appreciation of handwork. Through books, magazines, schools, and commercial companies the tenets of Arts and Crafts design were spread via textiles. ❖

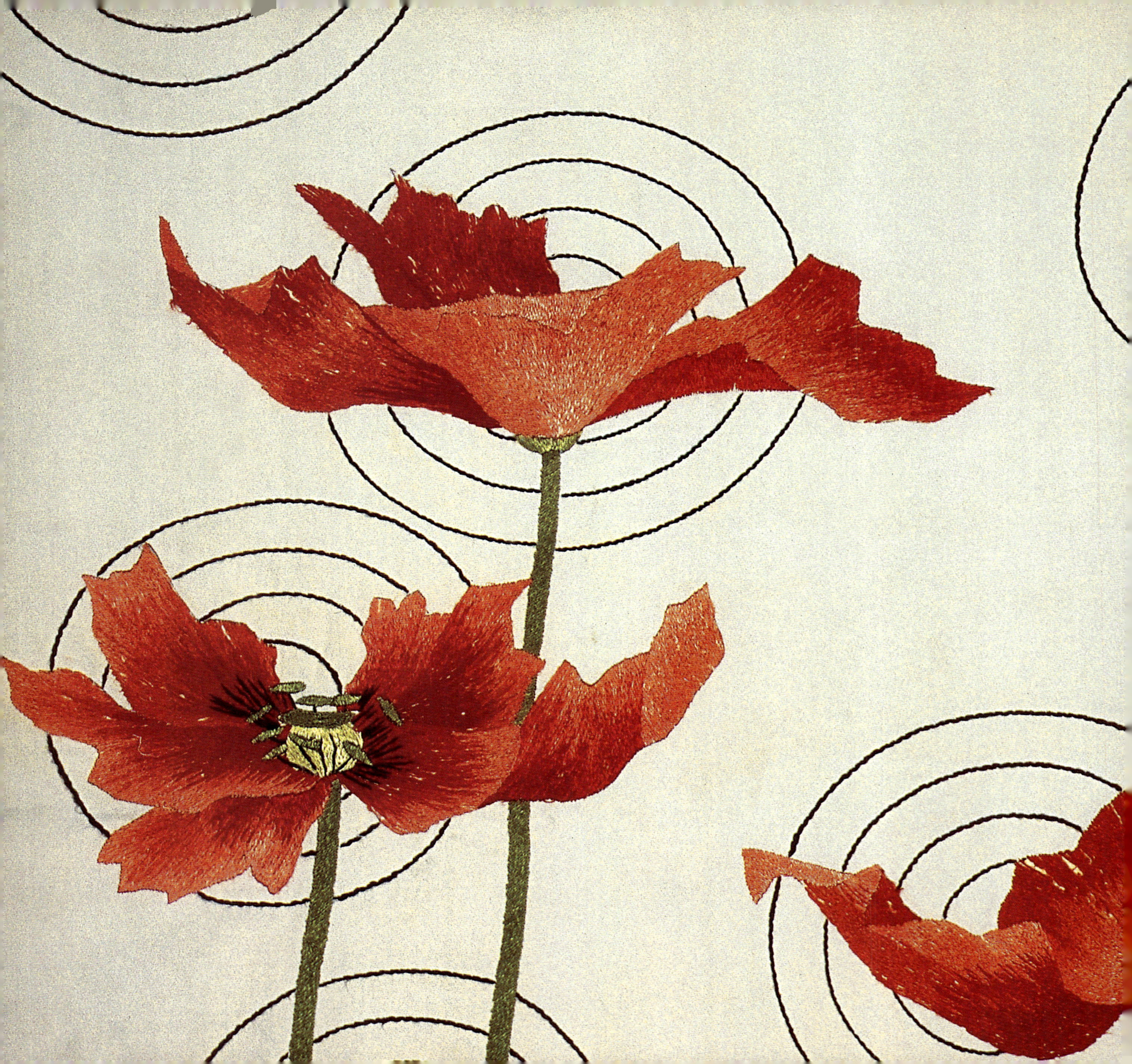

4 The House Beautiful: Textiles in the Arts and Crafts Home

The formation of the American home as an oasis where families could live according to the principles of "the simple life" was a primary focus of the American Arts and Crafts movement. The home was to provide its residents with space to retreat from the cares of the environment around them. It was to benefit and serve its dwellers. The artistic objects in the home served to educate and bring cheer. By being easy to clean and care for, the home would free its owners to pursue other interests. It was meant to be comfortable and welcoming and to reflect the personality of the individuals who dwelled within. The home was also a vessel, housing lovingly handcrafted objects from around the country. Participation in home-based do-it-yourself crafts democratized the decoration of the home, one of the lasting legacies of the American Arts and Crafts movement.

At the turn of the twentieth century, American design was affected by the changing styles of decoration that carried over from earlier decades. The philosophical ideas behind the Aesthetic movement stemmed from A. J. Downing and other mid-nineteenth-century architects who stressed the value of the home and the safe environment it created. The nineteenth-century Victorian home, with its profuse display of objects, was a conscious effort to excite the senses, to promote curiosity and education in children, and to impress visitors with one's wealth and sophistication. Downing, Calvert Vaux, and other architects of the era responded to this notion through their architectural designs, laying the foundation for the idea that a cheerful, comfortable, and friendly home atmosphere based on harmony was attainable to more than just the wealthy if the public applied basic principles of design and psychology to their home's design.[1]

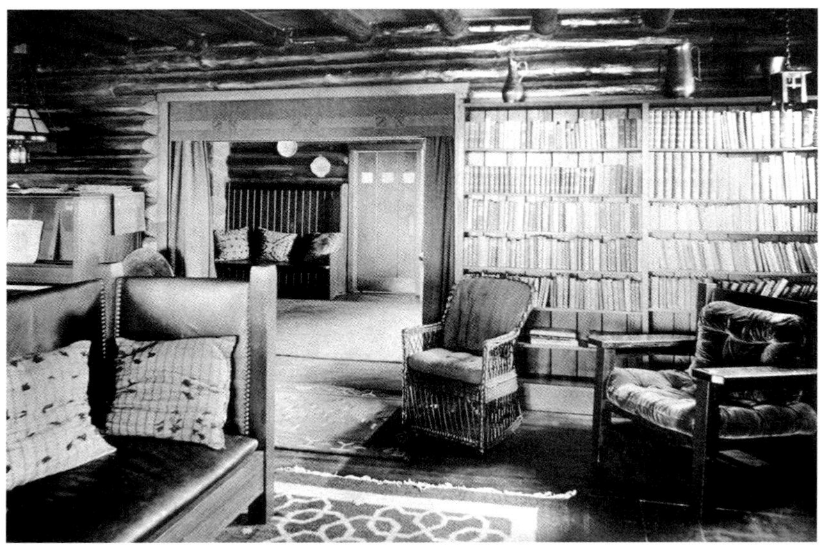

Nineteenth-century designers believed that ornament and objects joined together to create a complex and intriguing interior in which the beauty of art and the decorating choices of its owner provided cohesion. As the burgeoning middle class began to take an interest in interior decorating, tastemakers stepped forward to produce advice books and articles, including Clarence Cook's *What Shall We Do With Our Walls* (1880), Charles Locke Eastlake's *Hints on Household Taste* (1872), and *Artistic Houses, Being a Series of Interior Views of a Number of the Most Beautiful and Celebrated Homes in the United States* (1883–84). The styles available to consumers were abundant, and they were frequently combined to create an interior rich with references to other cultures and periods. Historical revival styles formed the basis of most nineteenth-century decoration. Candace Wheeler, the influential author, lecturer, and interior designer, transcended stylistic eclecticism, presenting many of the initial guidelines for what would become the Arts and Crafts home in her book *Principles of Home Decoration*. Although she advocated looking to past periods, her creative energies had gone into developing a new type of decorative textile that was of its time, employing conventionalized flower motifs rather than the naturalistic designs. Wheeler's significant contribution to the Arts and Crafts movement was to lay out principles of color and harmony for achieving the comfortable, attractive home. "In spite of the absence of authoritative teaching, we have learned that an art dependent upon other arts, as decoration is upon building and architecture, is bound to follow the principles which govern them. We must base our work upon what has already been done, select our decorative forms from appropriate periods, conform our use of colour to the

◀

Gustav Stickley's Log House at Craftsman Farms. View from the living room into the dining room. c. 1911

Stickley furnished his home with Craftsman textiles. Appliquéd rose portieres of "Craftsman canvas" adorned the doorways, and scrim pillows lined the settles and benches.

principles of colour, and be able to choose and apply all manufactures in accordance with the great law of appropriateness. If we do this, we stand upon something capable of evolution and the creation of a system."[2] Wheeler also emphasized the ways that anyone could use common household materials to beautify the home and recommended including textiles—from screens to curtains to mantle scarves—in all aspects of the interior.

Wheeler's book identified the need for the decoration of the home to serve as art, conveying character, cleanliness, color, and harmony. She noted that the various rooms and elements required specific attention and dedicated a whole chapter to curtains. She stated, "Consideration of draperies is second only to the wall and floor treatment in the scheme of home decoration. They have in truth much more to do with the effect of the room than chairs or sofas, since these are speedily sat upon and pass out of notice, while draperies or portieres are in the nature of pictures—hanging in everybody's sight. As far as the element of beauty is concerned, a room having good colour, attractive and interesting pictures, and beautiful draperies, is already furnished."[3]

The new approach Wheeler advocated in decorating was also taken up by social literature. The noted author Charlotte Perkins Gilman reasoned that if a woman was ever to develop to her potential she must emancipate herself from those duties of the home that were dispensable and "outgrow the magpie taste that hoards all manner of gay baubles."[4] Best known for her psychodramatic short story "The Yellow Wallpaper," in her time Gilman was a prominent author and lecturer with progressive ideas on economics and women's role in society. Hardly any facet of

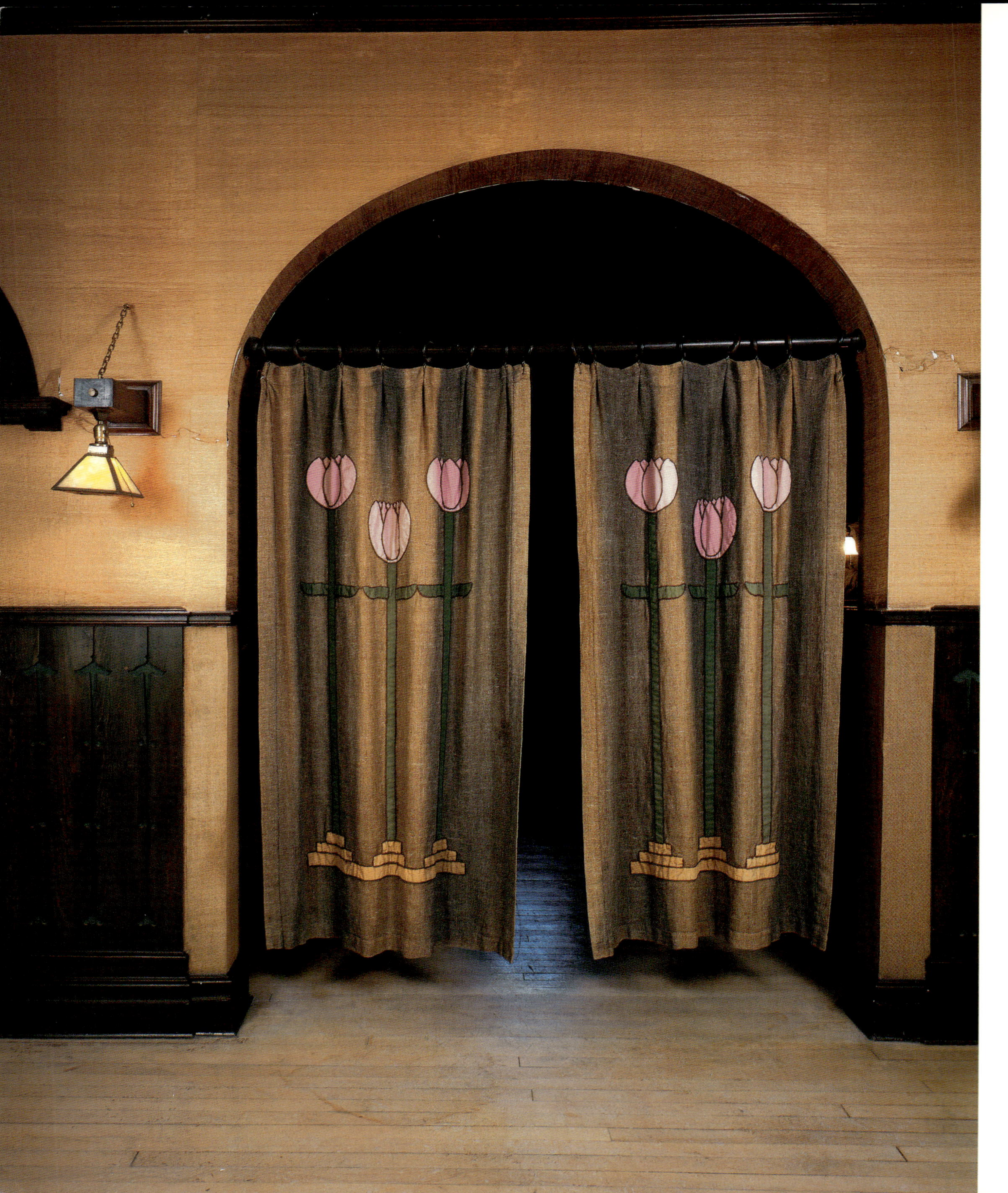

◀
Craftsman Workshops. Lotus portieres in the dining room of the Michael J. Riordan House. c. 1904. Flax and jute "Craftsman canvas" with cotton twill appliqué and hand embroidery, linen thread, 42 × 69" (106.7 × 175.3 cm). Collection Riordan Mansion State Park, Flagstaff, Arizona

life was to escape her pen, and of textiles she wrote:

> The most conspicuous field for the display of the beauty sense—or the lack of it—in our home life, is in the textile fabrics and their application to the body. The House is the foundation of textile art. People who live out of doors wear hides, if they wear anything. In the shelter and peace of the house, developed by ever-widening commerce, grew these wonderful textile arts, the evolution of a new plane for beauty. We find in nature nothing approaching it, save in the limited and passing form of spreading leaf and petal. To make a continuous substance soft as flowers, warm as furs, brilliant as the sunset—this was a great step in art.[5]

Hygenics also provided an argument for simplifying home decoration. Increased concerns about disease and infection brought calls for more fresh air and sanitary measures in the home. Lighter and less voluminous textiles let in light and air, trapped fewer germs, and were easy to maintain.

Wheeler's principles of harmony and color, and Gilman's social concerns publicized through their works continued to develop during the Arts and Crafts movement, especially through the influential designer and spokesperson Gustav Stickley. His promotional 1901 *Chips from the Workshop of Gustav Stickley* trumpeted the goal

> to produce, then, a home whose appointments render it a fitting scene for the work, pleasure, rest, and refreshment suited to the station and tastes of those who are to inhabit it, is a task that brings its own reward in the comfort and joy that it provides for both the habitual occupants and the occasional visitors. We can not over-estimate the value of symmetry in the

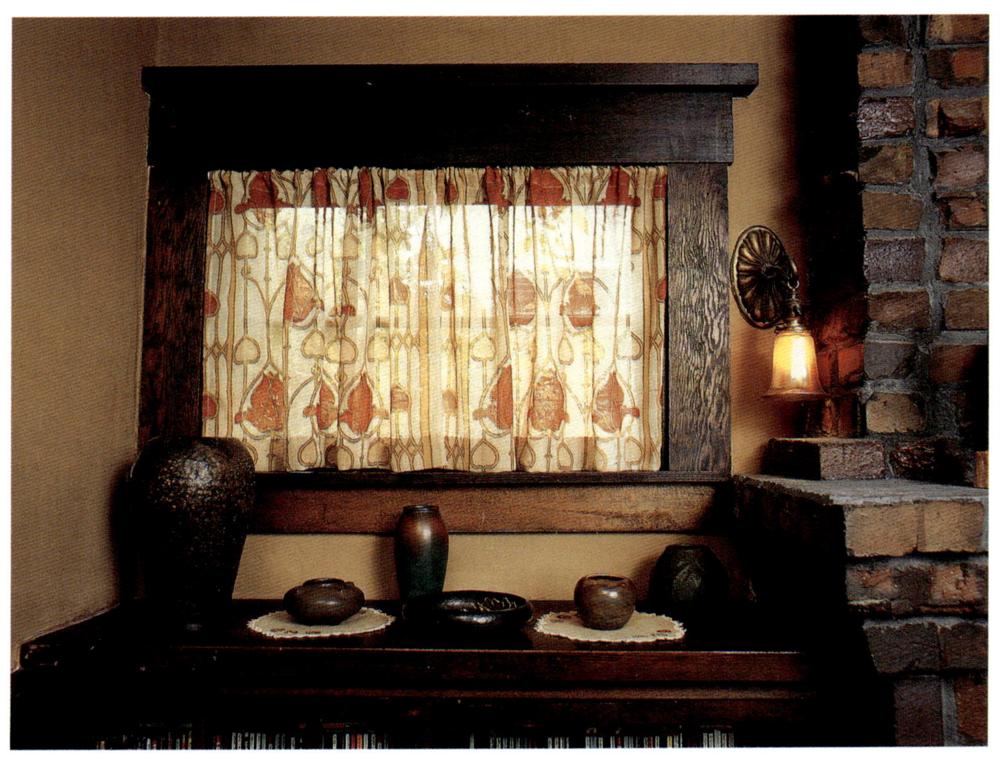

◀
Printed scrim curtain. c. 1912. Two panels, each 22 × 36" (55.9 × 91.4 cm)
The design of this period fabric is reminiscent of a stained-glass window pattern.

> objects that daily surround us, or the value of good color in the walls, curtains, and cushions upon which our eyes necessarily rest, as we think out the problems of existence. For fine color comes to us like food and like joyful news. It is invigorating.[6]

By 1900, Stickley had introduced his unique style of furniture and was in the process of developing an architectural style and a cadre of other decorative objects. He was reaching toward a vision of the unified home, "so step by step, we grew naturally into the designing and arranging, first of rooms, then of entire schemes of interior decoration, and lastly the planning and building of the whole house."[7] In 1909 he wrote: "we began ten years ago with the furniture; the metal work followed as a matter of course because it was the next thing needed; then the dressing of leathers to harmonize with the style of the furniture and the wood of which it was made. Then came the finding of suitable fabrics and the kind of decoration most in keeping with them, and from all these parts was naturally developed the idea of the Craftsman house as a whole."[8]

From 1901 to the first appearance of his own line of textiles in 1903, Stickley's reverence for textiles came through the pages of *The Craftsman* magazine. The second issue of *The Craftsman*,

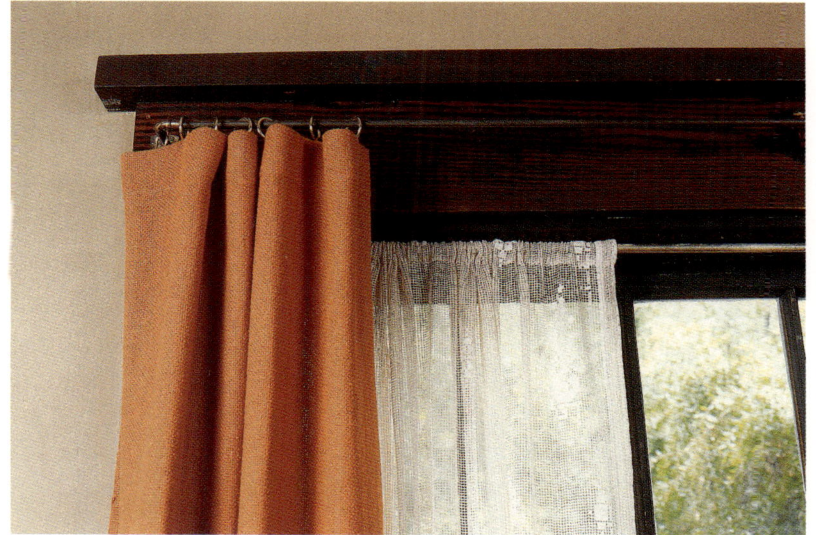

▶
Typical method of hanging curtains. The glass curtains of machine-made net, c. 1910, are mounted inside the window frame on a small brass rod. The monk's cloth overcurtains have brass rings sewn on and are hung on brass rods with gooseneck brackets.

published in October 1901, was dedicated to the development of textiles through time. Although earlier issues illustrated room settings containing textiles, the August 1903 issued marked the first appearance in the magazine of textiles produced by Craftsman Workshops. Stickley's own linens featured natural fabrics and blends that were patterned, plain, and embroidered.

Stickley was not alone in emphasizing appropriate textiles for the Arts and Crafts home In fact, the pages of *The Craftsman* report on many other individuals and enterprises working with similar ideas. Stickley, however, was important in bringing the various mediums of interior decoration together and for promoting the simple, comfortable, cheerful home across the country through the distribution of his retail goods, magazine, lectures, and catalogs. The magazine's coverage of the public's interest and participation in textile contests and Arts and Crafts competitions around the country helped bolster the movement's popularity.

In 1905, Stickley's contemporary Alice M. Kellogg reported, "the progressive spirit of the new century and the rapid artistic development throughout our country have awakened a widespread, intelligent interest in all matters relating to the Art of the House."[9] Her book, *Home Furnishing, Practical and Artistic* surveys the design styles available for decorating a contemporary home and provides a succinct view of the Arts and Crafts movement:

> A Continental attempt to introduce a new household art, called "L'Art Nouveau," has reached us but has not received sufficient encouragement on this side of the water to make it an

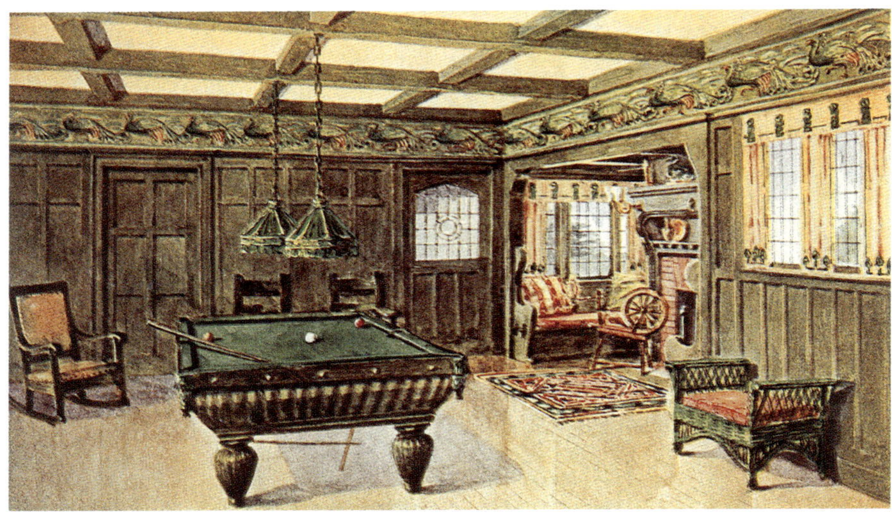

◀
Sherwin-Williams Company. "Oak Lends Itself Admirably to Handcraft Effects." Illustration from *Your Home and Its Decoration*. 1910

> established success. Its flowing curves, delicate ornamentation and exquisite workmanship demand special accompaniments in wallpapers and floor coverings, and when carried out with fidelity some charming interiors have been produced.
>
> The "mission idea" has, on the other hand, made a powerful impression in American homes, and the substitution of the straight line for the curved, the absence of applied ornament, and a simple in place of complex construction have made a distinct advance in furniture.
>
> The mission furniture, too, has made an opening for a simpler fashion in the accessories of furnishing and decoration—rugs, wall covering, curtains, pottery. The permanent hardware also is given to designers who can contribute to the atmosphere of the mission interior, and andirons and fireplaces are selected with regard to their specific fitness. Even the small item of a table mat or a flower holder is recognized as a successful adjunct or a disappointing feature in a room pervaded with mission principles.[10]

Mable Tuke Priestman's *Art and Economy in Home Decoration* (1908) became a popular general decorating book that completely embraced the Arts and Crafts movement. Stickley's *Craftsman Homes* and *More Craftsman Homes*, and Henry Saylor's *Bungalows* were also completely devoted to the Arts and Crafts movement but focused on the architecture. Others, such as *Homes and Their Decoration* by Lillie Hamilton French, *Furnishing the Home of Good Taste* by Lucy Abbot Throop, and Kellogg's book treated the style as the latest of many options in decorating fashion, often relegating it to the porch or summer cabin. Other writers were outright hostile toward it "A large portion of the worst furniture ever made belongs to the so-called mission or Arts-and-Crafts type," and "Mission is not a style but the negation of style," said George Leland Hunter in his book, *Home Furnishing*.

But detractors like Hunter made barely a ripple in the banners of champions like Priestman. She was an interior decorator, a craftworker, and author on these subjects, and she revealed her political leanings by documenting utopian communities. In *Art and Economy in Home Decoration* she quotes extensively from Charles Wagner's *Simple Life* (1901) and sums up her intent: "let us avoid ostentatious display, and cultivate the beauty of harmony and simplicity."[11]

The process Priestman recommends is to first get rid of anything that does not fit the scheme, employing William Morris's criteria: "Is this beautiful?" "Is this useful?" The homemaker must "have the strength of character not to put unnecessary ornaments back again unless they come up to these requirements."[12] One is then guided in choosing the wall color and treatment according to the quality of light coming in a room, its use, and the desired ambience. Her down-to-earth approach intersperses basic design principles on the use of color and proportion, gives practical suggestions of solutions to specific decorating problems, surveys the marketplace for items the homeowner should look for and beware of, and offers how-to advice on diverse subjects such as "How to Stain Floors," "Needlework in the Hands of the Craftsman," and "Ornamenting Fabrics by Means of Stenciling and Block Printing."

▼
L. & J. G. Stickley, Inc. "A Living Room." Illustration from Brown's *Book of Home Building and Decoration*. 1912
Copper-colored scrim curtains lend a warm glow to the light filtering through.

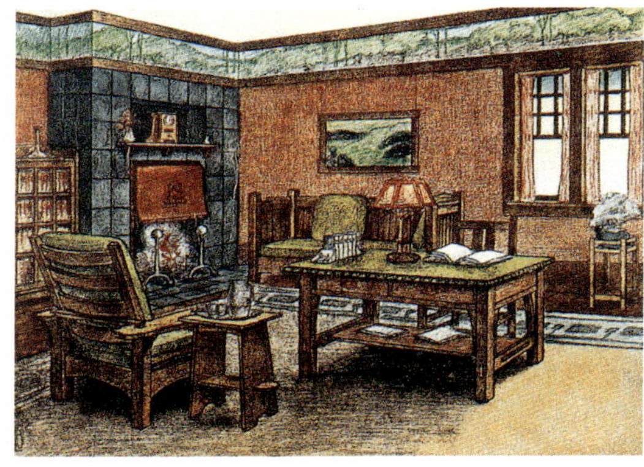

While Priestman offered a practical approach, Helen Binkerd Young presented the method for decorating and furnishing the modern home by academic analysis. She develops an argument for the type of home environment "on which home-loving people may unite," rejecting the previous generation's method of decorating a room by doing "something which would show up well."

> This we now know is not what we want. In fact, it is the very thing we do not want; for, in the main, walls are merely backgrounds for pictures, furniture and people and should be covered in such a way as to hold their place. Moreover, a home should be a place to rest. All things in it should encourage peace, harmony, repose and freedom. Mental and moral poise are impossible to persons engulfed in a sea of bright colors and aggressive patterns. Nervousness is the sure price paid for over-decoration. . . . Here is the parting of the ways between good taste and bad in home decoration: Good taste consciously emphasizes the welfare of people. Bad taste unconsciously emphasizes the possession of things. . . . So much is now known about the physical and mental effect of home environment that every intelligent person may acquaint himself with a few wise and reasonable principles. The psychology of the nervous system recognizes jarring colors and patterns as well as jarring sounds; hence mistakes in decoration can no longer be excused under the kindly mask of a difference in taste.[13]

Although Young's advice concentrates on wall color, this analysis of the psychological effect of decoration extends to other decorative elements as well. Some decorating manuals, such as Mary

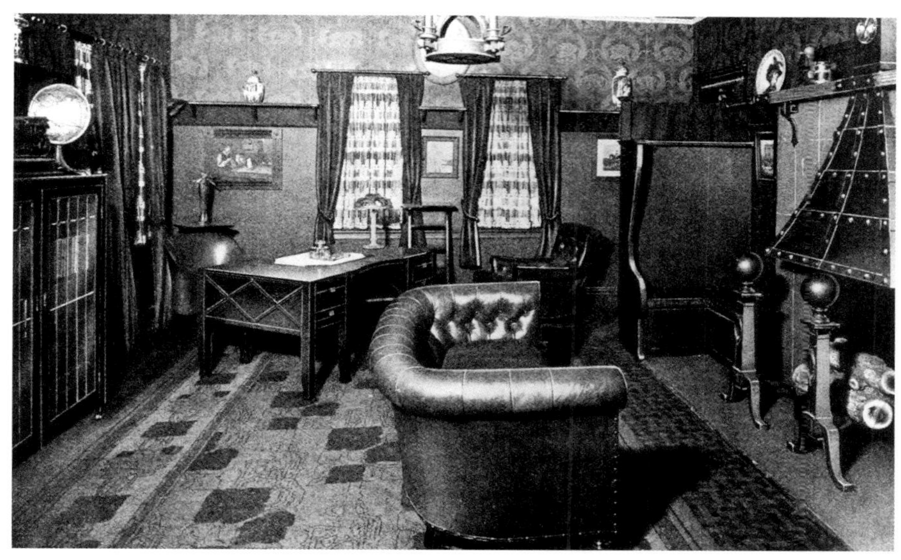

◄
Clifford & Lawton. "Modern Living Room, Arts and Crafts American." Illustration from *The Room Beautiful*. 1915
Patterned glass curtains to the sill are fronted by plain fabric overcurtains hung on large rods and rings. The overcurtains on the back wall hang below the sill, while those on the side wall hang to the floor

Ann Sell and Henry Blackman Sell's 1916 *Good Taste in Home Furnishing*, outlined general design principles based on perception of proportion and scale, and incorporated recent theories on the psychological effect of color. The Sells outlined a series of questions to help determine the color of the draperies or curtains for a room.

Many decorating books published during the Arts and Crafts period did not deal exclusively with the Arts and Crafts style; rather, it was simply one of many decorating choices included in the pages. Eventually, with some influence of European modernism, many decorative schemes took an extreme approach to the "simple life" idea, where everything was stripped down to bare essentials and all references to ornament were removed. A common thread between the Arts and Crafts style and later modernism was that both sought a new look that was appropriate for a changing world in a new century.

Hazel Adler in *The New Interior* created decorating schemes using aesthetic principles of unity, personal expression, utility, and color as opposed to the former method, which was to assemble an interior eclectically from many parts, i.e. furniture, fabric, objects, etc. Adler quotes an anonymous French writer "'The knowledge of being well dressed imparts a blissfulness to the soul which religion is powerless to bestow.' In a like manner the knowledge of being well housed, of having created for one's self an environment which is an adequate expression of one's tastes and individuality, of having established a harmony between the inner and the outer life, lends to living a certain poise and power which can seldom be derived from other sources."[14]

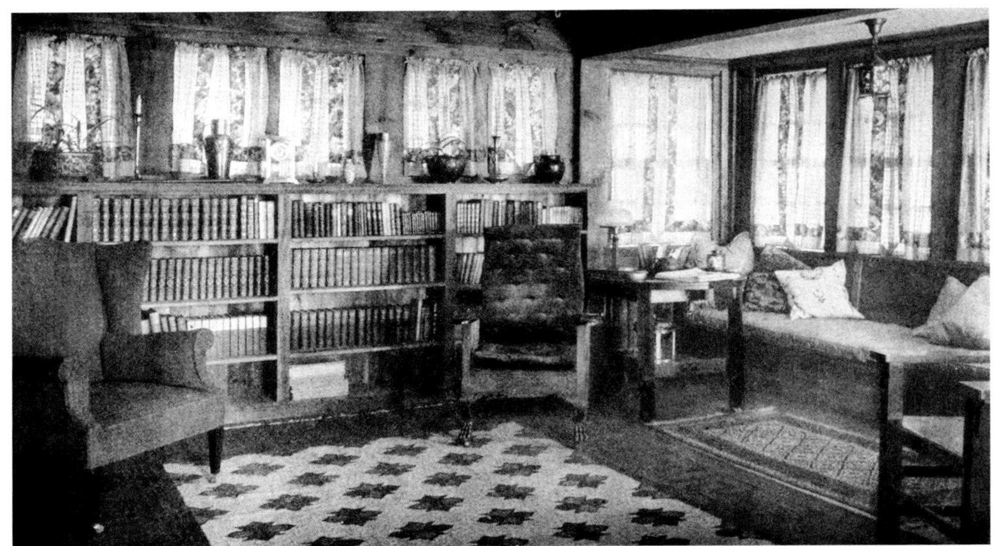

These ideas were spread and perpetuated through the education of children. In Charles F. Warner's *The Library of Work and Play: Home Decoration,* schoolchildren ages eleven to eighteen were reported to have designed, built, decorated, and furnished a house. They worked according to the "Ten Commandments of Decoration" delineated in the book, which included the mandate "No kind of decorative art offers greater possibilities for touching the right—or the wrong—chord than that which makes use of fabrics."[15]

Following the new principles of simplicity, women, the traditional homemakers, approached their homes with a more relaxed attitude. "It is not that the average woman loves housework less, but that she loves the companionship of her home and friends, books, outdoor life and recreation better. There is not an intelligent, happy family woman who does not enjoy adding to every way in the beauty and comfort of her surroundings. Her home is the background of her life, and she wants it to be attractive. She may not really enjoy housework. Why should she? But she will like to work for her home just as a man wants to work for his country."[16]

Textiles proved an inexpensive way for people to decorate the interiors of the new, middle-class American home, which was designed around practical needs. Home decoration became a way to unite domestic science and aesthetics. Open floor plans to create flow among the rooms were enhanced with cozy corners and custom built-in sideboards, bookcases, and other furniture, conceived to make life simpler in comfortable, simple, easy to clean, and harmonious interiors. Candace Wheeler summed up current sentiment when she wrote in 1894 that "a perfectly fur-

◀
Richardson Wright. "Library with Inappropriate Curtains." Illustration from *Inside the House of Good Taste*. 1918
Original caption: "A dignified treatment for a comfortable library and living-room combined. Visualize plain fabrics at the windows instead of the inserted cretonnes, and one immediately sees how the dignity of the room would have been enhanced."

nished house is a crystallization of the culture, the habits, the taste of the family and not only expresses but makes character."[17] In her own summer cottage, Pennyroyal, located in Onteora, New York, she incorporated the quote "Who Creates a Home Creates a Potent Spirit Which in Turn Doth Fashion Him That Fashioned" as a daily reminder of the importance of her work.

Color became an important way to set the mood of a house. Authors such as Charles Keeler, who wrote *The Simple Home* (1904), recommended avoiding cold colors and using warm tones. Nature's palette of buff, brown, red, deep blue, and rich green were all warm, comfortable, and inspiring colors. Maud Ann Sell wrote in more detail on the use of color and its impact. Yellow warms rooms and "expands" objects. Red intensifies a room, and blues diminish a room. Other colors follow the lead tendency of their primary color. Homemakers were warned that dark colors cannot assert themselves in the north light. Green and blue become black. Gold, orange, and red alone have sufficient power to hold their own and make one conscious of them in darkness.

For home renovators, the continuing development of textiles as a decorative art was a way to easily change an interior. Textiles were one of the easiest ways to introduce the new color theory into a space. Textiles for the home were available ready-made but, to afford quality goods, families participated in making their own curtains, portieres, pillows, and linens. The American Arts and Crafts house was meant to be "a home, not merely a dwelling-place," and its style, both in architectural plan and interior decoration, "is suggestive of a period of American life when architecture and furnishings were simple and beautiful, and perfectly adapted to American needs."[18]

▼
Dirk van Erp's studio, showing curtains with conventional lamp designs. c. 1910–20 photograph. Collection Oakland Museum of California
The curtains are possibly the design and handiwork of D'Arcy Gaw, a professional designer with whom van Erp had a short-lived partnership.

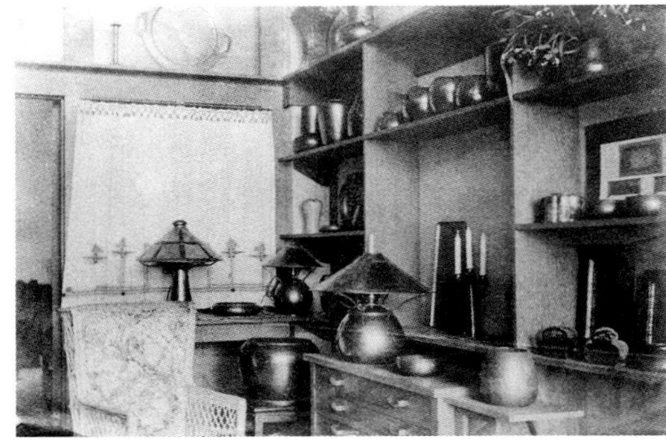

Textiles symbolized this metamorphosis. As Stickley wrote,

> Out of the dead past of "fancy work," a fresh and personal interpretation of beauty has grown; the womanly craft of the needle has again allied itself to art. All along the lines of needlework sincerity is replacing affectation as in all the decorative arts to hundreds of thoughtful people. The awakened desire for homes expressive of the simple beauty of life, reaches out for means of setting forth in all the departments of those homes the beauty which is simplicity; so the right kind of house leads on to the right kind of furniture and furnishings, till the reconstructive spirit has brought every detail of a little world into harmony with itself.[19]

Physically, the importance of textiles in the household was often reflected in the home layout. Since the nineteenth century, a small room in the servants' wing or in the main part of the house was set aside for household sewing functions.

Textiles were used in every room of the turn-of-the-century house, in the form of wallcoverings, curtains, and rugs. In Arts and Crafts style homes, burlap, canvas, and rough linens were applied to walls as decorative coverings. Patterned wallcoverings were also common, but it was important that the pattern appeared to be two-dimensional. This increased use of fabric for wallcoverings was aided by advancements in home utility options. For example, annual spring cleaning, once mandatory to control the sooty output of the coal furnace that took its toll on fabric, was no longer as necessary when cleaner steam heat became more common.

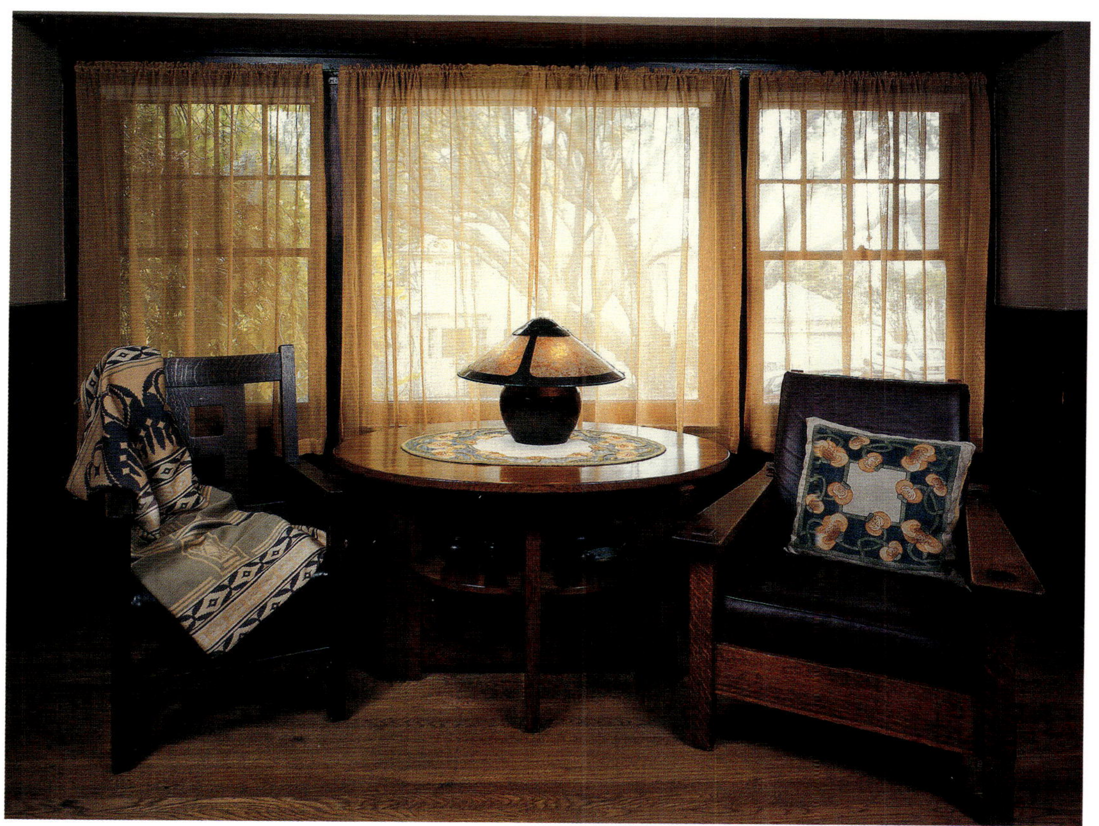

Living room with copper-colored linen scrim curtains, stenciled and hand-embroidered table linen and pillow, and tapestry-weave couch throw

Light was a contributing factor in the mood in Arts and Crafts homes. Stickley believed that since "the healthiest and happiest life is that which maintains the closest relationship with out-of-doors, we have planned our houses with outdoor living rooms, dining rooms, and sleeping rooms, and many windows to let in plenty of air and sunlight."[20] Window coverings were a critical element in all styles of interior decor, but particularly in the Arts and Crafts home.

Windows had long been likened to "the eyes of the house," but to the new interior decorators of the twentieth century they took on even more personality. It was thought that their treatment portrayed the character of the person within. Author Lillie French wrote: "I never escape the feeling of the face behind the pane, and seldom of the soul shining out of the face. Show me the windows of a house and I will show you the manner of person dwelling inside."[21] She scrutinized windows hung with "cheap Nottingham-lace," imagining the pretentious homemaker and her untidy children and another window hung modestly that "betokens refinement and order." In a similarly voyeuristic vein, Ruby Goodnow and Rayne Adams in *The Honest House* "'size people up' by the way they

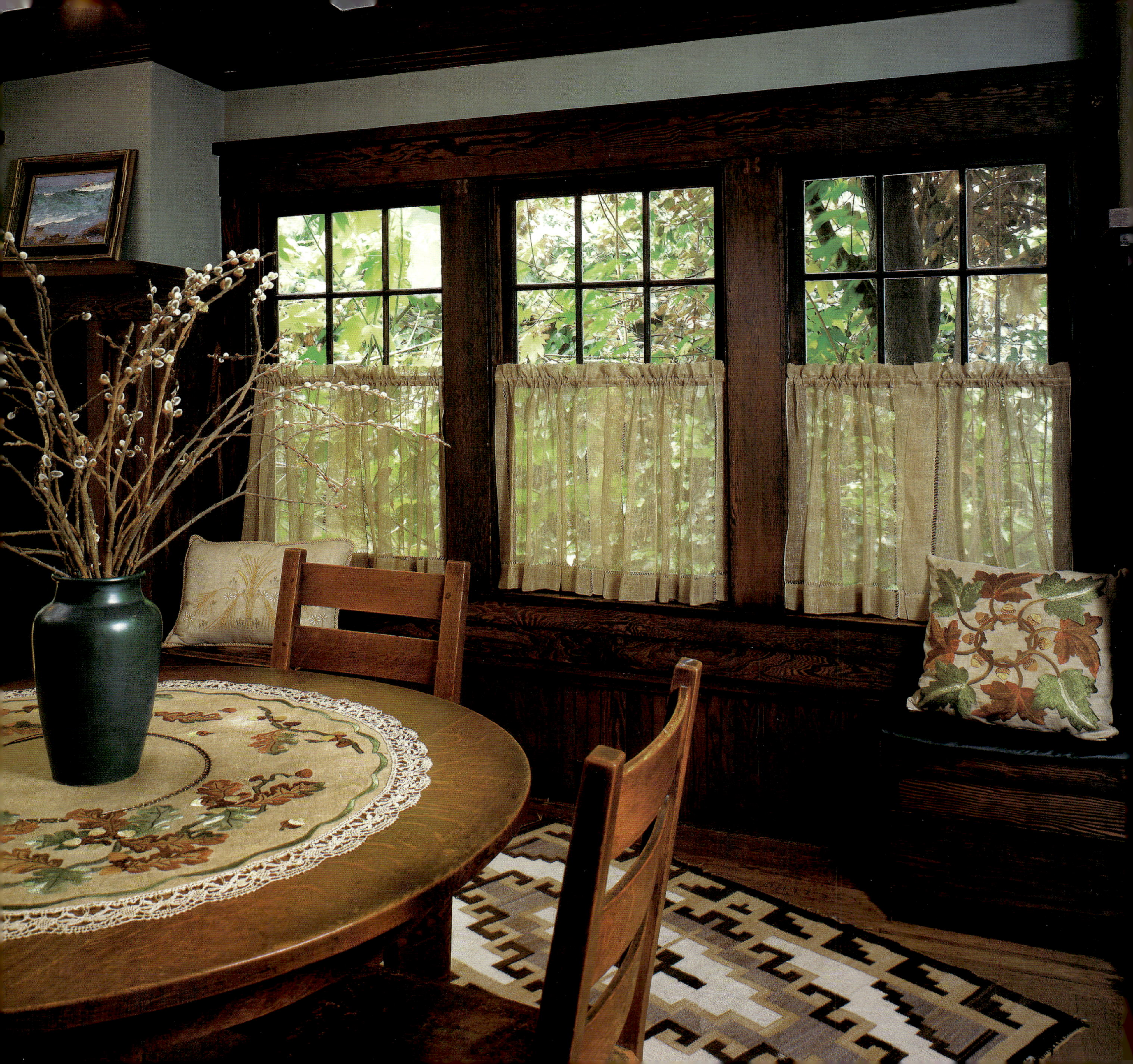

◀
Dining room with raw linen scrim curtains with hand hemstitching, and oak and acorn table linen and pillow. Hand stenciled and hand embroidered. Collection Caro Macpherson. Even where curtains are not required for privacy, they soften the effect of hard woodwork and add ambiance.

treat their windows." They reported on the "cave-dwellers" of New York City, "their pallid families in air-tight houses," the windows hung with layers of laces, shades, velvets, and brocades, lined and interlined, and topped with "the hideous lambrequins of the Victorian era of decoration."

Aside from the social and moral implications, the exterior appearance of windows demanded aesthetic consideration. "In deciding upon the window draperies one should view the question from both sides—that is, the effect from the exterior as well as that of the interior. . . . [I]t is best to have the general effect of the windows of an entire floor the same." One method suggested was "to hang net curtains close to the glass, in which case they show from the outside."[22]

Windows in the Arts and Crafts era, with its heightened sense of health consciousness and love of the outdoors, also took on a new role as purveyors of these attributes. "Health is the first essential of good homemaking. If our homes are to be wholesome and cheerful, we must make arrangements for the admittance of the best of nature's gifts—light and air. We must, therefore, not have curtains so costly that we dread sun, air, or dust."[23] Hygiene was also a concern to Theodore Dillaway in *Decoration of the School and Home*, ruling out bamboo and beads, or velvets and heavy wools. In addition to the choice of materials, this new sensibility affected the style and form of window treatments: "In keeping with this spirit of rationalism the cumbersome, dust-catching festoon drapery has been banished, and in the detached house the lace curtain and over-hanging that once swept the floor have disappeared in favor of simpler forms—the sill length hangings of to-day."[24]

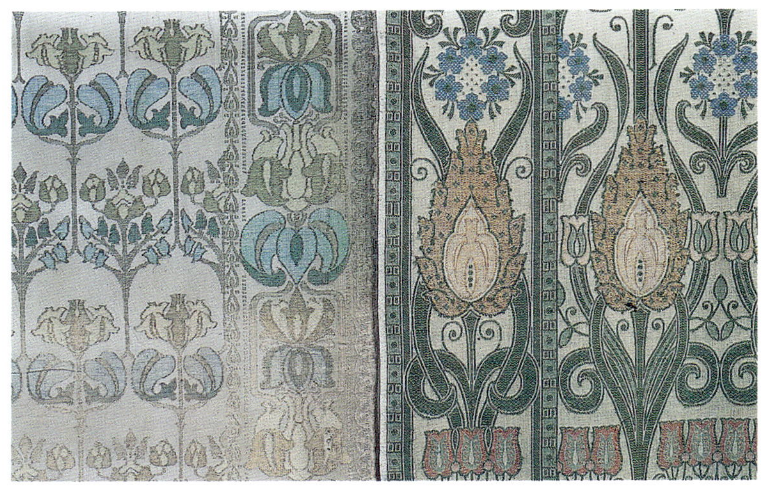

◄
Anonymous, possibly imported. Detail of commercially woven curtain fabrics: Madras (left) and Crete (right). c. 1900–20. Cotton; Madras panel: 96 × 44½" (243.8 × 113 cm), design repeat 13 × 5" (33 × 12.7 cm). Crete panel: 104 × 49" (264.2 × 124.5 cm), design repeat 26 × 8" (66 × 20.3 cm). Collection Timothy Hansen and Dianne Ayres
These curtain fabrics have woven borders along both sides and the bottom; the top could be cut to any length necessary.

While far less drapery was used than in previous times, it was generally assumed that most windows would be donned in some manner. In *Home Furnishing* (1913), George Leland Hunter put aside his disdain for the new style in his advice, "Yet bungalows quite as much as any other type of residence need draperies to soften the hardness of wood and plaster and brick and stone, and to introduce the rich and warm and picturesque textures possible only in the products of the loom."[25] Even when they were not required for functional purposes, such as light control and warmth, door and window hangings were often viewed as necessary for their decorative effect—adding color and pattern, and creating the cheerful, comfortable, and friendly atmosphere of an Arts and Crafts home.

Window hangings near the glass, often of a sheer fabric, were alternatively called "sash" or "glass" curtains. Most recommended treating each window individually with its own pair of curtains. These shielding devices provided privacy, particularly on the second story, while also protecting the fragile nature of the dyes used in textiles. Many windows in Arts and Crafts style homes had two sets of curtains, glass curtains and over-curtains, sometimes called "side" or "inner" curtains of a heavier fabric, which could be drawn during the day to keep out the heat and at night for privacy. Valances were also common in the Arts and Crafts style home, as were roller shades, generally mounted behind the glass curtains and/or obscured by a valance. Portieres, panels that hang at interior doorways, continued to be a common feature throughout the era. Few

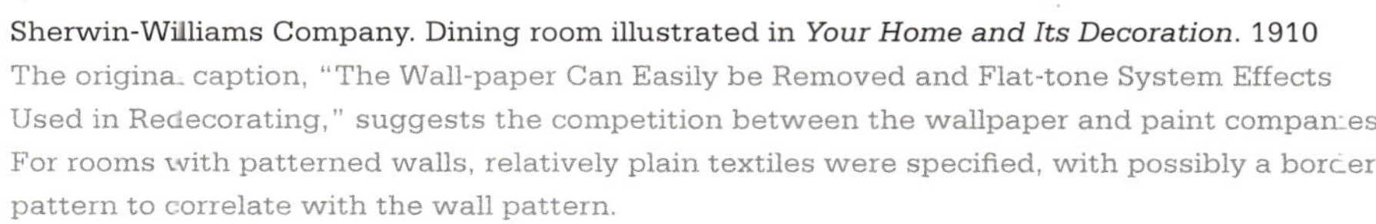

▼

Sherwin-Williams Company. Dining room illustrated in *Your Home and Its Decoration*. 1910

The original caption, "The Wall-paper Can Easily be Removed and Flat-tone System Effects Used in Redecorating," suggests the competition between the wallpaper and paint companies. For rooms with patterned walls, relatively plain textiles were specified, with possibly a border pattern to correlate with the wall pattern.

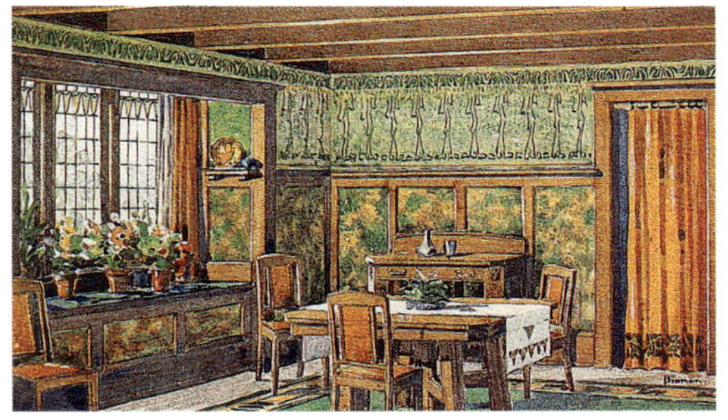

curtains from the era survive today because in their ordinary use, being subjected to sunlight, they deteriorated and were usually discarded.

Goodnow and Adams offer a good overall scheme for curtaining windows of the era, and while they are not specifically focused on homes of the Arts and Crafts style, their general advice applies.

> Glass curtains are nicest when they are of white or cream net or muslin or scrim. Natural-colored linen scrim also is good. A two-inch hem on both sides and the bottom and a two-inch casing on the top are the usual finish. Sometimes they are finished with hemstitching, if you care to take the trouble.
>
> These thin curtains are strung on a small brass rod and are hung as close to the glass as possible. The lower hem barely escapes the sill at the bottom. The curtains may hang in straight fold, or may be pushed to the sides by day. If they are made of net, it will not be necessary to push them aside, for net is thin enough to see through. Ruffled curtains, crossed and looped back, often appeal to us just because of their cleanly, fresh appearance, but plain ones are nicer. Ruffles belong on wearing apparel, not on house-furnishings. . . .
>
> Windows that go all the way to the floor of course should have glass curtains that barely cover the glass and side curtains that just escape the floor. French windows [or doors] are treated differently; here two small brass rods must be used on each panel, confining the top

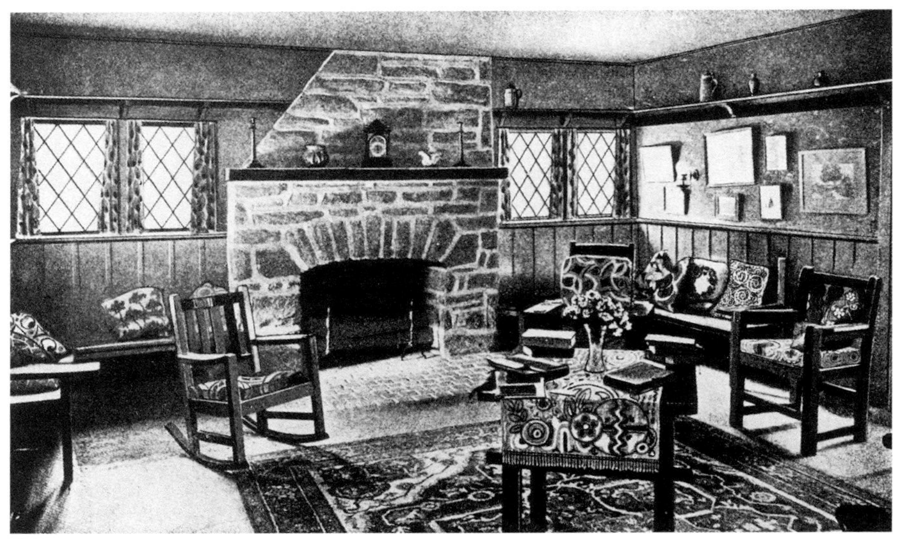

◄
Clifford & Lawton. "Mission Style Bungalow with Futurist Fabrics." Illustration from *The Room Beautiful*. 1915
Fashion changes in fabric more quickly than in architecture. Futurist textile designs had a short-lived popularity before World War I altered the course of fashion.

> and bottom hems of the thin curtains. Casement windows [windows hinged at one side] are often treated in the same way. Small casements may have short sash curtains, loose at the bottom."[26]

For casement windows that open outward, it was suggested to mount the curtain rod on the window jamb. For those that open inward, a rod could be mounted on the window itself, or, if mounted on the jamb, a rod on a hinged bracket was used. The typical type of construction was a simple casing at the top that the rod slid through. Occasionally, if mounted on the window casing or if only covering the lower portion of the window (café curtains), the sheer curtain had a flange of fabric, called a heading, that extended above the rod. For larger curtains which were purchased as ready-made panels, the extra length could folded and left to hang down at the top.

Priestman advises, "The new stenciled curtains are especially suited for bobbinets and scrims, and if properly done will stand sunlight and soap. Sometimes the design runs down the front and across the bottom of each curtain. Others are made with the design running across the top and also just above the hem at the bottom." Additionally, for a dark room, sash curtains of soft yellow "will give the effect of sunlight. If, on the other hand the room has a southern exposure, greens and blues will tend to soften the light."[27]

Gustav Stickley also recommended fabrics for curtains of "sufficiently loose weave to allow the light to come through with a translucent effect . . . in the warm, sunny tones of straw, ivory or corn color . . . and to bar all decoration save perhaps a shadowy stencil or a line of drawnwork or hemstitching that might let through an occasional sparkle of clear light."[28] In addition to these

▼

Alfred Peats' Wallpaper Company. "The Hall." Illustration from pamphlet, *A Modern Home*. 1907

Stylistic puritanism was not always required; Arts and Crafts portieres could be used with furnishings of other periods and styles as well.

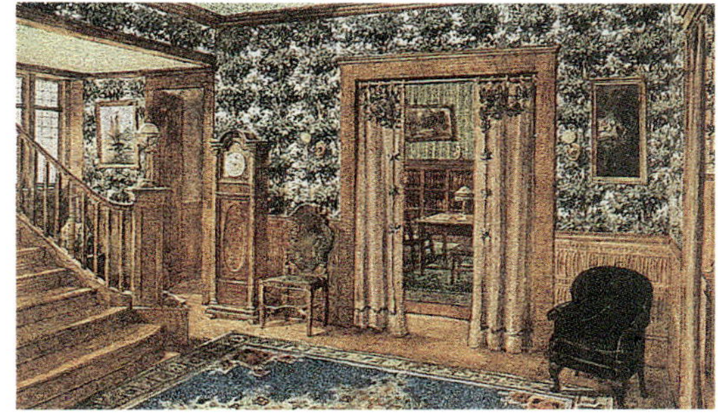

techniques, his Craftsman Workshops experimented extensively to develop designs for darned work upon a square open mesh that would complement his furniture and Craftsman homes.

Sash curtains often became the focus of needlework or stenciling projects in the magazines. "If one cannot afford expensive curtains, hand-drawn scrim ones are much more desirable than cheap lace."[29] Appliqué was generally not recommended for curtains of sheer fabric, but stenciling was common. Hand embroidery was generally limited to hemstitching, or cloth tape was stitched on in a geometric pattern, often a Greek key or a simple floral design.

Sheer fabrics with printed Arts and Crafts designs were also available. Depending on the maker, these fabrics varied from thirty-four to forty inches wide and usually had a border along each selvage edge. One width was usually ideal for use in a casement window. For a wider double-hung window, a pair of curtains could be made with two or more widths, the panels being sewn together or cut down and the sides hemmed, as required.

If it was not needed for privacy or light control, and if the view from the window was desirable, often the glass curtain was omitted. Goodnow and Adams suggest, "The most beautiful windows are treated architecturally, and require only a heavy side curtain that may be drawn at night."[30] As for the choice of that curtain, they add: "A heavy curtain has great possibilities for beauty When you choose the fabric, select some stuff that is good in design and texture, especially at night, for while almost any heavy curtain is attractive enough when pulled to one side in heavy folds by day, when it is drawn at night it should be even more so—it should be decorative."[31]

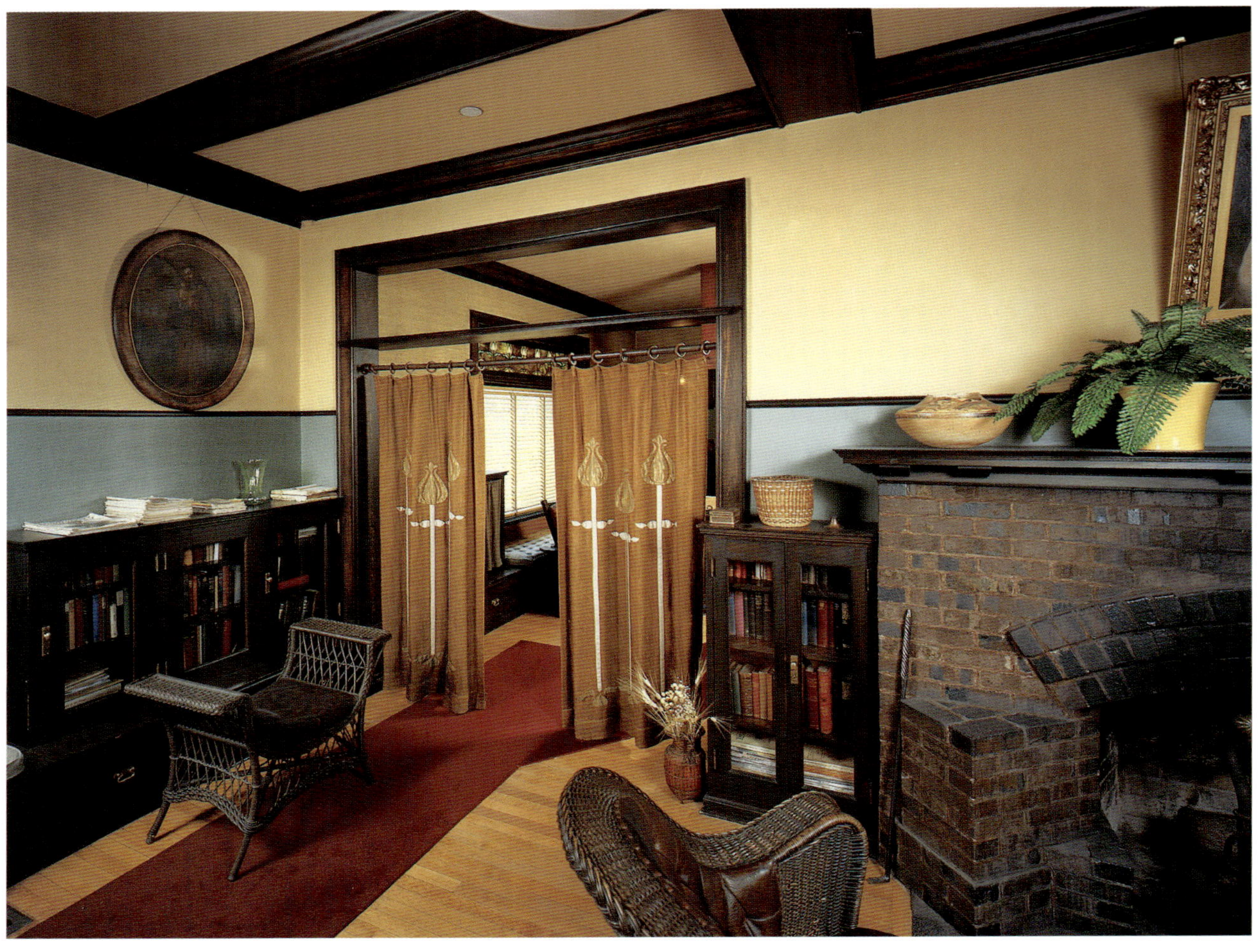

For double-hung windows, in addition to glass and side curtains, a valance may have been added. Goodnow and Adams's preference was for the valance to have its own rod so that the curtains behind it could be drawn at night, but they acknowledged that the common practice of shirring the valance on the same rod between the side curtains had a nice effect of framing the window. Another function of a valance was to block sun glare at windows that were not shielded by exterior awnings. Often used with café curtains, a valance was also frequently used across a group of adjacent windows as a unifying effect. In a small room, this horizontal emphasis would give the visual effect of enlarging the room. If decorative work was added they were constructed as flat panels or with inverted pleats placed at intervals; alternatively, the valance was gathered onto a rod.

◀

Attributed to Craftsman Workshops. Portieres in the living room of the Timothy A. Riordan House. c. 1904. Basketweave linen, possibly Stickley's "heavy flax canvas," with lamé and cotton twill appliqué and linen hand embroidery. Collection Riordan Mansion State Park, Flagstaff, Arizona
This fabric was originally a leaf-green color. The portieres are a single thickness of fabric with the same design in appliqué on the reverse, the flowers being cotton denim, the stems brown, and bottom elements green.

Much of the drapery hardware of the period was extremely simple. Glass curtains or light-weight side curtains were usually hung on a ⅜-inch diameter brass rod with gooseneck brackets, brackets with flat sides, or simple brackets for inside mounting. In some cases, extension rods with rubber ends were used. For larger windows and portieres a brass covered wood pole, brass tube, or a wood pole up to 1½ inches in diameter was used. Again, the brackets were quite simple, sometimes merely L-shaped heavy brass wires that screwed into the window frame. For mounting within the frame, most typical for portieres, a pair of sockets held the rod at each end. For outside mount applications spherical-shaped rod ends would be added; these were either plain, banded, or fluted. When rings were used, they were simple brass or wooden rings with small eyelets onto which the curtain was hooked or sewn. Traverse rods were yet to be marketed, but a draw system could be rigged with screw eyes and cord. Rings were used on curtains when they would be opened and closed frequently. If it was desired that the rings not show, or to eliminate the gap between the rod and ring, smaller rings were sewn onto the back of the curtain. Occasionally, small tucks were used at the heading (see page 121).

This simpler style of curtain required far less material than those of previous generations. One and one-half to two times the width of the window was sufficient to drape a window with pleasing folds. Usually this was split between two panels, a pair of curtains being typical for most windows. For narrow windows and sidelights the curtain was often one panel. As for length, the majority of curtains stopped just above the sill or "If the sill does not project far enough to receive

▶
Window and bookcase curtains and block-printed pillow in the living room of the Timothy A. Riordan House. Collection Riordan Mansion State Park, Flagstaff, Arizona
Opposite the fireplace and portiere shown on page 118, these curtains are faithful reproductions in construction and color. Additional hardware indicates that sheer curtains also hung at these windows. The pillow is likely original to the house.

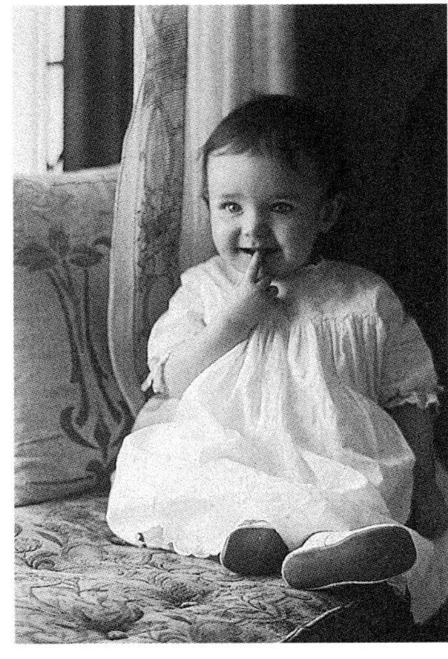

▲
Powers Photography, Claremont N.H. Baby in a window seat with conventionalized pillow and curtains. Undated photograph. Collection Timothy Hansen and Dianne Ayres

it, the over-curtain must continue until it reaches the bottom of the apron where it appears to come to rest."[32] This decree was not followed universally. Some illustrations from the period show curtains stopping just below the sill or at the middle of the apron. Floor-length curtains were occasionally used in the bedroom to enhance the feeling of softness and warmth and sometimes in a living room or dining room for a more formal effect.

Opinions varied on other details as well. Some sources approved of the use of tie-backs, but Priestman said: "An abomination constantly seen is a pair of heavy curtains meeting in the middle of a window and then held tightly back by a cord or band. They give a feeling of uneasiness to those who appreciate the fitness of things, and are in themselves a contradiction. Why hang them forward if you want them back? The same fault may often be seen in sash curtains. They are hung on a rod at the top and the bottom of a window, and then a foolish white band or cord holds them back in the middle."[33]

Portieres, or door curtains, common in the nineteenth and early twentieth centuries, were another popular textile item, often found throughout the house in interior doorways. These fabric dividers were welcoming and inviting, providing privacy and warmth, and encouraged a flow of movement. Designed to be seen from both sides, portieres could be hung singly or in pairs and were usually hung on rungs on the inside of a door frame. The panels were often embellished on both sides with stenciling or appliqué and embroidery in the colors appropriate for the room they faced. For doorways with sliding pocket doors, two pairs of portieres were used, lined with a

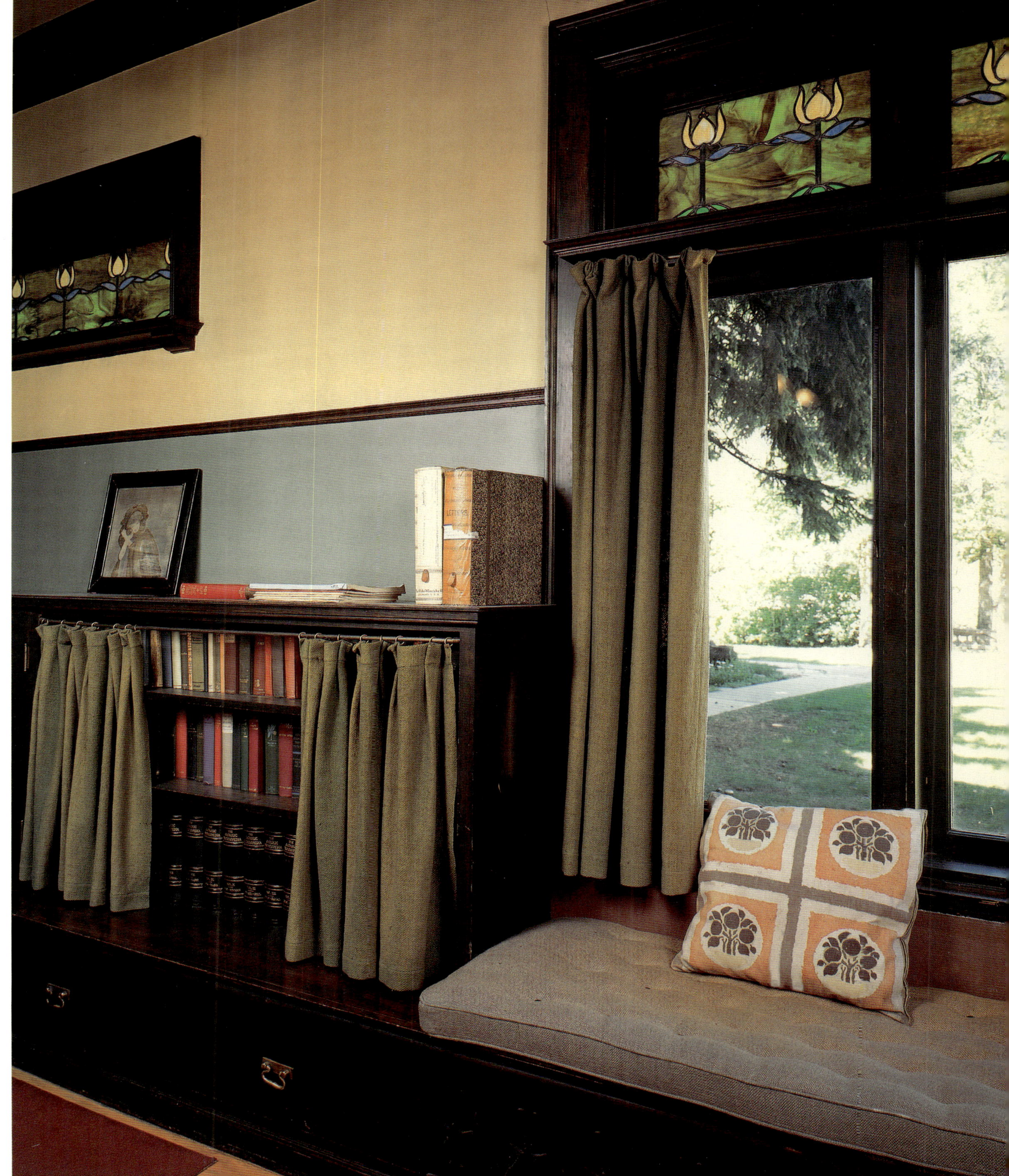

▼
Ekin Wallick. "Stenciled Textiles." Illustration from *The Attractive Home*. 1916
Table scarfs were used on many types of furniture, including dining, library, and lamp tables; bookcases; and sideboards.

▶
Anonymous. Tray with embroidered panel. c. 1910. Wood, metal, and linen with silk hand embroidery, 5¼ × 11¼" (13.3 × 28.6 cm). Collection Tommy and Beth Ann McPherson
Small decorative accessories were popular to scatter throughout the home.

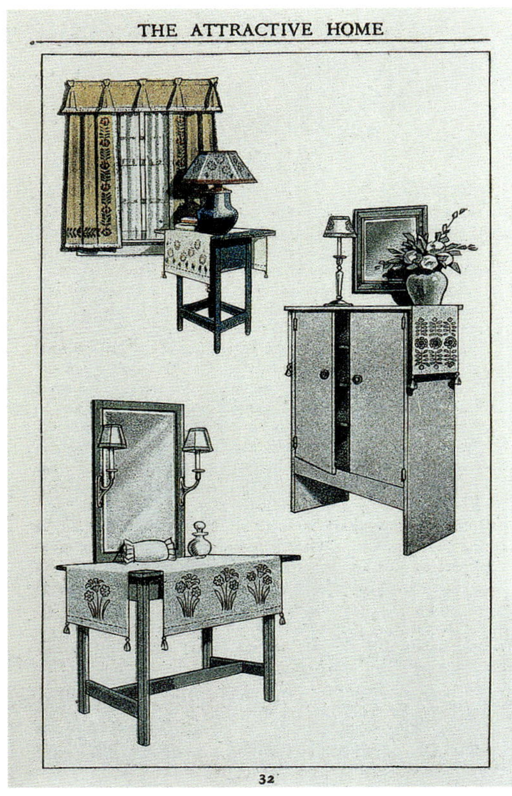

plain, inexpensive fabric. Home magazines recommended using bedspreads or tablecloths, if necessary, to lessen costs.

Writers recognized the important role individuals played in setting the tone of their homes. "It should be the aim of every one who has an appreciation of the beautiful to endeavor to get away from the commonplace. It is not practical or possible for many to make their own furniture or weave their rugs, but it is possible for every home to express the individuality of the owner in the choice of beautiful and original hangings."[34]

Within the realm of personal expression, however, there were guidelines for matters such as coordinating fabrics for all the hangings within a room and among adjacent rooms. Halbert White laid out rules for an individual room based on its size and character:

> If the room is large and somewhat formal in character, it is well to have all of the hangings exactly alike and of rich and heavy material. If the room is not so large nor so formal the portieres may remain rich and heavy and the over-curtains may be of some of the light-weight, sun-resisting materials, made to hang without lining. Many of these fabrics light up with a beautiful, soft glow when hung against the window, and admit more light to the room than do heavier materials. For small rooms it is frequently advisable to use these light-weight stuffs, both for the windows and the portieres, having them all of the same. There are rooms in which it is advisable to have the portieres and the valances of the same heavy material and the over-

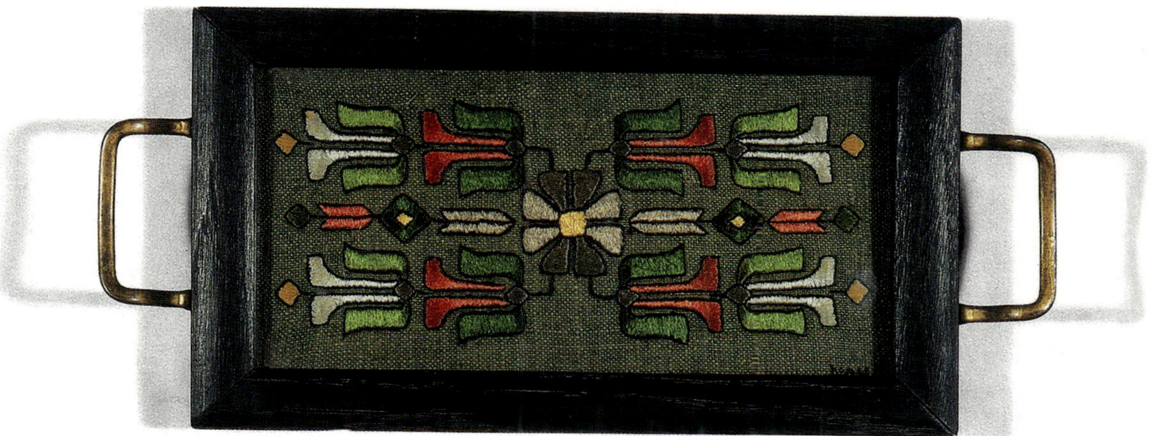

> curtains of a lighter weight stuff, like soft silk. When prints are used, especially in bedrooms, all of the hangings should be of the same.[35]

For coordinating between rooms, opinions varied. White wrote, "It is well that there should be a variety of fabrics in the various rooms, using distinctive, but harmonizing fabrics and colors in each room, having all the portieres in any one room exactly alike, but different from those in any other room."[36] Goodnow and Adams opined that if adjoining rooms have the same wall treatment, then the curtains should be the same. And the Sherwin Williams Company proposed, "For the wall treatment and draperies throughout (which must be considered together), a repetition of one or more of the colors in various combinations will be found restful and attractive."[37]

The use of a room was an important factor in determining its window treatment, considering not only privacy and function but also the effects of color and pattern.

> In the selection of fabrics apply the laws of reason. Select rich quiet materials for dignified rooms, less pretentious materials for less pretentious rooms. Let you morning-room be bright and cheery with a riot of color in its chintz hangings, if your temperament so dictates. Your living-room, where you spend most of your waking hours, should be subdued and quiet, but never gloomy. The library should have nothing to distract the eye.
>
> Are you fond of figured materials? Use them freely in the rooms in which you spend the least time. Your breakfast-room will take figured materials, so will your wainscoted dining-

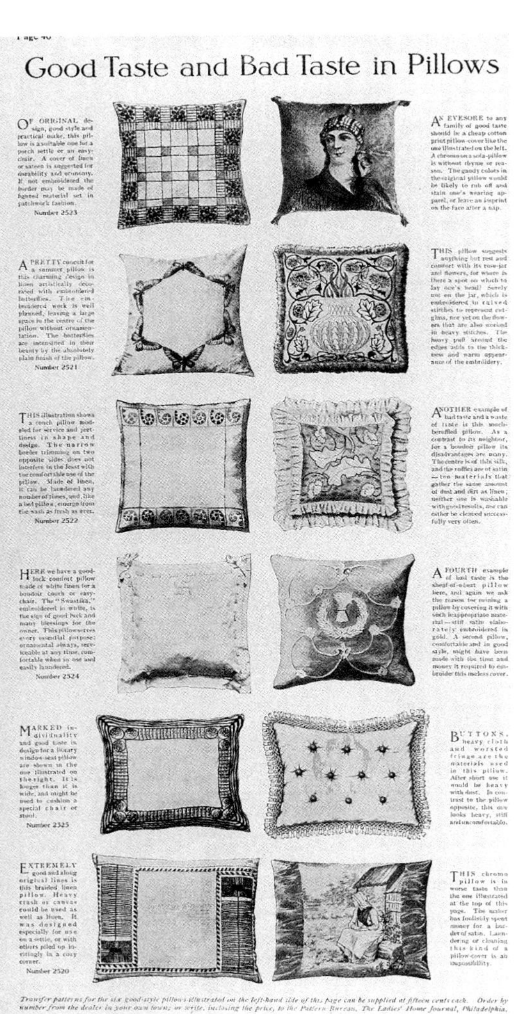

Page 40

Good Taste and Bad Taste in Pillows

Of original design, good style and practical make, this pillow is a suitable one for a porch settle or an easy-chair. A cover of linen or sateen is suggested for durability and economy. If not embroidered the border may be made of figured material set in patchwork fashion.

Number 2523

An eyesore to any family of good taste should be a cheap cotton print pillow-cover like the one illustrated on the left. A chromo on a sofa-pillow is without rhyme or reason. The gaudy colors in the original pillow would be likely to rub off and stain one's wearing apparel, or leave an imprint on the face after a nap.

A pretty conceit for a summer pillow is this charming design in linen artistically decorated with embroidered butterflies. The embroidered work is well planned, leaving a large space in the centre of the pillow without ornamentation. The butterflies are intensified in their beauty by the absolutely plain finish of the pillow.

Number 2521

This pillow suggests anything but rest and comfort with its rose-jar and flowers, for where is there a spot on which to lay one's head? Surely not on the jar, which is embroidered in raised stitches to represent cut-glass, nor yet on the flowers that are also worked in heavy stitches. The heavy puff around the edges adds to the thickness and warm appearance of the embroidery.

This illustration shows a couch pillow modeled for service and prettiness in shape and design. The narrow border trimming on two opposite sides does not interfere in the least with the comfortable use of the pillow. Made of linen, it can be laundered any number of times, and, like a bed pillow, emerge from the wash as fresh as ever.

Number 2522

Another example of bad taste and a waste of time is this much-beruffled pillow. As a contrast to its neighbor, for a boudoir pillow its disadvantages are many. The centre is of thin silk, and the ruffles are of satin — two materials that gather the same amount of dust and dirt as linen; neither one is washable with good results, nor can either be cleaned successfully very often.

Here we have a good-luck comfort pillow made of white linen for a boudoir couch or easy-chair. The "Swastika," embroidered in white, is the sign of good luck and many blessings for the owner. This pillow serves every essential purpose: ornamental always, serviceable at any time, comfortable when in use and easily laundered.

Number 2524

A fourth example of bad taste is the sheaf-of-wheat pillow here, and again we ask the reason for ruining a pillow by covering it with such inappropriate material — stiff satin elaborately embroidered in gold. A second pillow, comfortable and in good style, might have been made with the time and money it required to embroider this useless cover.

Marked individuality and good taste in design for a library window-seat pillow are shown in the one illustrated on the right. It is longer than it is wide, and might be used to cushion a special chair or stool.

Number 2525

Buttons, heavy cloth and worsted fringe are the materials used in this pillow. After short use it would be heavy with dust. In contrast to the pillow opposite, this one looks heavy, stiff and uncomfortable.

Extremely good and along original lines is this braided linen pillow. Heavy crash or canvas could be used as well as linen. It was designed especially for use on a settle, or with others piled up invitingly in a cozy corner.

Number 2520

This chromo pillow is in worse taste than the one illustrated at the top of this page. The maker has foolishly spent money for a border of satin. Laundering or cleaning this kind of a pillow-cover is an impossibility.

Transfer patterns for the six good-style pillows illustrated on the left-hand side of this page can be supplied at fifteen cents each. Order by number from the dealer in your own town; or write, inclosing the price, to the Pattern Bureau, The Ladies' Home Journal, Philadelphia.

◀

"Good Taste and Bad Taste in Pillows." *The Ladies' Home Journal*. July 1906

At first glance, this article seems like a frivolous example of blatant commercialism (one could purchase the "good" pillows), but it was part of a well-meaning and successful campaign by Edward Bok, editor of *The Ladies' Home Journal*, to educate middle-class women on basic design principles and elevate the quality of American home decoration.

> room, albeit patterns and materials should be more formal in character. A large hall with much wainscot carries well a rich, subdued design.[38]

While nets, muslin, and plain, printed, or hemstitched scrims were suggested for glass curtains, fabrics deemed suitable for inner curtains in Arts and Crafts homes were coarse-weave linens, printed cretonnes, heavy crepes, denim, raw silks, madras, and monkscloth. At the time, varieties of monkscloth were distinguished as cloister, friars', and druid cloths. "Where the size and importance of the window makes two sets of draperies necessary, the rough basket-weave cotton cloths called cloister, and friars', and druid, make splendid overdraperies. The warps and wefts of the coarsest [druid] are in groups over a quarter inch wide, producing a texture that is 'bungalowy' to the limit. It contrasts wonderfully well with scrim curtains beneath."[39]

Coarse linens such as arras cloth (offered by Craftsman Workshops under the name "Craftsman Canvas") and "agra cloth" were "coarse as burlap but soft and agreeable to the touch and [to] no end durable. Sometimes it is ornamented in a manner appropriate to bungalows, with border and edging in coarse, bright-colored embroidery."[40] Madras and crete woven with conventionalized Arts and Crafts patterns were used alone, as glass curtains with a plain overcurtains, or as thin portieres. Both have a scrimlike ground with additional threads woven in to form a pattern, the edges of which are fuzzy with the cut ends of the thread. Crete has the figures on the back side. Madras has the pattern on the front side, the sheer ground formed by twisting the warp thread in pairs around weft threads (see page 114).

▼
Craftsman Workshops. "A Craftsman's Library Table" with a seedpod table square. Illustration from Priestman's *Art and Economy in Home Decoration*. 1908

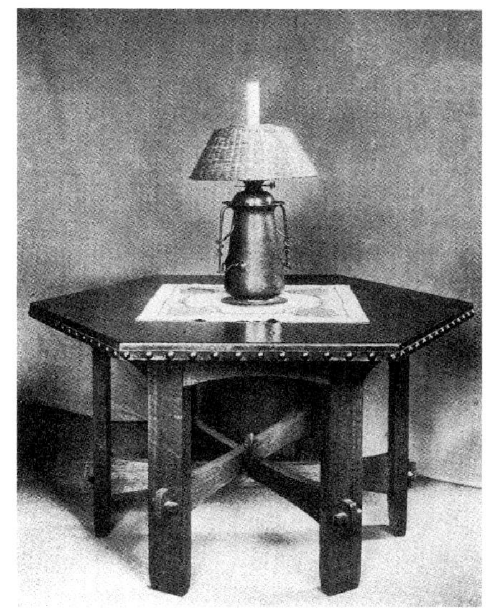

For more elegant homes, writers recommended reproductions of English eighteenth-century hand-block prints, "packed with fruit and leaves that glow with autumn golds and browns," and "shadow silks that excel in iridescence and drape back most gracefully where the introduction of curves is desirable."[41] In any case the "inner curtains must become part of the wall line, and be harmonious in color and design with the general treatment of the room in which they are used."[42]

In deciding whether to have plain or patterned curtains, the homemaker was advised: "You may with safety use plain hangings with plain walls to produce a quiet, restful room. Avoid figured hangings with figured walls, although a suitable figure looks well with a striped paper. In general terms, it is safe to use figured hangings with plain walls, or plain hangings with figured walls, as one acts as a foil on the other and thereby frequently adds interest to the room."[43]

The possibilities for embellishing side curtains were varied. Stenciling was frequently done, while appliqué and hand embroidery were utilized by the ambitious needleworker or those who could afford to order from companies such as the Craftsman Workshops or employ the services of a local artisan. Even then, these more labor-intensive techniques were generally reserved for portieres, which did not bear the brunt of direct sunlight—the window curtains being of the same fabric with no decoration or a coordinating fabric.

Periodicals urged homeowners to use decorative textile elements to modernize their homes. New suites of furniture might be too costly to switch in and out, but pillows, table squares, and table runners were inexpensive accents that together could transform a room. Recurring queries

▶
Attributed to Craftsman Workshops. Printed period pillow on a fainting couch. c. 1904. Linen. Collection Riordan Mansion State Park, Flagstaff, Arizona

▼
H. E. Verran Company. Table scarf from a kit by Royal Society. c. 1912. Linen, stenciled and hand embroidered, 21¼ × 60" (54 × 152.4 cm). Collection Timothy Hansen and Dianne Ayres

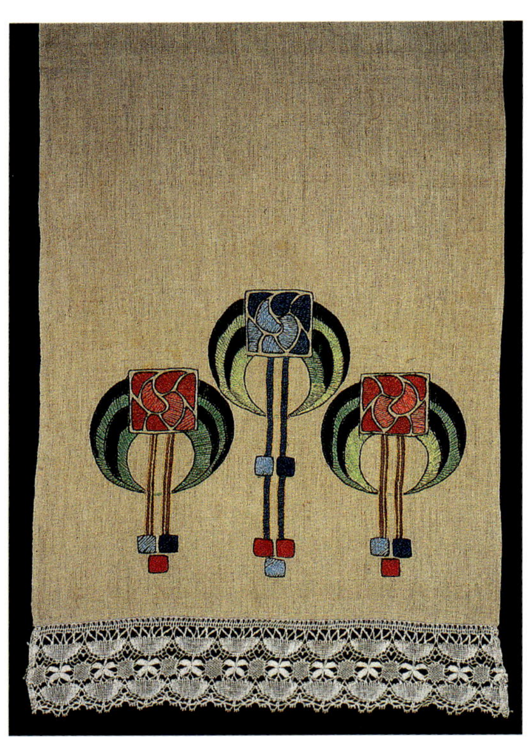

to advice columns in ladies' magazines asked how the readers might to unify all the patterns in their homes and redecorate in the new style. The repeated recommendation was to remove the problematic accessories and start over with harmonious, unified textiles.

The Craftsman Home Department summed up this philosophy in its March 1905 column. One reader from Colorado wrote, "I invite your attention to my needs in the shape of a table square, for a room with a mixture of colors, walls chocolate, woodwork red-brown, rug Smyrna, piano cover a large Paisley shawl, sofa cushions reds, golds, and orange, while the lounge cover is a dark blue with old gold pattern. I am aware that there are too many figured things in the room for harmony. What would you suggest doing away with and what colors for the table square?" The editor responded to the reader, "As you say, there is rather a mixture of colors in your room. Presuming of course that the wall covering, rug and woodwork are permanent fixtures, the easiest way to simplify your color scheme would be to remove or renew the minor furnishings of your room such as piano cover, sofa cushions, couch throw, etc. Instead of having these, introduce, in each case, an individual or separate color; they should repeat some of the main coloring of your room proper."[44] *Home Needlework* advised "handsome embroideries do not have to be elaborate. Sometimes the simplest designs are the most effective, but they should be in keeping with the general color scheme of the room in which they are to be used. A design may be very handsome in itself and yet not in harmony with other furnishings. If better judgement were used in the selection of designers and materials, these embroidered pieces should soon

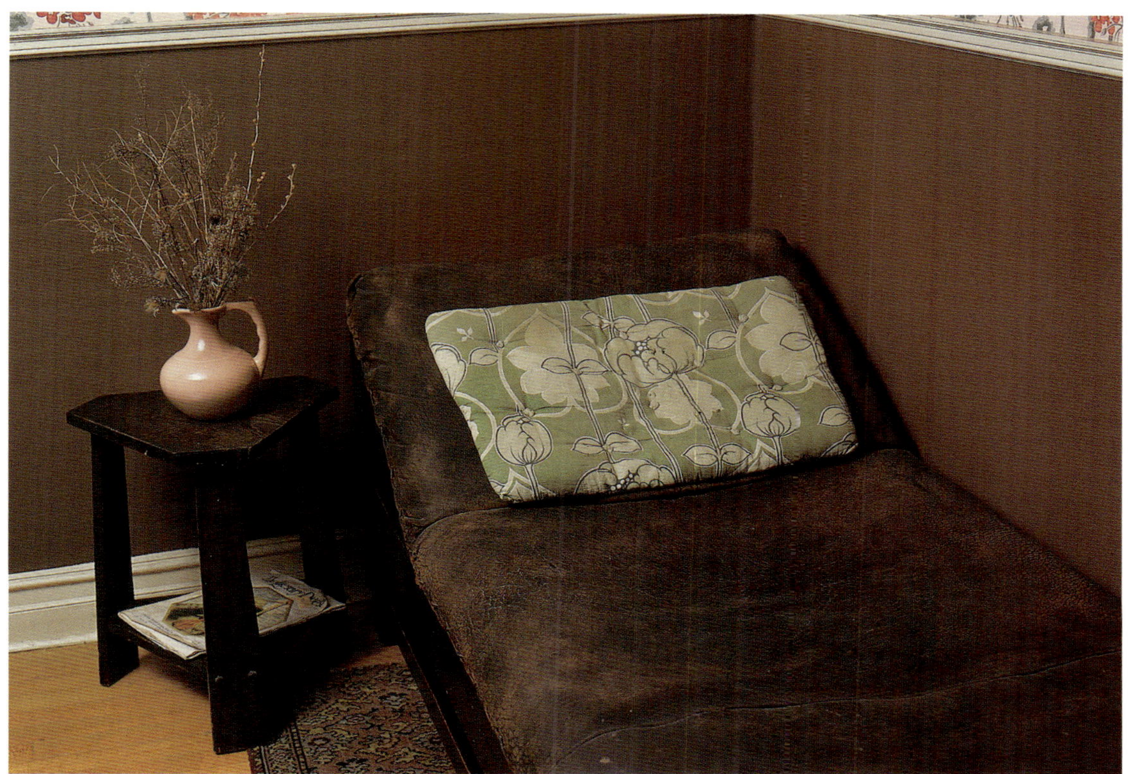

come to be considered a very important part of house furnishings and not designated by the term 'fancy work.'"[45] The homeowner was further advised: "Color contrasts can be supplied by sofa cushions, table runners, desk fittings, and in hundreds of other charming and spontaneous ways, but care must be exercised that there are not too many points of strong conflicting interest in a room."[46]

Table squares, rounds, and runners were some of the most popular accessories. The pieces bore simple designs that tempted needlewomen to try their hand. Their function varied from room to room in the house. In the living room squares and rounds served as accent pieces on center and side tables. Forms were adapted for specific functions, such as a decorative piano scarf, with extra length. In the dining room, runners were used as table and sideboard covers, offering protection for the furniture during dining as well as harmonizing the decoration of the room. Tables were dressed with cross runners, one long runner down the center and as many cross pieces as necessary to form place settings at each chair.

Table squares, rounds, and runners were sold as ready-made items through stores and mail order, but most were produced by embroidery kit companies as do-it-yourself pieces. Many designs

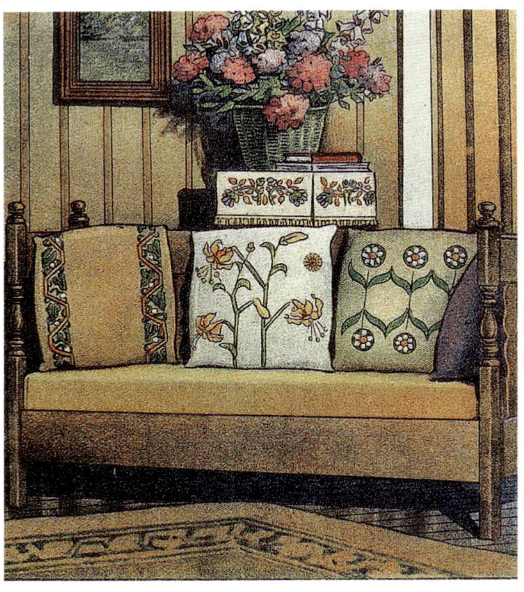

◀
Ekin Wallick. "Pillows on Settle." Illustration from *The Attractive Home*. 1916
Textiles added comfort, color, and cheer to the Arts and Crafts home. The accompanying verse to this illustration read: "Peace and rest at length have come, All the day's long toil is past; And each heart is whispering, 'Home, home at Last!' – Hood"

were offered in a variety of sizes and formats, giving embroiderers the opportunity to manufacture a set of linens for the room requiring them, whether living room or dining room. Linens came in relatively standard sizes. Runners frequently measured fifteen to twenty inches wide by seventy-two to ninety inches long. Squares commonly came in dimensions of twelve inches, twenty-two inches, twenty-four inches, and twenty-six inches. Table linens were positioned in a number of ways. A square could be placed in the center of a small table, leaving a few inches around the edges, or on the diagonal in the center of a round table. Rounds were frequently placed in the center of round tables as well. Oval linens were often used as centerpieces on rectangular dining tables or on oval-top tables.

Table linens were usually adorned with stenciling, embroidery, or appliqué for decoration. Stenciling could be the template for an embroidered design or a means of decoration in and of itself. Conventionalized organic and geometric designs were popular. The patterns were drawn or printed onto the fabric and then outlined, embroidered, or left plain as suited the stitcher.

Pillows were used throughout the house as accent pieces. Frequently they were coordinated with the table squares and runners in the room to form an ensemble. Commonly twenty-five inches square and executed in linen with silk or cotton embroidery, pillows appeared in chairs, angled on benches, and piled on settles. As Arts and Crafts furniture often did not have upholstered backs, pillows were crucial for comfort. Although some deemed pillows as necessary for comfort, others classed them with the rest of the fads—the "hand-painted craze," the "drapery

▸

Pillows. Linen with hand embroidery

Arts and Crafts pillows came in various shapes and sizes, but were generally large. The printed scrim curtains with a peacock feather design show a typical construction method, with small rings sewn on the back at each tuck.

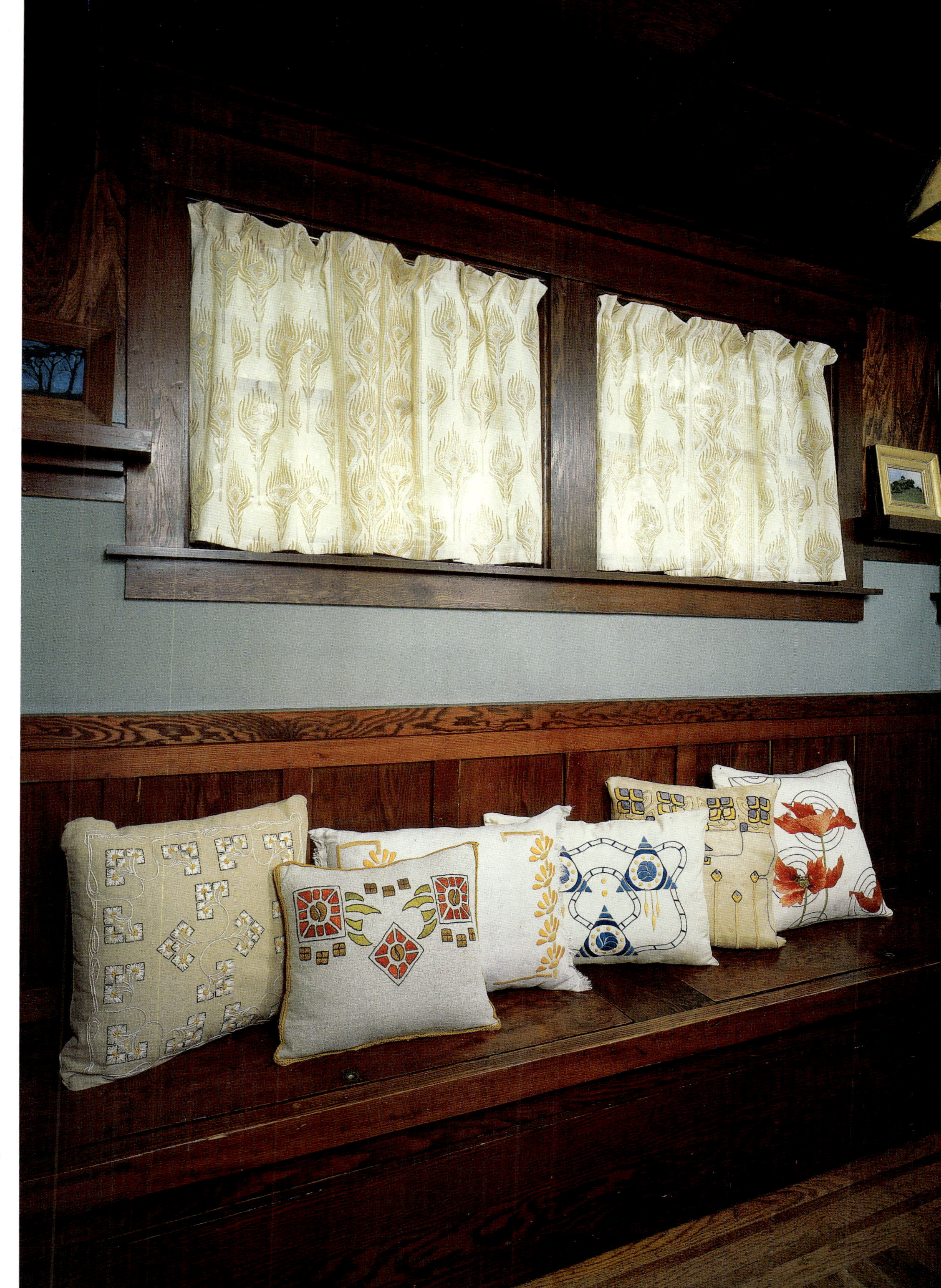

▶
Craftsman Workshops. Three-panel folding screen with conventionalized rose design. 1902–16. Flax and jute "Craftsman canvas" with linen appliqué and hand embroidery; each panel, 66 × 22" (167.6 × 55.9 cm). Marrin Collection

epidemic," and the "Bric-a-brac habit"—pronouncing that the "pillow epidemic is still in full sway. Fortunately, beautiful pillows, well-designed furniture, rugs of rich, good coloring, and artistic draperies are to be found by those who have the taste to select what is good."[47]

The ladies' magazines featured countless articles on pillows, demonstrating their universal nature. One such article, "Couch Pillows of Artistic Design," featuring pillows with conventionalized Arts and Crafts motifs as well as simple geometric designs, emphatically stated: "couch pillows are quite an indispensable item in house furnishings. There is hardly a room in which one or more is not needed and this gives opportunity for the embroiderer to do some very practical work, for naturally the covers should be in keeping with the character of the room in which they are used, as well as in harmony with the color scheme."[48] Novelty pillows with catchy phrases such as "Life? It's Just One Darn Thing After Another" or "We Pine For You" (page 60) were frequently used on pillows destined for the casual sanctums of the den, the porch, and the boat.

Articles on the appropriateness of pillows for the home often concentrated on specific areas, such as the veranda of the country house. Numerous options were presented, including stylized geometric forms or naturalistic decoration. It was often noted for which type of furniture they were most suitable: for the "Craftsman's sofa . . . instead of being filled with fluffy pillows of light colors, the heavy straight-backed pillows of craftsman's canvas ornamented with appliqué are absolutely in keeping."[49]

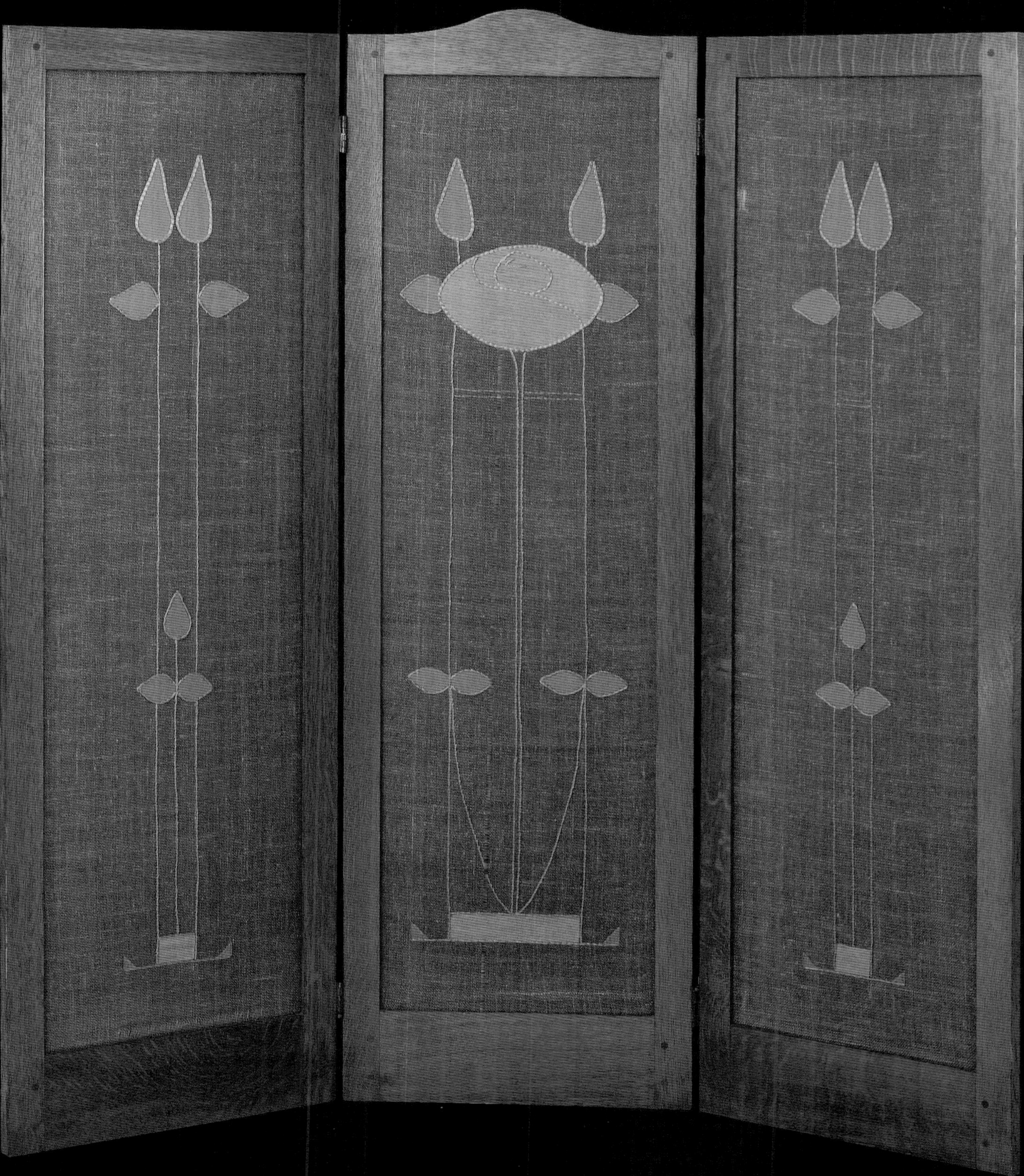

▶
Colonial Drapery Fabrics. "Outdoor Living with Textiles." Illustration from *The Home Beautiful*. c. 1909
Healthy outdoor living was a mainstay of the Arts and Crafts lifestyle.

Various materials from around the world were used in the creation of household textiles. Ireland and Holland were known for their classic linen. On a more specialized note, German linen filled the niche for heavier materials, and Italy and France provided linen lighter in character, frequently trimmed with lace. Russia was responsible for producing the heavy, coarse crash used in such great quantities during the Arts and Crafts period.

Trifold screens with patterned or embroidered insets were sometimes an alternative to portieres for dividing a room and were frequent additions to living rooms, dining rooms, and bedrooms. Screens rose to new popularity in the late nineteenth and early twentieth centuries for both their practicality and exotic nature, conjuring up images of the Orient. Fire screens, banner screens, drawing-room screens, and tea screens are just a few of the various forms. Many major companies, such as Morris & Co. and Stickley's Craftsman Workshops, sold screens.

Specific rooms in the household developed specialized textile forms to meet their individual needs.

Porch

Furnished with plain and portable furniture of willow or light woods like hickory, porches functioned as both interior and exterior rooms. The main porch frequently served as a family living space with casual and comfortable furnishings fit for exposure to the elements. Fabric awnings, particularly green and white, were common as shade devices. Rolled canvas in tan or green as

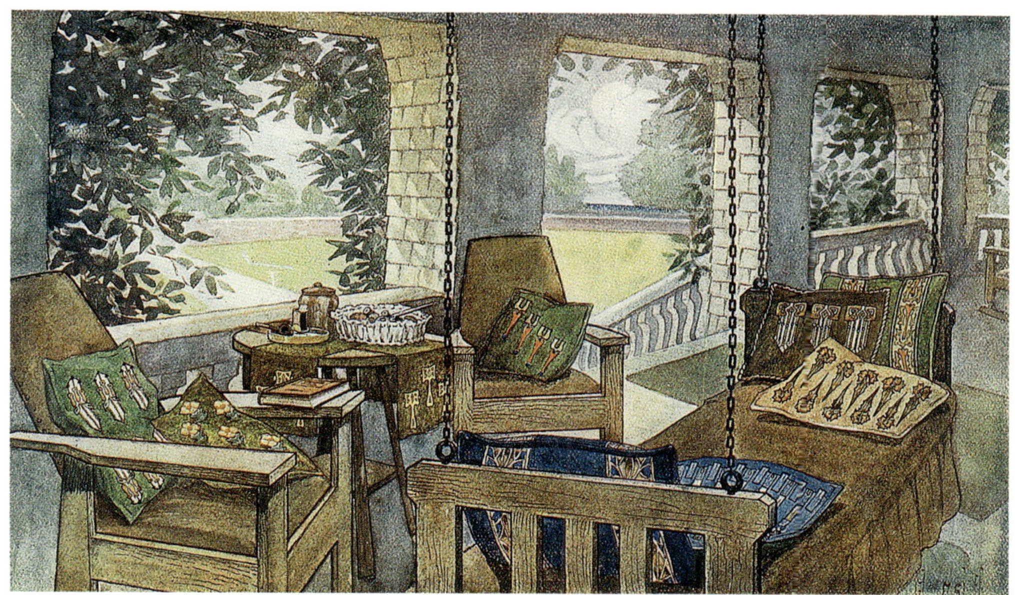

well as straw shades were also used on porches, but these were subject to wind, which made them problematic. Cushions made of materials suitable for the outdoors, such as linen, denim, or cretonne, were recommended for the furniture. Natural decorative motifs that harmonized with the outdoor environment—flowers, birds, and pinecones were favored embroidery designs as were the lighthearted motto pillows.

Floor coverings commonly used in the porch area were hemp or straw mats. Rag rugs, often made by the females of the house, were seen as well. Indian rugs and Navajo blankets, with their simple designs and basic colors, were also recommended for porches. Welcoming and practical, they further added to the roomlike atmosphere.

Halls

As public rooms in the home, where the family would spend the greatest percentage of time reception halls, living rooms, and dining rooms were the most important areas of the house in which to display textiles and other decorative objects. Curtains, table covers, rugs, and pillows chosen for the public spaces set the tone for the entire house.

During the Arts and Crafts period, halls returned to their former level of importance as the primary area in which to welcome people into the home. Providing the first impression of the home's occupants, the hall "is the preface to all the rest and in a well planned house it strikes the keynote of the whole scheme of interior decoration."[50] Halls came in numerous shapes and sizes.

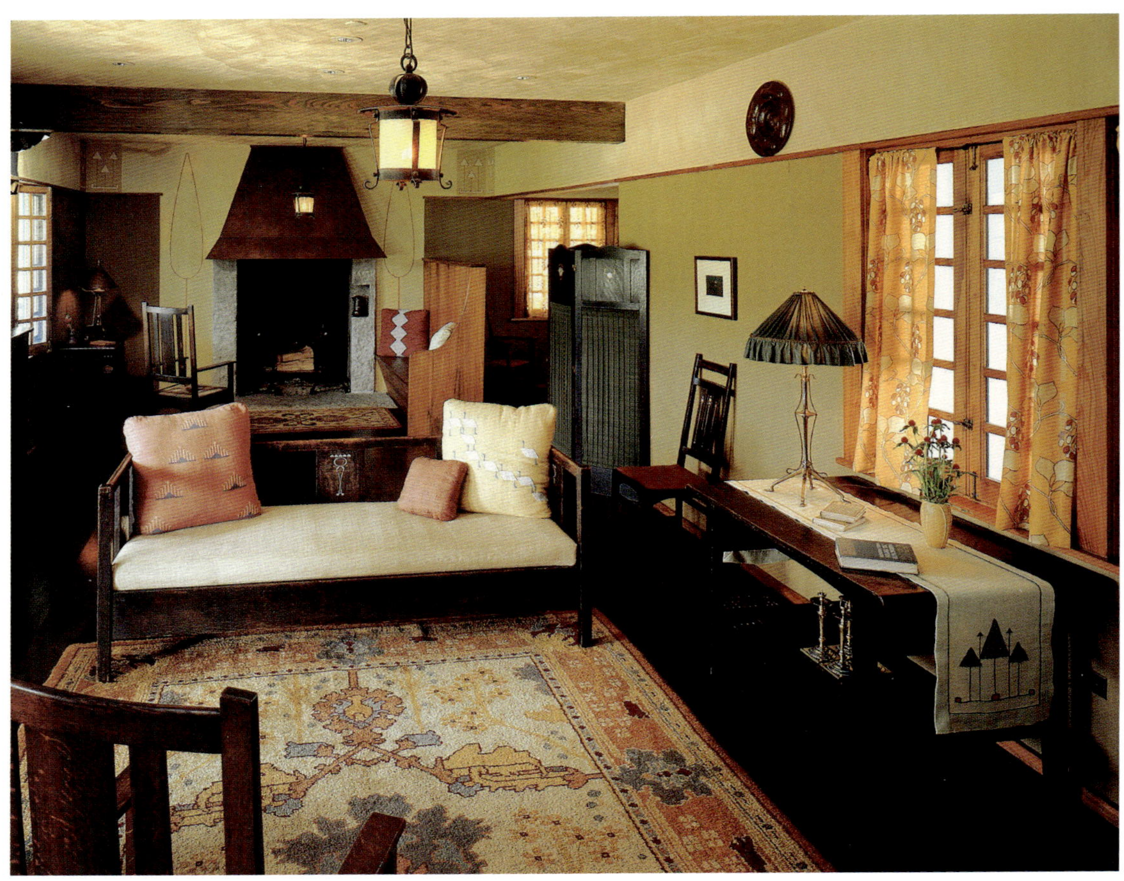

◀
Harvey Ellis. Living room. Collection Crab Tree Farm
Based on Harvey Ellis's "Windmill Cottage" design, the living room in this cottage is a prime example of the American Arts and Crafts style. Textiles, scattered throughout the room, help to tie the decorative scheme together.

In cold climates, an area was often screened off of a larger room to serve as a vestibule that protected the main areas of the house from inclement weather. In other plans, the hall and living room were combined as both a reception and gathering area.

Architectural details of the hall often included a fireplace and a deep recess near the stairway that served as a seating area with built-in benches frequently accented with pillows. The second-story hall was an open space that replaced the nineteenth-century sewing room and upstairs sitting room. The upstairs hallway was often lined with throw rugs and accented by curtained windows.

Living Room

The living room was where all "the business and pleasure of the common family life may be carried on."[51] There was a pronounced move toward comfort in the turn-of-the-century house. Eighteenth- and nineteenth-century house plans emphasized the formality of the separate front parlor, whereas the plan of the new twentieth-century home purported that the main floor needed

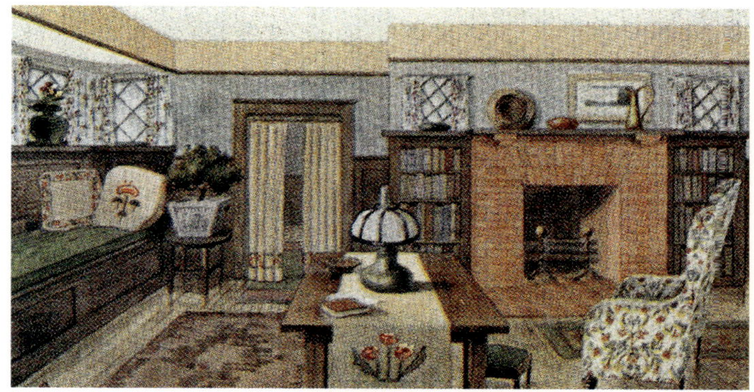

▶
Colonial Drapery Fabrics. Living room illustrated in *The Home Beautiful*. c. 1910
Textiles could be coordinated throughout a room by cutting the designs from prints and appliquéing them on pillows, table scarves, and portieres. Slipcovers and overstuffed furniture were often used in homes of the time.

only a hall, kitchen, and living room to serve the family's basic needs. Family life centered in the living room, and social reformers stressed its importance as the heart that shaped the character of the family—and, in turn, the nation. The room served to comfort its inhabitants, providing an environment where they could be at ease with their thoughts and pursuits, and a haven for the young to learn and grow. This formal room of the house was meant to express the family's wealth and station honestly, which entailed eliminating unnecessary accessories.

Inglenooks, built-in architectural benches, symbolized the comfort, coziness, and relaxed nature of the new Arts and Crafts home. The built-ins added "pleasant nooks and corners which give a comfortable sense of semi-privacy and yet are not in any way shut off from the larger life of the room. Such an arrangement has always seemed symbolic of the ideal conditions of social life. The big hospitable fireplace is almost a necessity, for the hearthstone is always the center of true home life."[52] Inglenook benches and settles lined with cushions and table covers scattered throughout the room continued the color scheme established by rugs and curtains.

Rugs received added attention in Arts and Crafts homes. Area rugs were recommended to accent the natural wooden floors, shellacked, waxed, and polished to ensure cleanliness. Floor coverings were to be "low" in tone, forming a "base" level in the room. Imported rugs from China, India, Turkey, England, and France were used in this country. Wealthy homeowners purchased William Morris's rugs, and Stickley's Craftsman empire imported rugs from both the Eastern and Western hemispheres for sale to its well-to-do clients.

▶
Dining room with crossing runners. Collection Crab Tree Farm

In reaction to machine-made ornament, decorators discouraged the use of modern figured rugs with their mechanical, ordered patterns. Monochrome carpets, or those broken with unobtrusive designs several shades darker than the room were often recommended to sustain balance, and occasionally they united several rooms.

Dining Room

The dining room was "the center of hospitality and good cheer,"[53] equally important as a site for family interaction. Arts and Crafts ideology promoted simplicity and comfort as the new family values. In the typical plan, the dining room was placed conveniently in the house, near the kitchen. Convenience and cheerfulness were primary factors in the room's decoration. Furniture was comfortable, including chairs lined with cushions, and surfaces were protected with fabric that would clean easily.

Frequently, one part of the room was screened off by a portiere or a portable screen, which demarcated the area without destroying the openness of the room. These devices afforded privacy during meals without permanently impacting or altering the flow of space that was characteristic of the Craftsman house.

Stickley's *The Craftsman Home* emphasized this point, stating: "Even where the owner prefers to have the dining room a good-sized separate room, it always seems well to leave a wide opening

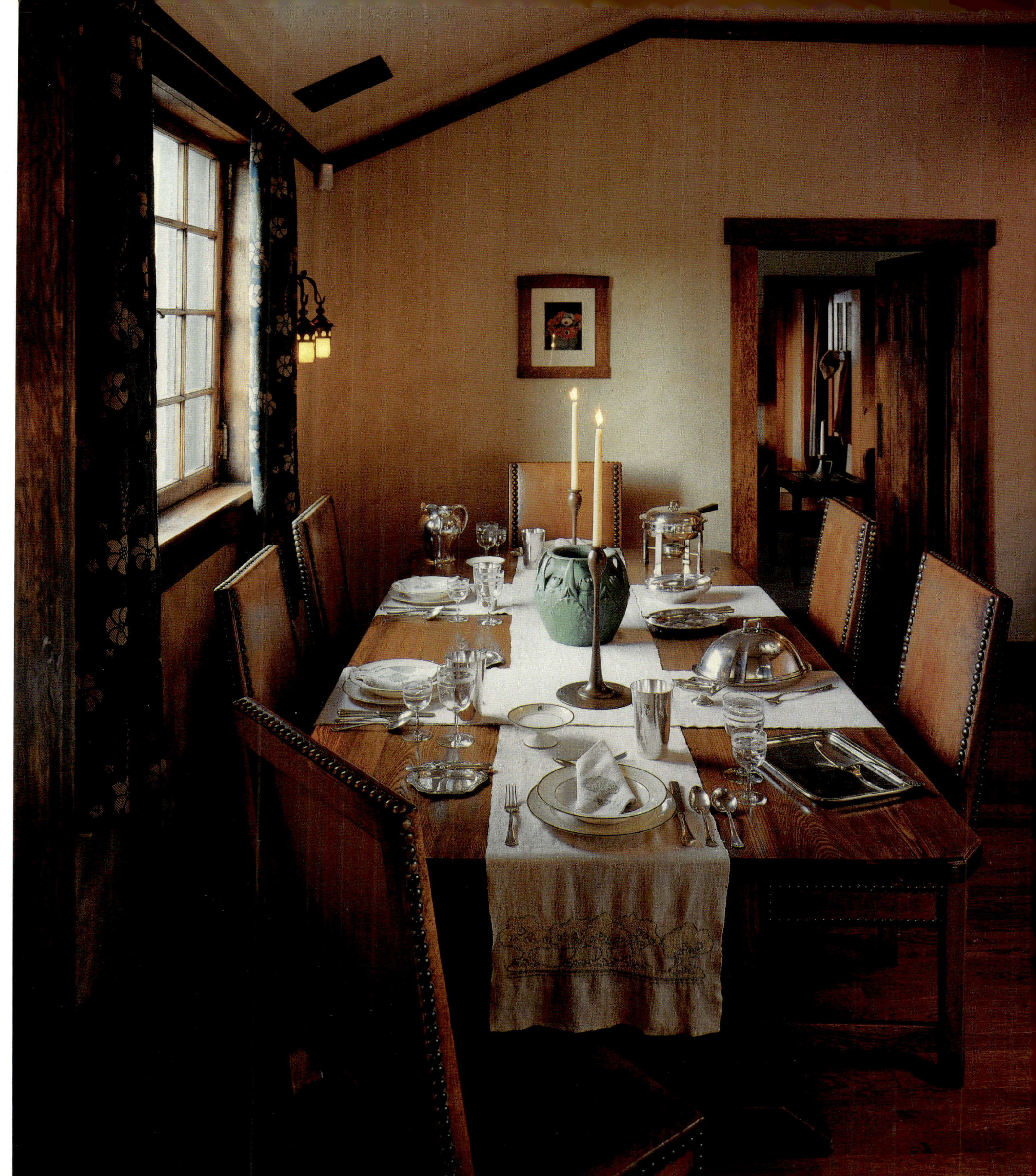

into the living room or hall, so that while portieres or screens can be used to close it off for privacy during meals, the floorplan can still be left as open as possible the greater part of time."[54]

Dining rooms appeared in multiple color schemes. In August 1903, a dining room in an urban house was described in detail in *The Craftsman*. Below the wainscoting, the walls were a burnt orange-colored leather accented by plaster. The wood trim was brown and the floor black, and there was a French blue tile hearth. Textiles in the room tied it all together, including a yellow and green Donegal rug and pale canary silk window hangings.

Popular magazines such as *The House Beautiful* emphasized the distinct nature of the Arts and Crafts style dining room as well. "When the dining-room furniture is of Mission style the natural linen with embroidered ends and borders makes a beautiful harmony of color and can be used for covers or mats or scarfs for luncheon or tea with excellent effect. The dinner table should always be laid in white. . . . Some of the natural linen scarfs for the luncheon or breakfast table have the same design as the dishes. A breakfast table laid with two of these scarfs crossed in the center with the mats between and the color of the embroidery the same as the dishes, is most attractive."[55]

Corticelli's *Home Needlework* suggested, "Table runners or scarfs are especially suited for square dining tables, or tables of the mission type. Three scarfs will dress up a table for six people and four will accommodate eight. When four scarfs are used it will be necessary to have a linen centerpiece, as otherwise the center of the table is bare. . . . If the 27 inch (centerpiece) be chosen the edges of the piece will rest on the scarfs. The use of scarfs is certainly to be recommended

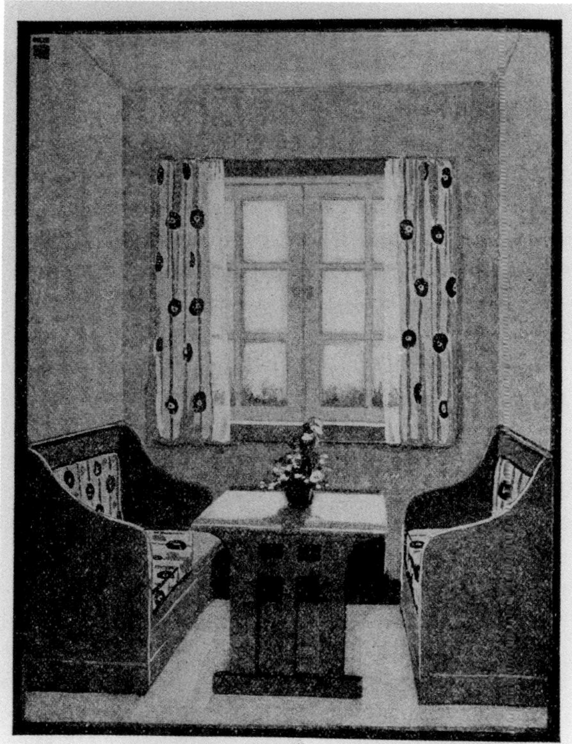

▶
Katherine Porter Brown. Breakfast nook illustrated in Izor's *Costume Design and Home Planning*. 1916

when one has a handsome polished table to display, and does away with the many fancy doilies of different shapes."[56]

More elaborate house plans included a study, billiard parlor, and other "luxury" rooms. Many of these rooms had extensive bookcases, which were often curtained. These rooms also had benches with cushioned seating.

Kitchen

Primarily the woman's domain, the kitchen underwent a transformation in the early twentieth century, modernized with new technology such as the cooling room and ice box. Kitchens were full of pantries, lockers, and sinks arranged according to modern and scientific ideas of sanitation. Painted woodwork was a common effort to improve cleanliness.

Windows were designed to let in light, which meant they might be with or without curtains. Magazines also encouraged that kitchens be equipped with a breakfast nook for easy dining, accented by pillows and table linens.

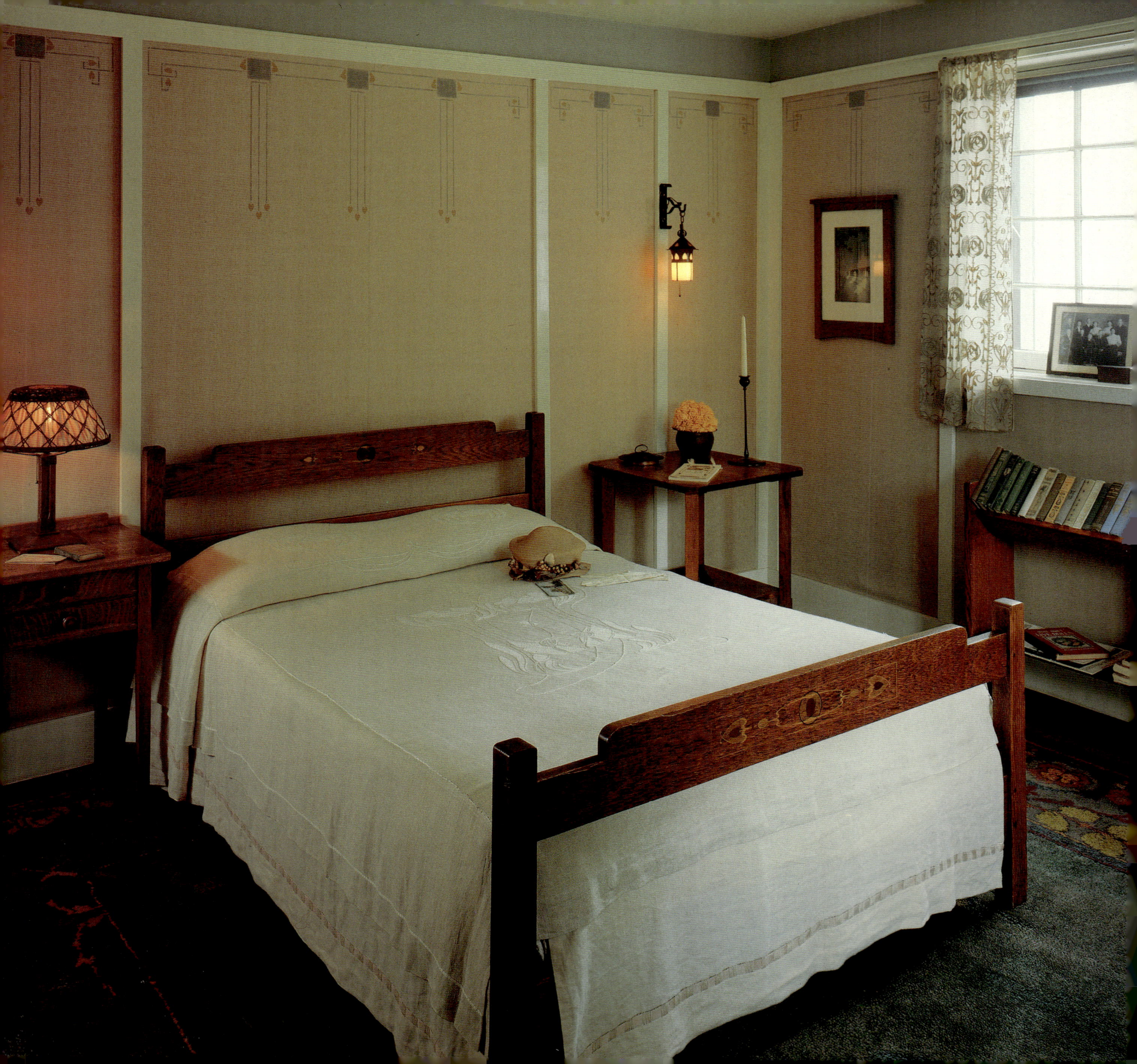

◀
Craftsman Workshops. Bedroom featuring "Zinnia" bedspread in white on white. Collection Crab Tree Farm

Bedroom and Nursery

The individuality of the bedroom was hearalded in a February 1906 issue of *The Craftsman*, which noted:

> Of all rooms in the house, the one where individual taste has the fullest play is the bedroom. The dwelling rooms must necessarily reflect the life of the whole family and the several occupations which are carried on in them, but the bedroom is the inner sanctum of each individual, and is intended above all for privacy, comfort and repose. It is the place for one's personal belongings, those numberless little things which are such sure indications of individual character and fancy and it is the one room where purely personal preference may be freely exercised. But in addition to this, it is, or should be, a place where one can go to sleep at night with nothing in the surroundings to depress, distract, or annoy, and awaken in the morning to a first unconscious impression of peace and cheerfulness.[57]

Periodicals recommended homemakers keep three principles in mind when decorating bedrooms: simplicity, convenience, and cheerfulness. Walls should be quiet and pleasant in color, the furniture suited in design and scale to the room's proportions, and the hangings harmonious in tone and of simple, washable material. The emphasis on bright, airy, and hygienic bedrooms and nurseries was new in the era. In an effort to prevent infectious diseases, people strived for sanitary conditions in all aspects of furnishing and outfitting the home.

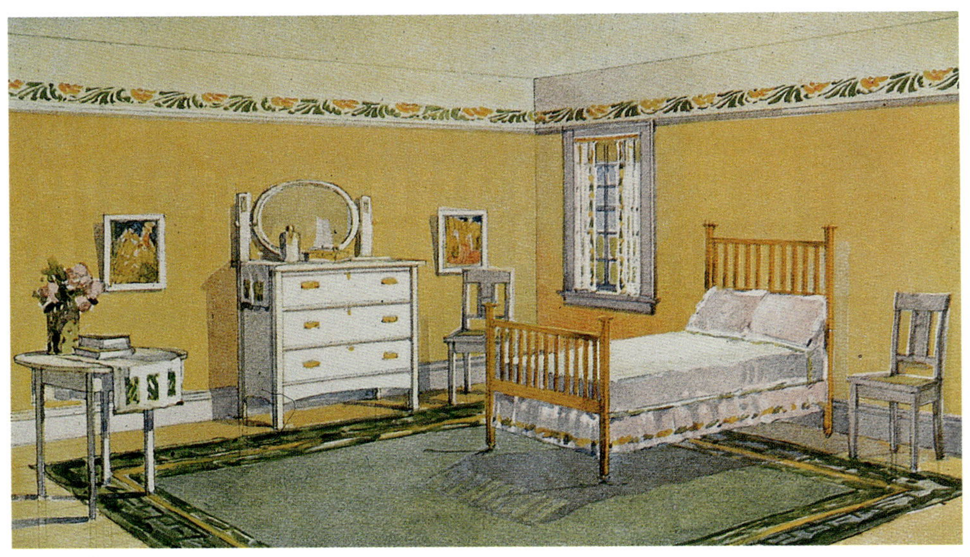

◀
Sherwin-Williams Company. "Stencil Decoration Gives Individuality to the Room." Illustration from *Your Home and Its Decoration*. 1910

> By following a well-defined general plan, a beautiful bedroom may be made at comparatively little cost. The simplest and most inexpensive materials are often the most appropriate and effective for a bedroom, and the plainer the furniture, the better. All it needs is a good color sense, a realization of the fitness of things and the courage to be simple, remembering always that the most perfectly arranged bedroom is the setting for all that makes for the comfort and individuality of purely personal surroundings.[58]

Color was a critical factor in crafting the temperament of a bedroom. "The color scheme of a bedroom is usually carried out in cool and delicate tints, giving the best possible chance for subtle accents here and there in the way of color and form, such as only needlework can give."[59] Bedrooms usually had light woodwork, sometimes of natural wood, and sometimes finished with a light stain that changes the tint of the wood without changing the character. "Upstairs, where privacy rather than openness is the characteristic of the plan, and where the hangings and decorations are more delicate in both material and coloring than those below, the woods most in keeping are those having a finer and less pronounced grain and a smooth surface."[60] The woodwork was often finished in soft grays and browns that harmonized with the furniture.

Periodicals of the day mention several potential decorating schemes for consideration. One proposed bedroom included a stenciled frieze in yellow, designed to harmonize with a cream ceiling, and yellow tiling. The textiles in the room included rugs of green and blue and curtains of cream linen printed with a poppy pattern in old rose, green, and blue. Gray oak furniture provided

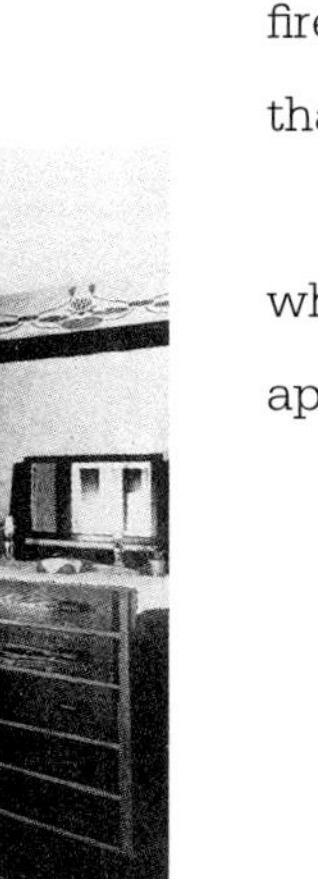

Mabel Tuke Priestman. Bedroom of "A New Jersey Bungalow." Illustration from *Artistic Homes*. 1910
Roller shades were often used in the early twentieth century.

a pleasant accent. A second example of a proposed bedroom is green going to grey with corresponding red rugs, draperies, and pillows. Still another example, a Craftsman-designed bedroom was executed in soft gray-blue, with enameled woodwork. The furniture was willow and silver-gray maple. The bedcover and bureau scarf in the room were natural, homespun linen with an appliqué and embroidery design in green and old rose. Other schemes include a yellow tiled fireplace, old blue walls, and blue and gold rugs. Each of these proposed rooms is based on colors that are considered restful and harmonious.

Textiles in the Arts and Crafts bedroom were often ivory or natural linen, replacing the pure white, lacy bedroom linens of the nineteenth century. They needed to be somewhat delicate in appearance, yet have the ability to sustain extensive wear and washing.

> No matter what are the furnishings of a room, the small accessories, such as the bedcover, scarves for the dresser and chiffonier, tablesquares, etc. should be white or pale in color and of a character to stand many visits to the tub. . . . [F]ortunately the era is passing of ruffled and belaced scarfs and covers shown up pitilessly the moment the first crisp freshness is gone, by the tinted silk pads beneath them. Their prettiness is so effervescent that they are the most extravagant of bedroom accessories—or, if not frequently renewed, the most untidy. At any time, they are more suggestive of luxury than of comfort. Pure, white linen, with touches of white embroidery, is always dainty, but in many rooms is too cold and characterless to produce the best effect. The greatest charm is usually found in linen of smooth weave and some delicate

▶

Bedroom. This linen bed ensemble descended in the family of Leopold Stickley, Gustav Stickley's brother. The natural linen is accented with eye-catching red trim. Collection Crab Tree Farm

> tint that brings it into harmony with the general color scheme, or in the irregular texture and pure color of the natural gray homespun linen that "wears like iron."[61]

The Craftsman published several articles on potential patterns for embroidering linen suites. These typically included bed coverings, chair cushions and upholstery, dresser scarves, bedspreads, and curtains. The linens furnishing the bedstead had been simplified and included a bedspread, often embroidered or stenciled with a motif in the center of the bed or along the sides. Window treatments usually consisted of one set of lighter weight curtains with a shade behind that could be drawn for privacy. Often, bedroom curtains were stenciled and a matching valance was hung between the panels or over them.

Nurseries and children's rooms were considered important areas to keep clean and bright. Parents, educators, and professional decorators were realizing the impact the environment in which they placed their children had on their well-being. In September 1903 *The Craftsman* published an article "In the Children's World" that discussed the importance of children's rooms. The author pointed out "it is well, both as an educative measure, and an a source of innocent pleasure which makes for the well-being of children, to give them, as far as the family resources permit, their own apartments, fully appointed, just as they are of necessity given their garments, their books, and their toys." *The House Beautiful* echoed this sentiment: "The room a person sleeps in has such influence on his attitude toward himself, consequently his relation to his neighbor, that it permanently forms character."[62]

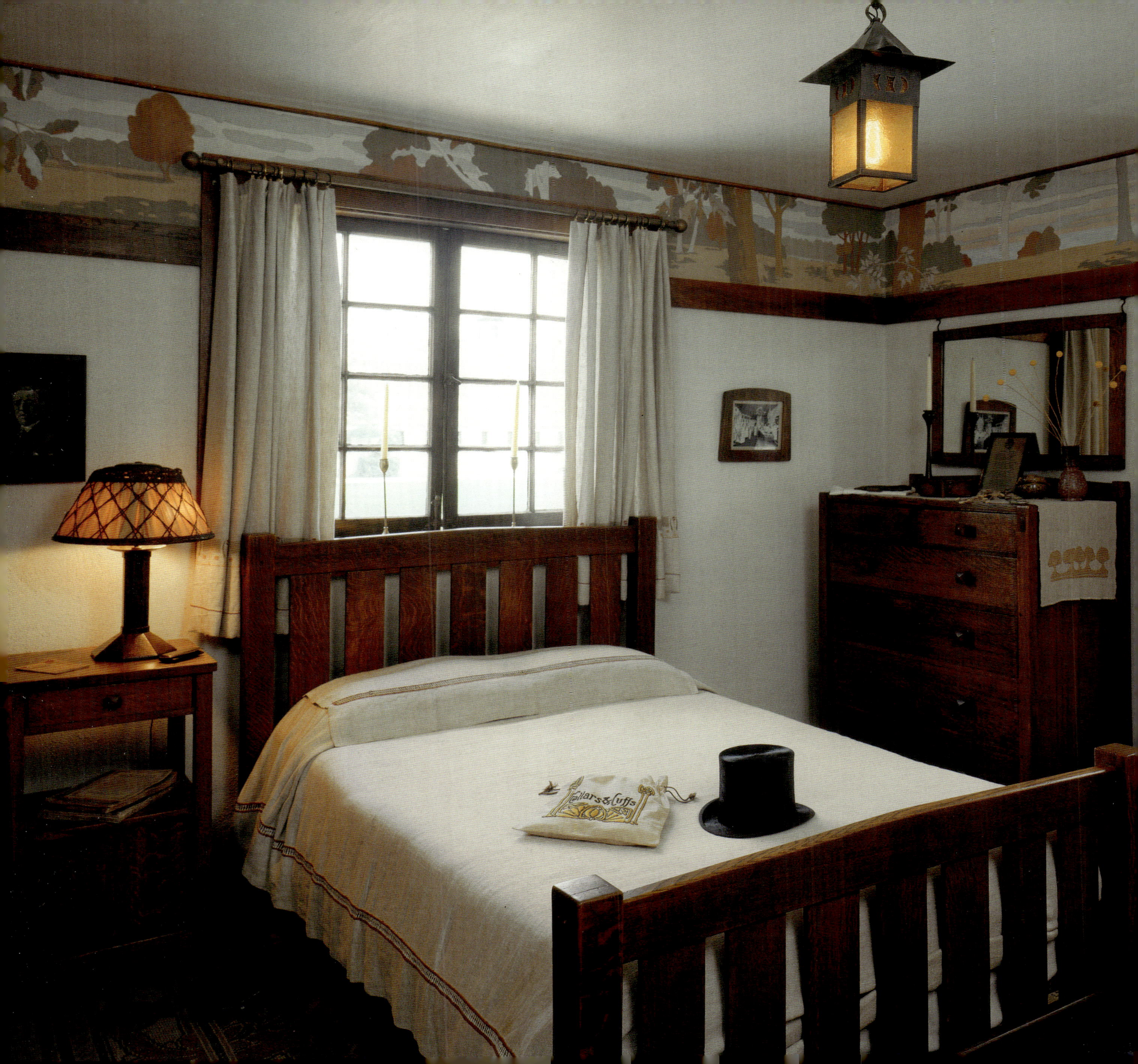
Collars & Cuffs

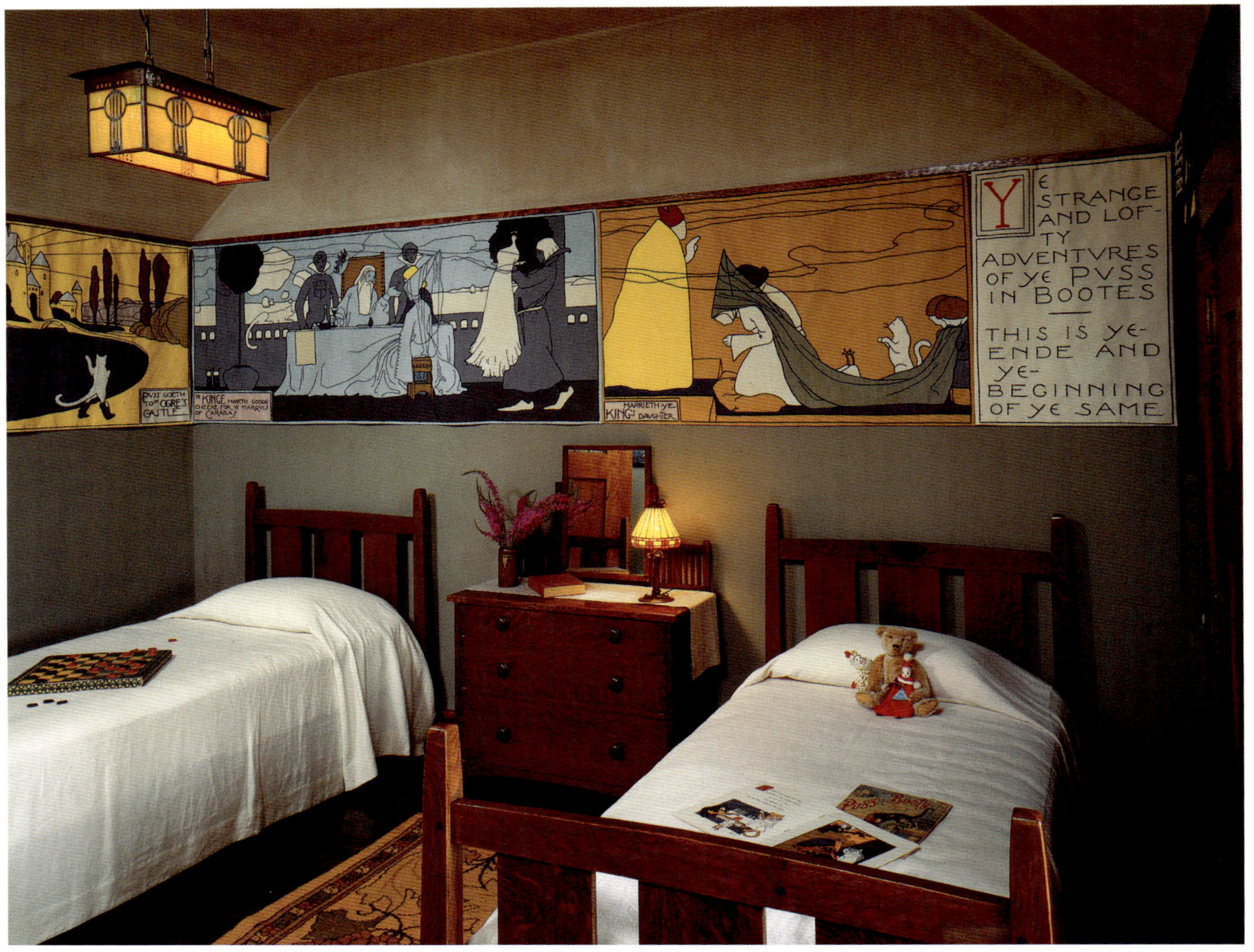

White and pastel colors such as a restful green, cool blue, and warm buff or rose were frequent color choices for nurseries. Sometimes these were brightened up with stencil and wallpaper borders. Textiles in these spaces needed to be practical and durable, such as washable throw rugs. Curtains were lightweight, to allow light and air into the room. Specially sized children's furniture required its own specially sized linens. Window seats with cushions were a common feature of the room as well.

In her book *Home Furnishing*, Alice M. Kellogg noted that "three connecting rooms for sleeping, playing, and bathing, with each item of furnishing and decoration carefully planned, form the ideal suite for the child. In the sleeping room there need be few articles of furniture—a crib or

◀
Nursery. Collection Crab Tree Farm
Children's rooms were frequently decorated with educational friezes and wallpapers. This contemporary embroidered rendition of a Harvey Ellis–designed nursery frieze published in *The Craftsman* (August 1903) illustrates classic tales and fables.

bedstead, a chair or two, a chiffonier or chest of drawers, with closets conveniently fitted up for holding clothing. . . . In making a study of the needs of the child, chairs may be selected for comfort, bookshelves placed within reach, and tables chosen of the right height. Artistic furniture for the use of children has never until lately been manufactured in much variety; but nearly all of the shapes made for older people may be found now in miniature sizes."[63]

An article on the child's bedroom in *The Craftsman* suggested "all design allowed in the rugs, hangings, friezes, and cushions must be rational and restrained, since familiarity with distortion is certain to produce evil effects upon the taste, as well as upon the manual skill of the child."[64] Objects and textiles in the room should match, including the cushions lining the wicker chairs and benches, the bed and crib linens, which included skirts, crib liners, and pillows and the decorative painting on the toys. *The House Beautiful* author Mary Mount encouraged the use of crash weaves, chintzes, and strong fabrics in this space. Designs were usually conventionalized nature motifs worked in silk floss on linen or hand-hewn cloth. Favorite colors included two shades of gray-blue, or all white on a natural background.

The curtains in children's rooms were practical and pretty. White glass curtains of scrim, dotted swiss, or other equally plain fabric were the most popular choices. Three-panel screens with textile inserts were also common, providing protection for the child from drafts while providing an architectural plaything. Bookcases and shelves for toys often had curtains, sometimes with playful scenes stenciled on, which could be drawn shut to eliminate the appearance of clutter.

▶
John Scott Bradstreet. Acorn curtains. Date unknown. Linen, machine embroidered. Collection Crab Tree Farm
Interior designers and architects such as Bradstreet, Greene and Greene, and Frank Lloyd Wright frequently designed or selected the textiles for their buildings.

Recommended rugs were washable cotton or wool creations. Authors encouraged decorators to cover the whole floor to protect children from drafts while playing. Rag rugs, if made of clean, new rags, provided an good surface.

The nursery represented

> the kingdom of childhood, surrounded by all the fun and adventure of the Golden Age—the magic realm you once inhabited, before you wandered "farther from the East." . . . This room is not like others. In the living room, for instance, a rug is merely a floor covering plus a certain aesthetic value, the ceiling is a blank architectural surface above, and the table is a useful and perhaps beautiful article of furniture. But in the nursery such things have other and vastly more important attributes. The rug is an ocean across which pirate ships are steered or Columbus sails for unknown shores; the ceiling is the home of the Old Lady who went up in a basket to "sweep the cobwebs off the sky"; and the table is a cavernous mountain beneath which are hidden grizzly bears or mischievous gnomes. Indeed, everything in the room is full of symbolism and delightful mystery.[65]

Bathrooms

Bathrooms, located off or near bedrooms, were simple and clean. Curtains were often plain. As the shower developed, shower curtains became necessary. Often canvas, the tight weave made them waterproof.

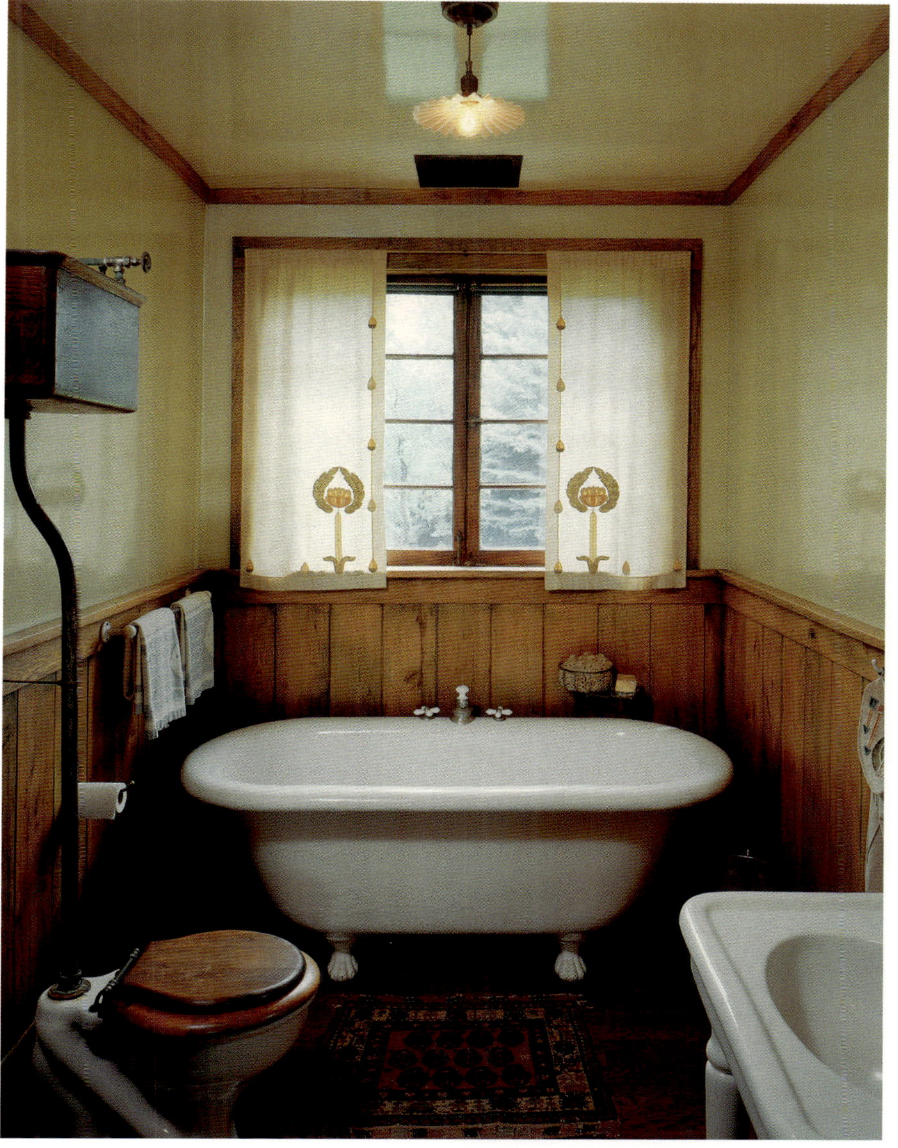

All of the rooms of the house had characteristics in common. Each space incorporated and depended on textiles in its own respective way to fill both practical and aesthetic functions. Numerous writers discussed the principles of home decoration for the benefit of the American public. Candace Wheeler believed "we need only fall back upon the principles of absolute fitness, actual goodness, and real beauty. If the furnishings of a well-coloured room possess these three qualities, the room as a whole can hardly fail to be lastingly satisfactory."[66] ❖

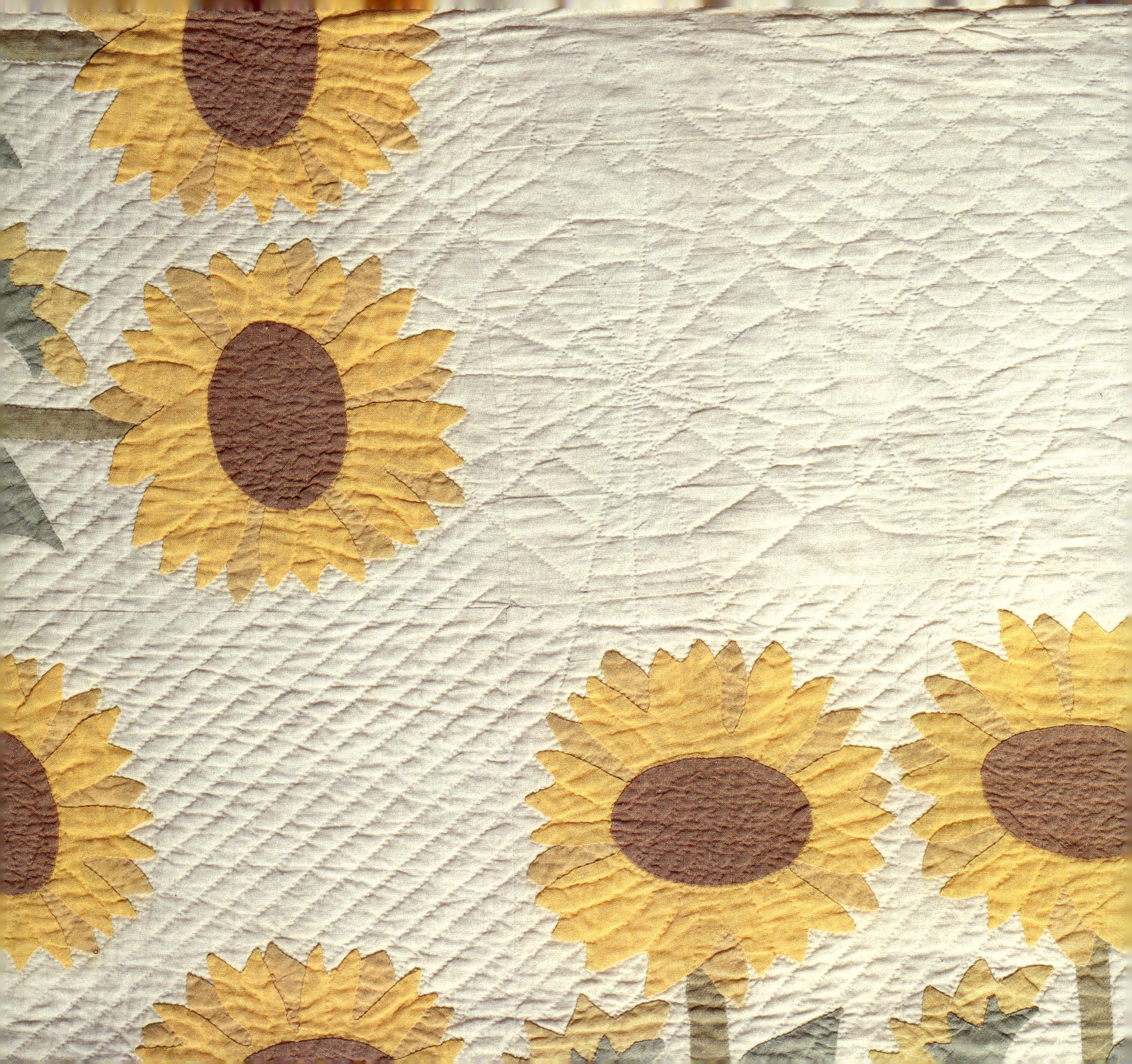

5 With Needle and Thread: The Craft and Construction of Arts and Crafts Textiles

The Arts and Crafts movement, with its complex underpinnings ranging from a reverence and revival of handicraft to a quest to create a uniquely new American style, fostered experimentation with many textile techniques. For the home crafter and the cottage industry, the relative low cost of the materials, equipment, and supplies made textiles one of the most accessible mediums for the ultimate ideal of the Arts and Crafts movement—to have one individual carrying through the design, creation, and sale or use of the object. In commercially produced textiles, the era prior to 1900 saw a dramatic change from hand-processed to machine-made goods, thus offering the benefit of the availability of these new technologies. The ever growing influence of published sources and the new emphasis on museum collections to be utilized for scholarship and artistic inspiration gave access to ancient crafts and those from other cultures. The movement had at its disposal many tools as well as eager participants to use them to conceive new forms.

To fully appreciate and accurately identify Arts and Crafts textiles, an understanding of the techniques employed in their construction and a familiarity with materials is essential. The processes encompass many industries and crafts. The time-honored traditions of handwork, the technologies available at the time, and the interrelationship among technique, function, and design all played a role in the textiles that were produced. Even for an item as seemingly simple as an embroidered pillow, the fibers may have traveled across continents and been subjected to a sequence of machinery before the hands of the artisan worked their craft upon it.

◀ Marie Daugherty Webster. Detail of sunflower quilt illustrated on page 199. Linen appliquéd on cotton, 88½ × 81" (225 × 206 cm). Indianapolis Museum of Art, Gift of Mrs. Gerrish Thurber

▶
Geo. Riggs & Company. "Old Bleach Linens." Advertisement in *Harper's Bazaar*. September 1904

All textiles are made up of fibers. Linen, cotton, silk and later rayon were the most prevalent fibers used in American textiles associated with the Arts and Crafts movement. Once cultivated, grown, and harvested, the fibers were processed and spun into threads. The quality of fiber determined the use for which the thread was appropriate, be it weaving, knitting, crocheting, or lacemaking (i.e. forming a cloth structure), or for use in sewing, embroidery, or other needlework techniques. The cloth may then acquire surface decoration consisting of various types of dyeing, printing, embroidery and appliqué work. It may also be further manipulated through cutting and sewing into its destined end use.

Materials

In 1913 America was the largest producer of cotton worldwide and exported two-thirds of its crop. Some cotton was also imported, primarily from Egypt and Brazil, to fulfill uses for which the American fibers were not suited. The New England states, which had long been dominant in the spinning and weaving of cotton, were losing much of their work to the South, where most cotton was grown and labor costs were lower. Sea Island cotton, grown along the coast and on small islands off the coast of South Carolina, Georgia, and Florida, was considered the best quality domestic cotton and was primarily used for fine fabrics, sewing, and embroidery threads. Cretonne, a heavy, plain-weave cotton printed with a large-scale pattern, along with denim, madras, and

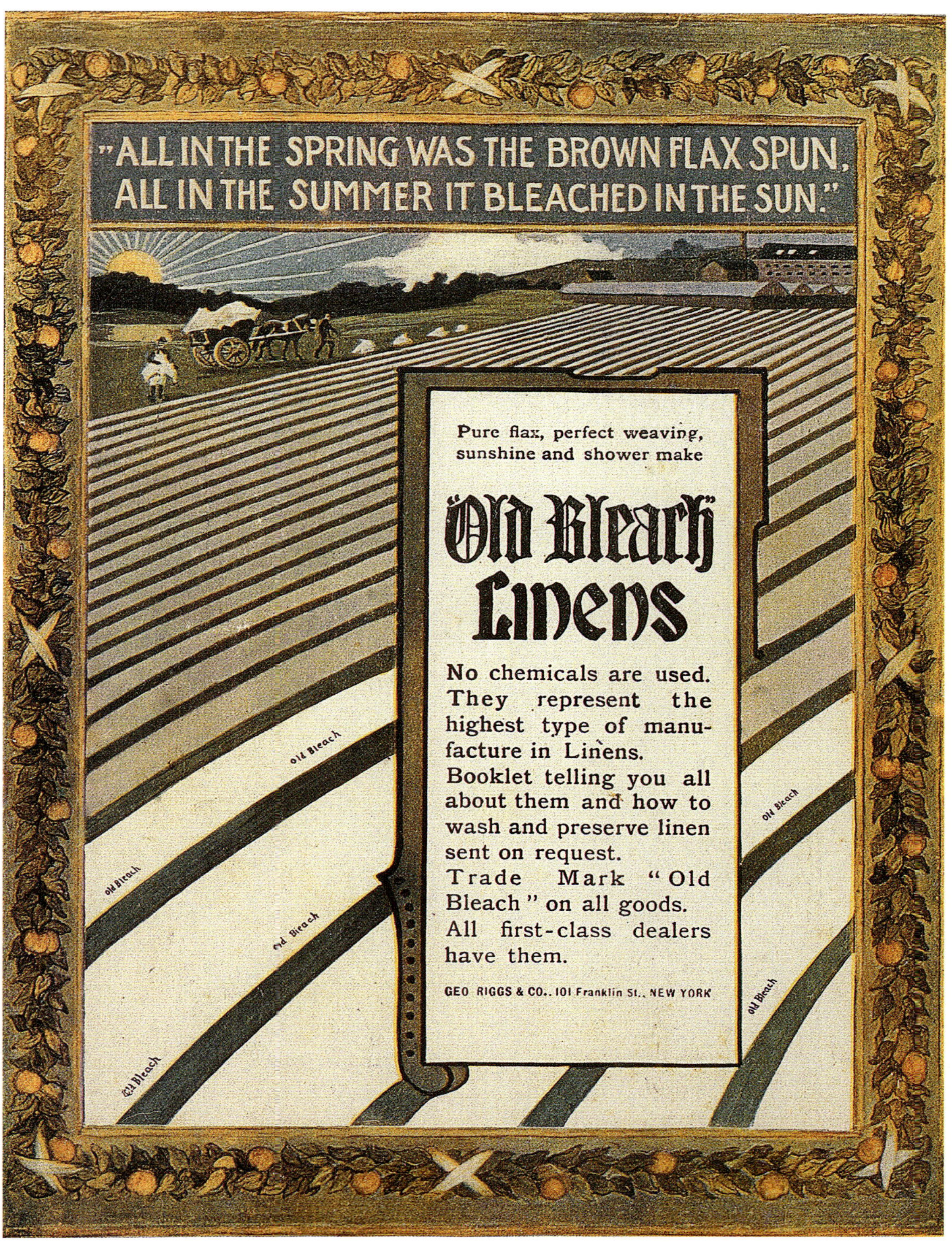
"ALL IN THE SPRING WAS THE BROWN FLAX SPUN,
ALL IN THE SUMMER IT BLEACHED IN THE SUN."
Pure flax, perfect weaving,
sunshine and shower make
"Old Bleach"
Linens
No chemicals are used.
They represent the
highest type of manu-
facture in Linens.
Booklet telling you all
about them and how to
wash and preserve linen
sent on request.
Trade Mark "Old
Bleach" on all goods.
All first-class dealers
have them.
GEO. RIGGS & CO., 101 Franklin St., NEW YORK
Old Bleach
Old Bleach
Old Bleach
Old Bleach
Old Bleach
Old Bleach

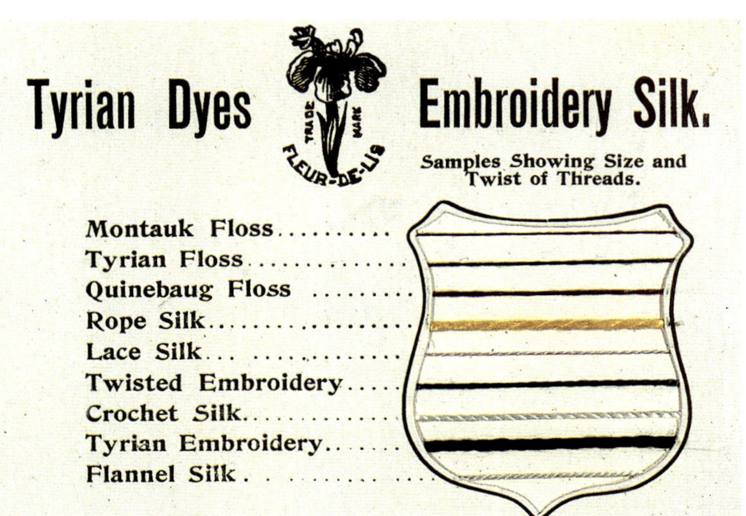

◀
New London Wash Silk Company. "A Guide for Art Needlework, Tyrian Dyes, Embroidery Silk Absolutely Fast Colors," thread sample card. c. 1900. Collection of Timothy Hansen and Dianne Ayres

monkscloth were commonly used cotton fabrics for home furnishings (see Chapter 4). In addition, cotton fabrics were widely used in clothing.

Linen is obtained from the flax plant. For the best quality flax is harvested by pulling the plant from the ground to yield the greatest length of the fibers. It is allowed to dry in the field, then rippled (or combed to remove the seeds and leaves), retted (a fermentation process to separate the fibers from the bark and woody core), and dried again. It then goes through the processes of breaking (to crack the inner wood and begin to remove it), scutching (to remove more of the woody parts and bark), and is further cleaned, then combed, sorted, and arranged into roving for spinning. The processing of flax from field to fiber takes a number of months and is labor intensive, accounting for the high cost of linen (page 153).

Nearly all flax grown in the United States at the turn of the century was cultivated for seed; some fiber from this crop was used for coarse and medium grades of linen fabric. In 1890 there were three establishments in the country for weaving linen, and by 1900 there were eighteen, mostly in Massachusetts.[1] Flax fiber and linen threads were imported for weaving fabrics here, but the finer grades of linen fabrics were imported from Ireland, Scotland, France and Germany. Fine qualities of flax for fiber were also grown in Russia, but primarily its coarser "crash" was imported (page 156 top).

Crash was also woven in the United States, but Russian crash was highly regarded for its coarse texture. Loosely woven from thick, loosely spun threads, it was usually in a natural color

▼

"Hand Embroidery Stitches Most Commonly Used." Adapted from illustrations from *Bucilla Blue Book of Embroidery*. 1916

1. darning stitch; 2. couching; 3. buttonhole stitch; 4. blanket stitch; 5. outline stitch; 6. cross stitch; 7. on upper leaf: left side, satin stitch; right, French knots; on right leaf: long and short stitch; 8. chain stitch; 9. honeycomb stitch

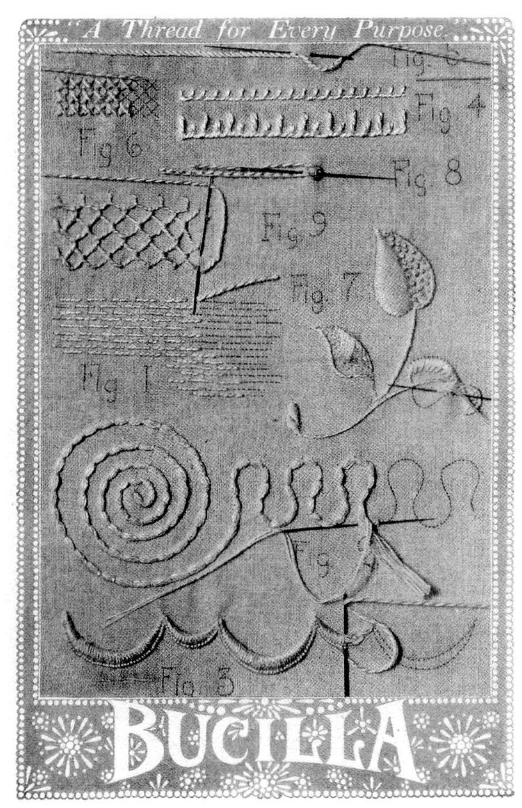

ranging from gray to a light brown. The cloth varied in width but was mostly fifteen to twenty-two inches wide, as its original purpose was for toweling, but its texture, color, width, and affordability made it the most commonly used base fabric for Arts and Crafts style embroidered pillows and table linens. Linen is well suited for use on tables, as its leathery texture helps to hold its place on the wooden surface. Sheer scrim fabrics for curtains were often woven of linen, and many other types of linen fabrics were used as well. Stickley's Craftsman Workshops offered nearly a dozen different weaves of linen, some in a variety of colors, among them linen velour, loose woven flax canvas, heavy flax canvas, homespun linen, hand-woven linen (crash), flemish linen, colored linens, bloom linens, and block-printed linens in at least three patterns. Bloom linens were "confined almost entirely to appliqué, as the two-toned effect caused by the different colors of warp and woof gives a shimmer that is charming when it is seen as part of a design applied upon some rough lusterless material." It came in combinations of dull rose and green, blue and green, red and dark blue, and two varieties of yellow and red.

In general, union fabrics—those woven of differing fibers for the warp and weft—were not often used, but arras cloth, in which the fibers were spun together, was highly praised. Craftsman Workshops was one of the first to import arras cloth from Scotland, which they offered under the name of "Craftsman canvas." It was similar in texture to firmly woven burlap but the threads were spun of a mixture of flax and jute. The cloth was then dyed, the two fibers accepting the dye differently "giving to the fabric the quality of unevenness in color that [is] so desirable in anything

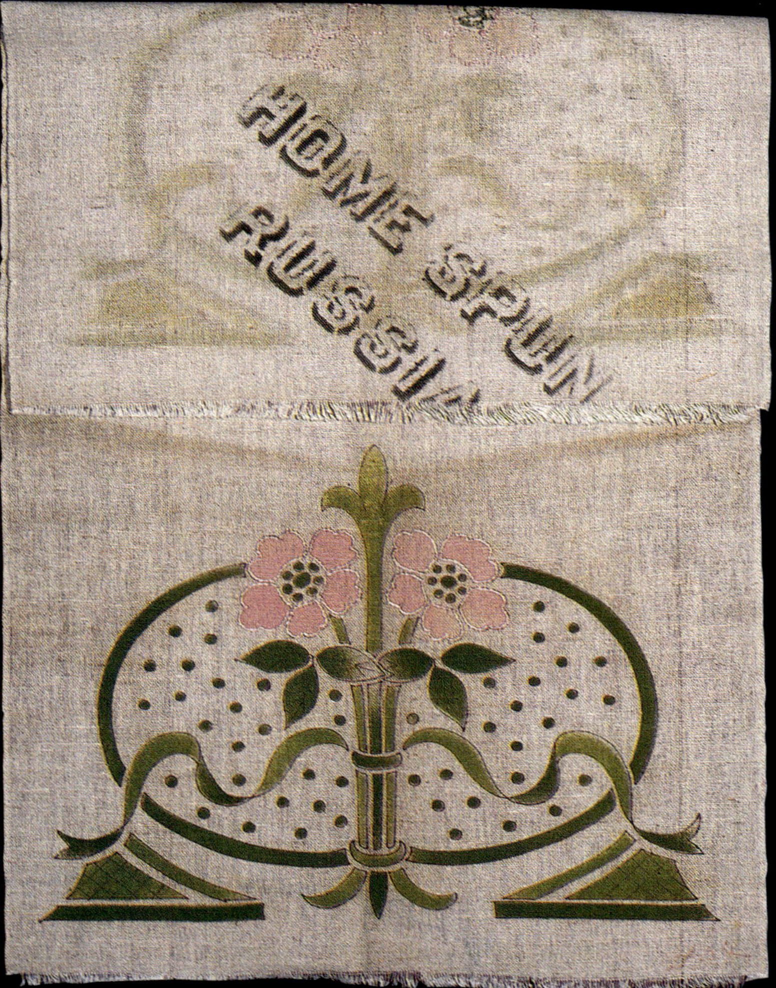

◄

Anonymous. Table linen kit, not completed, stamped "Home Spun Russian" on back. c. 1912. Linen crash with stencil, 18 × 50" (45.7 × 127 cm). Collection Tommy and Beth Ann McPherson

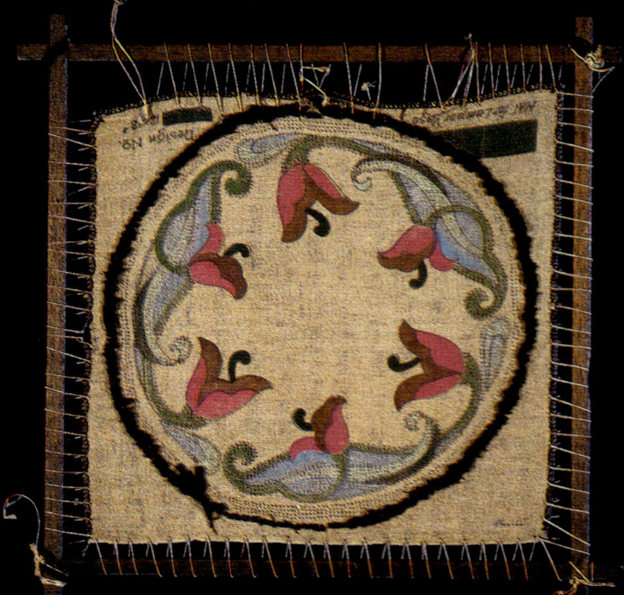

►

Anonymous. Mat for a lamp base, in a stretcher frame. c. 1910. Linen cloth, 12 × 12" (30.5 × 30.5 cm). Collection Tommy and Beth Ann McPherson

This is an example of punched work, with some of the loops removed. It was worked from the back with the thread punched through, leaving a loop with a short nap.

▶
Anonymous. Linen panel with hand embroidery in cotton, 15½ × 12" (39 × 30 cm). Collection Timothy Hansen and Dianne Ayres
This design captures a conventionalized flower as well as its process of regeneration, the dropping seeds and spreading pollen represented as dots.

used for a background." It was available in a wide range of colors, including wood browns, russet brown, rusty pine-needle green, deep leaf green, brick red, blue-greens, dull rich yellow "like ripe wheat," and old rose with a "yellowish tone like a frostbitten maple leaf." It was suggested for portieres, pillows, upholstery and table linens and was also used for folding screens with appliqué designs upon the panels.[2] While flax, if not abused, will last for centuries, jute is not a long-lived fiber, thus not many items made of arras cloth have survived.

Throughout the nineteenth and twentieth centuries, the manufacture of silk goods in the United States was dependent on Europe and the Far East for its supply of raw silk. In colonial days, royalty had encouraged farmers to put aside the cultivation of tobacco and take up the culture of silk, and, while it was not nearly as profitable, cottage industries in silk survived until the 1840s. At that time, a convergence of economic factors and a mulberry blight virtually ended domestic cultivation of the silkworm and its precious filament.

In 1913 there were hundreds of companies involved in the manufacture of silk goods. Silk was primarily imported in its raw state, hanks of fibers that had been reeled from the cocoon and readied for processing into sewing or embroidery thread or the threads for weaving. The most noteworthy use of silk in Arts and Crafts style textiles was its role as a thread for hand embroidery. While silk does not survive particularly well with exposure to sunlight, sheer silk fabrics were sometimes used for glass curtains in the Arts and Crafts home. Silk fabric was also used for apparel.

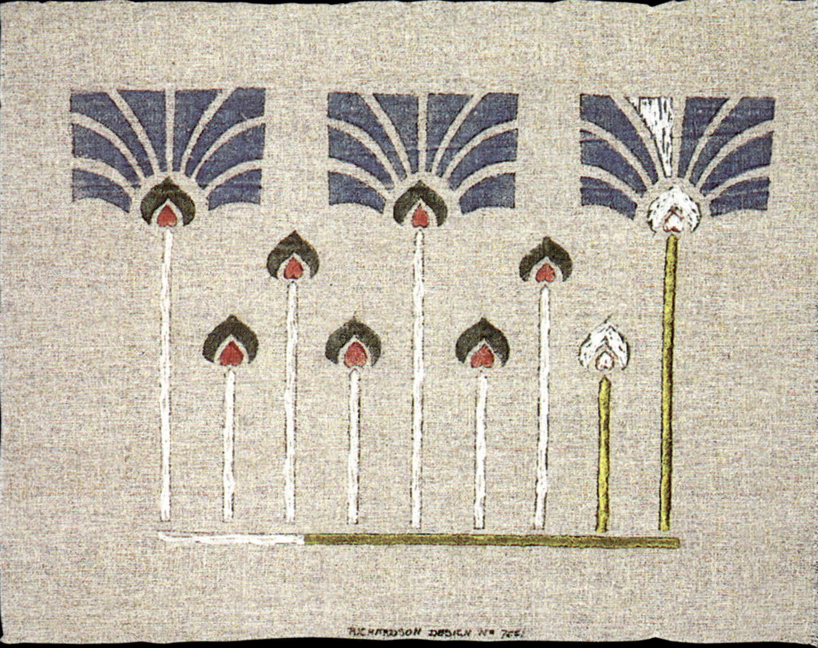

◀
Richardson Silk Company. Pillow kit, not completed, showing padding
worked before satin stitch. 1911. Russian crash linen with padding sti
in cotton cord and satin stitch in silk, 17 × 21" (43.2 × 53.3 cm). Collect
Timothy Hansen and Dianne Ayres

rran Company. "Royal Society" pillow, completed from a kit. c. 1912.
ith cotton hand embroidery in satin stitch, outline stitch and couching
cord and metal thread, 15½ × 26" (39.4 × 66 cm). Collection Chris
and Susan Stockton

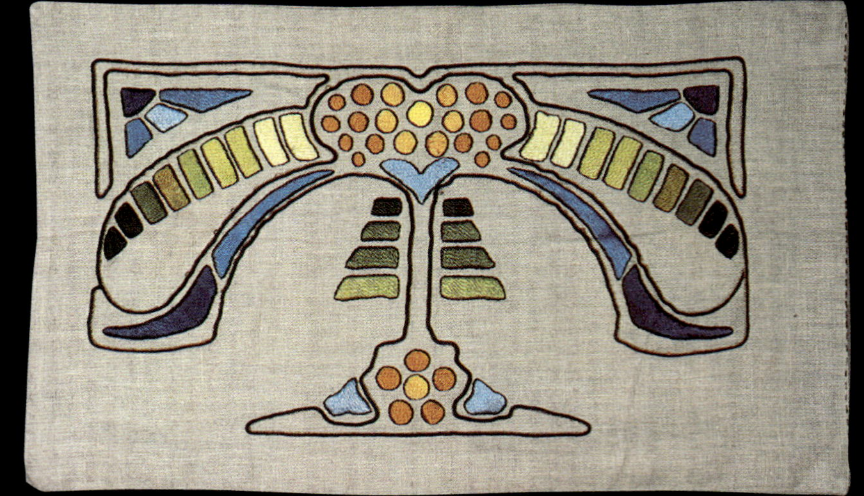

▼

Attributed to Bucilla Manufacturing Company. Pillow with thistle design, "No. 805 Work with Glossilla Skein No 84–86–88–3–56–58–60–62–64–66–69..." c. 1914. Linen with stencil and hand embroidery in rayon, 20 × 20" (50.8 × 50.8 cm). Collection Tommy and Beth Ann McPherson
The edges of the leaves are worked in long and short stitch, and the stems and flowers are worked in stem stitch.

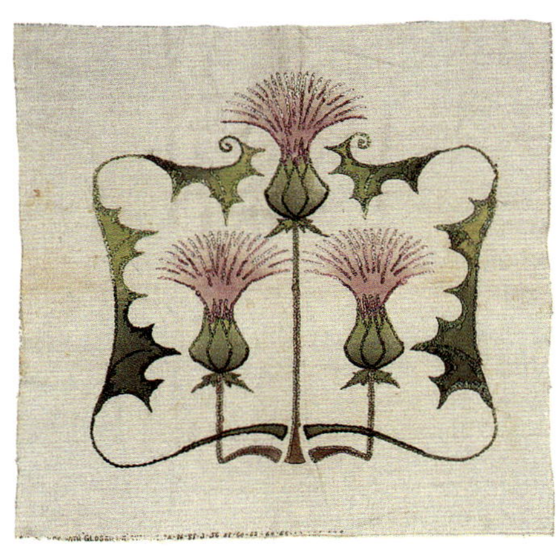

But industry in the early twentieth century was not content to be limited to these naturally occurring fibers. Due to the desirability of silk, efforts were made to produce "artificial silk." In 1912, Charlotte M. Gibbs reported:

> Because of the high cost and beauty of silk there have been many attempts to find substitutes for it. Efforts have been made to spin the spider's web and to use the filaments spun by other moths, but so far these have been unsuccessful. A single exception is the byssus of the shell-fish, Pinna. This byssus is a tassel-like appendage by which the mussel attaches itself to rocks, and it may be combed out and spun into a thread which is used sometimes for gloves, purses, and other small articles. The natural color of this silk is olive green or brown.
>
> Chemists have experimented for years to find a substitute for silk, and have produced several artificial silks from different substances. The most successful of these is Chardonnet silk, so called for the man who succeeded in producing it.[3]

Chardonnet silk was produced from cotton fibers, but it was viscose, produced from wood pulp, that became the most commercially viable "artificial silk." It was first commercially offered for embroidery thread in 1912, causing an upheaval in the industry. The 1924 edition of *The Story of Silk* reported, "The stigma attached to the word 'artificial,' and the fact that artificial silk was at first definitely intended as a really false substitute for silk, made it difficult for many years for the fibre [sic] to gain for itself the place in trade and popular esteem that its merits warranted."[4] An

▶
Water lily table mat and pillow completed from kits. c. 1910. Linen with hand stencil and hand embroidery
Even the pre-stamped kits allowed for individual expression. These two pieces were made by different embroiderers. The crafter of the table mat worked the petals and stems in satin stitch and the border lines in couching, while the pillow maker chose to leave most of the stenciling to show and worked mainly in stem stitch. Both worked French knots in the flower centers, but the different threads and methods of working gave very different results.

▼
Acorn and leaf pillow. c. 1906. Linen with silk hand embroidery, the stems and acorns in satin stitch with couching across the acorn caps, the leaves in long and short stitch, 20½ × 20½" (52.1 × 52.1 cm). Collection Caro Macpherson

addendum placed in this book reports that the industry, trade associations, and government had recently settled upon a new name for the fiber; it was to be called "rayon."

While wool was used extensively during the period, it did not play a large part in textiles associated with the Arts and Crafts movement. Mohair and other wool upholstery fabrics were occasionally used for portieres, but its use was generally discouraged due to its propensity to attract dust and pests. Dress goods, suitings, and knitted underwear were staples for cold climates. Some hand weaving, particularly in the South, incorporated wool.

Other minor fibers occasionally were used. Burlap, woven of jute, was often applied on the walls. Fabrics of hemp or ramie sometimes substituted for linen. Fabric made of piña, or pineapple fiber, was imported from the Philippine Islands. Some embroideries were done upon a piña fabric, dyed and printed to simulate arras cloth.

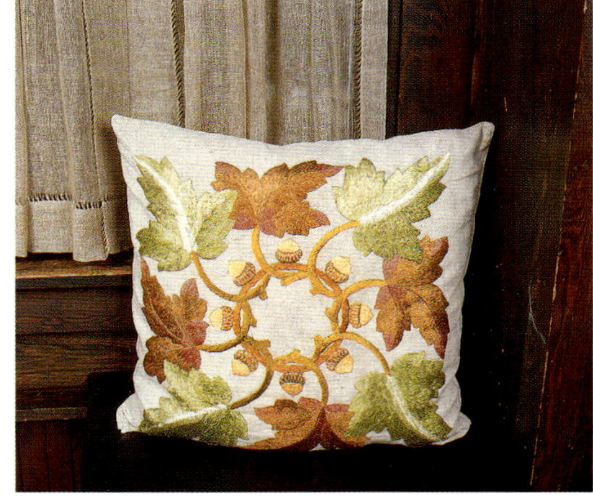

Of course, the majority of fabrics in use in the early twentieth century were commercially spun and woven. In part, this easily obtainable resource freed the homemaker from much drudgery and allowed for the indulgence of creating decorative textiles.

> At the present day [1912], machine-made fabrics are, of course, most important. Today it is impossible to use hand-made materials for most purposes, but there is a plea to be made for the industry, in that it offers a field for the true expression of the individual, and there is a combination of the honest wearing quality, beauty, and a certain distinction in the fabrics, not to be found in machine-made materials. The machine-made is not to be discarded, but neither

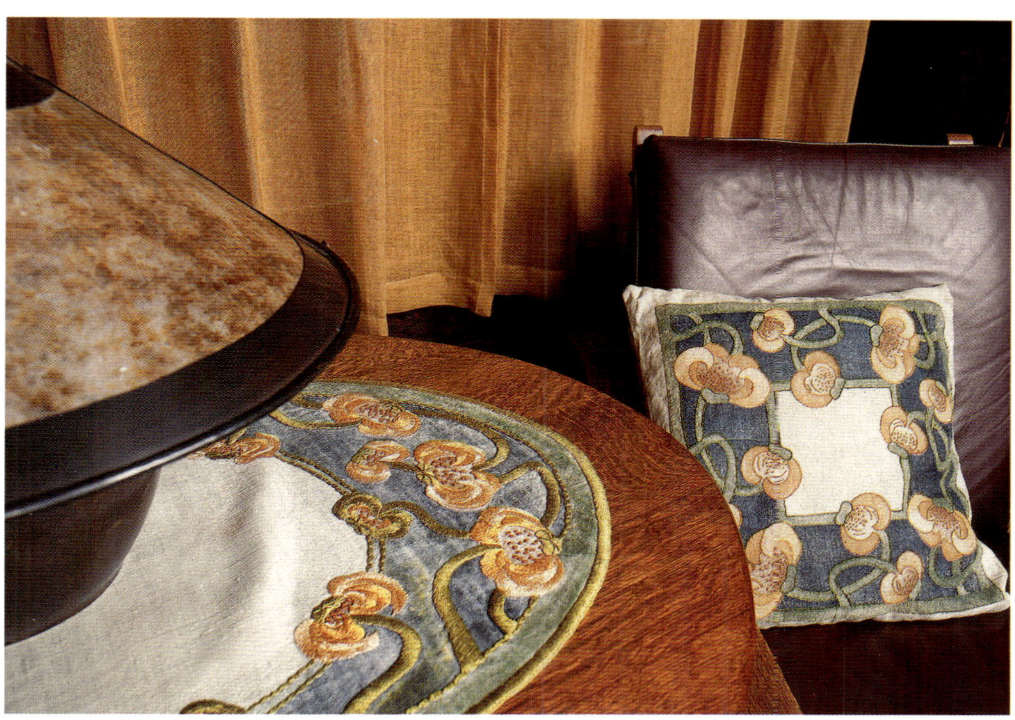

should the hand-made be allowed to disappear. It is finding renewed expression today in the Arts and Crafts movement.[5]

Techniques

Many techniques were championed under the banner of Arts and Crafts, each finding its niche of participants and patrons. Most techniques had their roots in ancient history or other cultures and were revived for or adapted to the precepts of the movement. Many were employed by a range of people, from artists and artisans to homemakers and schoolchildren, each producing objects of utility—be it the utility of art, education, or function. Each technique offered particular constraints, thus rendering it useful for certain types of objects and requiring design adapted for its processes. The following is not an inclusive list of all techniques executed at the time, only those which were most in use and most closely associated with the movement. Nor is it intended as a how-to, as there are many other contemporary and period sources for more in-depth instructions; rather, as information to help identify and appreciate surviving textiles from the period, their artistry and craft, and some of the important participants.

▶
Anonymous. Table centerpiece. c. 1913. Linen with hand embroidery in rayon, machine lace edging, 24" (61 cm) diam. Collection Timothy Hansen and Dianne Ayres
Padded satin stitch was used for the green, light tan, and reddish brown forms, the latter outlined with stem stitch, with masses of French knots between them. A line of couching connects the forms.

Embroidery

The technique most commonly associated with textiles of the Art and Crafts movement is hand embroidery. Embroidery is the ornamental application of thread upon fabric, using a needle. While the craft is ancient and was practiced in nearly every culture, particular varieties of embroidery are associated with certain regions and time periods. The Arts and Crafts movement drew upon these regional and historical styles and developed its own unique styles of embroidery.

Most women at the turn of the century had some experience in needlework; the training of most young girls (and many boys, too) deemed the skill necessary in keeping a home and for cultural discipline. But, as styles changed, further instruction was required for the worker to successfully carry out the new type of work and contemporary designs. Until one gained an intimate knowledge of the materials and techniques "she will have results worthy of the name of 'fancy work,' but not of 'art embroidery.'" This 1899 *Lessons in Embroidery,* jointly published by Brainerd & Armstrong and Corticelli, offers that information.

> We need the proper tools for our work. The requirements for hand stitches are fewer than for "full" or "solid" embroidery, which is done in a frame or hoop.
>
> The first requirement for framed work is a high table. It should stand about thirty inches. The chair used should be low. One usually sits slightly sidewise to a hoop, and a rocking chair is therefore usable and comfortable because the position can be shifted. It is necessary to sit squarely in front of a bar frame, therefore a low straight chair is better. The reason for a high

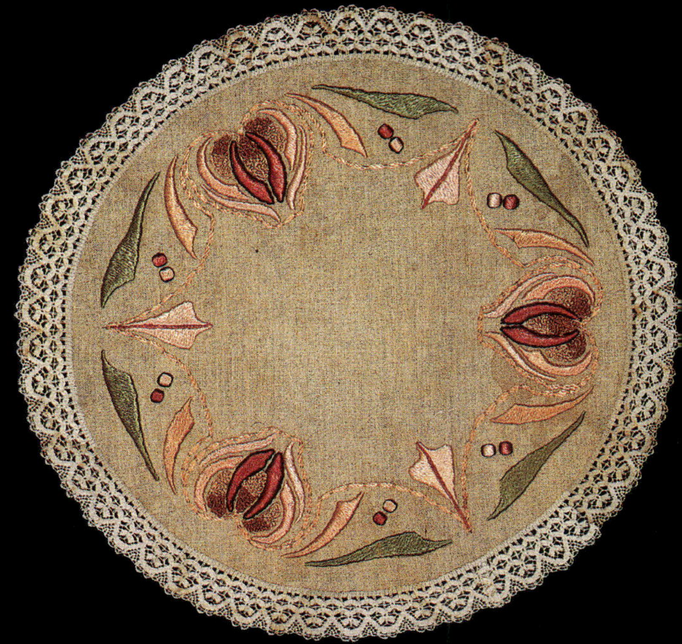

▼
Anonymous. Wallachian table centerpiece. c. 1909. Linen with hand embroidery in silk, buttonhole stitch hem, 24" (61 cm) diam. Collection Tommy and Beth Ann McPherson

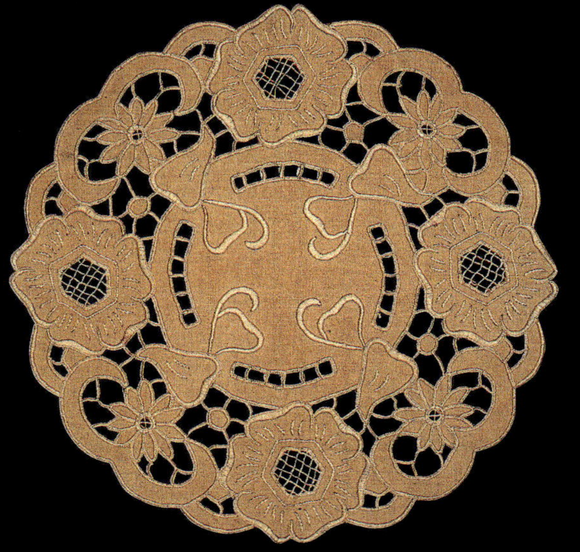

◀
Anonymous. Table linen in cutwork. c. 1905–20. Linen with hand embroidery, buttonhole and stem stitches, 20" (50.8 cm) diam. Collection Timothy Hansen and Dianne Ayres

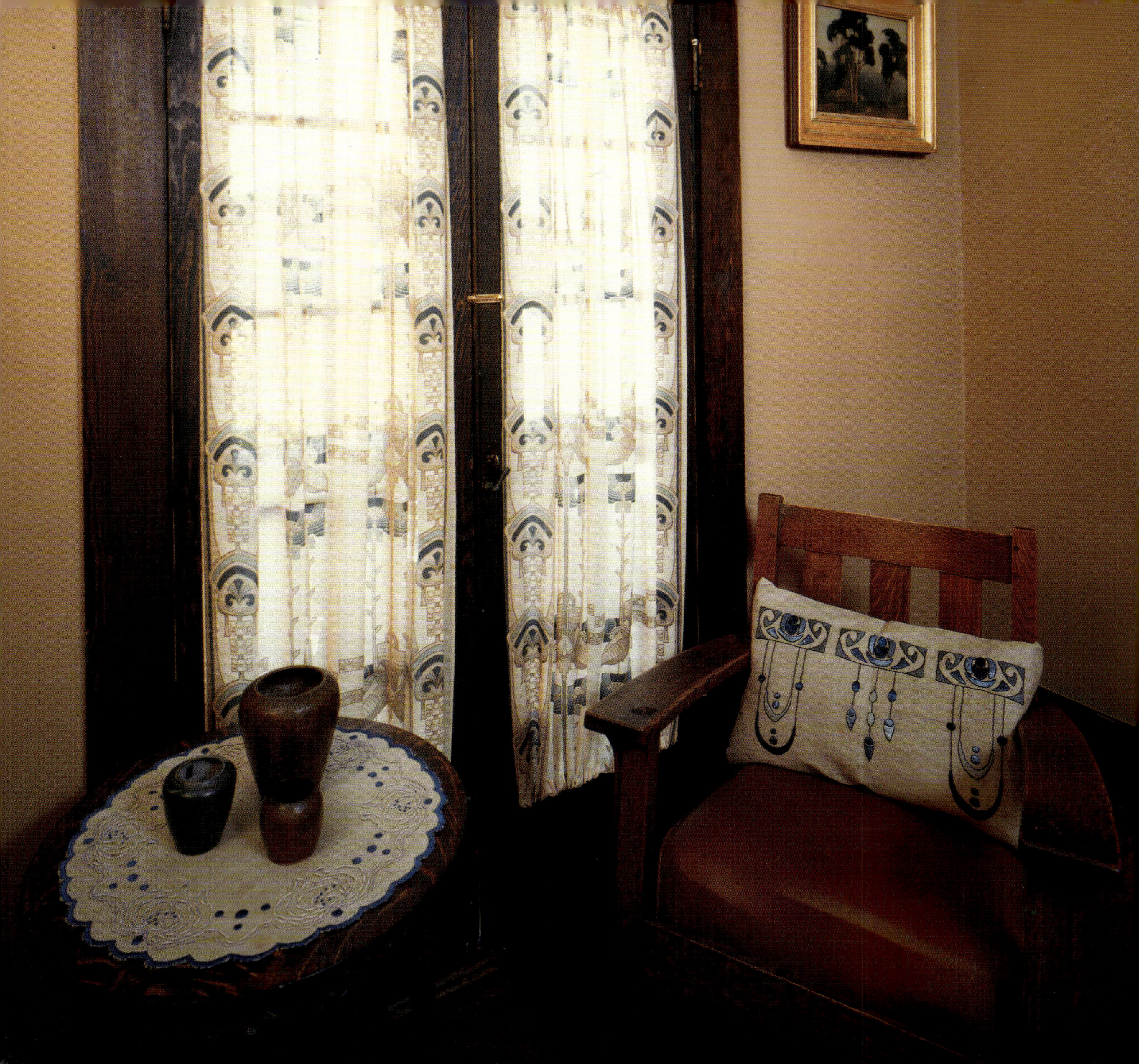

◀
Stairway landing. c. 1910
The small table linen has the design couched with coronation thread, highlights of satin stitch, and the hem worked in buttonhole stitch. The pillow is worked from a kit by Richardson Silk Company, in which the crafter used both cotton (green) and silk (blues) embroidery threads in satin stitch, giving and interesting textural effect. The stem stitch in black outlines and completes the forms. The linen scrim curtains were commercially roller printed.

> table and a low chair is evident. It forces one to sit straight. The lungs are not compressed and one can work for hours without fatigue.

Once the work was attached in a frame (page 156 bottom) or a hoop—the hoop being the "less elaborate or may we say less professional way"—the edge was clamped or otherwise secured to the table, and the table placed with its left side against a window. The lower part of the window was to be curtained and a dark apron worn to prevent glare and reflection on the work.

> Of the other instruments necessary the needle is of especial importance. Two thimbles should be used when embroidering in a frame. The scissors should be true and sharp and not too small. A medium sized pair will be far more convenient for cutting the silk and certainly for cutting out the scalloped edges than the little ones often called "embroidery scissors." Anything which tends to make the work "puttering" should be avoided. We need freedom and perfect ease in embroidery. An amateur at a frame has a tendency to make very hard work of it, to tighten and cramp the hands, to make every muscle rigid, not infrequently to hold the breath and struggle as a boy at his first writing lesson. The frame, the low chair, the high table, are insisted upon for no other reason than to make the worker perfectly comfortable and to secure to her every convenience. She has, then, but to accept these easy conditions, relax the fingers and wrists, hold the needle between the forefinger and thumb, secure, yet not tight, and let the thread fly loose and take care of itself.

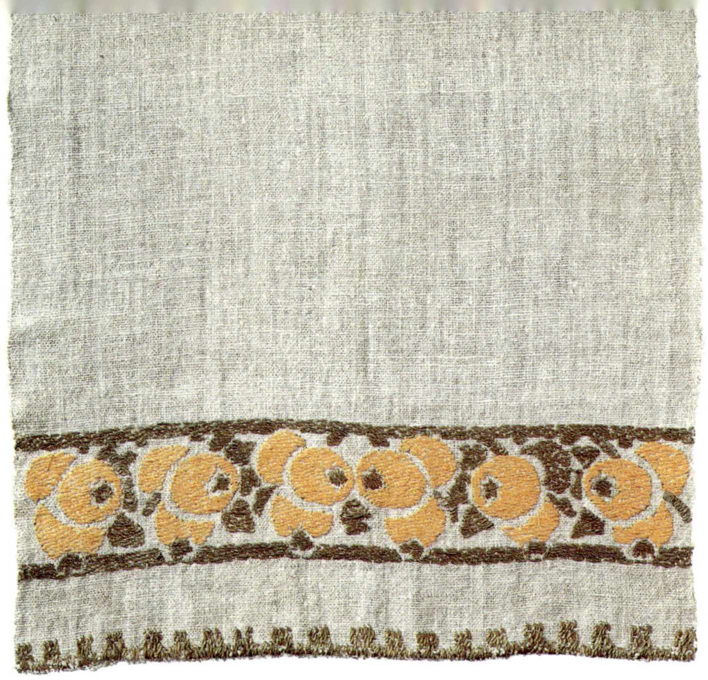

◀
Craftsman Workshops. Table scarf with crab apple design. 1902–16. Linen with hand embroidery in linen, darning stitch, 14¾ × 17½" (37 × 44 cm). Collection Crab Tree Farm

Later instruction manuals were less exhaustive (the above being only small excerpts from a lengthy article on the topic) and also not as insistent that a frame be used, as the type of work requiring them became less common. By 1910, the "hand stitches"—those stitches that did not cover large areas of the fabric and could be done holding the work in the hand—were typical in the evolving style of embroidery.

Cotton or silk thread was most commonly used in Arts and Crafts style embroidery, but linen and, later, rayon threads were also used. Cotton embroidery thread was almost exclusively of the variety which is today termed *pearl* or *perle* cotton; at the time it is was sometimes called *floss* but was generally referred to as *rope*. Two plies, each loosely spun, were then twisted together to form a heavy thread. Rope was most typically used on table linens and pillows. In addition to rope, Royal Society offered a similar finer thread called "India." Both were offered in approximately 250 colors. Finer yet, they offered "flosselle," in eight different weights in white and in two weights in a selection of thirteen colors. Flosselle was mainly recommended for embroidering monograms, children's ginghams, and towels. By 1915, they also sold "strand floss" in which the ply could be split, recommended for use on flannels and soft materials.[6]

Each worker had her individual preference for embroidery threads. Some found silk difficult to work with, while others would use nothing else. Cost was also a factor in the choice of threads. A skein of Royal Society rope (cotton) gave eight yards of thread and cost about six cents in 1915. Depending upon the design, a pillow could require from twelve to thirty skeins, this at a time

▼
Craftsman Workshops. China tree napkin. 1902–16. Linen with hand embroidery in linen, darning stitch, 6¼ × 6" (16 × 15 cm). Collection Crab Tree Farm

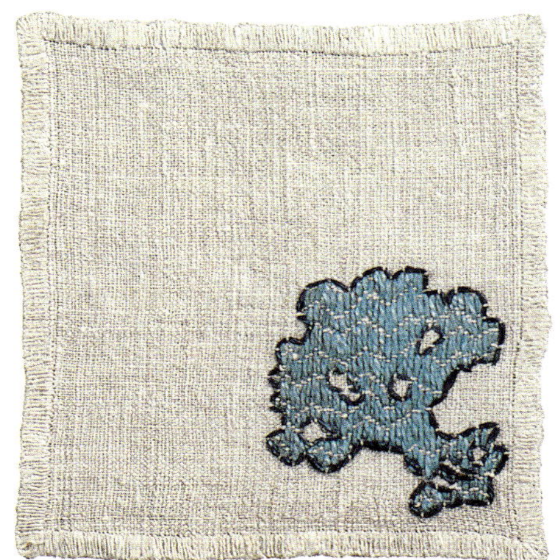

when the average working woman earned five dollars per week. Rope silk was pricier, ten to fifteen cents for a ten-yard skein. Packing closer, it often required thirty or more skeins for a pillow, double for a table linen with the design on both ends.

The thread manufacturers devised names for their threads, selecting names to fit the character they wished their company to display. Most offered a rope and a "filo"—the very finest embroidery thread—but, beyond that, many got creative. Richardson's chose "Sicilian" and "Grecian"; Heminway selected "Spanish," "Turkish," and "Japan floss," the latter their filo; and the New London Wash Silk Company, in addition to the ancient Phoenician "Tyrian," paid homage to Native Americans with "Montauk" and "Quinebaug" (page 154). Brainerd & Armstrong prefaced all their thread names with "Asiatic" to credit the origin of the silk and attached names like "Roman," "Medieval," and "Caspian." The flosses were not to be divided, but often a number of strands of filo would be held together when working.

Linen embroidery thread was not widely available, but Craftsman Workshops used it extensively. It had a nice sheen and was durable. Rayon embroidery thread, as noted above, became available in 1912 and was readily accepted by embroiderers. It had a high gloss like silk but was about half the cost. It can be identified as having a "greasy" feel whereas silk feels somewhat prickly.

Each type of thread had a corresponding needle that was recommended by the thread manufacturers. It was important to use a needle large enough to form a good hole so as not to fray the

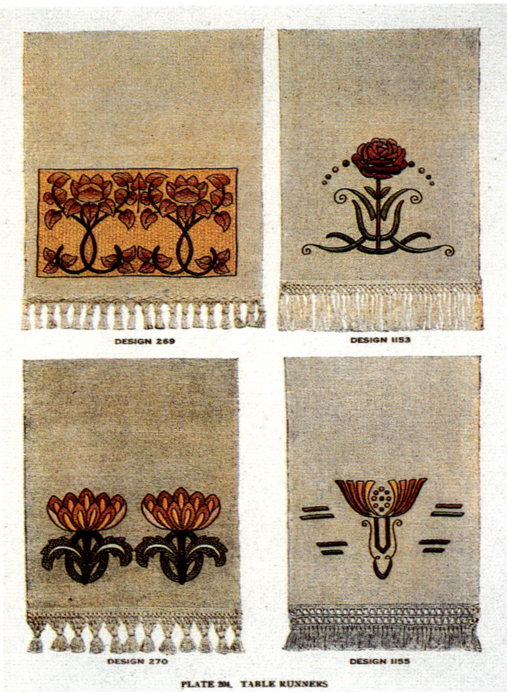

◀
Belding Bros. & Company. "Plate 204" table runners. c. 1913. "Design 269" stenciled, with goblin embroidery; "Design 270" stenciled, with satin stitch, French knot, and outline stitch; "Designs 1153 and 1155" with satin and outline stitches

thread as it passed through the cloth. For the most part, crewel needles, with long eyes and sharp points, were used. Richardson's offered its own special embroidery needle, which was longer than normal, and also a Japanese embroidery needle with a round flattened eye, "Warranted to the good graces and warm attachment of the worker."[7]

A limited number of embroidery stitches were typically used for American Arts and Crafts textiles. It was uncommon for a piece to be done all in one stitch; usually two or more different stitches were incorporated. The most commonly used stitches were stem stitch and satin stitch. The names and method of working of many stitches varied according to the needlework authority. In America, usually the working thread was kept below the needle in stem stitch, but the English style kept the thread above, resulting in a finer line due to the twist of the thread. This came to be known as Kensington stitch in America. Either variation could have been referred to as outline stitch. Depending upon how much the stitches overlap and the embroiderer's unique hand, the stitches can vary considerably in appearance (page 155).

Satin stitch, a stitch used to fill an area, involved taking parallel stitches across a form. The maximum length of a satin stitch was determined by the particular combination of fabric, thread, and intended use of a piece but generally was no more than three-quarters of an inch. In essence it was quite simple, but keeping a good edge and even tension were key factors. To give more dimension to the work, a layer of stitches was laid perpendicular to the direction of the intended satin stitch. This was often done in a cheaper cotton cord, keeping the bulk of the padding on the

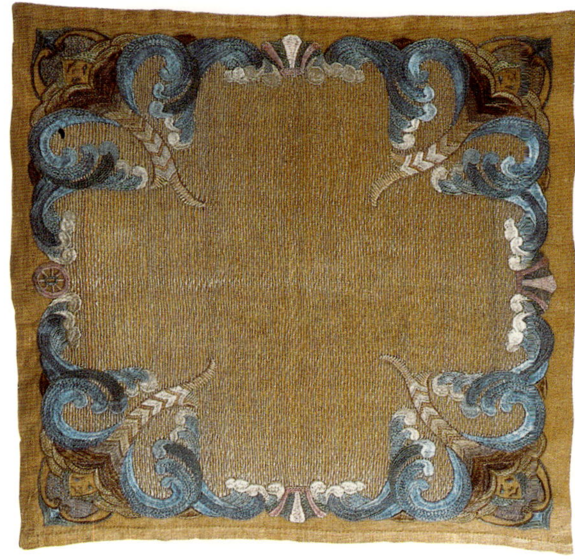

▶
Deerfield Society of Blue and White Needlework. Table Square "The Golden Sands and Mermaid." 1905–15. Embroidered linen on linen, 20 × 19½" (50.8 × 49.5 cm). Memorial Hall Museum Collection, Deerfield, Massachusetts
The piece is stitched with a border of blue waves and a mermaid at each corner, the interior covered with a running stitch on brown linen.

face of the piece (page 158 top). Often, satin stitch was worked and then outlined in stem stitch. This covered any unevenness of the edge, and, when a black thread was used for the outline, made the color of the fill more vibrant.

Related to satin stitch was the long and short stitch, its name being self-explanatory. A single row could outline a form (page 159), or, when an area was too large to be covered by simple satin stitch, interlacing rows of long and short stitches were used (page 160). Satin stitch and its variations required a considerable amount of thread. As much or more thread is on the back of the piece as on the top side, thus it was often specified in kits produced by thread manufacturers.

Buttonhole stitch and blanket stitch use the same basic stitch, the difference being in buttonhole the stitches are spaced close together. Buttonhole was often used as an edging for table runners and centerpieces (page 161) and for the edges of cutwork (page 163 bottom). In both cases, the embroidery was worked upon the solid cloth and then the edges of the table linen or the interior spaces of the cutwork were cut away adjacent to the stitching. In addition, buttonhole stitch was the basis of Wallachian embroidery, an import from Romania that was the rage in 1908 and 1909. Buttonhole stitches close in on themselves to fill a round or oblong shape, often a leaf or flower petal form (page 163 right).

Couching is an embroidery technique in which a thread or group of threads is laid on the surface of a fabric and another thread is used to stitch it down. Often, the laid thread was metallic or coronation braid—a cord, regularly spaced thin and thick. In couching with embroidery

▶
Newcomb College. Table scarf. c. 1902–15. Linen with hand embroidery in darning stitch, 19½ × 76" (50 × 193 cm). Collection Crab Tree Farm

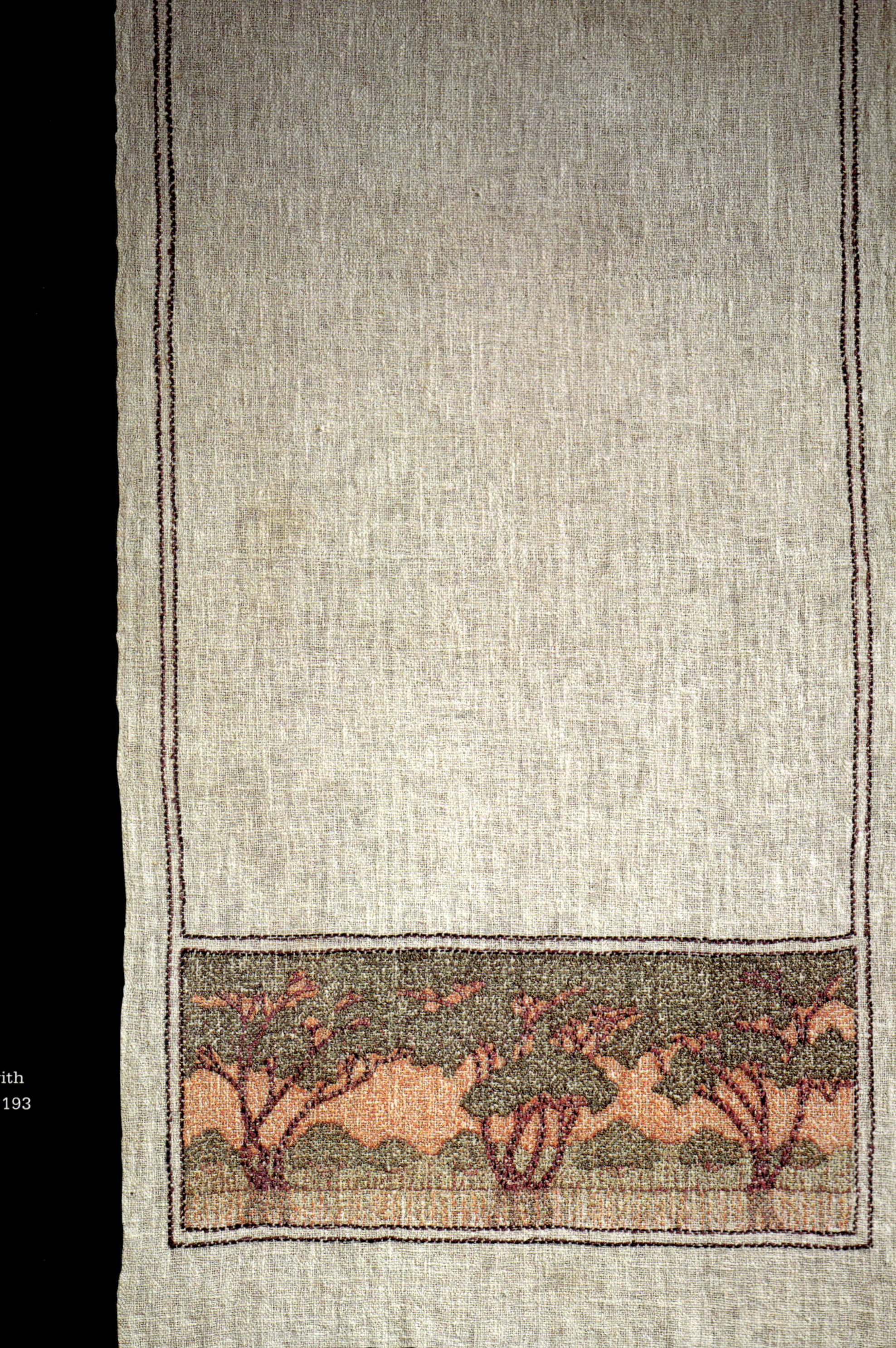

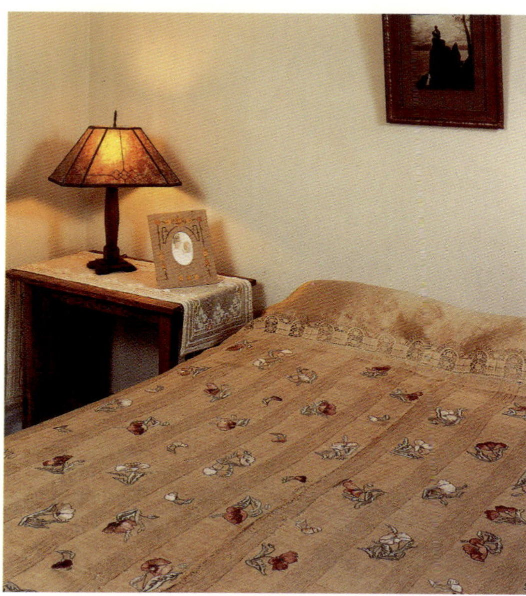

▶
Bedroom textiles. Collection Caro Macpherson
The bedpread, made of linen with hand embroidered poppies dancing across it, is the project of an ambitious needleworker. The edging is silk and handmade lace. The table scarf is darned net, 14½ × 55" (36.8 × 139.7 cm). The "Arabian" color net has embroidery in white and tan of a thick soft thread. The picture frame is linen with hand embroidery.

threads, variations in the number and size of threads and the stitch spacing gave different effects. Successive rows of couching were sometimes used as a fill stitch, and it was often used to outline forms. Couching was usually embroidered along the edges of appliqués as well.

French knots were worked singly as a dot of color, or used as a fill when worked in mass (page 163 top). They were often used for flower centers and anywhere a raised uneven texture was desired.

Darning stitch was very much akin to weaving with a needle, a thread stitched in at intervals. The stitches could run straight with the grain of the fabric or follow the form of the design. Darning stitch had long been used in decorative needlework as a background fill, but Arts and Crafts embroiderers took it to new, artistic heights. Stickley's Craftsman Workshops produced many designs worked in darning stitch, either with the entire design work in one color—as in the Zinnia Bedspread (page 140), or with different monochromatic forms making up the motif—as in the Crab Apple Table Scarf (page 166). Mostly, the stitches were taken straight across the grain, and sometimes a running stitch of a second color outlined the design (page 167). Many Craftsman Workshop embroideries of darning stitch exhibit a chevron pattern set up by the stitches, this being simpler than randomizing the stitch pattern.

Few kits offered by the embroidery thread companies employed darning stitch, other than where it was used as a fill for the background or where the stitches were to be taken following a sparsely stamped pattern of black lines. This later was called "Goblin" embroidery, and a number

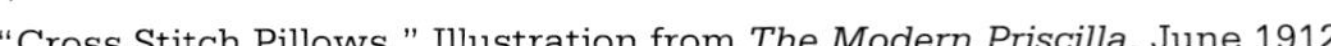

"Cross Stitch Pillows." Illustration from *The Modern Priscilla*. June 1912
Kits for cross stitch were not common in the Arts and Crafts period, as a good method of marking had not yet been devised. The article states, "one cannot expect to follow the graceful curves of the stamped outlines of flowers and leaves exactly; in fact, the charm of the embroidery would be lost if one could do so."

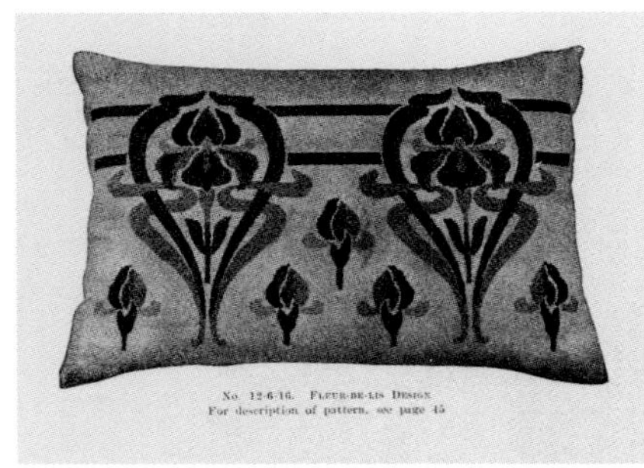

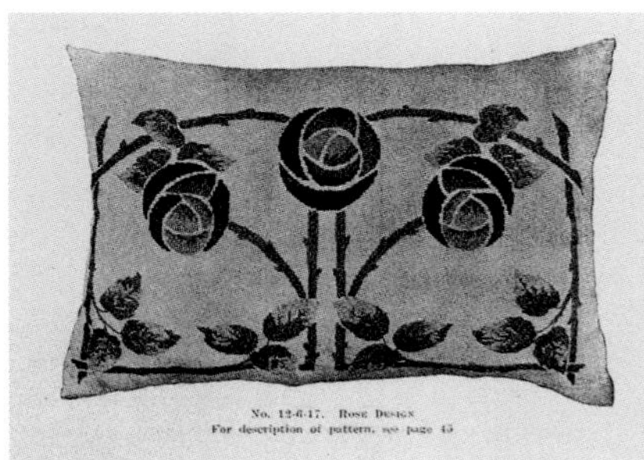

of designs were offered by Belding Brothers (page 168). For a description of various companies involved in hand embroidery, see Chapter 3. While a kit for the more detailed darned work designs was difficult to produce and complete successfully, Craftsman Workshops did offer them, their clientele being more willing to take on an artistic learning endeavor than that of the mainstream kit manufacturers.

Nowhere was darning work carried out with as much artistry as at Newcomb College (page 170). Many of the designs were conventionalized representations of the local flora and scenery. The darning stitch was often worked with the grain of the fabric, the warp or weft, sometimes both directions on the same piece—horizontal stitches taken for the ground and foliage and vertical stitches for tree trunks. But the artists did not restrict themselves and followed their instincts to create unique and exquisite table linens, wall hangings, and myriad other items.

Some of the fabric of which the items were made was spun and woven by the Newcomb craftsmen as well. Occasionally a piece was spun, woven, designed, and embroidered by a single person. More frequently, they used Russian crash and cotton and linen fabrics woven by Louisiana Acadian weavers and Tennessee weavers. Imported silk embroidery thread was used.[8] Random stitch lengths were used and placed so as not to set up a pattern unless one was desired. Any given area of the design is worked in two or more colors. The use of color and the visual mixing achieved within a form and across the work contribute to the strong artistic statement made by Newcomb textiles.

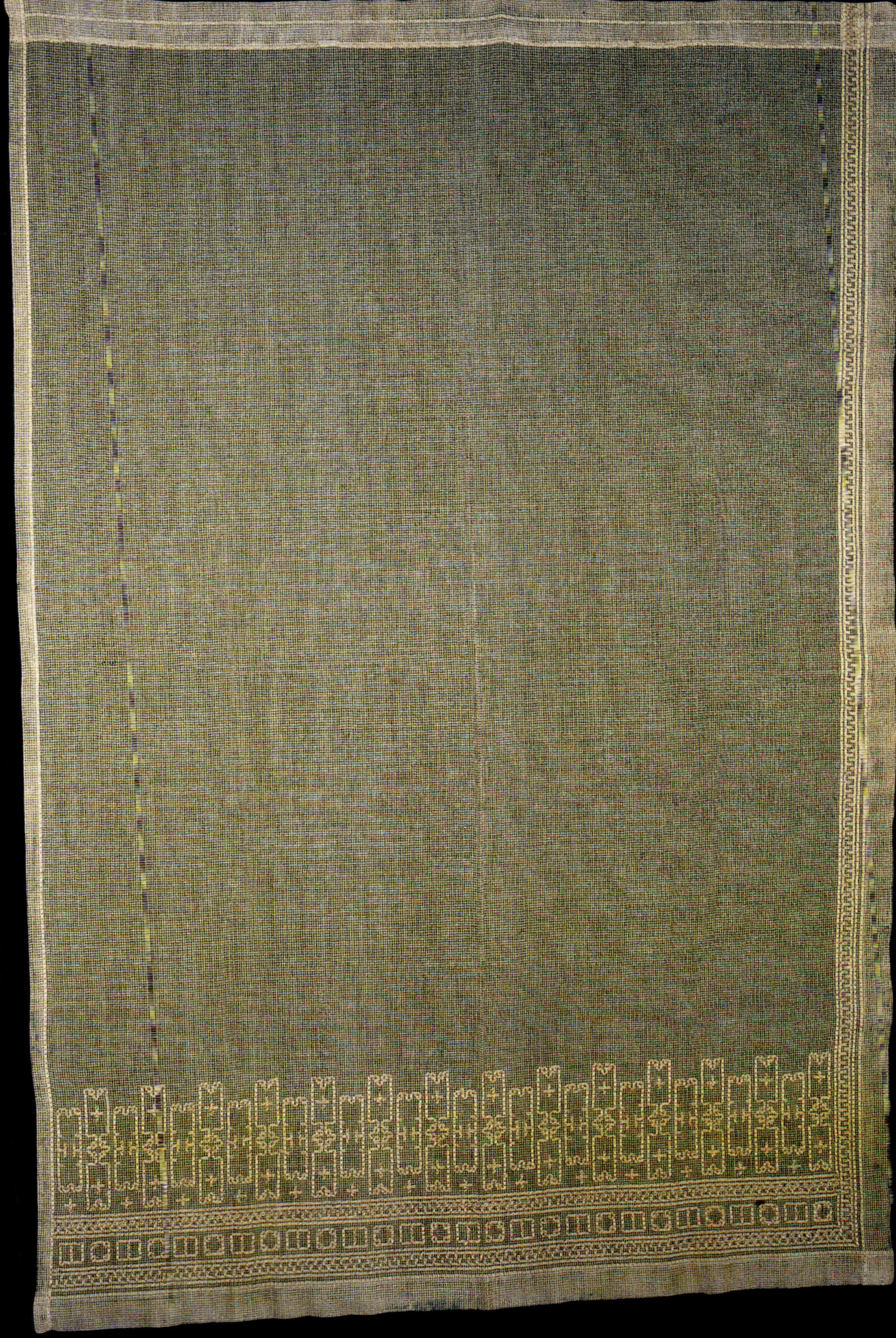

▶
Craftsman Workshops. Craftsman darned net curtain, left panel of a pair. c. 1908–16. Cotton net with linen hand embroidery in darning stitch, 55 × 38" (139.7 × 96.5 cm). Collection JMW Gallery, Boston

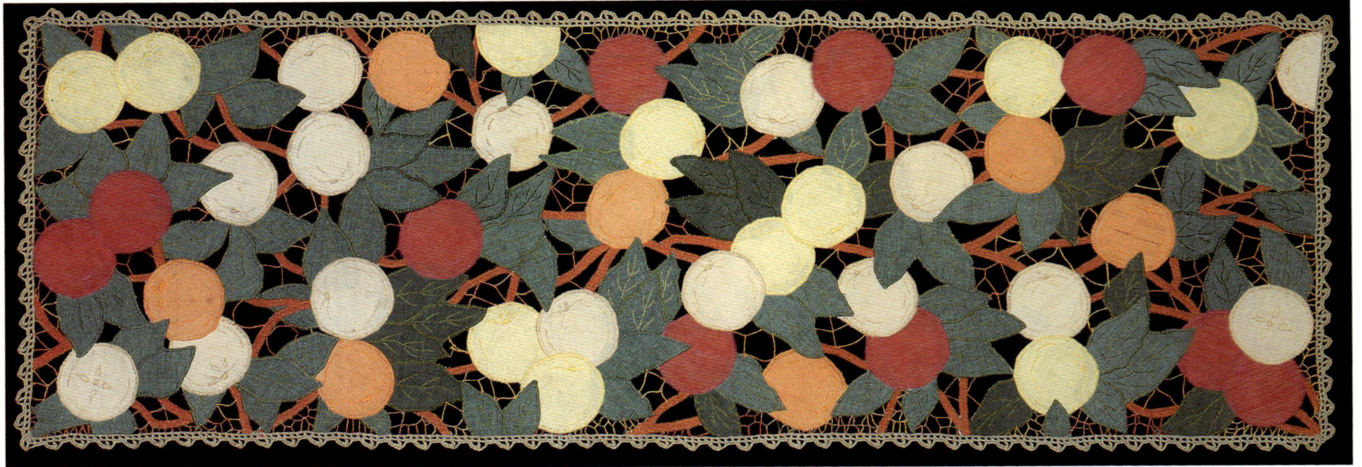

▲
Anonymous. Fruit table linen in appliqué and Spachtel embroidery. c. 1908. Cotton with hand embroidery in buttonhole and stem stitch, 17 × 51" (43.2 × 129.5 cm). Collection Timothy Hansen and Dianne Ayres

Darning work was also carried out on open mesh fabrics for curtains and table linens (pages 171, 173). Craftsman Workshops sold completed curtains and published an in-depth article to aid the housekeeper to make her own.[9] A filet net, with an even, square, open weave, was used for the basic curtain. The embroidery thread recommended was mercerized cotton, approximately the same thickness as the holes of the weave, in white, ecru, or colors fitting to the scheme of the room. A blunt needle was used for the work. Unlike most darning work, which spanned a number of threads before a stitch was taken, the thread was stitched in and out with each mesh, like weaving. While the technique was not unique to Craftsman Workshops, they recommended simple geometric designs that were more in keeping with the Craftsman home and the technical requirements of the darning process itself, rather than the more common ornate floral patterns.

Cross stitch was not commonly used in Arts and Crafts embroidery, but there are some examples of it. In theory, nearly any conventionalized design could be adapted to the grid pattern that the stitch produces (page 172). More appropriately, the design was specifically devised for the geometric nature of the stitch (pages 175, 176).

In drawnwork embroidery, threads are withdrawn from the fabric, either the warp, weft, or both directions, and stitches are taken to form a pattern with the open spaces. It can have very different appearances depending upon the fabric used. It can be worked on the field of a piece of fabric, as shown on the pillow on page 177. When worked toward the edge of the fabric, as a hem finish, the stitch is called hemstitching. On fine table linens this appears as a series of small open-

▶
Anonymous. Conventionalized botanical table runner in cross stitch. Date unknown. Wool with hand embroidery in cotton, 19 × 48" (48.3 × 121.9 cm). Collection Tommy and Beth Ann McPherson

ings (on the bottom left example on page 177). On scrim curtains, a larger swath of threads are drawn, creating longer openings for light to come through (page 160).

Ribbon embroidery enjoyed a revival around 1908, much of the work being done in a more delicate manner, but occasionally the technique was taken up by an artisan working with Arts and Crafts design. Usually the ribbon was not stitched thru the fabric, excepting to fasten the ends, but was laid on top, the loops and twists of the ribbon sewn with small stitches. "The twist of the ribbons where they turn gives interest to the surface of the embroidery, which is always more or less in relief upon the stuff"[10] (page 178).

In addition to the above-mentioned Wallachian, several styles of embroidery were introduced, particularly during the period from 1906 to 1909 when the purveyors of needlework kits had yet to develop the mature conventionalized designs associated with the Arts and Crafts style. Biedermeier (also Biedermair), worked with colored embroidery threads, was based on designs of a seventeenth-century German man. "The name Biedermair . . . means good or simple man. Since its revival, to-day, when one hears so much of the simple life, it is singularly appropriate"[11] (page 179). Other styles included shadow embroidery, stitching on the back of a semi-sheer fabric; eyelet embroidery, the pattern mainly defined by round holes edged with embroidery; and styles imported from Europe: Mountmellick embroidery, elaborate designs using heavy raised stitches on a heavy firm fabric; Spachtel embroidery (page 174), a type of cutwork with ties across the openings; and Shelksting, made up "entirely of Outline stitches, worked closely together. The

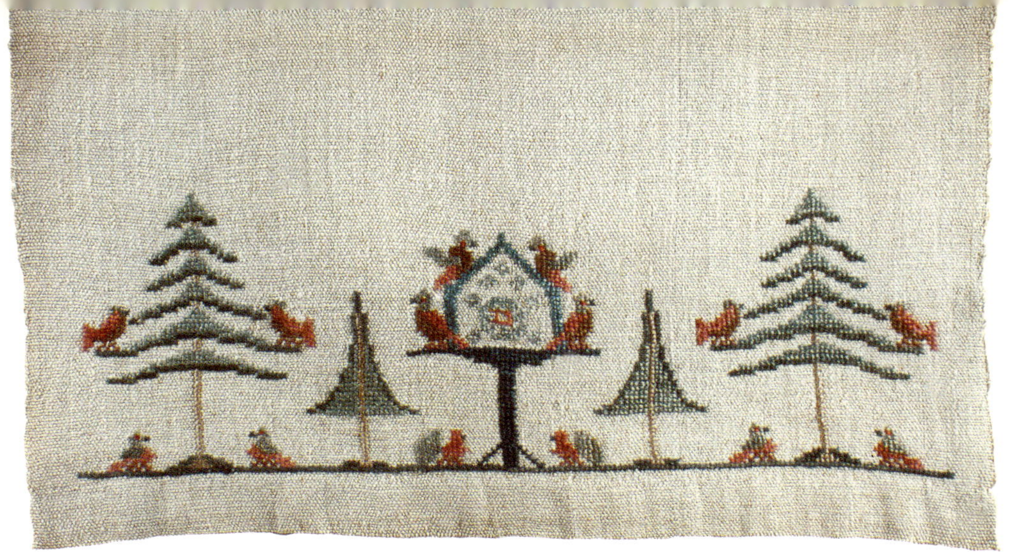

◀
Deerfield Society of Blue and White Needlework. Chairback "Dovecote" or "Aviary." 1909. Linen on linen in cross stitch, 31 × 51¼" (78.7 × 130.2 cm). Memorial Hall Museum Collection, Deerfield, Massachusetts

character of the design depends greatly upon the direction of the Outline stitches; each curve must be carefully followed, and each corner turned sharply."[12]

But all of the discussion was not technical when it came to embroidery. Many writers discussed the philosophical underpinnings. "Embroidery is not one of the things which *has* to be done, and must be done, therefore, as best one can do them. It is in the nature of a superfluity; the excuse for it, that it is beautiful."[13] Clara Kellogg's audience in the professional journal *Interior Decoration* had the means to purchase their embroideries rather than make them, thus if it was to be worth their time, it must be done well.

Nowhere was an article on embroidery as inspirational as in *The Craftsman*:

> No applied art is more interesting in its modern development than embroidery; and it is a good thing that in a department so intimately connected with the home, vital art is taking the place of unimaginative labor. Out of the dead past of "fancy work," a fresh and personal interpretation of beauty has grown; the womanly craft of the needle has again allied itself to art.
>
> All along the lines of needlework sincerity is replacing affectation and making its appeal in embroidery, as in all the decorative arts, to hundreds of thoughtful people. The awakened desire for homes expressive of the simple beauty of life, reaches out for means of setting forth in all the departments of those homes the beauty which is simplicity; so the right kind of house leads on to the right kind of furniture and furnishings, till the reconstructive spirit has brought every detail of a little world into harmony with itself.[14]

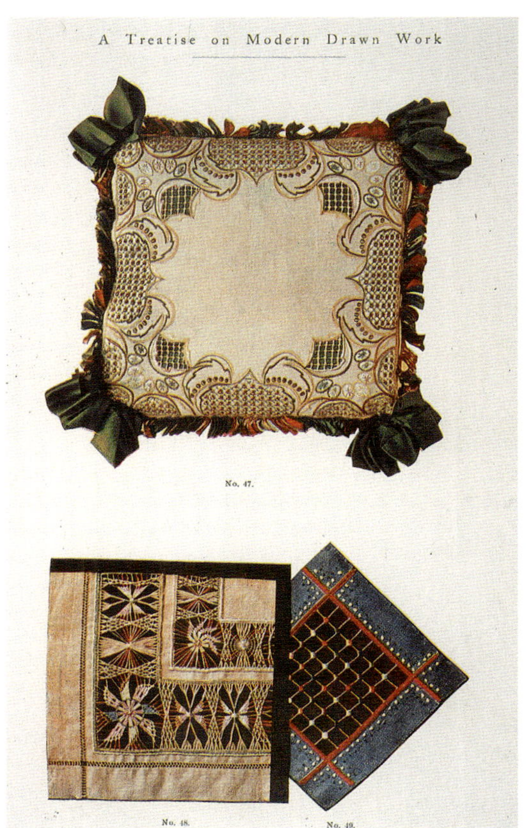

▼
Mrs. Isaac Miller Houck. Illustration from *A Treatise on Modern Drawn Work*. 1904
Often drawn work is seen on white linen, appropriate for the bedroom and some dining rooms in the Arts and Crafts home. Houck developed striking drawn-work designs in bold colors that would be equally at home in the living room or den.

It was not only the theory of embroidery about which *The Craftsman* was so lyrical. Brinley continues:

> To those who are interested in this new embroidery, and have perchance a bedroom which awaits the proper note of decoration, the accompanying designs for bureau scarf, bedspread and curtains may be of value. They are based on the pasture thistle. Sitting under August skies, watching through a golden haze their purple glory, they seem to typify the joy of life,—and not, as their name in Latin signifies, "Tribulation,"—the joy that can spring up in stony places, with hardly a grain of comfort to give foothold! These purple blossoms, beloved of bees and butterflies, held in their green vases of classic shape, have been, of course, conventionalized, and fitted to their various positions.

Craftsman Workshops developed a unique style that they originally promoted as "peasant embroidery." The work was designed to be "easily executed by needlewomen with no special training" and, in harmony with the coarse linen, to be worked with "slight irregularity and imperfection—not to say carelessness—were it only to avoid the appearance of machine-wrought embroidery."[15] They dropped this term quickly in reference to the needlework from their own workshops—possibly the upwardly mobile of the early twentieth century did not like to think of themselves in terms of peasantry—but other sources perpetuated the term.

"Surely no name ever fitted better the form of decorative art it was intended to designate than 'peasant embroidery' now being brought to the attention of the public by some of the best designers. There is a simplicity and a strength about the designs employed and the manner in

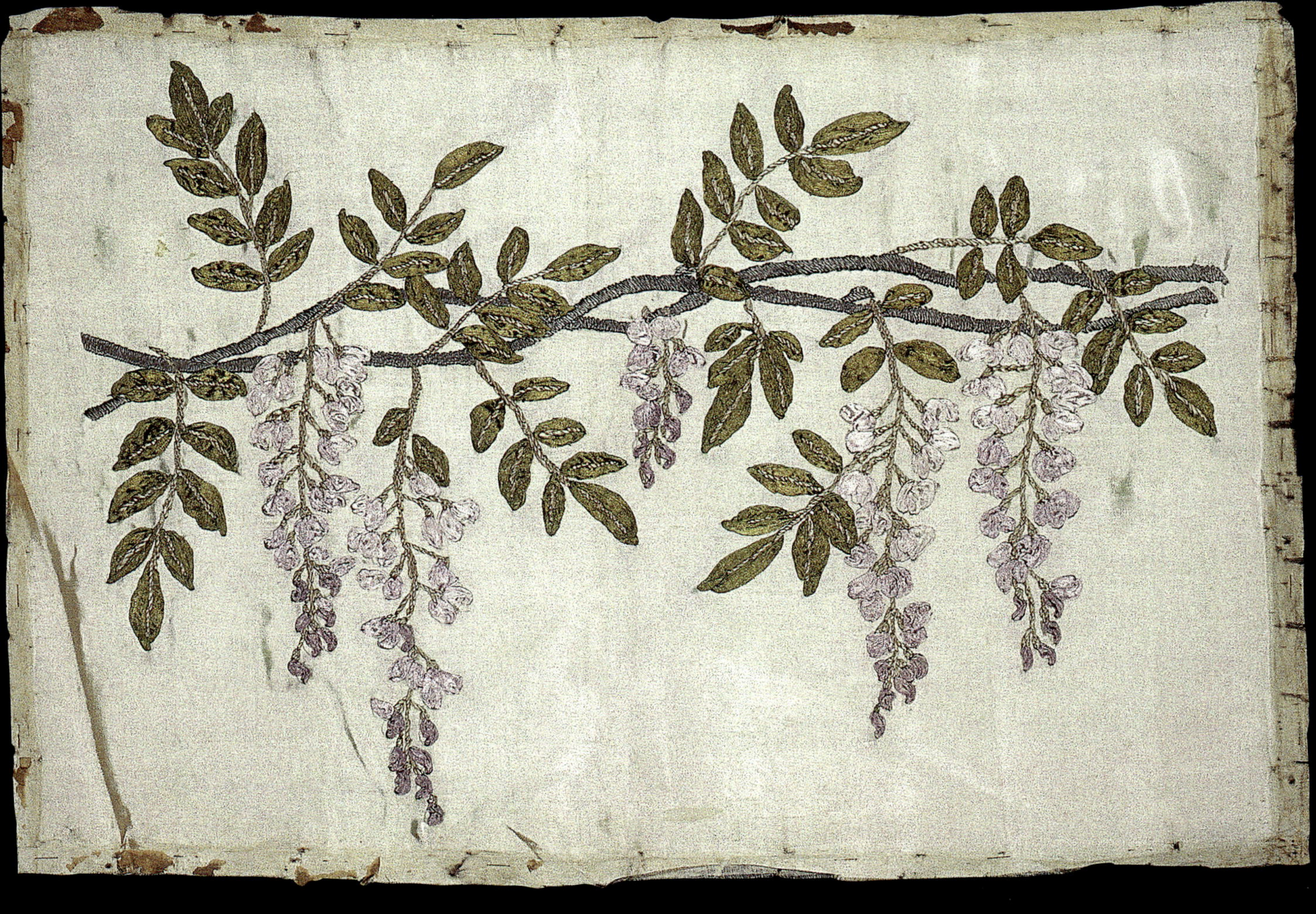

▲

Anonymous. Wisteria panel in ribbon embroidery. c. 1912. Silk with silk ribbon and har
embroidery, 19 × 27" (48.3 × 68.6 cm). Collection Timothy Hansen and Dianne Ayres

Some of the colors in this piece have faded; the flowers were originally shades from lil
intense purple, and the stem-stitch embroidery between the flowers and the leaves w

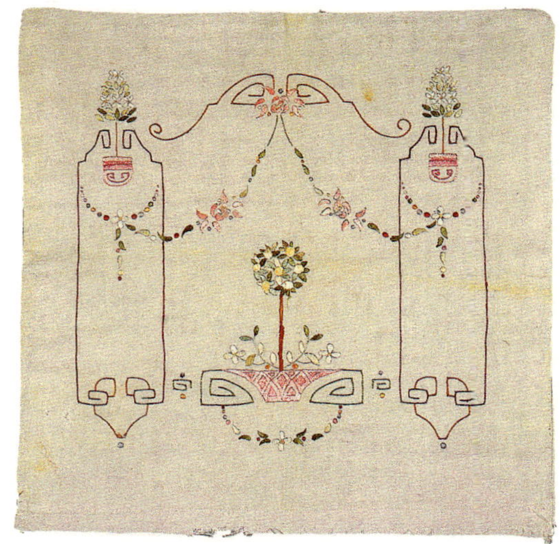

▶
Anonymous. Biedermeier pillow. c. 1909. Linen with silk hand embroidery in satin stitch and stem stitch, 19 × 19" (48.7 × 48.7 cm). Collection Tommy and Beth Ann McPherson

which they are worked out that brings back recollections of the golden age of craftsmanship, when artist and artisan were one, and when each piece of work had in it the significance of individuality."[16] The designs shown for portieres have "an equally vivid expression" of simplicity and massiveness as the newly emerging furniture and architecture.

Appliqué

Peasant embroidery often incorporated appliqué as a method to quickly achieve large areas of color. Appliqué is essentially the application of one piece of fabric on top of the base fabric. Usually the appliqué fabric is lighter in weight than the base cloth but, depending on the desired effect, the opposite may be done. For some pieces, particularly quilts, the edges of the appliqué are simply turned under and hidden stitches secure it to the base cloth. In Arts and Crafts textiles, however, appliqué was usually worked in conjunction with embroidery along the edges.

The edge embroidery could be done in satin stitch—this being most typical of the Glasgow style work—or couching stitch. Craftsman workshops did a variation of couching, using a blanket stitch to fasten the laid threads (page 180). Embroidery could also be stitched throughout the appliqué to define more lines of a design, but: "It must, nevertheless, be borne in mind that appliqué work is dependent on its outline for much of its beauty. The outline, therefore, should be well defined, and form part of the design, as lead lines do in stained glass."[17]

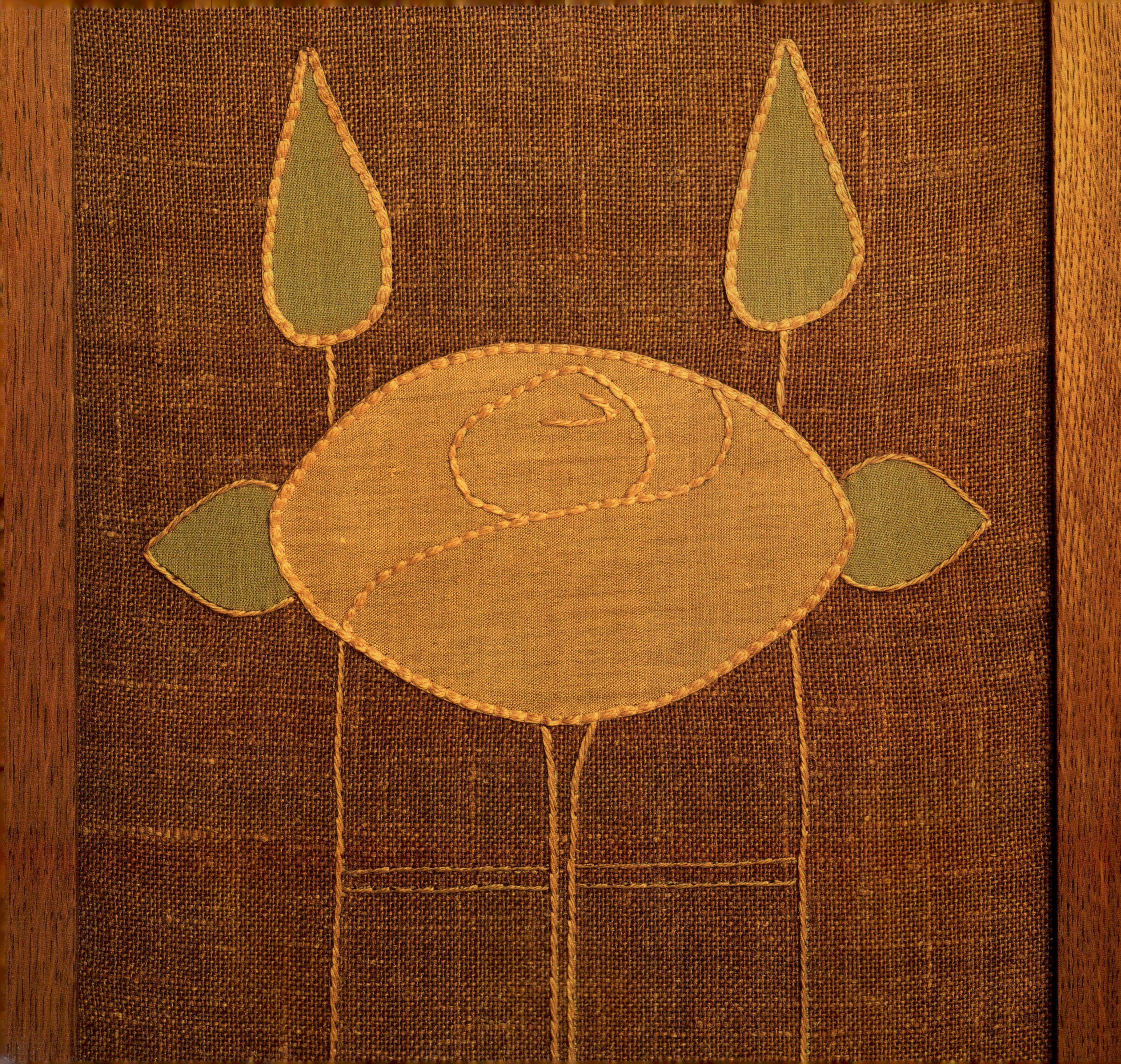

◀
Craftsman Workshops. Detail of three-panel folding screen with conventional rose design. 1902–16. Flax and jute "Craftsman canvas" with linen appliqué and hand embroidery. See illustration on page 131. Marrin Collection
Much of the appliqué work from the Craftsman Workshops is couched with a blanket stitch, as seen here.

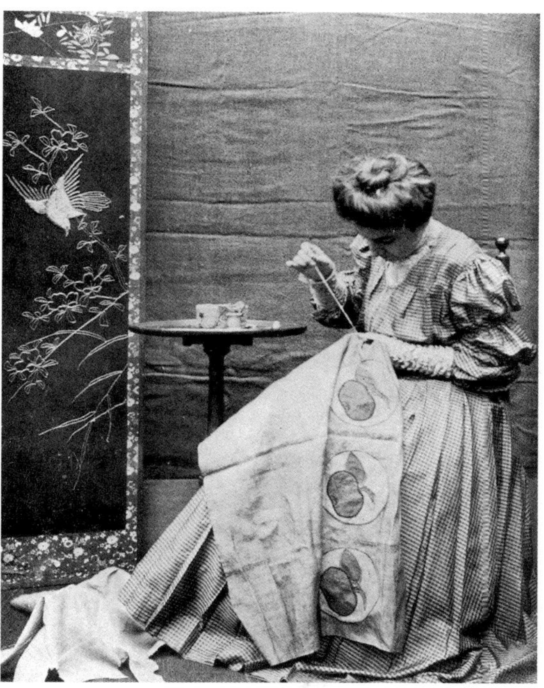

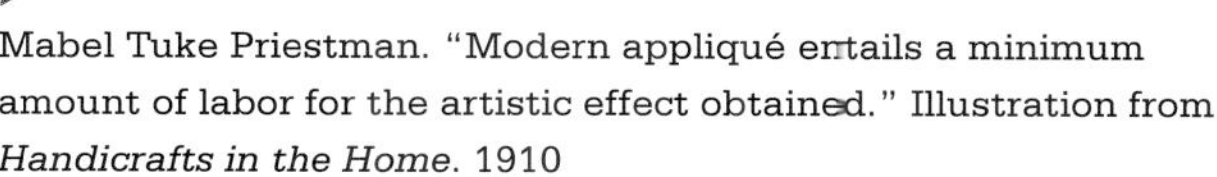

▶
Mabel Tuke Priestman. "Modern appliqué entails a minimum amount of labor for the artistic effect obtained." Illustration from *Handicrafts in the Home*. 1910

It was a widely practiced technique and useful for many types of items. "Beautiful hangings, table covers, pillows, and screens may be made of this most effective work . . . nothing could be more thoroughly in keeping with the popular Mission furnishings."[18] Few pieces with appliqué survive from the period, its somewhat fragile nature hastening its demise.

Stenciling

"The artistic stencil, long known to decorative art in Japan, Germany and England, did not come into general use in this country until the arts and crafts introduced it about three years ago."[19] This statement, published in 1908 in *The Good Housekeeping Manual of Home Handicraft*, may indicate a somewhat myopic view. Victorian Americans had frequently stenciled their interiors, and the budding Arts and Crafts guilds around the country usually included stencil artists in their ranks, but it is true that the early part of the twentieth century did see a blossoming in the use of stencils. The December 1903 issue of *The Craftsman* illustrated stenciled wall friezes of fabric and a portiere. In subsequent issues stenciling migrated to pillows and curtains, first in combination with embroidery, and then used alone. From 1906 through the teens, *The Ladies' Home Journal*, *The Modern Priscilla*, *Home Needlework*, and many other magazines widely promoted

◀
Deerfield Society of Blue and White Needlework. Table Square "Pomegranates." 1900–16. Appliqué and embroidery on linen, 15 × 15½" (38.1 × 39.4 cm). Memorial Hall Museum Collection, Deerfield, Massachusetts

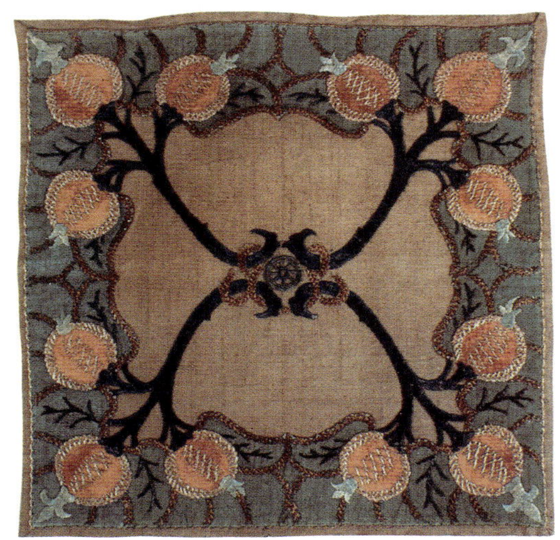

stenciling as being a quick method to ornament furnishings for the Arts and Crafts home and "one of the most easily learned of the useful arts."[20] They published how-to articles and often offered for sale stencils of the designs they illustrated.

Stencils could be purchased, either individually or in sets, sometimes including paints and brushes. Many companies offered the designs as perforated patterns that needed to be transferred to stencil paper, or as cut stencils. Stencils were relatively inexpensive: one eight-by-ten-inch perforated floral pattern from Samuel Pryor, Art Designer, cost fifteen cents, whereas the cut stencil was fifty cents. Other companies that primarily sold stencils and stencil designs were: Herrick Designs and Blue Label Stencil Works, both of Chicago; National Stencil Company, Columbus, Ohio; Perforated Pattern Company, New Haven, Connecticut; The Bell Company and the French Art Stencil Company, both of New York City; and Arthur Capper, Publisher, Topeka, Kansas. Possibly the largest selection of stencils was offered by H. Roessing of Chicago; its 1921 catalog of "Excelsior Fresco Stencils" contains more than twenty-four hundred designs, many of which were appropriate for use on textiles. The Articraft Company of Springfield, Massachusetts, and the Tapestry Paint and Stencil Company of Chicago offered fabrics, stencils, paints, finished stenciled table linens, pillow tops, and curtains. Many of the major paint companies also offered stencils, initially to provide competition with wallpaper companies for those who desired patterned walls, but they soon recognized the market for those stenciling on fabric as well.

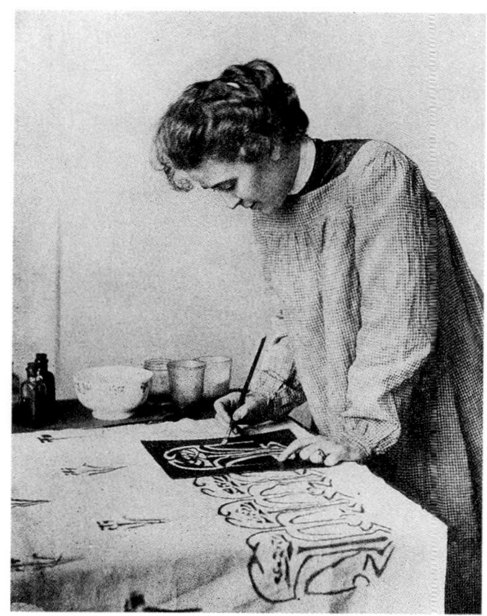

▶
Phelps Publishing Company. "Stenciling, Applying the Color to a Design." Illustration from *The Good Housekeeping Manual of Home Handicraft.* 1908

Stenciling was also employed by artists, the technique lending itself to limited-edition items or a single item with a repeating pattern (pages 185, 186). Those skilled at the design, color use, and workmanship required for the technique could make "good money," but "buying ready-made designs would be out of the question, for her work should be an expression of herself, and must be individual to obtain recognition."[21] While most stencil artists remained anonymous, a few did obtain some recognition through the books and magazine articles of Mable Tuke Priestman: namely, Anna Duane, Elma S. Ritter, and Hanley H. Parker (page 184).[22] Ritter and Duane also published articles themselves on the craft.[23]

The economy of stenciling made it popular for the furnishing of a new home, since the types of items it was useful for—curtains, pillows, and other textiles—were usually left for last, when the budget had been exhausted. It also afforded the middle-class home unique items for little expense, particularly when the homemaker designed the stencil herself.

For home crafters who wished to make their own designs but were less than artistic, it was suggested to look at designs from wallpaper (embroidery, china painting) and adapt them to the technique by breaking the design into cut-out areas with sufficient ties for the stencil paper to hold together. At the same time, the ties needed to be integrated into the design. By 1906, a pre-coated paper was sold at artists' supply stores; for those who were unable to procure it, directions were given for making manila paper water resistant by soaking it in linseed oil, turpentine, and Japan drier, or coating it with shellac after the design was cut out. Cutting the stencil

▼ Mabel Tuke Priestman. "Individuality in Stenciling." Illustration from *The House Beautiful*. September 1910

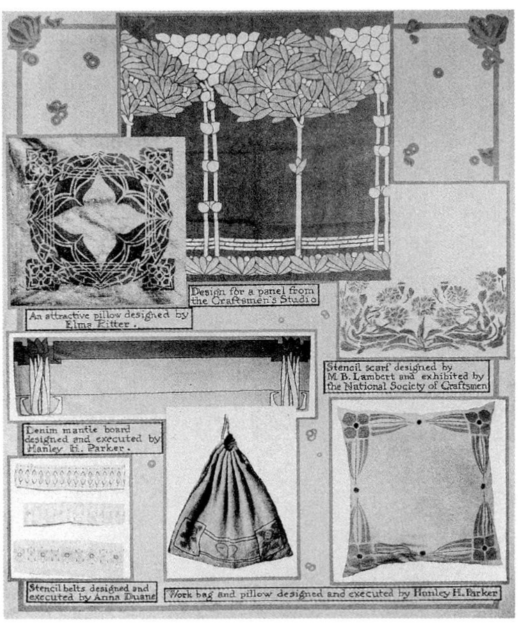

was an arduous task as well, since most home crafters on a budget would not have purchased a special weighted stencil knife but instead would have used a penknife. These tasks combined made purchasing a ready-cut stencil quite appealing.

Conventionalized designs particularly lent themselves to stenciling; in fact, the act of adapting a design to the technique often further conventionalizes the design. Designs inspired from nature—flowers, leaves, insects and birds—and geometric patterns were employed. The scale at which stenciling was done was also versatile. The area of design could be from a fraction of an inch up to quite large—it was not uncommon for a stencil to be twenty-four to thirty-six inches in its largest dimension. Often the stencil was made for one repeat of a continuous design. Larger areas could also be decorated with a set of coordinated stencils—with corner, end, and field, or repeating, elements.

Both dyes and paints were used, depending on the individual's preference and the type of item being stenciled. Dyes were available in powder form but the tubes were often preferred for their convenience. The concentrated dye was mixed with water; after dipping the brush, most of the liquid needed to be blotted off before stenciling lest it bleed under the stencil edges and spoil the design. Dyes were recommended for use on thin fabrics. To try to make them resistant to fading and washing out, it was suggested to add the white of one egg or to steam the stenciled fabric with a hot iron, but often the process was not successful. For linen, paints were required, as it did not take the dye well. Sherwin-Williams and other paint companies offered formulations

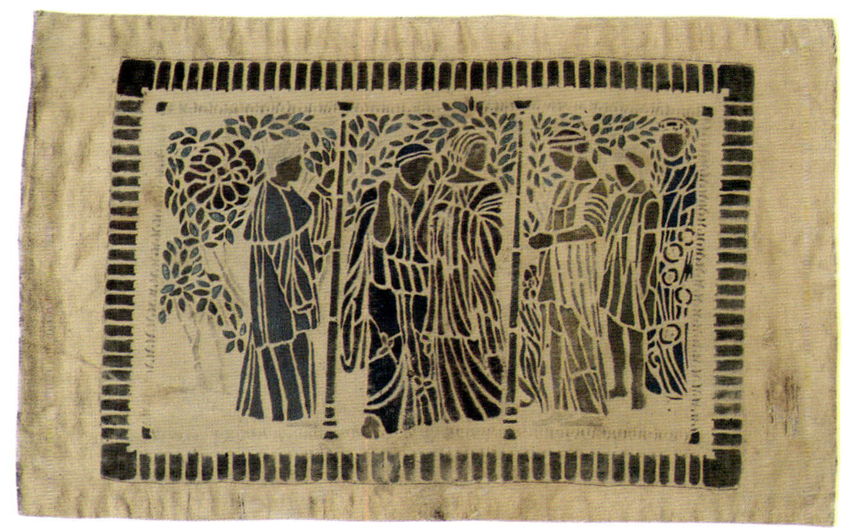

▶
Anonymous. Triptych. c. 1910. Stenciled silk, 16¼ × 25¼" (41.3 × 64.8 cm). Collection Caro Macpherson

specifically for stenciling but often artists' oil paint was used. Tips for using oil paints varied from squeezing it onto blotting paper to allow the oil to be absorbed, to adding turpentine, benzene, gasoline, or chemicals sold to specifically to improve colorfastness. The creamy consistency of oil paints made them more controllable than dyes but required a firmer hand, often tiring the worker on a large project.

One article in *The Modern Priscilla* promotes the use of crayons for use in stenciling, particularly on a cotton crepe fabric. This article is accompanied on the page with advertisements for "'Crayola' for Stenciling and for Arts and Crafts" and "Serpentine Crepe" (page 187). This blatant promotion did not seem to have converted many to the use of crayons for stenciling but later crayons found a new niche in "Crayonex" wall hangings (page 50 bottom).

In general, little paint was to be put on the surface of the fabric, so that it retained its original hand, i.e. its texture and suppleness. For some, the aim was to achieve an even color, although for others the unevenness inherent in the process was part of its charm. This, along with the nature of the design and the ability to shade or blend colors are keys in identifying stenciled textiles. In working multiple colors on a leaf form, Priestman suggested, "The less care given to shading the better; it should look haphazard, like the turning autumn leaves on the trees."[24]

She also advised, "The intentional effacing of the ties should never be done. The frank acceptance of the limitations of a stencil print is craftsmanlike, and makes the stencil more interesting."[25] This, apparently, was a hot debate among decorators. Vanderwalker, in *New Stencils*

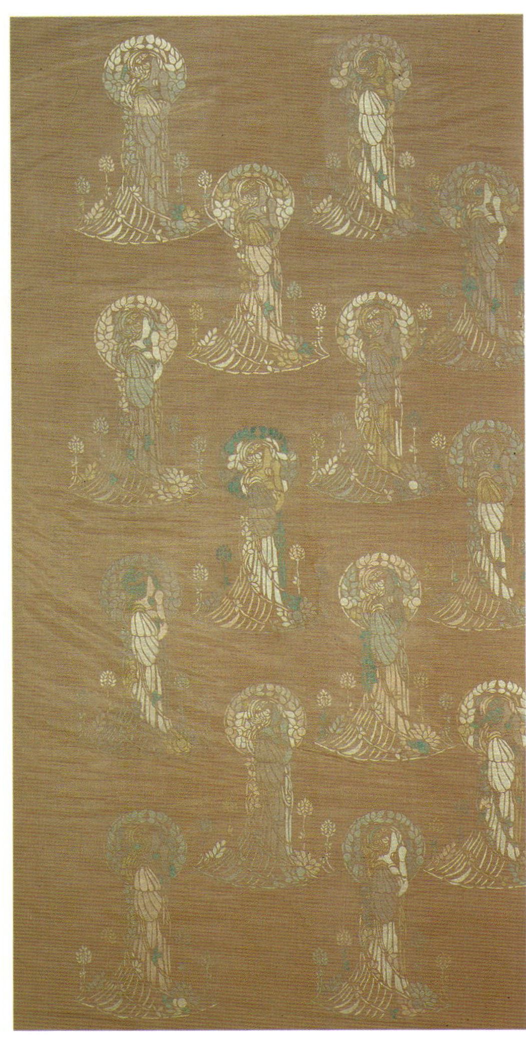

◀
Attributed to Lucia Mathews. Piano cover. c. 1910. Stenciled silk. Collection Oakland Museum of California, Gift of Concours d'Antiques

and Their Use, agreed in principle but makes the exception for some Greek key designs that would otherwise appear unfinished.

As in most arts, knowing when to stop and not overworking was an integral factor in the success of stenciling, both in the process itself and in the extent to which it was employed in a room. Hardly any item escaped the pursuit of the avid stenciler (page 189 top). In addition to embellishing curtains, pillows, table and bed linens, stenciling was employed for wall frieze fabric panels, upholstered furniture, floor mats, and myriad other objects. Stenciling was also suggested for use on seasonal Christmas items, both for its quick results and economy as well as its environmental impact: "the ideal decoration[s] for this season [are] holly, mistletoe, running cedar, ferns and laurel, all of which are delightfully suggestive of the Yule-tide; but it is not always practical to obtain these living greens, and even if it were and every family took a sufficient quantity the woods would soon be denuded, so for more than one reason we have to resort to some other method of expression."[26] Stenciling allowed both the artist and the craftsperson to express themselves and represent nature in a range of moods.

Block Printing

Like stenciling, block printing on fabric had deep historical roots by the turn of the century and was utilized in inventive ways by American artisans. It did not reach the same wide popular usage, however, since the carving of blocks was a greater challenge and required tools less

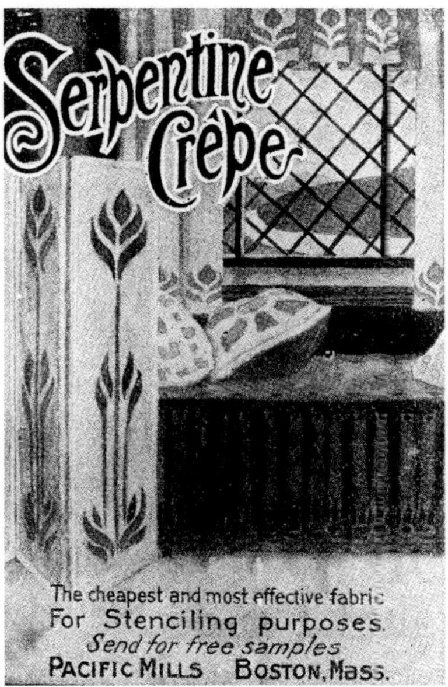

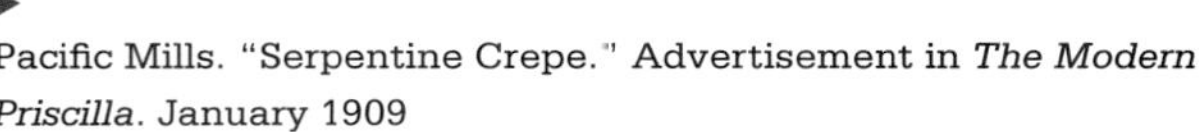
▶
Pacific Mills. "Serpentine Crepe." Advertisement in *The Modern Priscilla*. January 1909

commonly found in the home. Unlike stenciling, companies did not offer pre-cut designs for the technique, and few magazine articles were published to encourage the home crafter to try her hand at the art.

Still, Mable Tuke Priestman, the ever-ardent promoter of handicrafts, included sections on the technique in both *Handicrafts in the Home* and *Art and Economy in Home Decoration*. She reports that, once the block is cut, the printing takes about one-third the time of stenciling, the results being somewhat similar but not as sharp and clear, giving an iridescent effect. She describes the traditional process of transferring the design to a block of holly, boxwood, maple, or basswood that has been planed and sand-papered and cutting it with a sharp knife or carving tools. A thick pad of muslin was then made, to which the color, in a creamy consistency, was applied. Oil paints were preferred for their permanence but dyes were also recommended. Once the pores of the block were filled with the color, the printing proceeded. Muslin, denims, monk's cloth and all types of linen, especially Russian crash, were recommended fabrics for block printing. For fine materials, the pressure as applied by hand was sufficient but for those of a coarser texture the block was struck with a mallet to transfer the color. Priestman acknowledges some of the anxiety that probably prevented many from exploring the technique. "It takes a little nerve at first to print, as, of course, the block cannot be moved when it has once touched the fabric."[27] But she also attempts to reassure those with less skill in obtaining consistent results: "the patterning with a block has the charm of uncertainty about it as to the result of each impress."[28]

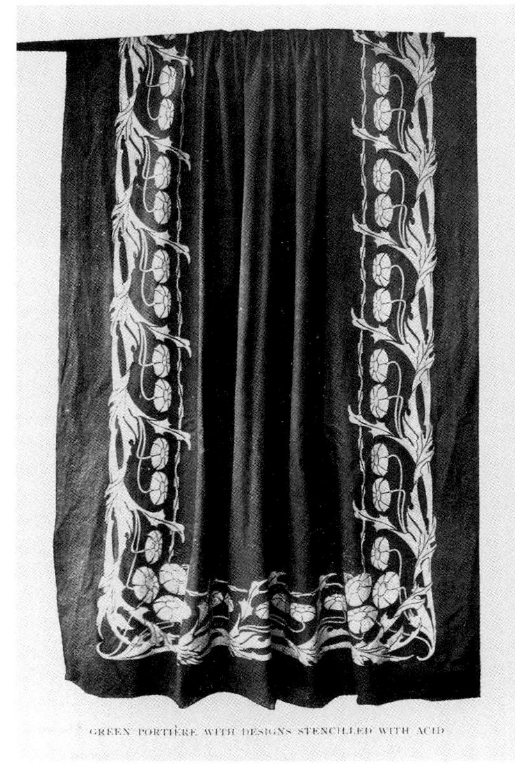

◄
Mabel Tuke Priestman. "Green Portiere with Designs Stenciled with Acid." Illustration from *Handicrafts in the Home*. 1910

Other sources[29] suggested, instead of carving the design from a block of wood, cutting it from a thin piece of wood with a fret saw or from a thick felt and attaching it to a block. This method was particularly preferred when block printing was employed in the classroom. Block printing provided not only a method to ornament objects but was also useful in exploring design principles by experimenting with various arrangements of colors and masses in repeating patterns. The Waldcraft Studios offered instruction manuals and supplies to print with pegs or sticks in various geometric shapes. These were useful in the beginning study of design to teach the arrangement of colors and masses, but could also be utilized as elements in the design of more complex patterns on textiles.

The method of inking the block on a pad of color resulted in the printing of one color. The majority of block printing on textiles was of a single color. For designs of multiple colors, a set of blocks was made, one each for each individual color area. Less commonly, the colors were painted directly on the block, as was sometimes done in fine-art block printing. This allowed gradations of colors to be printed, and each print was unique (page 190).

Today, distinguishing a block-printed fabric from one made by other techniques is not always a simple task. While designs for block printing were not as restricted as those for stenciling, which required ties, often similar designs were used. The previously mentioned iridescence is one hint, although it is not universally found in all block printing. Depending on the workers' hand, the printed area may show a darkening around the perimeter where more paint built up on the cut edge of the design. But, in general, finding identifiable block-printed period textiles is rare.

▶
Jessie Tarbox Beals. Room stenciled in rose design. Illustration in "Stenciled Furnishings for a Girl's Room." *The Modern Priscilla*. November 1913

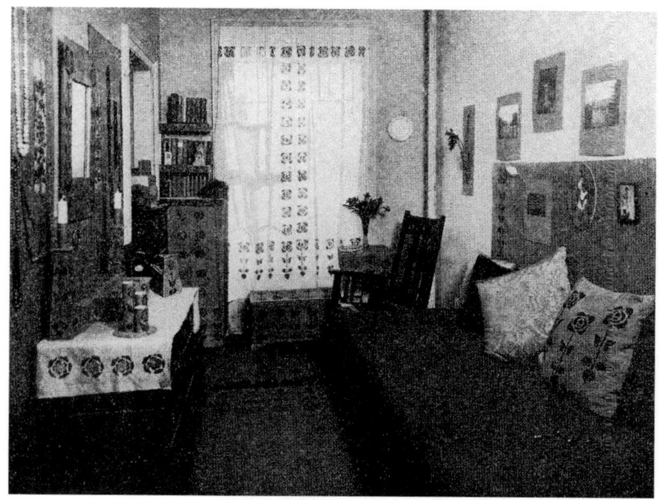

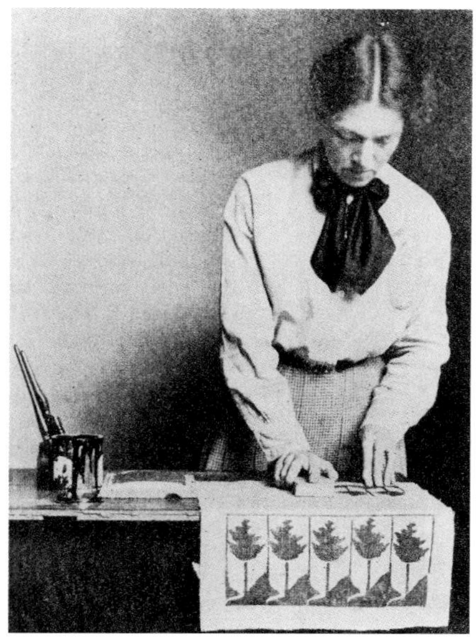

▲
Phelps Publishing Company. "Printing with the Wood Block." Illustration from *The Good Housekeeping Manual of Home Handicraft*. 1908

Batik

In 1908 Mabel Tuke Priestman reported, "Craftworkers are beginning to do a modern form of Batik. . . . This industry is only in its infancy in America, but it is an interesting field open for immense developments."[30] Two years later, she gave a brief description of the process and discussed the work of Mrs. Wegerif Granestein in Holland, suggesting that craftworkers in this country should develop designs for batik from American Indian motifs.[31] Preistman's earlier reference was probably to the work of Amy Mali Hicks of New York. Hicks had a studio and exhibited in the Arts and Crafts Society in New York and at the National Arts Club.[32] Her earlier work was a variation of batik, known today as tie-dye.[33] While Hicks also published on the subject,[34] it was another Dutch person, Pieter Mijer, who became the main proponent of batik in America. Mijer spent his childhood in Java, where batik had been practiced for centuries. His book, *Batiks, and How to Make Them*, first published in 1919, became the standard reference on the subject for a generation of craftsworkers.

Batik involves applying a dye-resistant substance onto fabric, dyeing the fabric, and then removing the resist. The process is repeated for each color of the design, covering those areas which are not to take that particular color. The resist substance, usually a combination of beeswax and paraffin, was applied with a brush or with a *tjanting*—a special tool with a spout and a reservoir for the hot wax. The European and American method progresses from the lighter to the darker colors, adding resist between successive dye baths. When a piece incorporates different

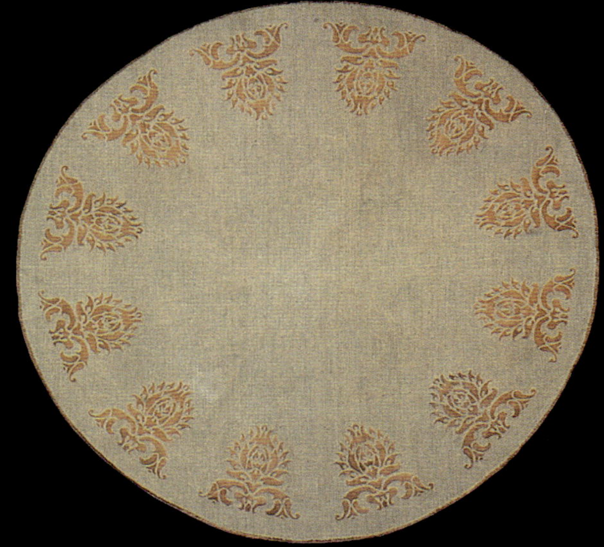

▲
Anonymous. Table centerpiece. c. 1910. Linen with block printing and hand-embroidered hem in cotton, buttonhole stitch, 36" (91.4 cm) diam. Collection Tommy and Beth Ann McPherson

▼
Oakley. Block-printed panel, sea horse, fish, and jellyfish with seaweed. Date Unknown. 36 × 25" (91.4 × 63.5 cm). Collection Tommy and Beth Ann McPherson

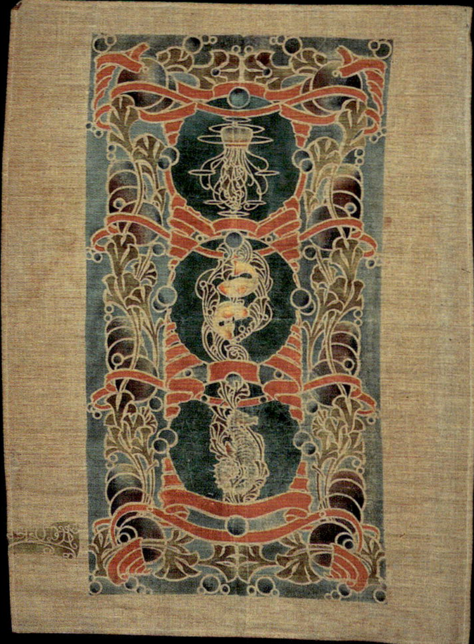

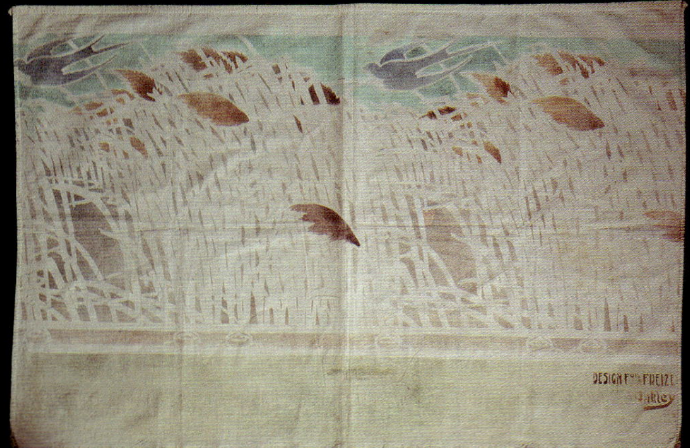

◄
Oakley. Block-printed freize. Date unknown. 24 × 35" (61 × 89 cm). Collection Crab Tree Farm

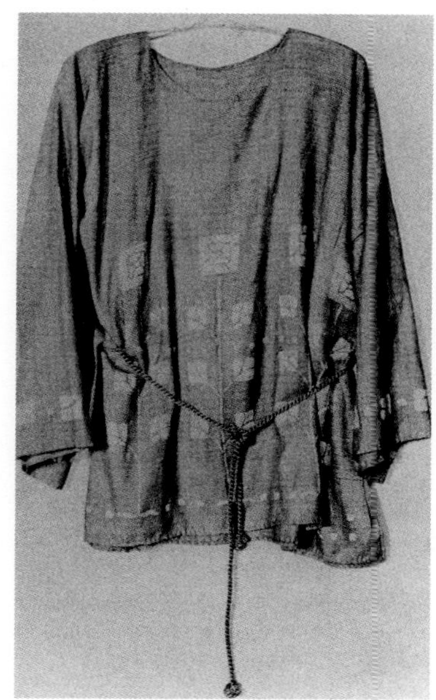

▶
Miss Blanche Stillson. Batiked blouse. Illustrated in *Batik and Other Patten Dyeing*. 1920

families of color, the color from previously dyed areas is removed and the procedure continued in the new color range. As in block printing, single-color projects are the simplest to carry out. Batiks with multiple colors require a great amount of planning.

Mijer cautions, "As with any other art or craft, one needs to study the medium before using it and another fact that has only been too often forgotten, is, that batik has design and knowledge of colour as its foundation and I would like to advise readers who have not studied these essentials, to leave batik alone until they have acquired some understanding to them."[35] For the most part, the hobbyist and popular magazines did "leave batik alone," its messiness and use of uncommon tools probably being more of a barrier than their lack of design acumen. Batik was practiced on a limited scale in the public schools, primarily promoted by the Waldcraft Company of Indianapolis, which illustrates a number of successful projects by high school students in its book, *Batik and other Pattern Dyeing*.

The process lent itself to designs ranging from a simple motif to pictorial scenes. In addition to its use for wall hangings and other household items, batik was often employed for articles of clothing, its boldly patterned effect harmonizing well with the unfitted, loose shapes of apparel of the late teens and twenties (above).

A number of artists trained in the Arts and Crafts school of design also worked in batik into the 1930s and beyond, some transitioning to either avant-garde or period revival styles, and others continuing to work in the Arts and Crafts style. Among them are Lydia Bush-Brown,[36]

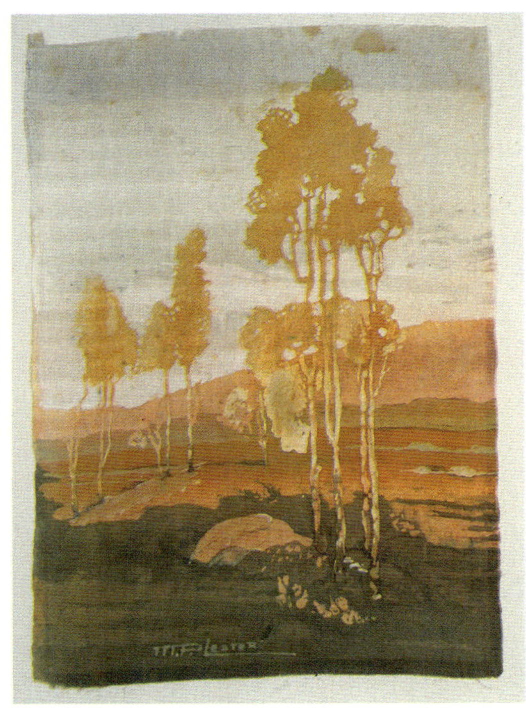

◀
Marian Plummer Lester. Batik of landscape with eucalyptus trees. c. 1931–40. Batik dye on silk. 15 × 10½" (38.1 × 26.7 cm). Collection San Diego Historical Society; Gift of Jim Stelluti

who was trained at Pratt Institute and probably learned the technique from Charles Pellew. Pellew was a chemist at Columbia University who published a series of articles on dyeing and the batik process in *The Craftsman*[37] and offered seminars to artists on the those topics.

Marguerite Thompson Zorach also explored the technique extensively, creating artistic "Bohemian" clothing and wall hangings, possibly for use as theatrical backdrops. Batik items won top prizes in a series of competitions organized by *Women's Wear* between 1916 and 1920. At least two progressive-minded textile manufacturers, Cheney Brothers and H. R. Mallinson, took notice and soon offered commercial printed fabric with batik style patterns.[38] But Mijer cautioned against the use of batik for the commercial production of materials, concerned that it would lose its connection with the hand of the artist.

Hand Weaving

The turn of the twentieth century saw a renewed interest in hand weaving, both in the revival of past styles and in new work done following the principles of Arts and Crafts design. Woven coverlets and runners, typically white with blue, but sometimes woven in other color combinations, became very popular (page 65 bottom). Associated with the Colonial era, their often geometric designs coordinated well with Arts and Crafts furniture. Some illustrations from Craftsman Workshops show woven coverlets on beds. For more information on the hand-weaving revival, see Chapter 1.

▼
Elizabeth Fox Herr. Batik of woman reading a book. c. 1914–21. Batik on velvet, 26 × 14" (66 × 35.6 cm). Collection Timothy Hansen and Dianne Ayres

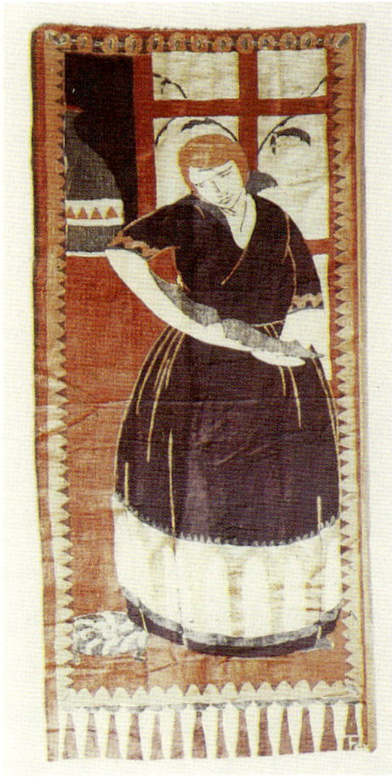

Among the few weavers to embrace the new design principles of the Arts and Crafts style, Anna Nott Shook was influential. She haled from Missouri and the Black Hills of South Dakota, where she owned and operated a chain of specialty fabric stores. She then set up Homekraft Studios in Peekskill, New York, to teach weaving and had a studio in New York City. She also taught through correspondence courses, wrote numerous magazine articles, and in 1928 wrote *The Book of Weaving*. The illustrations in the book are mostly the work of her students, and many show a sophisticated use of design and color (page 195 bottom). She also rightly recognized the importance of this work.

> Our pioneer grandmothers, toiling over heavy looms to make the necessary clothing for their families, would hardly understand the reverence with which we speak of the handmade product. . . . Within the memory of most of us home-weaving was held in little esteem. No more than fifty-five years ago weaving in the home was considered a petty economy of which to be ashamed. Do you remember the old rag-carpets, woven on one of those clap-trap looms which made more noise than an elevated train? . . . This was the lowest ebb in the art, to be followed by the present revival.[39]

Another artisan weaver was Kate Watson of Chicago. Designs for her rugs, laundry bags, and pillows were inspired by Peruvian, Norwegian, and Egyptian art, but her work was described as "especially attractive in combination with furniture of the mission or craftsman types; its rich, subdued coloring and sturdy texture harmonizing with the ample lines and rich, wood-tones of chair and settle"[40] (page 195 top).

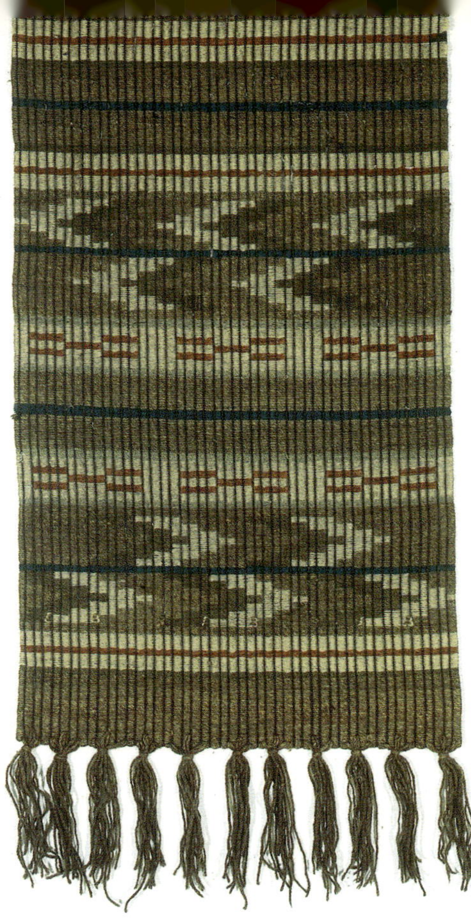

▲
Anonymous. Handwoven runner. Date unknown. Wool, 16 × 64" (40.6 × 162.6 cm). Collection Beth Ann and Tommy McPherson

▶
Mrs. Kate Watson. Rug with a tree border. Handwoven in light tan, brown, and green. Illustrated in Harriet Joor's "An Artist of the Loom." *The House Beautiful.* July 1909

Many weavings of the era, if found today, may go unrecognized for their importance within the Arts and Crafts movement. For pieces whose provenance is lost, the continuity of design and the subtle simplicity that made them so appropriate to the period make identification today difficult. To establish an attribution in textiles, so often an anonymous art, requires a sensibility that comes only with longstanding experience. For weavings with no pattern, we are left only to judge the qualities of the fibers and threads and their apparent age. Like any living being, time can be kind or harsh, complicating this inexact science.

Quilting

While the majority of Mable Tuke Priestman's *Handicrafts in the Home* (1908) is directed toward middle-class women looking for a leisure pursuit and to those who wish to earn a living from their crafts, the short chapter on "Old-Time Quilting" primarily imparts an appreciation of quilts that readers may have inherited from their grandmothers. She also acknowledges the role quilts played in the social interactions of Colonial times and the more recent past, but views the activity as too time-consuming for her contemporaries. While quilt work was at an ebb in its popularity during the Arts and Crafts period, the movement fostered achievements that brought about the popular revival of quilting for decades to follow.

Certainly, quilts were made, particularly in the South, where "from the cradle to the grave the women make quilts," to quote Elizabeth Daingerfield,[41] author of "Patch Quilts and Philosophy,"

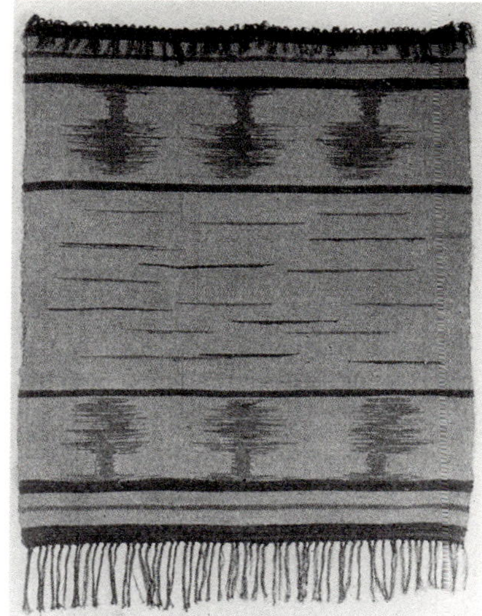

▼

Top left: Mable Frerich. "The Bridge." Handwoven silk and wool. Top right: Lamp shade texture. Handwoven silk and wool, in design stitch and tapestry. Bottom left: Mable Frerich. "Autumn Tree." Handwoven silk and artificial silk. Bottom right: Fine linen piece, mounted on neutral background. Handwoven linen and silk. Illustration from Anna Nott Shook's *The Book of Weaving*. 1928

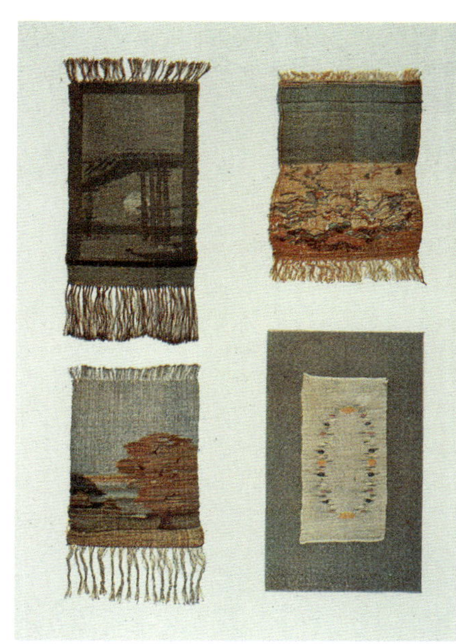

published in *The Craftsman* in August of 1908. She continues:

> To every mountain woman her piece quilts are her daily interest, but her patch quilts are her glory. . . . The piece quilt, of course, is made of scraps, and its beauty or ugliness depends upon the material and colors that come to hand, the intricacy of the design and one's skill in executing it. I think much character building must be done while hand and eye cooperate to make, for example, a Star quilt, with its endless points for fitting and joining. But a patch quilt is a more ambitious affair. For this the pattern is cut from the whole piece and appliquéd on unbleached cotton. The colors used are commonly oil red, oil green and a certain rather violent yellow, and sometimes indigo blue. These and these only are considered reliable enough for a patch quilt, which is made for the generations that come after.

This article and two subsequent articles in *Ladies' Home Journal* by Daingerfield[42] are illustrated with both standard, known quilt designs and original designs by mountain women. While these women were relatively isolated from the contemporary design influences of the time, publication of their work was a significant episode in the revival of quilting.

In 1905, Bok's *Ladies' Home Journal* commissioned several well-known artists to provide designs for children's quilts. The series consisted of designs for appliquéd quilts by Ernest Thompson Seton, "A Wild-Animal Bedquilt" (January); Maxfield Parrish, "A Circus Bedquilt" (March); Gazo Foudji, "A Dragon Bedquilt" (May); Peter Newell, "An Alice in Wonderland Bedquilt" (September); and Jessie Wilcox Smith, "A Child's Good-Night Bedquilt" (November). But

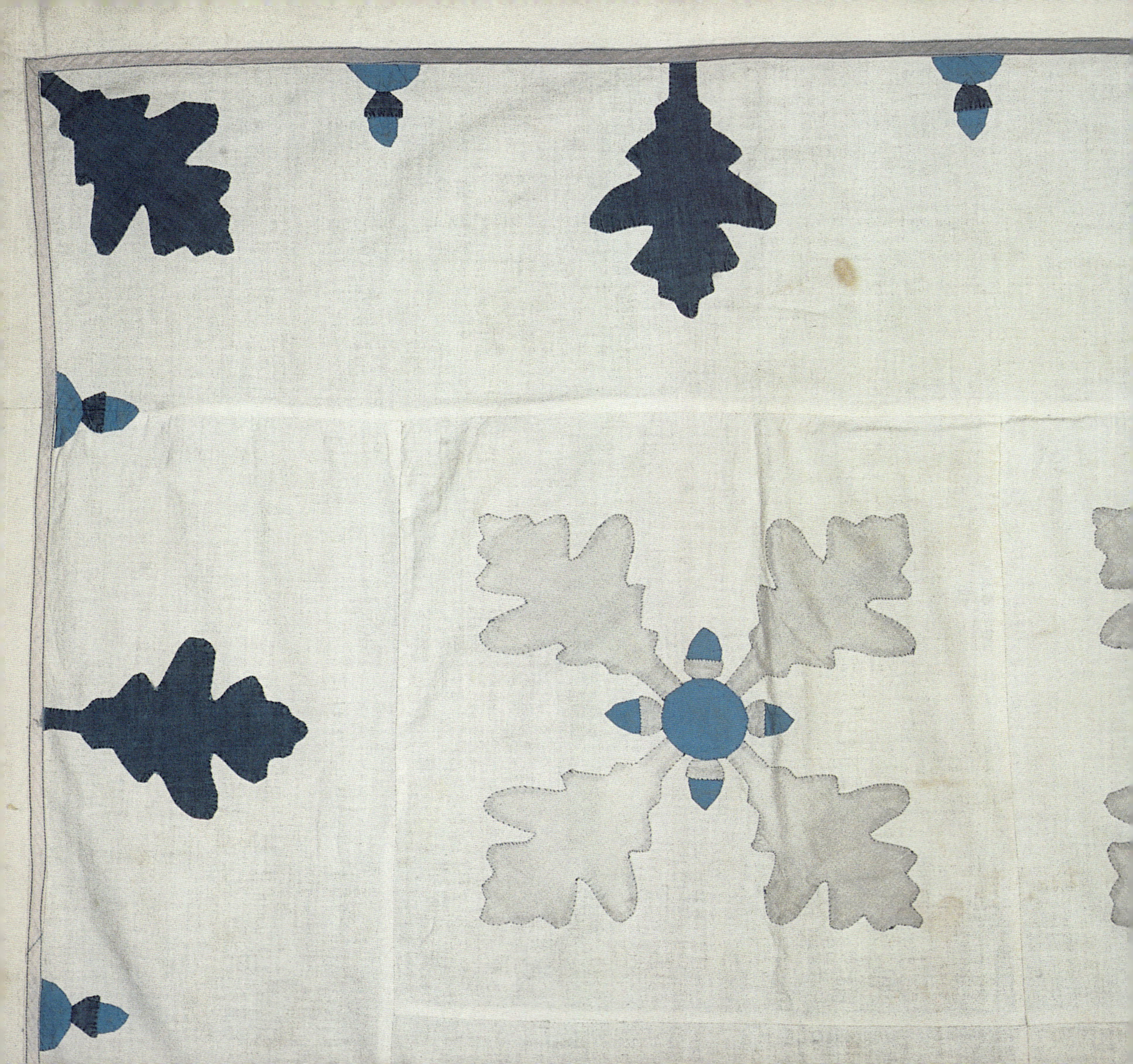

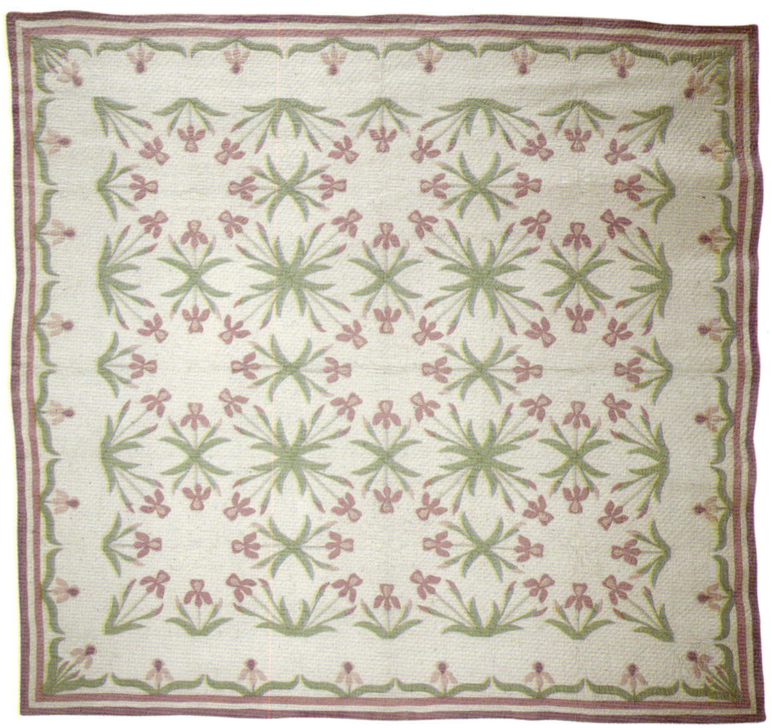

▶
Marie Daugherty Webster. Iris quilt. 1910. Quilted and appliquéd cotton, 83 × 82" (211 × 208 cm). On loan to the Indianapolis Museum of Art, Collection Rosalind Webster Perry

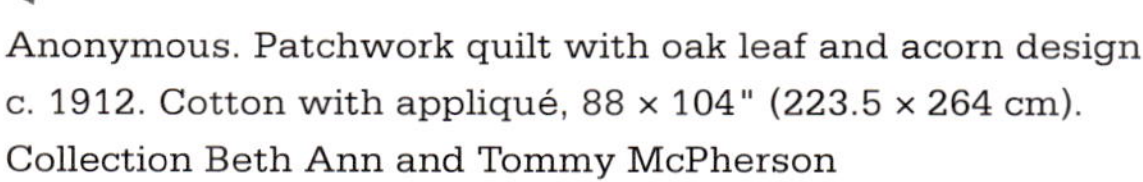

◀
Anonymous. Patchwork quilt with oak leaf and acorn design. c. 1912. Cotton with appliqué, 88 × 104" (223.5 × 264 cm). Collection Beth Ann and Tommy McPherson

it was Bok's cultivation of the work of a previously unknown Indiana woman, Marie Daugherty Webster, that produced some of the most stunning quilts of the Arts and Crafts era.

Marie Webster made her first patchwork quilt about 1908, at the age of fifty, to decorate a new home. She had, no doubt, been exposed to the Arts and Crafts and Art Nouveau movements during her grand tour of Britain and Europe in 1900, and while the house itself was Colonial Revival, some furnishings reflected the new design styles. Her quilt, "Pink Rose" was a variation of the historic "Rose of Sharon" pattern, and, when brought to the attention of Bok, compelled him to write, asking her to submit more designs. Taking inspiration from flowers in her garden, she created numerous patchwork quilts and cushions that were published in *The Ladies' Home Journal* during 1911 and 1912. Many were exhibited at Marshall Field and Company in Chicago and reviewed as "striking creations which represent a new development in artistic handiwork." She began to offer patterns of her designs to satisfy the many requests; then in 1921, along with two friends, Ida Hess and Evangeline Beshore, she formed the Practical Patchwork Company. In addition to her newfound design career, Webster researched the history of quiltmaking and, in 1915, *Quilts: Their Story and How to Make Them* was published, the first American book on the

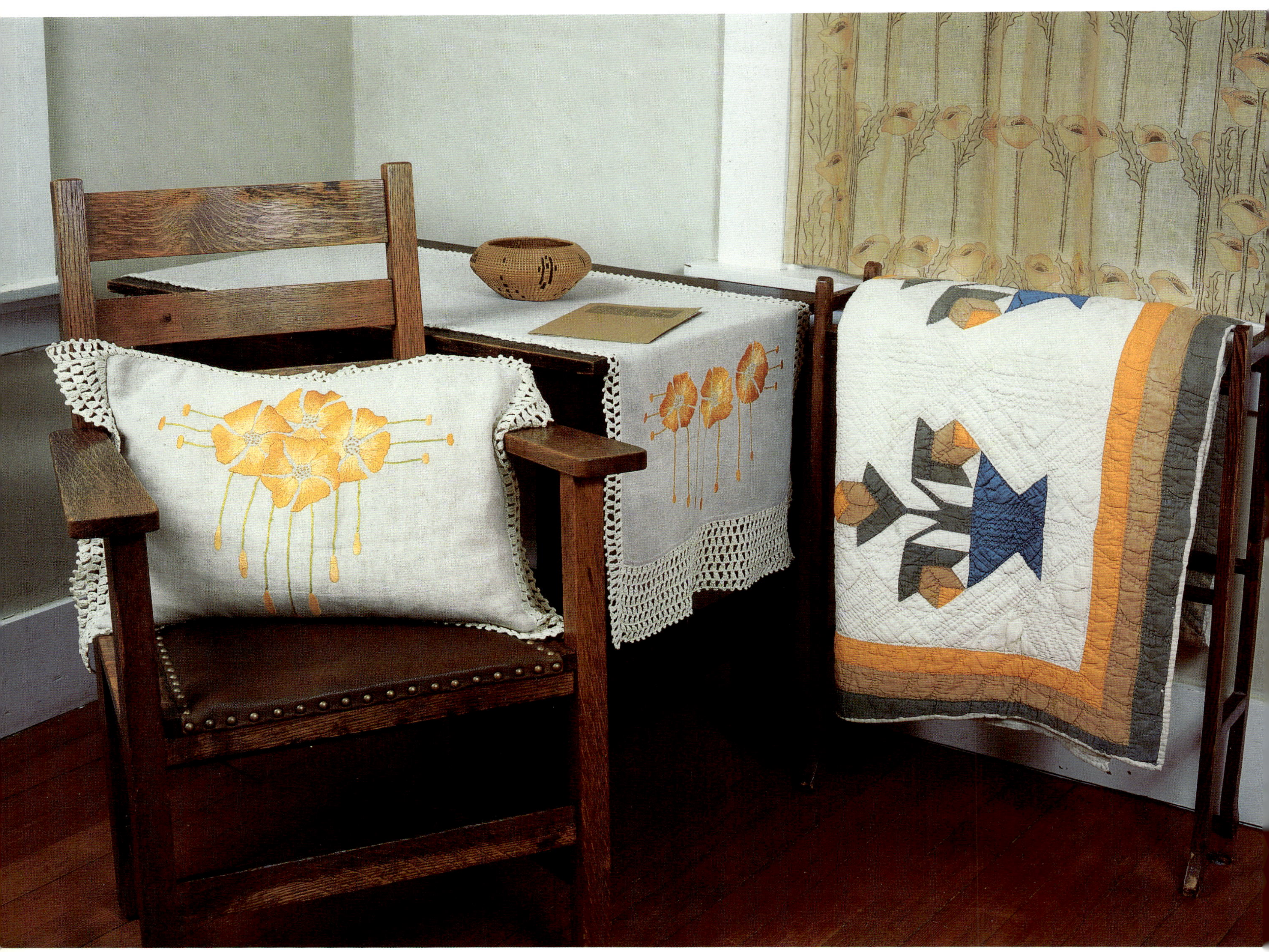

◀
Piecework quilt. c. 1915. Cotton, pieced and quilted. 90 × 72" (228.6 × 182.9 cm); Colonial Drapery Fabrics. Poppy curtains. 1913. Roller printed on "Colonial Artcraft casement cloth" cotton, 36" (91.4 cm) wide. Collection Timothy Hansen and Dianne Ayres; Poppy pillow and table scarf. c. 1912. Linen with hand embroidery in satin and stem stitch and filet crocheted edgings, pillow: 15 × 24" (38.1 × 61 cm), scarf: 18½ × 66" (47 × 167.6 cm). Collection Caro Macpherson

▼
Marie Daugherty Webster. "The New Flower Patchwork Quilts" Illustration from *The Ladies' Home Journal*. January 1912

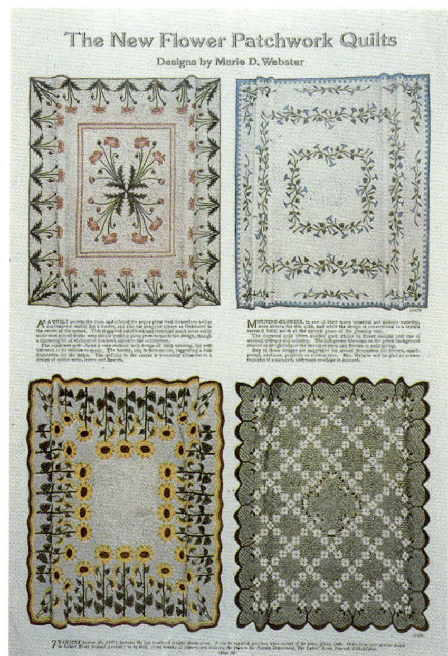
The New Flower Patchwork Quilts
Designs by Marie D. Webster

topic and still considered a classic reference today. While Marie continued designing through the 1920s, her designs and color palette changing with the times, her initial inspiration from the Arts and Crafts movement blossomed to create new generations of quilters.[43]

Lace Making

At first thought, lace seems antithetical to the core principles of the Arts and Crafts movement, but, in fact, there was great interest in lace making during the period. Many entries in Arts and Crafts exhibitions were handmade lace, although few images and little description of the work survive. In addition, a number of programs were established for disadvantaged women to learn lace making and produce items for sale. Much of the work was a revival of the handicraft, employing historic Italian techniques and designs.

One such program reported in *The Craftsman* was the work of Mrs. Sophie R. Miller who taught the craft to Indian women living on a reservation at La Jolla, California. "Since their contact with civilization has deprived the Indians of almost all their native industries by destroying the balance of primitive economics, and robbing them equally of materials and opportunities for work . . . [under] these circumstances, the white man's industry, however exotic or inappropriate in theory, becomes a means of salvation both to life and character, and a whole community . . . The fabrics [lace] wrought by the bronze work-women are the marvel of their white-skinned sisters

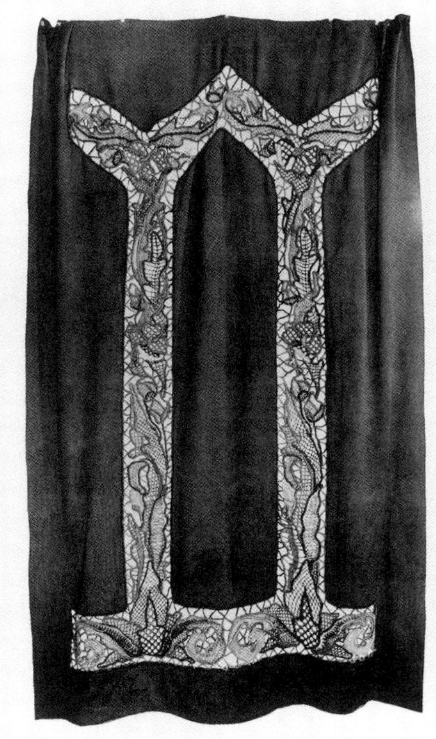

◄
Mabel Tuke Priestman. "Showing how hangings may be beautified by Pratt Point. The colouring is exquisitely soft." Illustration from *Handicrafts in the Home*. 1910

who purchase them."[44] While prejudice was often condoned at the time, the article takes a pragmatic stance: "it is easier for the hand trained for generations to acts of individual expression to acquire new arts than for the idle fingers of the rich to excel as quickly in similar occupations."

In New York City, Katherine Lord established a similar program at Greenwich House, a social settlement, for "two classes of women, foreigners skilled in some form of hand-work who needed direction in design and choice of material, and girls and women physically unfit to enter the regular industrial field."[45] Italian pillow laces, filet, Carrickmacross and Limerick laces, Italian cutwork, and finer needle laces were produced. Once the women were technically proficient in producing work of historic designs, new, original designs were executed. Many of these new designs were by Katherine Lord, and some illustrated in her other articles on lace techniques exhibit Arts and Crafts style conventionalized designs.[46] She mainly employed the Limerick and Carrickmacross lace techniques that are worked upon a net—often commercially made—either with a crochet hook or a blunt needle, and filet lace which is made from a single thread, knotted to form a mesh and the pattern worked upon it.

Another notable innovation in lace making occurred at Pratt Institute. Priestman reported on their adaptation of Italian point, a technique in which a cord is attached to a backing fabric in the outline of a design, various needle lace stitches fill the intervening spaces, and then the backing is cut away. This variation used manila cord and colored linen threads, giving the work characteristics of stained glass (above).

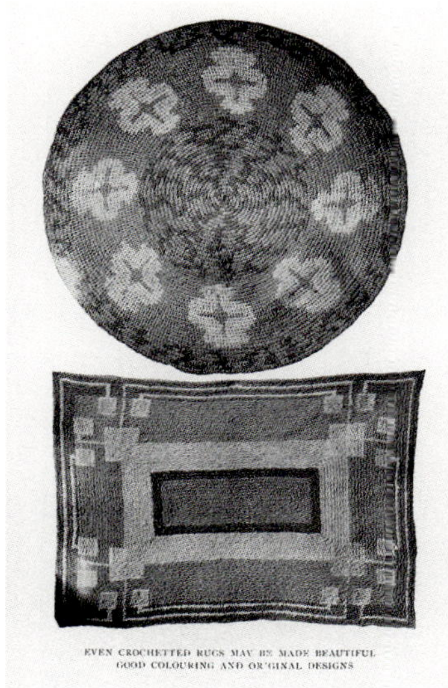

▶
Mabel Tuke Priestman. "Even Crocheted Rugs May Be Made Beautiful—Good Colouring and Original Designs." Illustration from *Handicrafts in the Home*. 1910

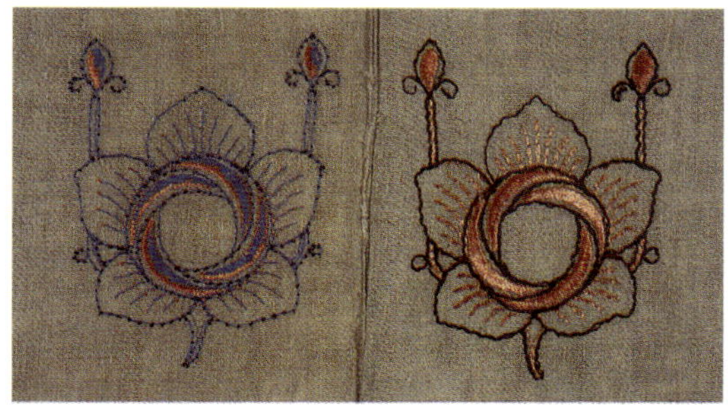

▼
Anonymous. Table scarf with machine embroidery. c. 1915. Linen with machine embroidery in cotton and silk, scarf: 17 × 55" (43.2 × 139.7 cm), each motif: 5 × 4" (12.7 × 10.2 cm). Collection Timothy Hansen and Dianne Ayres
The motif on the left shows the back; a bobbin thread, here quite obvious in blue, reveals that this is machine embroidered.

Crochet

Crochet work is carried out with a single strand of thread and a hooked needle. A limited number of stitches form the repertoire, but in various combinations and with differing threads the work can take on many different characteristics. It was employed for items as varied as sheer curtains, lacy edgings on table linens, and small rugs. Filet crochet is related to filet lace only in that the base is a network of squares; the pattern is worked in as the crochet proceeds (see pillow and table linen on page 198). For small rugs, crochet was done with a heavier thread, the stitches being taken over a cord to add thickness and add stability to the piece (above).

Unraveling the legacy of handmade textiles from the Arts and Crafts movement reveals not only their artistry and craftsmanship but also their entwined associations to the culture of the time. Each piece is a unique expression of the maker and reflects her position within the social fabric. Producing and possessing these distinctive pieces was and is a passionate pursuit for individualistic Americans. But mass-produced goods also formed an important piece of the patchwork of textiles for the home and dress in the early twentieth century.

> No textile renaissance, however, which is dependent for its existence upon whole or even partial handwork can ever be far-reaching in its results. No matter how stimulating the work of individual craftsmen may be, it is in the hands of the manufacturer that the ultimate power lies. While some of the American manufacturers have been far-sighted and broad-spirited

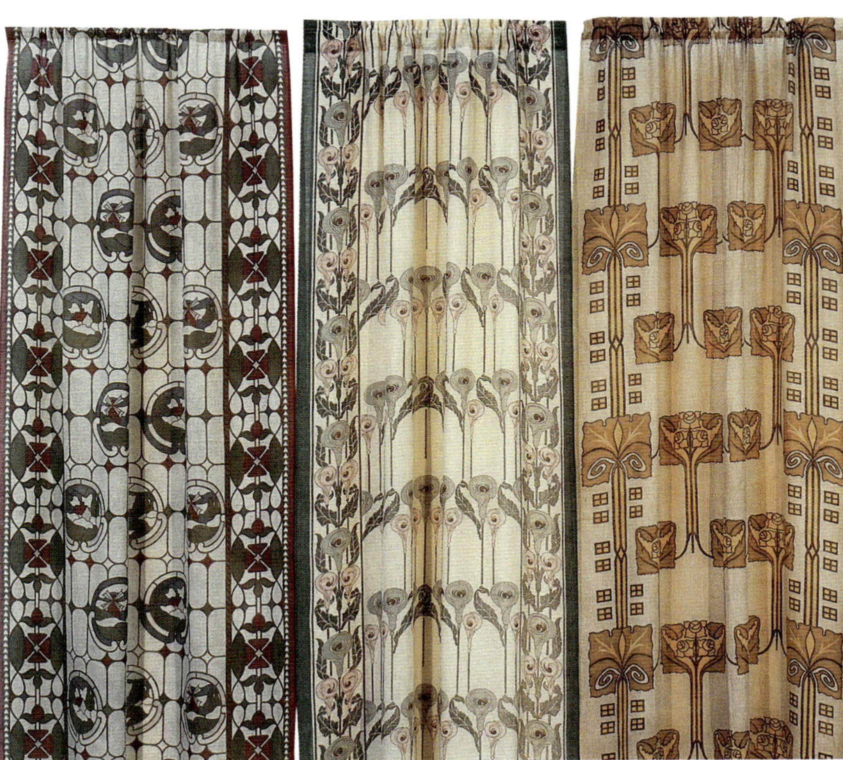
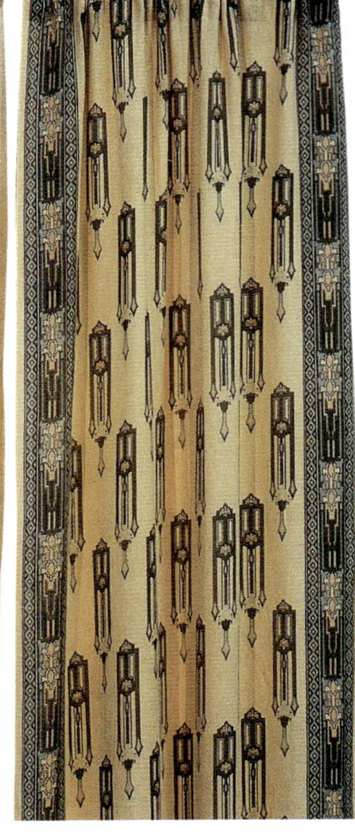

◀ Printed scrim curtains. c. 1912. Collection Timothy Hansen and Dianne Ayres

> enough to express modern influences, they are greatly in the minority. The great body of our manufacturers of decorative textiles seem still laboring in the Dark Ages, continuing to copy fifteenth- and sixteenth-century designs which are a far cry to the modern spirit.
>
> It is high time that the American manufacturer should awake to the realization that the demand of to-day for a high standard in decorative textiles, necessitates their conception by artists and not by draughtsmen.[47]

Surviving textiles and printed records from the period are consistent with Adler's statement made in 1916; not many American textile manufactures embraced the new design style. The few that did primarily produced printed yardage for use in home decoration (above). Colonial Drapery Fabrics printed "conventional designs" on etamine—an open-weave scrim fabric—and "new 'Arts and Crafts' designs" on their Colonial Artcraft casement cloth—a sheer, finely woven cotton. These fabrics were intended as curtain materials, but many other items constructed of them are found, including purses and bedcovers. The company also suggested the designs may be cut from the casement cloth and appliquéd onto plain background fabrics to make pillows, curtains, table runners, etc. (page 133). Other companies that produced printed fabrics of Arts and Crafts

◀ Philadelphia Tapestry Mills. "Artloom Tapestries." Advertisement in *Harper's Bazaar*. September 1904

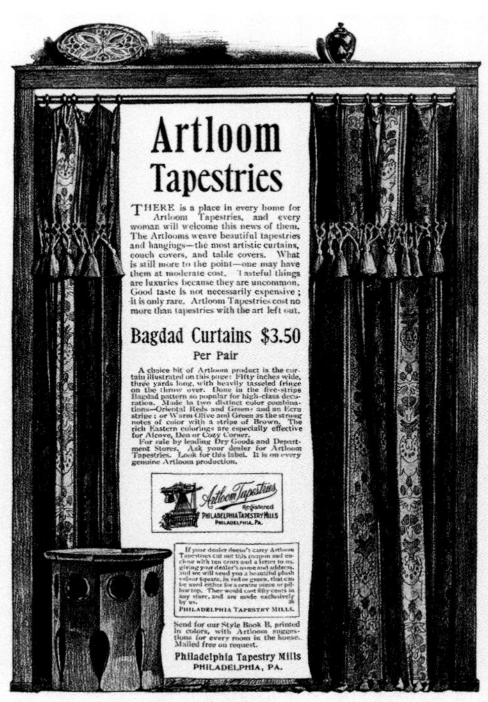

designs include Cheney Brothers in South Manchester, Connecticut, and Arnold Print Works in North Adams, Massachusetts.[48]

Tapestry weave fabrics were also produced for use as portieres and couch throws (left; page 111). The weave process for these results in a double-faced fabric, with the colors in the pattern reversed on the other side. The pattern is often woven for the particular size of the portiere or throw with a border on one or both ends. In addition to being offered in specialty catalogs of companies that produced them at the time, these textiles were often sold through mail-order catalogs and department stores.

Occasionally, machine-embroidered textiles are found from the period. The stitching was of two types. A standard sewing machine that did zig-zag could be set up to simulate stitches appearing as satin stitch and couching (page 201 bottom). The other type of machine embroidery was done with a Cornely Machine, which did a chain stitch. The designs of items made with it are distinctive in usually having one continuous line of stitching, often in black. Accents of satin stitch, either by hand or machine, completed the design. Pillows and table linens with machine embroidery were sold completed, making what, on first glance, appear to be Arts and Crafts heirlooms, available to those who could not craft them. ❖

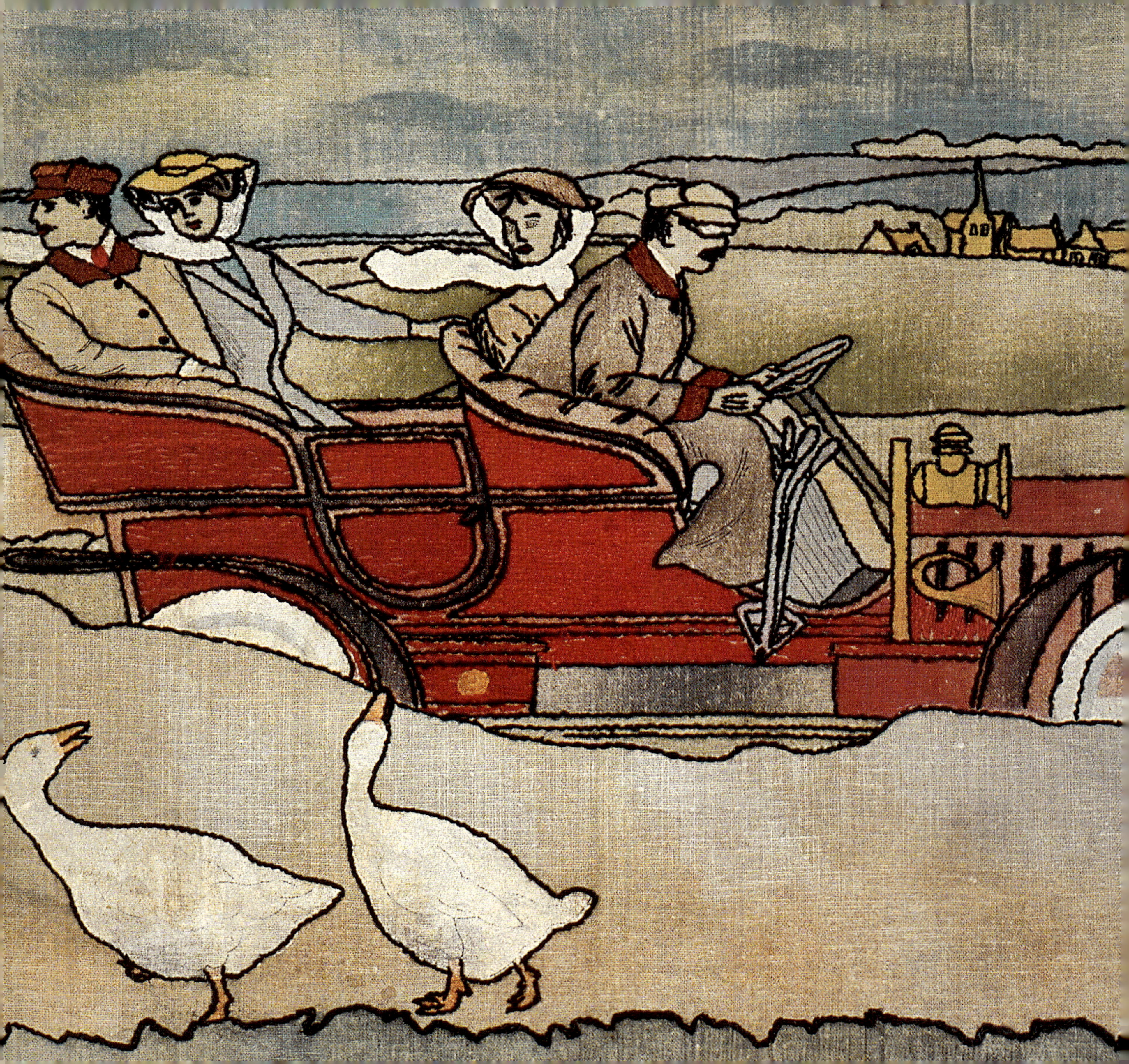

6 The Art and Ethic of Dress: Arts and Crafts Clothing

> She, in fact, expresses herself in her work, and so her work is related intimately to her life, the way she has decided that she wishes to live. This is absolutely as true of clothes as of housekeeping or handicraft work or of painting. If a girl is trained to use her brain in planning and making her clothes, her dresses and hats and scarfs and belts will all be related to her personality and express the degree and kind of cultivation her mind has absorbed.
>
> *The Craftsman*

During the Arts and Crafts period, the manufacture and choice of clothing represented one's personal philosophy as much as it demonstrated participation in current design trends. Styles of dress at the turn of the twentieth century were intended to incorporate the basic tenets of the Arts and Crafts movement: simplicity, honesty, health, and individuality. Women's clothing was the most radically affected, both by the economic climate of the time and by the cultural freedom characterizing the intellectual and artistic output of the day. Prior to this interest in clothing reform, fashionable clothes for both sexes were cut unnaturally, forcing the body into contours that were uncomfortable and often impeded physical activity. Women's clothing, in particular, was of concern. The cut of both the garments and the foundation undergarments pinched and twisted the female figure into an exaggerated, unnatural form. This contortionism impacted female health and well being, providing a catalyst for reform.

Dress began evolving in new directions in the 1870s with the impetus coming from Europe. The new mode of beauty emphasized a return to "naturalness." Mrs. H. R. (Mary Eliza) Haweis,

▼

Anonymous. Bonnet. c. 1890–10. Linen, cotton embroidery thread, and silk ribbon, 38 × 10½" (96.5 × 26.5 cm). Collection Tommy and Beth Ann McPherson

Historically influenced textiles such as this bonnet were frequently created to be used in historical pageants and theatricals. Loosely based in period accuracy, this bonnet alludes to nineteenth-century women's headgear but is adorned with a contemporary geometric embroidered pattern on a natural fabric base.

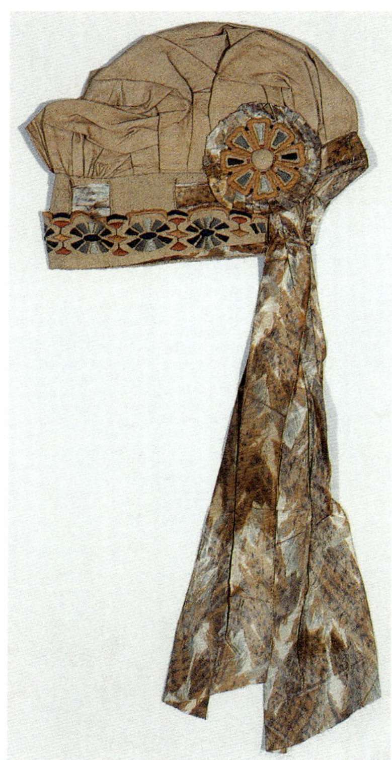

noted in England's *The Queen* (1878): "The primary rule in beautiful dress is that it will not contradict the natural form of the human frame; and the secondary rule, growing out of the first, is that the proportions of the dress shall obey the proportions of the body. . . . A woman who studies artistic dress will first study the human figure."[1]

How "naturalness" was defined varied from writer to fashion editor to wearer. "Artistic dress," as this new concern was deemed, drew from many sources for information. Mrs. Haweis commented on the new fashion in *The Art of Beauty* in 1878:

> Morris, Burne-Jones, and others have made certain types of face and figure, once literally hated, actually the fashion. Red hair—once, to say a woman had red hair was social assignation—is all the rage. A pallid face with a protruding upper lip is highly esteemed. Green eyes, a squint, square eyebrows, whitey-brown complexion, are not left out in the cold. Now is the time for plain women. Only dress after the Pre-Raphaelite style, and you will be astonished to find that so far from being an "ugly duckling" you are a full-fledged swan.[2]

This new approach to dress was even more clearly defined in England by the *The Queen*'s correspondent A.C. in 1879. Visiting "aesthetic cousins," he was initiated into "the dogma that dress should be to the body what speech is to the mind. Dress should have a character and expression—that there should be harmony between the wearer and apparel."[3]

In pursuit of such harmony, dress reformers became interested in the natural body and its expression through time. Exploration revealed that for the previous century and a half, the contraflexive serpentine curve of the idealized human figure in art had symbolized naturalness. Hogarth, for example, had popularized the curve in decorative arts and fashion in the *Analysis of Beauty* (1753). Philosophers who later carried the torch, including John Ruskin, dwelled on "the infinite curves of nature."

The historic dress of the ancient Greek and Roman periods, as well as the medieval and Renaissance periods, was known from art, literature, and theater. These styles influenced dress reformers, as is reflected in the magazines of the time. An 1880 article dealt with concern over the appropriate average size of waist for a woman of from 5'3" to 5'5" in height, pointing out that the waist of "The Venus de Medici measures twenty-six inches."[4] Critics viewed the waist as key to the appearance of the human figure. A sarcastic critic commented on the waist's relationship to health and beauty:

> The first aim is to have an "antique waist"—which a vulgar mind would pronounce horribly thick—thick like the Venus de Medici's, thick like that far nobler Venus of Mil [sic]. And why? Because the proportion of the figure, the grace of action and carriage, are so dependent on the waist being the right size, that it is impossible to preach too strongly the folly and ugliness of tight lacing. The coarse, abrupt curve which is formed by a small waist and broad hips is very far removed from Hogarth's true "line of beauty" which is a curve extremely gradual. What is gained by an ugly waist like a v? Nothing but a long list of hideous maladies which sap the health and spoil the complexion. What is gained by a somewhat "antique waist?" Good

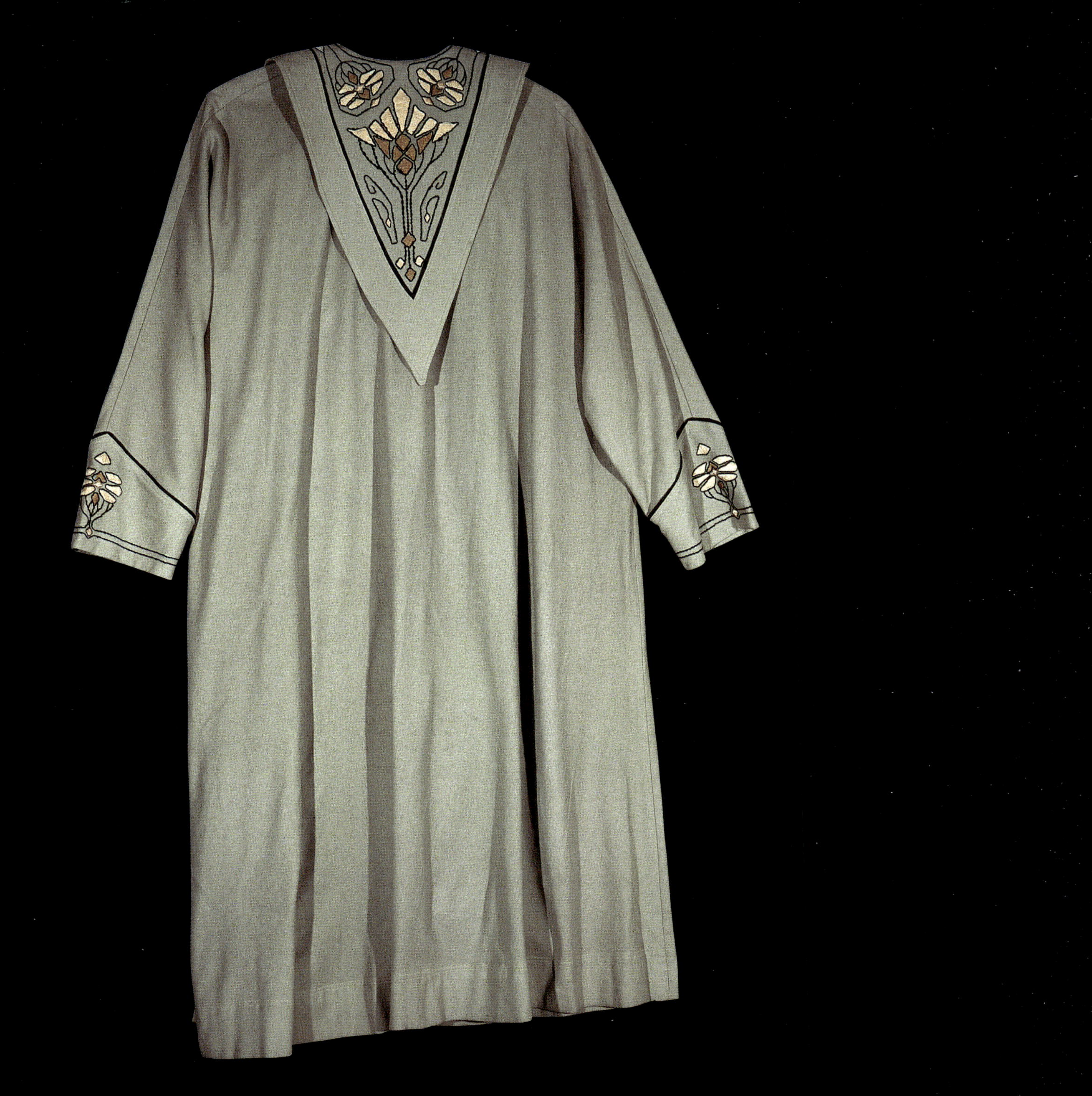

◀
Anonymous. Coat with embroidered collar and cuffs. c. 1915. Wool with silk threads, 46 × 22" (117 × 56 cm). Collection Tommy and Beth Ann McPherson
Coats, both machine manufactured and handmade, were frequently embroidered with Arts and Crafts designs. The loose, full cut of the coat fit over the looser cuts and shorter skirts of the 1910s.

> proportion in an artist's eye, ease and grace of movement, often a really statuesque carriage—impossible to the slaves of la mode, with their hard, bony cuirasses on.[5]

The new mode continued to grow in popularity internationally. In 1884, Arthur Liberty opened a dressmaking department in London. Although the idea of a "Liberty's Art Costume" department met with much speculation, he claimed that it was not to be a department driven by fashion, but rather to create distinct Liberty gowns tied to an interest in historical costume. For example, the gowns seen in Kate Greenaway's books—which were praised by Arts and Crafts figures, including the renowned John Ruskin—inspired costume designers to create comfortable smocks and clothing as children's wear. Her popularity spawned journals such as the *Kate Greenaway Almanack*, which sold ninety thousand copies in America, England, France, and Germany, influencing the clothing of children on two continents.

"Artistic dress" popularized itself in Europe. Englishmen such as Oscar Wilde and others from his circle were influenced primarily by illustrators such as Greenaway, who emphasized a romantic Regency style of dress.[3] William Morris, Charles Rennie Mackintosh, and leading pre-Raphaelites expressed their interest in the human figure by designing costumes that drew from the softer lines and relaxed, simpler silhouettes of medieval times. Pre-Raphaelite and Art Nouveau artists and illustrators popularized this look, giving it a romantic status that made it more acceptable and desirable. Jessie Newberry, an embroidery teacher at the Glasgow School of Art, designed many of her own clothes, including her wedding dress, and other tunics and dresses. The artistic gown

▼

"Street Costumes." *The Modern Priscilla*. April 1912

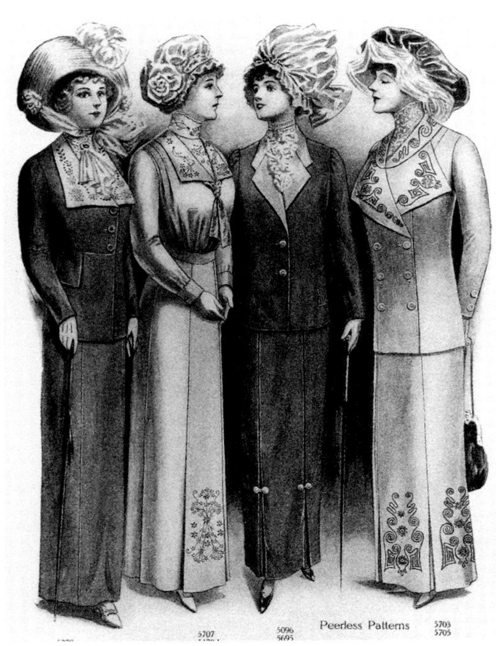

was seen as "appropriate to the occasion on which it is worn; it is of good material, neat, convenient, graceful, healthful, allowing for free movement of the body, It is free from superfluous trimming, it is restful to look at rather than disquieting, in color and design it is alluring and persuasive, not self assertive; it emphasizes in every possible way the charm and personality of the wearer. Such a costume requires intelligent thought and study, which is more than justified by the result"[7] (page 208).

Americans not only watched the changes in fashion in Europe during the nineteenth century; the wealthy participated in European fashion by shopping in London and, Paris, and others could absorb the trends through the ever-topical ladies' magazines. Thus, the everyday woman found her dress reform closer to home, where some had pushed for such change for decades. As early as 1842, American author Catherine Beecher suggested that functional house apparel was necessary to the running of a good home. Others followed in her footsteps, and in 1855/56 a National Dress Association was founded. The national organization dissolved during the Civil War, but the movement had begun.

Many of the extreme changes in dress were focused on women's garments, which had to meet different needs as women's roles changed. As part of the health and social reform movements, a contingent began pushing on a broad level to free women physically as well as spiritually. The physical damage caused by the corset began to be addressed. The corset and other tight-lacing devices displaced the internal organs, affected breathing, and damaged the muscular structure

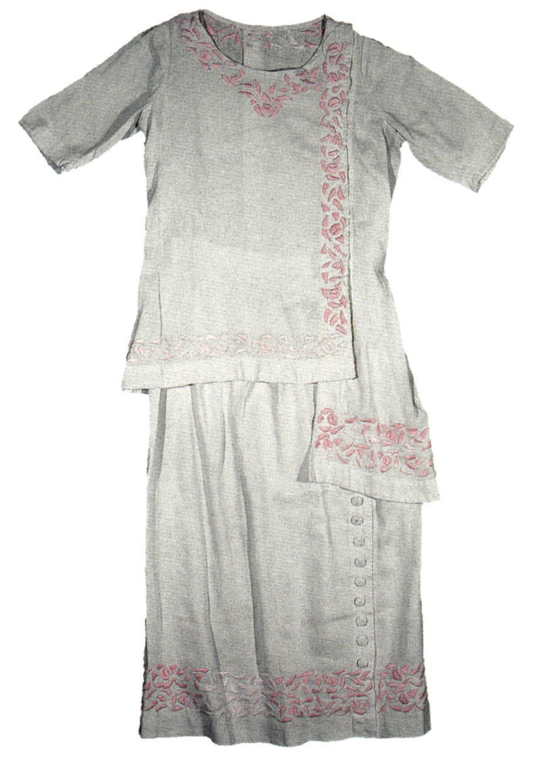

◀
Anonymous. Walking suit. c. 1910. Linen and silk embroidery thread blouse: 34 × 19" (86 × 41 cm), skirt: 36 × 22" (91 × 56 cm). Collection Tommy and Beth Ann McPherson
The boxy cut of this two-piece ensemble accommodated the freedom of movement expected by young women in the early twentieth century.

of the body. Exercise and fresh air were recognized as ways to achieve good health. The movement to free the body from harm and place it in unrestrictive garments was referred to as "dress reform." Some, but certainly not all, of the leaders of the movement were linked to feminism and socialism. Small groups sprang up around the country and began reaching out to women. A distribution network slowly formed as some groups sold patterns; others sold actual clothing.

The American dress reform movement achieved wide exposure at the Philadelphia Centennial Exposition in 1876, where a number of reform garments were on display, including a group by the Alice Fletcher Depot of New York, a firm offering undergarments and a woman's "emancipation suit," combining chemise, drawers, corset, and corset cover. At the 1893 Chicago Columbian Exposition, *The Jenness-Miller Magazine* exhibited the American costume, which consisted of a wool tunic covering a divided skirt. Thus, slowly and with exposure, "aesthetic dress," achieved primarily by the upper classes, evolved into "dress reform," attainable by all classes.

Many aspects of reform dress were in accord with the basic tenets of the Arts and Crafts ideals. During the time, "Numerous dress-reform styles started, many of which were freakish, but the aim of every girl in relation to dress should be to evolve for herself something simple that will not necessitate an undue amount of time and show, something pleasing and artistic in its adaptation to individual appearance, and comfortable enough to permit freedom."[8] International reformers stressed the importance of incorporating the principles of classical dress in their wardrobes. Changes in fashion between the Victorian and Edwardian periods expressed

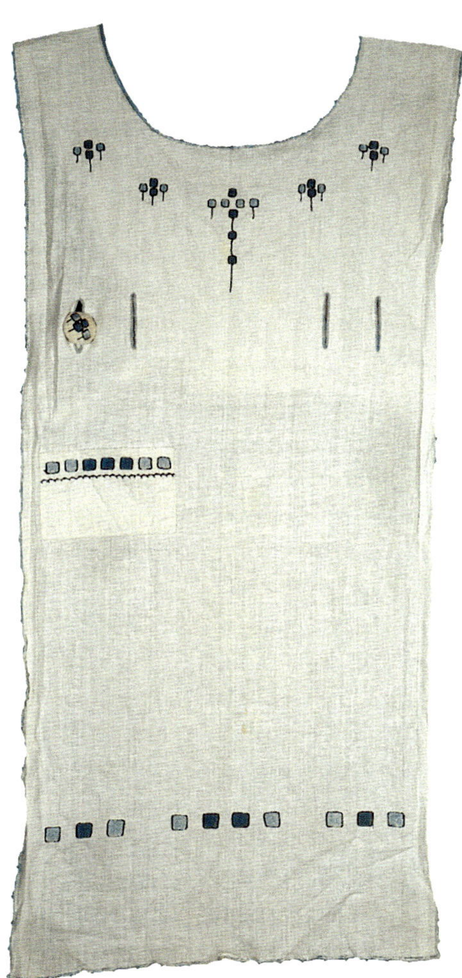

◀
Anonymous. Smock. c. 1912. Linen with silk embroidery, 40 × 19" (101 × 48 cm). Collection Tommy and Beth Ann McPherson
This three-quarter-length smock typifies the work clothes donned by American women as they cared for their homes or participated in artistic and craft pursuits.

themselves most cohesively in undergarments. Naturally, if the goal was to free the body from confining undergarments, underclothes were going to change radically to meet new expectations.

In England in 1884, a Dr. Jaeger introduced principles of health and hygiene to the mass populace and advocated woolen undergarments—including a woolen corset, with double layers over the chest, stomach, and throat—as the means to achieve good health. According to Dr. Jaeger, wool was porous and allowed breathing. Although his influence was widespread, its impact waned through time. Other porous materials were designed and recognized as more comfortable.

Another advocate, Mr. Lewis Haslam, pushed the importance of fresh air and breathable fabrics. He recognized cotton had these qualities and founded the Aertex Company in 1888 to work with cellular materials, manufacturing vests, combinations, and corsets. Cellular materials were designed to be cooler in the summer and warmer in the winter. Viyella, a blend of cotton and wool, was one such combination. Some undergarments were more delicate and began to be called lingerie. The first all-silk underwear had been invented in the 1880s and by 1900 had taken the country by storm.

These lighter materials also fit better under late-nineteenth-century clothing. Skirts fitted smoothly across the hip area and then fell into folds, drawing the eye downward. Until 1898, bodices fit tightly across the bust area and were usually decorated other material, epaulettes,

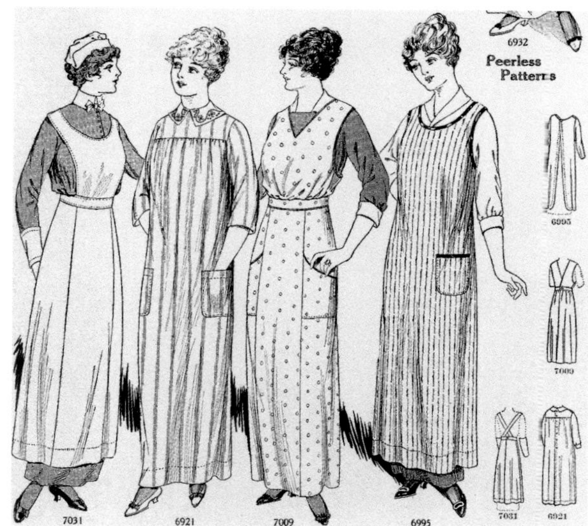

The Modern Priscilla. March 1915
Peerless patterns marketed patterns for the famous coverall "bungalow aprons" aimed at the new American homemaker.

lace, and trim. Skirts remained plain with the exception of some occasional braiding. Sleeve size shrunk and ballooned, expanding in width only to taper back down. Dressmaking materials were fairly stiff in nature, including cloth, serge, tweed, plush, heavy silk, damask, and velvet (page 210).

Increased international media and communication only strengthened the impact of fashion. Journals and publications shared news of the latest couture trends in America and Europe, with Paris leading the new movement. Madame Gaches-Sarraute designed corsets that were intended to improve the health of the female body instead of endangering it. She understood the importance of supporting the abdomen, removing all sources of pressure from female organs, yet leaving the thorax free. Charles Worth who established one of the first Paris couture houses, disliked the current indented corset and introduced a straight-busked corset. This created the bow-fronted "Gibson girl"–type figure (named for illustrator Charles Dana Gibson) who prevailed in the popular literature of the time. Due to its lines, the new corset left the bust widely unsupported. Bust pads, camisoles, and other artificial shape makers were all designed to help alter this. Edwardian clothing was cut to accentuate a full bosom and a small waist.

Despite decreased expectations for women to continue to wear corsets, a number of women did choose to keep wearing them. The straight-fronted corset rose in popularity. It started farther down the body, creating a much flatter profile. To cover the new silhouette of the body without corsets or the bulky undergarments that had taken their place, gowns loosened dramatically.

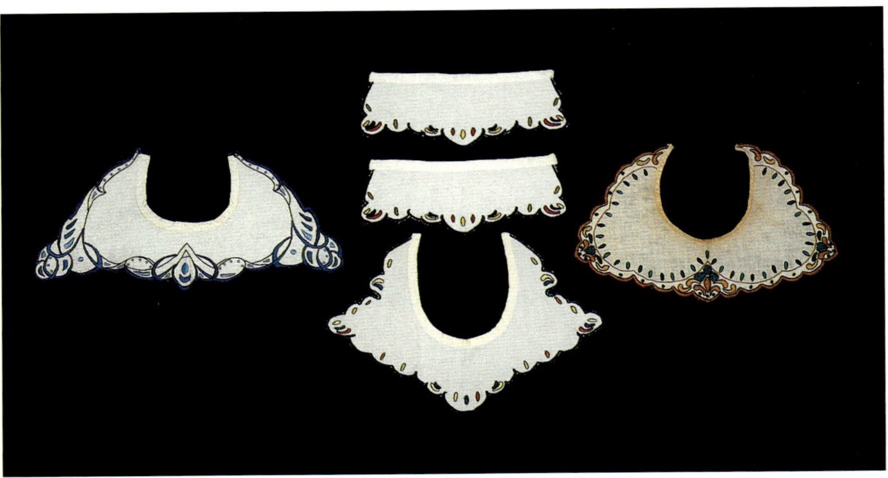

◀
Anonymous kit company and magazine patterns. Collars and cuffs. c. 1900–15. Linen and embroidery silk and cotton threads, approx. 3 × 12" (7.6 × 30.5 cm). Collection Tommy and Beth Ann McPherson
Collars and cuffs provided decorative interest and flexibility for otherwise plain and serviceable shirtwaists that were designed for wear at work and at home.

Dress materials became flowing and softer. Choice materials included fine cloth, mohair, cashmere, tussore, and linen for more tailored cuts and crepe-de-chine, voile, muslin, net, and chiffon for softer day and evening gowns. Garments adapted to accommodate the new materials, as they needed support. Decorative designs and embroidery were necessary to hide the tucks and seams that stand out on filmy materials. Flounced skirts helped support the filmy fluted skirts. Waistlines tapered toward a central point. Sleeves retained a slight puff at the top, smoothing out to a straight line by the end of the century. High collars were of lace or net and backed so they remained semi-transparent, supported by boning.

"Separates," or the fitted skirt and blouse, gained popularity between 1890 and 1900. The outfit of plain skirt and blouse was a practical option. Flexible clothes were desirable at a time when women were beginning to fulfill multiple roles. Trimmings could also be used to transform the blouse and skirt into an ensemble appropriate for many occasions (above).

Skirts went through three major incarnations in this decade. The skirt worn around 1890 was cut with hip gores, or darts, and gathered in the back. In the first few years of the decade, skirts were worn snug at the hips and wider at the hem. The umbrella skirt, or one-piece skirt, was cut from one circular piece and was unseamed. In the middle of the decade, the skirt became bell-shaped. Skirts were narrow to the knees, with flounces or darts added below the knees.[9]

Between 1895 and 1910 skirts straightened and became more form-fitting. The 1895–1900 period saw the popularity of the s-curved, Art Nouveau influenced, wasp-waist skirt. Corsets

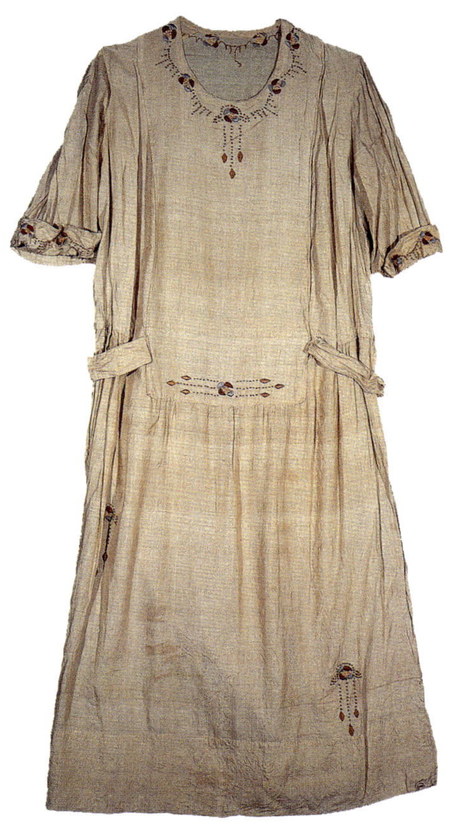

◀
Anonymous. Dress, New York State. c. 1915. Silk and silk embroidery thread, 44 × 20" (112 × 51 cm). Collection Tommy and Beth Ann McPherson
The loose cut of this dress illustrates the evolution of women's apparel in the second decade of the twentieth century. The handmade dress is embroidered with an asymmetrical design in natural colors of mustard, rust, khaki, and blue, on the skirt, sleeves, and bodice. Placed off center, the composition represents the principles of Arts and Crafts design.

were still worn at this time. Year to year the waist began to loosen up and the silhouette relaxed, although skirt shapes became narrow and high-waisted, briefly becoming so narrow at the bottom they impacted walking and hobbled the wearer, hence the nickname "hobble skirt."

But things were due to change, as commentators such as Cynthia Asquith noted in *Remember and Be Glad*:

> Many of our clothes were far from comfortable or convenient. . . . Walking about the London streets trailing clouds of dust was horrid. I once found I had carried into the house a banana skin which had got caught up in the unstitched hem of my dress! I hated the veils that, worn twisted into a squiggle under my chin, dotted my vision with huge spots like symptoms of liver trouble. They flattened even short eyelashes. Our vast hats which took the wind like sails were painfully skewered to our heads by huge ornamental hatpins, greatly to the peril of other people's eyes. I couldn't endure high choking collars with boned supports that dug red dints in my neck, so I wore low square-necked blouses long before these became the fashion—a non-conformity for which I was severely criticized. . . . Feather boas were regrettably in fashion, and in these if you couldn't afford a new one you soon looked like poultry in very poor condition.[10]

The clothing of the first decade of the twentieth century was designed for the new body type. Prior experience left older generations of American women unsympathetic to the young who did not fully appreciate the nature of the undergarments being left behind. Helen Kinne and Anna Cooley commented in *Shelter and Clothing:*

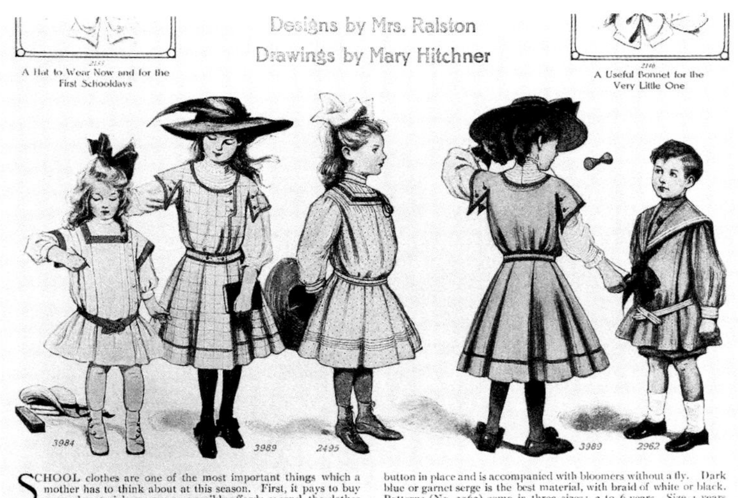

◀
Designs by Mrs. Ralston, drawings by Mary Hitchner. "School Clothes for Younger Children." *The Ladies' Home Journal*. August 1908

> Few young girls appreciate the necessity for careful consideration in the selection of the first corset or corset waist. The test for such a garment is that it should leave no marks on the body. Corsets cause an atrophy of the abdominal muscles and if not properly fitted interfere seriously with the circulation of the blood and cause displacement of the viscera—when lacing is resorted to the thorax is deformed and uglified. These displacements caused by ignorance, lead to the ill health and inefficiency of about one half the women. . . . Tight bands or corsets interfere with the circulation and cut off the supply of blood needed by the brain and internal organs. The corset should fit snugly over the hips, but allow plenty of freedom at the waistline. . . . Most girls wish to preserve the lithe graceful waistline with which nature has endowed them. Notice the beautiful hip and waist curves of the Venus de Milo, or the Winged Victory of Samothrace. Are they not more beautiful and artistic than the corset made lines. Girls can preserve this vigorous graceful form through proper exercise of the muscles at the natural joint the waist. Fat easily accumulates. . . . [a] corset does not prevent this accumulation. Tennis, golf, gardening, hoeing, sweeping, and horseback riding, mountain climbing, walking, all help to prevent the excessive development of fatty tissue. The waist may not then with proper development be called slender, but it is lithe and graceful like the beautiful ideals of the "Venus" or "Victory (of Samorthrace)."[11]

The cut of women's clothes continued to evolve. The bodice became less fitted, and by 1904 was loose all around. The exterior fabric, however, was mounted to a built-in foundation, often of light silk, with or without boning, which anchored it. Sleeves again became fuller and were gathered in at the elbow. As the bodice became fuller, the skirt did as well, although it retained the three basic shapes it had held previously. Skirts again stayed mounted on a foundation lining for support. Many skirts contained so many yards of material that they could be remade into more current fashions when the wearer was ready.[12] The waist became an important focal point for uniting the two pieces and became tight-fitting, though not as exaggerated as before. The look had strong eighteenth-century references, which were recognized by the fashion commentators of the day. By 1906, the belt developed into a supported high waistband attached to the skirt, called a corselet. The look was emphasized by a blowsy shirtwaist.

Separates continued their rise in popularity, and the shirtwaist, or woman's blouse, with a skirt became a national uniform. More women were working and needed clothing appropriate to their duties, clothing that combined simplicity, utility, and beauty. Many shirtwaists had detachable collars and cuffs for practicality. Dresses and shirtwaists were often embroidered, as were collars and cuffs, such as those shown on page 214.

The voluptuous, S-shaped female figure so popular in the first years of the twentieth century was no longer fashionable by about 1907. Instead the slender, willowy form began to take the country by storm, becoming the basis for twentieth-century style. Tailored coats, such as the gray wool embroidered coat on page 208, straightened the figure to a tubular form. Bodice cuts loosened by 1910, becoming simply cut with fullness arranged in the center front. Kimono cuts, with the

▼

Anonymous. Driving cap. c. 1910. Linen and cotton embroidery thread, 5 × 9 × 11½" (12.7 × 22.86 × 29.21 cm). Collection Timothy Hansen and Dianne Ayres

In the first decades of the twentieth century, driving caps became a necessary accessory for the new automobile.

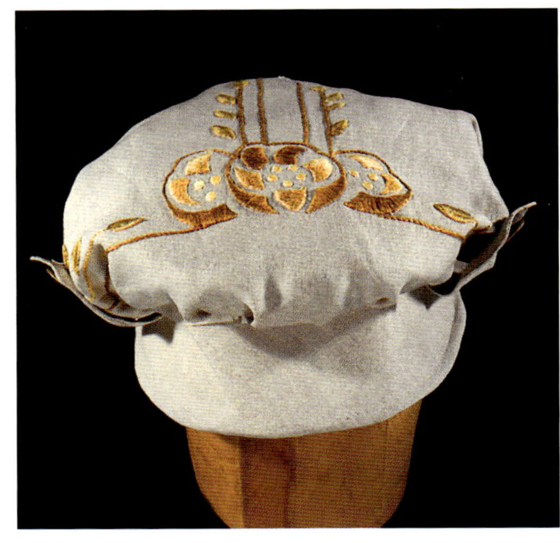

sleeve and bodice in one, and princess cuts became popular as well. The skirt narrowed, using less material and fewer gores. The mermaid skirt, with its narrow top and full bottom, was one such extreme example. Jackets came in many shapes and sizes. Boleros and Zouave jackets, both popular at the beginning of the century, continued to be worn. The stylized fitted jacket remained popular for walking, shooting, and other athletic endeavors. Sack coats and dusters were the appropriate wear for traveling.

The early twentieth-century woman had a lifestyle in which days were filled with a variety of duties. Most women still participated actively in the care of the home, even when help could be afforded, making comfortable work clothing a necessity. Aprons from the period are rare to survive, as they were used until retired to the rag basket. They sometimes incorporated simple embroidery work (page 212). Not to be overlooked in the ladies' magazines this article was made as fashionable as possible. *The Ladies' Home Journal* and *The Modern Priscilla* illustrated the "bungalow coverall"—a shapeless over tunic with a back closure—demonstrating that the new middle-class consumer building and furnishing the bungalows was considered an important market (page 213).

Middle- and upper-class turn-of-the-century women faced several wardrobe changes in the course of a day. For housework, often in the morning, a straight-line dress would be worn under a smock or apron. The afternoon and evening of social activities required more formal attire. After finishing with the care of the house, in the afternoon, a "porch dress" replaced the afternoon dress

▶
Audley B. Wells. *The Art and Ethic of Dress.* 1915
Wells characterized the modern, active woman through illustration and prose. The caption for this plate noted "Grace of motion is a finer quality than faultless proportion. A marble statue may be exquisite in form but cannot be compared to an elastic spirit woman, whose every gesture indicates soul."

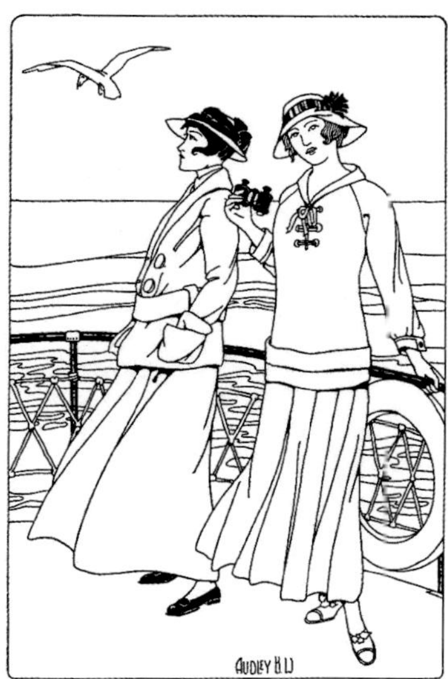

as the appropriate attire for healthful Arts and Crafts period women. Such a garment was worn while reading, participating in craft projects, or visiting with friends. Work could intervene at this time of the day, so it was imperative that the dress be practical as well.

Women acquired these outfits from several sources. Porch dresses were available by mail order and through dry-goods stores, although ready-made clothing was not considered to be of great quality. Many women used dressmakers or made their own clothing from patterns or magazine articles. Ladies' magazines such as *The Delineator* and *Ladies' Home Journal* included patterns and designs for making clothes. Cotton, linen, lawn, mull, a sheer muslin, and "tub silk"—a woven cotton-silk blend—were all popular choices. Many dress patterns included designs to adorn the clothing, and needlework or iron-on transfer patterns could be purchased separately. Often, the cuffs, collar and covered buttons sported single- or multicolored conventionalized motifs. Lace, if incorporated, was used as a flat panel and not a ruffle. The cut was often asymmetrical, with embroidery placed to follow the form.

The placement of ornament was a challenge to reformers. Arts and Crafts ideology encouraged a decrease in the use of ornamentation on garments. However, embroidery was a popular, accessible art, in which all economic classes and ethnicities had the skills to participate. Other methods used for adornment had long historical traditions. Soutouche braiding was one such decorative technique. The braiding was laid on top of the garment and couched down, similar to work seen in the medieval English embroidery admired by William Morris and other leaders of the

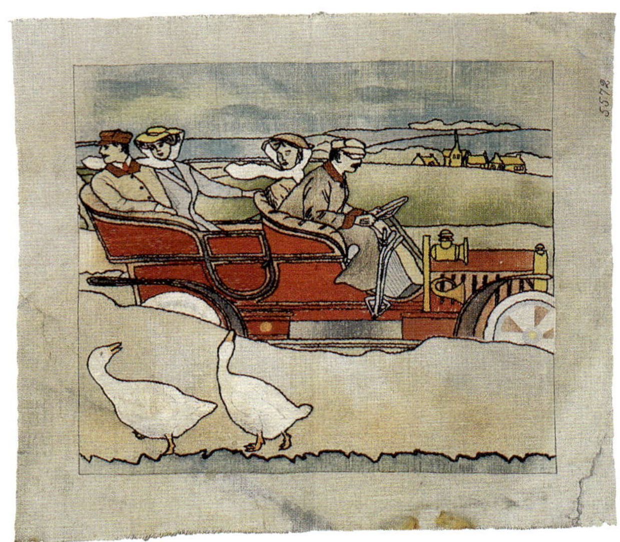

▶
Anonymous. Novelty pillow. c. 1915. Linen, stencil paint, and silk embroidery thread, 21¼ × 24" (53.97 × 60.96 cm). Collection Timothy Hansen and Dianne Ayres
Recommended for use on the porch or in the den, novelty pillows featured leisure activities of the day such as golf, tennis, and motoring.

Arts and Crafts movement. Appliqué was occasionally done in conventionalized forms or nature motifs on garments requiring less rigorous wear or cleaning.

Muted colors and natural, undyed materials were emphasized in dress, like in many other components of the Arts and Crafts aesthetic. For many reformers, it was important to create the same harmony and expression of personality on the body as in the home. Natural silks, linens, and cottons were all praised for their texture. Varying the thread thickness in many of the woven materials deliberately created a homespun look and feel to the material that was greatly prized in this aesthetic. The raw beauty of the fabric was sometimes accented with adornment, as in a raw silk dress embroidered in an asymmetrical floral pattern that demonstrates the artist's hand (page 215).

Reformers were very cautious about the materials from which clothing was manufactured. It was a concern that fatigue and ill health were prompted by heavy clothing that restricted ventilation and circulation. Some also felt strongly that there was a close relationship between the regulation of body temperature and the texture and fibers of materials, believing underwear worn next to the skin should be in coarse mesh, because the body produced heat that needed to be eliminated by radiation, evaporation, and conduction. Clothing that absorbs and retains moisture was not as healthful as that which eliminates it more quickly—quicker in linen than most fabrics. Many cotton garments were woven loosely and treated to absorb easily. Silk was also seen as excellent, but costly.

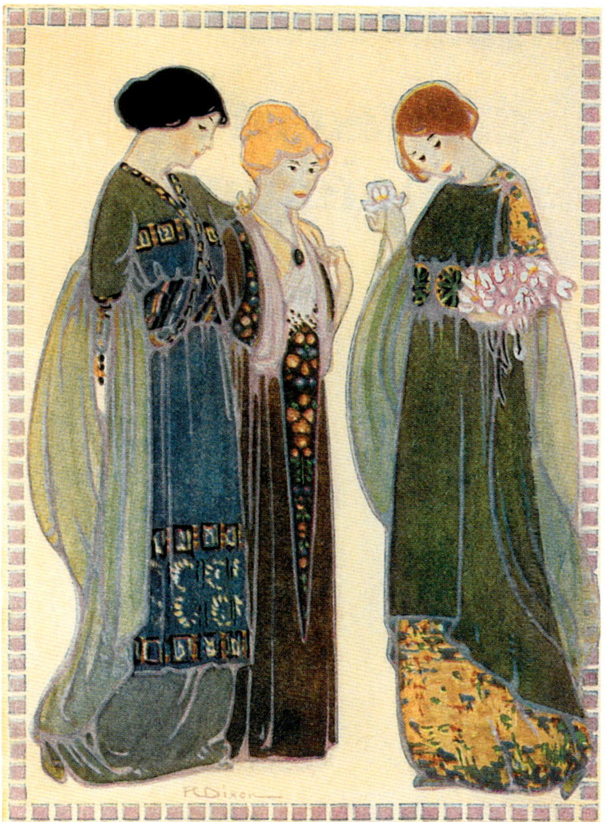

Rachel Taft Dixon. Illustration from *Costume Design and Home Planning*. 1916

Practical fabrics were chosen for the day, dressier fabrics for the evening. A necessary item in England, tea gowns caught on in America as well. The gowns were loose and romantic, often with an empire line and Watteau-inspired back pleats in the medieval manner of the pre-Raphaelites. A fashion journal reported, "at 5 o'clock they will don the picturesque teagown and adopt an air of drooping languor which savours of mystery, while striking an Oriental note of passion and colour."[13] Similar lines were used in some evening wear, particularly if it involved an over dress.

But a large segment of American women were still looking to Paris for its dictates on fashion. Edward Bok, editor of *Ladies' Home Journal*, was "constantly amazed at the audacity with which these French dressmakers and milliners, often themselves of little taste and scant morals, cracked the whip, and the docility with which the American woman blindly and unintelligently danced to their measure."[14] With the largest circulation magazine in America at his command, in 1909,[15] he took up a campaign to promote American fashion design. This was not the first of his crusades; he had successfully rallied against patent medicines, effectively shamed many cities into cleaning

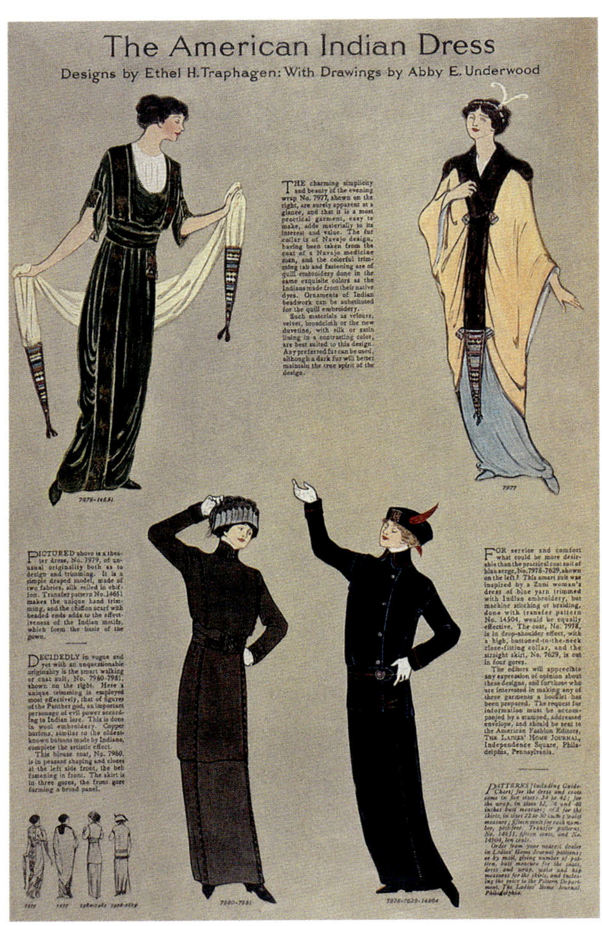

The American Indian Dress

Designs by Ethel H. Traphagen: With Drawings by Abby E. Underwood

THE charming simplicity and beauty of the evening wrap No. 7977, shown on the right, are surely apparent at a glance, and that it is a most practical garment, easy to make, adds materially to its interest and value. The fur collar is of Navajo design, having been taken from the coat of a Navajo medicine man, and the colorful trimming tab and fastening are of quill embroidery done in the same exquisite colors as the Indians made from their native dyes. Ornaments of Indian beadwork can be substituted for the quill embroidery.

Such materials as velours, velvet, broadcloth or the new duveline, with silk or satin lining in a contrasting color, are best suited to this design. Any preferred fur can be used, although a dark fur will better maintain the true spirit of the design.

7979-14651

7977

PICTURED above is a theater dress, No. 7979, of unusual originality both as to design and trimming. It is a simple draped model, made of two fabrics, silk veiled in chiffon. Transfer pattern No. 14651 makes the unique hand trimming, and the chiffon scarf with beaded ends adds to the effectiveness of the Indian motifs, which form the basis of the gown.

DECIDEDLY in vogue and yet with an unquestionable originality is the smart walking or coat suit, No. 7980-7981, shown on the right. Here a unique trimming is employed most effectively, that of figures of the Panther god, an important personage of evil power according to Indian lore. This is done in wool embroidery. Copper buttons, similar to the oldest-known buttons made by Indians, complete the artistic effect.

This blouse coat, No. 7980, is in peasant shaping and closes at the left side front, the belt fastening in front. The skirt is in three gores, the front gore forming a broad panel.

7980-7981

7978-7629-14504

FOR service and comfort what could be more desirable than the practical coat suit of blue serge, No. 7978-7629, shown on the left? This smart suit was inspired by a Zuni woman's dress of blue yarn trimmed with Indian embroidery, but machine stitching or braiding, done with transfer pattern No. 14504, would be equally effective. The coat, No. 7978, is in drop-shoulder effect, with a high, buttoned-to-the-neck close-fitting collar, and the straight skirt, No. 7629, is cut in four gores.

The editors will appreciate any expression of opinion about these designs, and for those who are interested in making any of these garments a booklet has been prepared. The request for information must be accompanied by a stamped, addressed envelope, and should be sent to the American Fashion Editors, THE LADIES' HOME JOURNAL, Independence Square, Philadelphia, Pennsylvania.

PATTERNS (including Guide-Chart) for the dress and coats come in five sizes: 34 to 42; for the wrap, in sizes 32, 36 and 40 inches bust measure; and for the skirts, in sizes 22 to 30 inches waist measure; fifteen cents for each number, post-free. Transfer patterns, No. 14651, fifteen cents, and No. 14504, ten cents.

Order from your nearest dealer in Ladies' Home Journal patterns; or by mail, giving number of pattern, bust measure for the coats, dress and wrap, waist and hip measures for the skirts, and inclosing the price to the Pattern Department, The Ladies' Home Journal, Philadelphia.

◀
Ethel T. Traphagen, with drawings by Abby E. Underwood. "The American Indian Dress." *The Ladies' Home Journal.* November 1913

up blighted areas, and played a major role in directing consumers' taste to simpler, more practical architecture.

Bok engaged experts and the actress Sarah Bernhardt to expose that "the designs sent over by the so-called Paris arbiters of fashion were never worn by the French-woman of birth and good taste; that they were especially designed and specifically intended for 'the bizarre American trade,' as one polite Frenchman called it; and that the only women in Paris who wore these grotesque and often immoderate styles were of the demimonde."[16] He investigated and revealed that even the best American merchants were selling garments that had been constructed in the United States with knockoffs of French labels sewn in. He also argued his case on grounds of patriotism and commissioned American designers to create styles based on American Indian motifs and historic costumes from the Metropolitan Museum of Art (above). He subsequently launched a campaign against the wearing of aigrettes, the plumage sported on the fashionable hats of the day, by illustrating photographs of the slaughter of the mother birds and starvation of orphaned baby birds. He appealed to women's mothering instincts. But, after protracted campaigns, he found that they were to no avail. The aigrette campaign only succeeded in publicizing their desirability and increased their sales fourfold. Nor was the American woman to be swayed from her fascination with the allure of sophistication denoted by wearing a Parisian model, or one that could be represented as such.

Stickley's *The Craftsman* took a more philosophical approach in attempting to influence American women to free themselves from the treadmill of fashion. Their audience was a select one, in quest of a different mode than that of the mainstream.

> Fresh styles, new modes, the usual whimsicality designated as fashion has no place in *The Craftsman*; but dress as an expression of character, as related to daily living, as a part of personality like one's home and friends, is very closely and inevitably woven in the woof of life. It is the new Philosophy of Dress, not a contribution to the utterly silly, unworthy subject characterized as "Fashions," which this magazine desires to present, believing that women who think will be glad to do their share in reorganizing the present scheme of dressing, both for their own comfort and happiness and to contribute to a "better and more reasonable way of living."[17]

The new principles of dress, design, and health were also disseminated through the industrial and household arts programs at colleges and universities, including Teacher's College

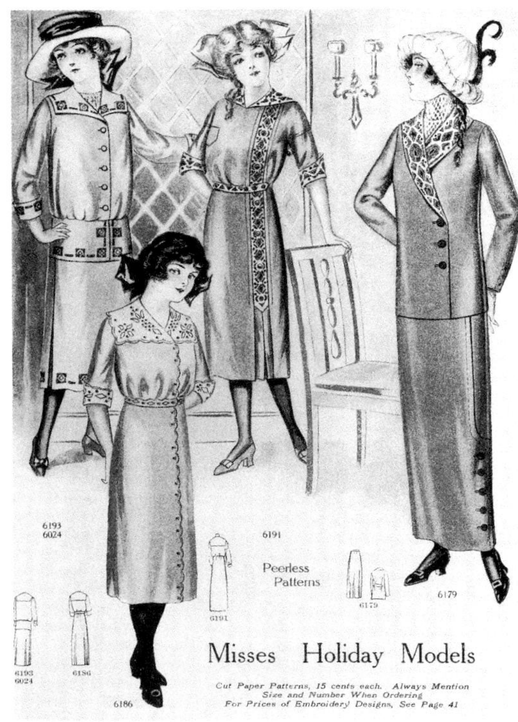

◀
"Misses Holiday Models." *The Modern Priscilla*. June 1913

at Columbia in New York City. These programs had wide impact. Students studied architecture, art, sculpture, and historic costume. Helen Kinne and Anna Cooley, two of the instructors in the Columbia program, wrote a textbook, *Shelter and Clothing,* which reminded readers that all aspects of dress and the home should both suit their purpose and surroundings and express the personality of the wearer.

> In our costumes we should have a higher ideal than mere fashion. . . . To be merely fashionable is to be of the thousands; to wear artistic and individual costumes is to be well-dressed. It is not for the benefit of womankind that the fashions are made to change so frequently, but to enrich manufacturer, modiste, and fashion-book maker. . . . Each generation is in the grip of social customs; we submit unconsciously to the survivals of style. It is not a matter to be treated lightly, so much of health, comfort, and good looks depend on the garments we wear that they deserve intelligent thought. We are frequently unaware of how much our clothes hinder us in our daily tasks, so much disability comes below this level of our consciousness. The full, plaited walking skirts when too long require energy better devoted to something else, in order to support them. . . . Change we want, but let us accept only such change as is for the better, either in the direction of comfort or beauty, or both.[18]

The younger generations that Kinne and Cooley and other instructors were teaching grew to become adults during the Arts and Crafts movement and were products of the new American health consciousness. Their clothes allowed movement, were made of sturdy, breathable materials, and, of course, were washable. Popular forms included the romper, the smock, and a bloomer-and-tunic combination known as a Russian suit (page 216). Starting out their lives in free-flowing gowns and coveralls, children were able to easily transition into becoming active adults, free to bicycle, and participate in the changing world around them.

The reform movement influenced men's clothes too. Young boys were started out in sailor suits and linen playclothes. These boys grew up to favor relaxed clothing, such as the sack suit worn by Gustav Stickley, Elbert Hubbard, and Frank Lloyd Wright. A soft shirt and loose bow tie was a mode of dress adopted by William Morris, Hubbard, and others.

Many influential teachers and figures were involved in clothing. Wright designed garments for his wife that were executed by a seamstress. Claude Bragdon, a period designer, designed costumes for the theater. Art education advocate Arthur Wesley Dow, poet Charles Keeler, and others were also involved in theatrical and pageant costumes (page 206).

In order to assist the new dresser, some fashion guides went so far as to suggest wardrobe lists. The lists included basic items such as undervests, drawers, corset covers, stockings, and union suits. Footwear included high shoes, low shoes, rubbers, and sandals. Sleepwear and casual wear included nightgowns and kimonos. Spring and summer essentials included white skirts, petticoats, and outing flannels. Outerwear included wool sweaters, rain coats, and umbrellas. Winter wear included woolen waists/scotch flannels, wool dress skirts, and winter suits. A silk waist would be kept for "best" with a suit. A long coat, winter hats, and summer hats

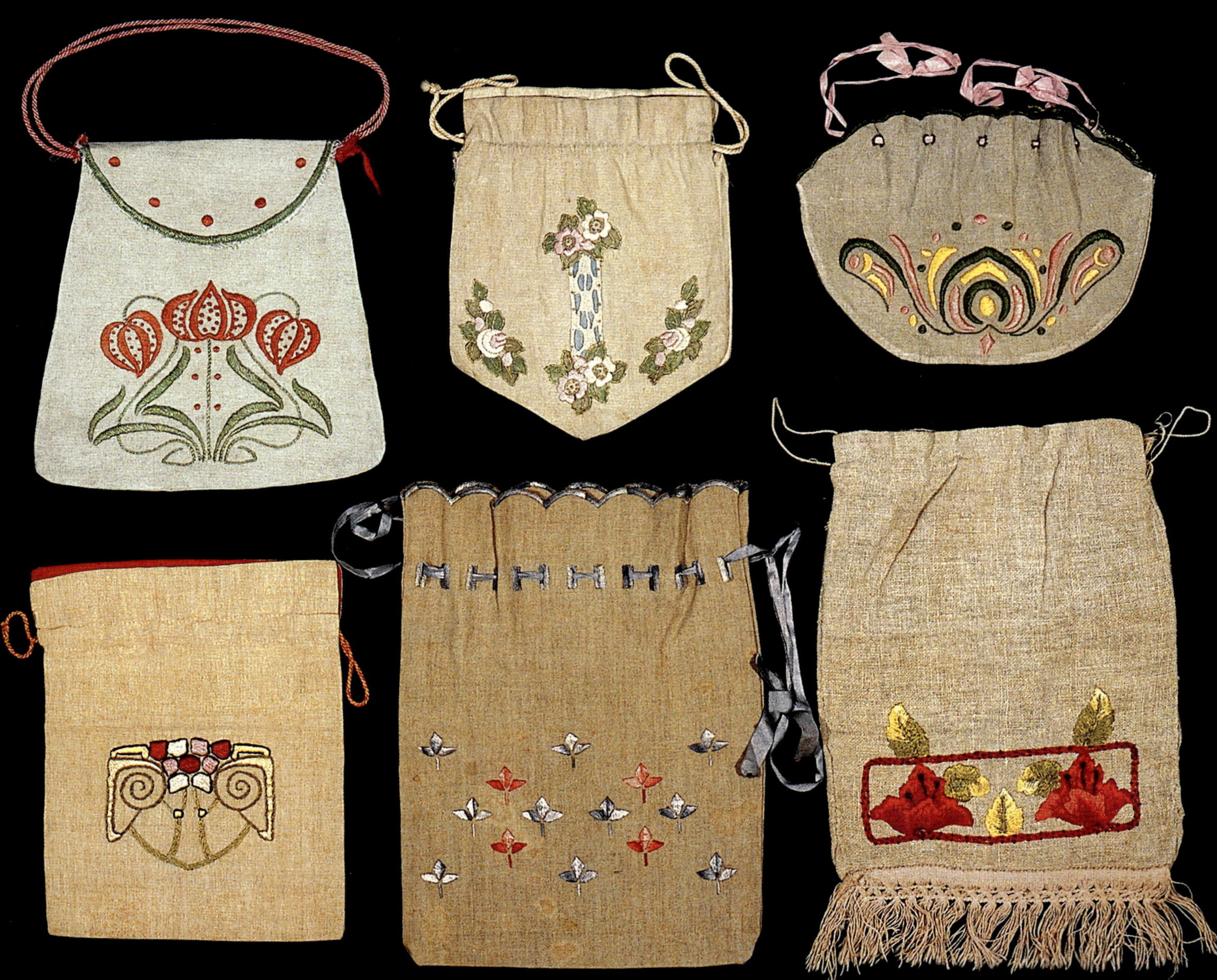

◀
Assorted embroidery thread companies. Bags. 1905–15. Linen, silk, and cotton embroidery thread, approx. 12 × 20" (30 × 48 cm). Collection Tommy and Beth Ann McPherson
A popular kit choice offered by the embroidery thread companies, bags came assembled or unassembled, depending on the company of manufacture. Geometric and stylized designs adorned the fronts, backs, or flaps.

would protect the wearer. A silk dress for the afternoon, a linen skirt, a lawn dress, a tailored waist, and lingerie white waists completed the spring/summer list. Accessories included collars, ties, belts, and handkerchiefs and dogskin, kid, and cotton gloves.

Fitting to the idea of form following function, increased physical activities necessitated appropriate attire as well. Despite an interest in feminine ruffles and frivolous undergarments, silk undergarments were simply not conducive to heavy activity. Thus, practical, healthful undergarments and costumes appropriate for sports were developed. Golf, cricket, tennis, hockey, fishing, skating, skiing, mountain climbing, bicycling, archery, and croquet began to play a role in women's lives. New, washable clothing items such as knickers and bloomers were designed to accommodate these activities. On an everyday basis, walking became more common, and skirts were shortened and flared as a result. Mail-order and pattern companies produced many of these goods, allowing Americans nationwide to participate in the new trends, no matter their whereabouts (page 219).

The introduction of new leisure activities also affected women's clothing. Motoring was one such example. In the early years, the new mode of transportation was open, without shield from wind or rain. To preserve one's appearance required the appropriate accouterments, including hats, caps as on page 218, motor veils, gloves, goggles, dusters, capes, and costumes (page 220). Eventually, cars were closed in and dress became of less concern.

Suits took many shapes, cuts, and forms, looser for country wear and more tailored for city wear. The tailored, or walking, suit, shown on page 211, representing both the modern silhouette and

▶
Anonymous. Shirtwaist. c. 1906. Cotton and silk, 19 × 18" (48 × 46 cm). Collection Tommy and Beth Ann McPherson
Shirtwaists, or women's blouses, provided a flexible means for middle-class women to dress up or dress down their basic separates. Shirtwaists were both plain and decorative. This particular example is a striking Arts and Crafts design, with its geometric motifs and strong colors.

women's newfound level of activity, became indispensable. Tailored costumes, such as the 1909 director suit, were designed to appeal to a new generation of women. The suit's cut-away coat with close-fitting sleeves and a false waistcoat was worn with a narrow or mermaid skirt.

About 1910, designers such as the theater-inspired French couturier and costumer Poiret ensured that designs did not become stagnant by introducing draping and knee-length tunics over narrow skirts, which gradually became shorter. The materials of choice for these new drapes included linen, tussore, soft woolens, and silks. Serges and tweeds were used as face cloths in suits. Blouses were of delicate fabrics, often embroidered. Evening gown bodices became diaphanous.

Clothing's narrower shape and the loosened silhouette required appropriate undergarments. The new line required slim hoops and a long, boned, loosely laced corset with stocking suspenders to support the lengthened look. Large bust lines continued to stay popular. For those less endowed, corsets with pleated fronts were made to assist in exaggerating this area of the body. This look continued to evolve through the teens.

Petticoats declined in use as the slim lines rose in popularity. More and more women donned "knickers," both open and closed, under their garments. One of the earliest was the split or divided skirt knicker developed between 1906 and 1908. The split kicker buttoned up the legs, allowing it to function as either a petticoat or knickers.

The introduction of the brassiere was a major moment in the history of female clothing. Illustrations of the garment appeared in *Vogue* as early as 1907, and the term was used widely

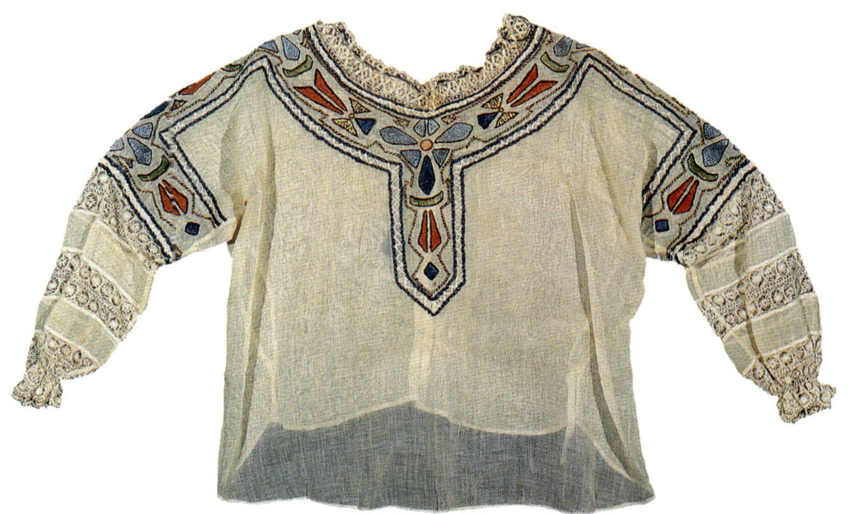

enough to be included in the Oxford English Dictionary in 1912. In 1913, Caresse Crosby (Mary Phelps Jacob), a New York City debutante, developed a new style of brassiere. Jacob disliked the boning still present in corsets. Attempting to find comfort, Jacob used two handkerchiefs and ribbon to create a brassiere that separated the breasts and bared the midriff, allowing a great deal more comfort for the wearer. She patented the "backless bra." The materials used in the production of these undergarments continued to evolve.

Throughout this evolution, accessories were important to the formation of an ensemble. However, the type of accessories underwent a transformation. Gloves are one such example. Although the rigid etiquette of glove wearing faded, various shapes and sizes were still offered. Men's gloves retained the relatively serious formal appearance of the nineteenth century. Women's gloves, however, followed the current trend and became plainer. As in other areas of manufacture, technical developments in glove making in the late nineteenth century made it possible to produce the finished product faster and less expensively. New means of tanning leather with minerals, such as chrome, were developed in 1885, producing water-resistant and sturdy lambskin gloves. Other materials were used as well, but the primary selling point was that the gloves were washable. The new means of production increased the acceptability of fabric versus leather gloves. By 1920, a change in attitude became apparent in the period literature, in which gloves were approached as purely functional accessories. By 1921, gentlemen were wearing gloves only at state or court functions.[19]

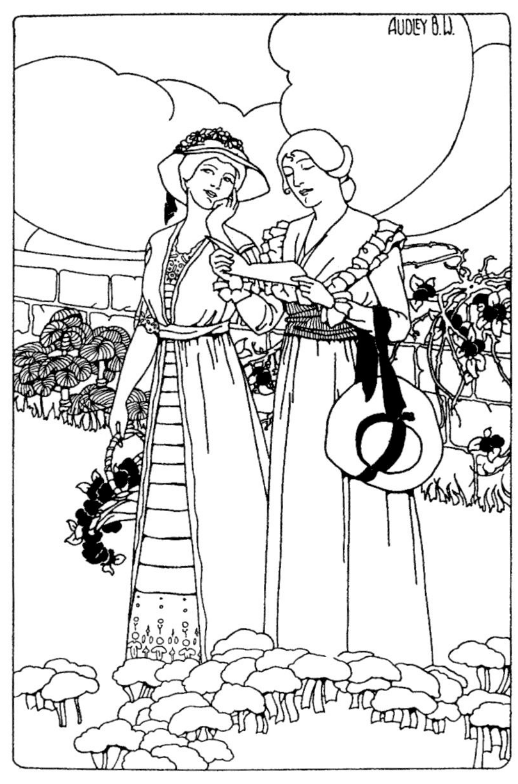

◀
Audley B. Wells. "Summer gowns that are always beautiful." Illustration from *The Art and Ethic of Dress.* 1915

As the twentieth century entered its second decade, the public's dress both clung to the past and reached toward the future. Magazines commented on the increased level of activity in women's lives.

> This is the keynote of modern fashion, for La Mode at the present time is an expression of no particular period, and of no definite style. . . . With the conclusion of the first decade of the twentieth century, the result of continually living at high pressure has reflected itself not only in feminine fashion but also in feminine character. In the feverish rush to get through her engagements, the modern elegante has but little time except for dining in restaurants, motoring, bridge, and weekend visits. In the most giddy times of the Second Empire, she never lived at so rapid a pace as she does now.[20]

New ideas and philosophies for how life was to be lived were in the air. In Europe, the pre-war/Edwardian period was considered one of the last great eras of social standards and behavior. Traditional mores were both questioned and challenged. The women's fashion magazines and company catalogs show the prominent mode of dress as the sway back, narrow silhouette of Edwardian dress. By 1915, skirts flared out slightly again and silhouettes loosened even further, creating the boxy look of the late teens. Necklines also loosened, continuing the trend toward comfort and demonstrating the influence of Japan's kimono dress on American female silhouettes.

During World War I, materials were in short supply, and there was not extensive time or interest in fashion. As women took to the factory, the need for practical dress only heightened. Suits remained popular, with the waistline riding above waist level. Skirt length rose seven or eight inches off the ground. Necklines came round or v-shaped. Blouses and tunics took on a longer, loose form, held in at the hip by a belt. Next came "all-in-one" dresses and jumpers. By 1919, the boyish figure of the flapper, with slim hips and a flat bosom was gaining attention. The new mode was adopted primarily by young working women with disposable income. For the first time in history, many women had money to spend at their own discretion. Perhaps in an attempt to demonstrate their increased emancipation, many women began choosing clothes that lessened the physical differences between themselves and their male counterparts.

Although the Arts and Crafts movement faded from the forefront of American style in the 1920s, its impact on women's dress left a lasting legacy.

> This question of good dressing is much simpler than "reforms" and "movements." It does not need to force a woman to "take a stand" and in any ostentatious way differ from prevailing modes; all that is necessary is for her to study her own color scheme, to understand the merits and faults of her own body, to select for that body the clothes that are just suited in line and color, to avoid useless ornamentation, and to see to it that the color, texture, and cut of her clothes are suited to her occupation in life.[21] ❖

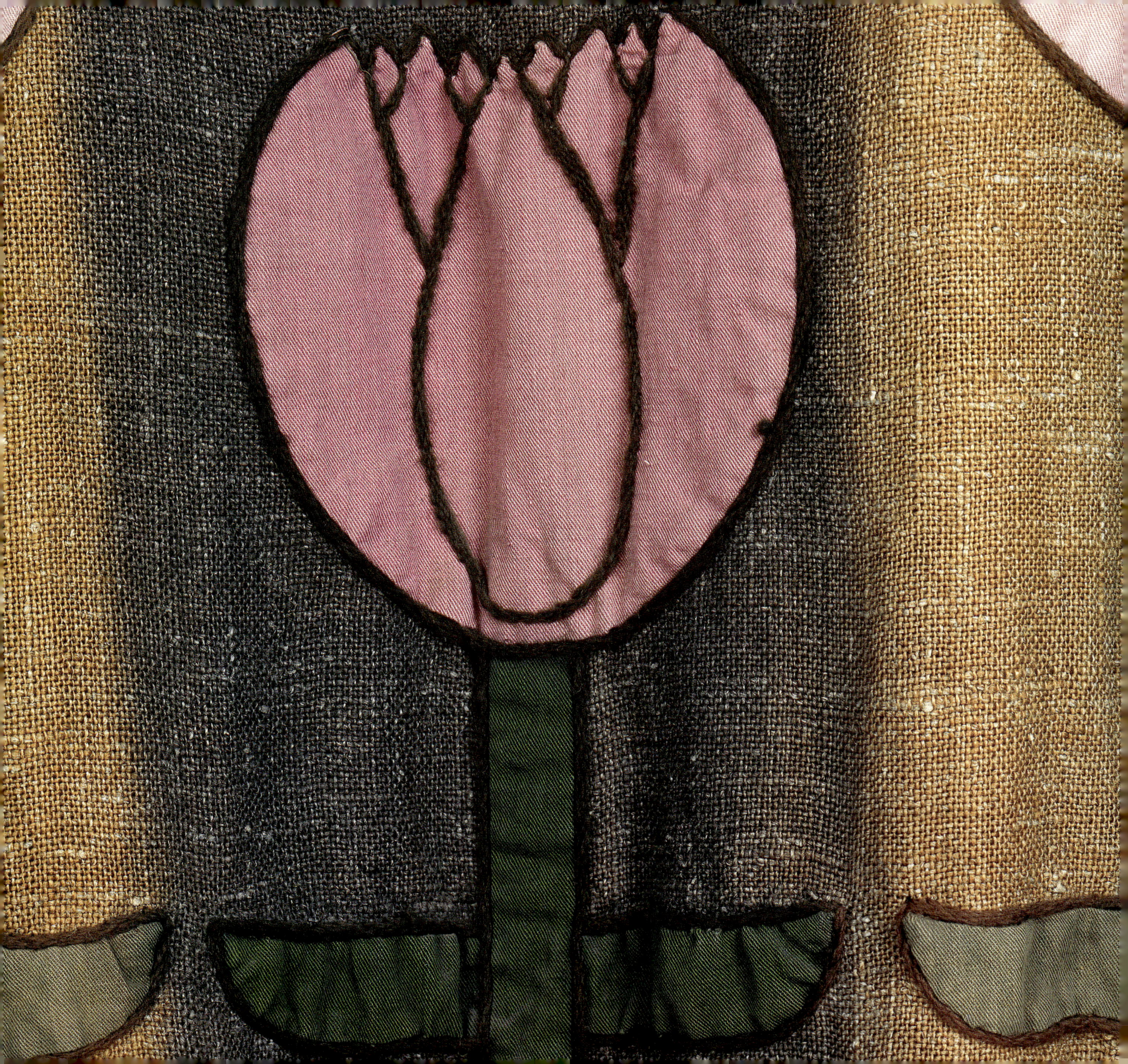

7 Stitches in Time: The Care of Antique Textiles

◀
Attributed to Craftsman Workshops. Riordan Mansion portiere. c. 1904. Collection Riordan Mansion State Park, Flagstaff, Arizona

Because of the deep folds in the portiere, some areas were exposed to sunlight for a prolonged time and not other areas, resulting in uneven fading. Originally, the base cloth was uniformly green. The flowers have also faded.

Arts and Crafts Textiles are an important part of our heritage. Yet many museums and other institutions, while having furniture or pottery in their collections, have few or no textiles from the period. Hence, it falls upon collectors to preserve for future generations our Arts and Crafts textile heritage. The textile collector, as a caretaker of this heritage, must confront the following issues: whether or not to use the textiles as they were originally intended; how to store textiles; the pros and cons of cleaning textiles and, finally, the preservation of the textiles. For information on dealing with specific pieces, we urge you to consult a textile conservator.

Textiles, by their nature, are ephemeral. Curtains, if exposed to sunlight, will only last a few years. Clothing, if worn, will need periodic cleaning, and will have a relatively short life. The same is true for pillows, table runners, and other household items. Textiles surviving from the Arts and Crafts period, even if they appear to be in excellent condition, will not last as long with use as their modern day counterpart. This is because the fibers have slowly but constantly been breaking down since their date of origin.

Different fibers break down at different rates. Jute and silk are among the shortest-lived fibers common to the Arts and Crafts period. Jute was commonly used for table runners, pillows, and wall coverings. Today, jute textiles are rarely found because the fibers have long ago turned brittle. When these items are folded, they tend to break on the fold. Jute was occasionally blended with linen; these textiles are also very fragile and should not be folded. Silk was commonly used for embroidery thread, as material for clothing, and for some high-end printed fabrics for use in the

▼
Peacock table scarf. c. 1905. Silk embroidery on linen, 18½ × 67" (47 × 170 cm). Collection Timothy Hansen and Dianne Ayres
This detail shows the results of improper hand cleaning with water. The purple and green dye from the embroidery has bled into the area surrounding the linen base cloth.

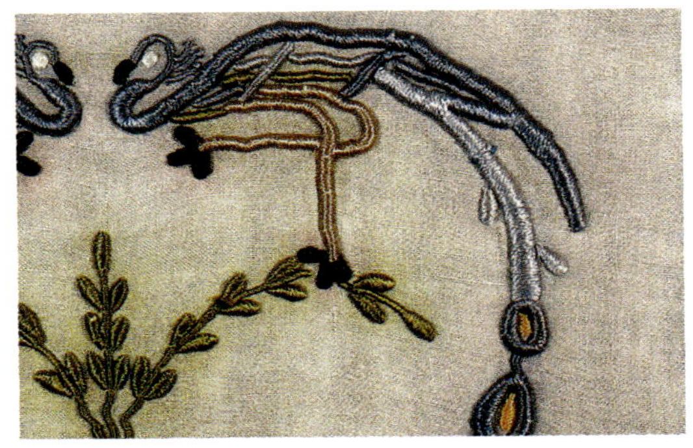

home. These items should be treated with extreme care, as today they are undoubtedly very fragile. A silk embroidery on linen, if folded, will stretch the silk thread. This stretching can break the silk fibers and cause the embroidery to fall apart. Even dusting can hurt some silk embroideries.

Fortunately, not all the fibers common to the period are so fragile. While not "as good as new," linen, cotton, and artificial silk (rayon) may still be in relatively serviceable condition. Often these fibers are dyed or pigmented with colors that are not light fast. Exposure to light can quickly cause fading, sometimes in as little as a few months. If these items become soiled, cleaning can also present problems. Often colors will run or just wash out, leaving the piece as only a shadow of what it once was. For these reasons, extreme care should be exercised if vintage textile items are to be used in the home, or clothing from the period worn. In light of this, many collectors frame their textiles archivally and enjoy looking at them instead of using them as originally intended.

Whenever possible, vintage textiles should be stored flat, in archival boxes, with each piece separated from the others by archival tissue or cotton cloth. The reason for separating textiles with a layer of archival tissue or cloth is to prevent the possible transfer of some dyes from one piece to another. The boxes should be stored in a cool, dry place. Every six months or so the boxes should be unpacked and the items inspected for problems like color transfer, bugs, deep creases, and the like. If a piece is folded, it should be folded in a new place when packing and the old fold gently straighten out.

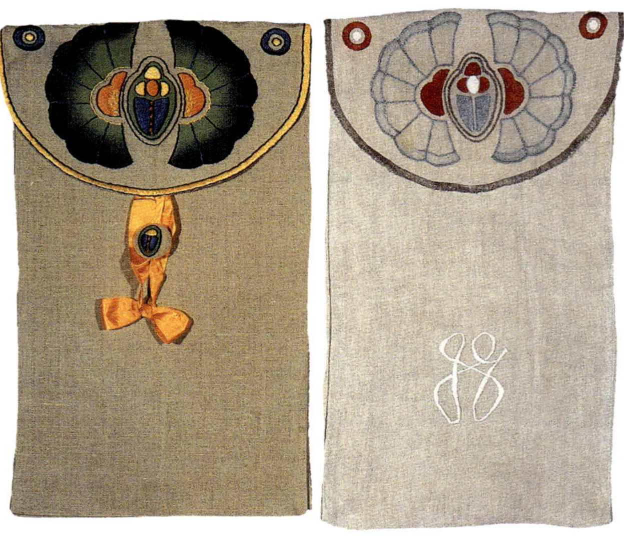

◀
Linen bags. c. 1911. Cotton embroidery and stenciling on linen, 20 × 12" (51 × 30.5 cm). Collection Timothy Hansen and Dianne Ayres
The base cloth and stenciling of the bag on the right were originally the same as the bag on the left. The choice of embroidery colors is different. Because of repeated laundering the bag on the right has significantly deteriorated.

Large items, like runners or curtains, are sometimes rolled onto tubes with layers of archival tissue or cotton keeping the piece from touching itself, the tube, or other pieces. Textiles should not be stored in plastic bags, as sunlight can cause the plastic to break down, forming chemicals harmful to the textiles. In some cases it may be advisable to wear cotton gloves while handling the textiles to keep oils in the skin from being absorbed into the textiles. The archival boxes of textiles should not be stored next to an exterior wall, as often these walls fluctuate in temperature because of the changing weather conditions outside and sunlight heating up the wall. Changing temperatures can cause humidity or even condensation, which can foster the growth of mold or cause some dyes to transfer to other pieces.

Bugs, like silverfish and moths, are also a hazard to be guarded against. It was a common practice to starch household items during the Arts and Crafts period, which prolonged the life of the textiles by making them less susceptible to wear and made them easier to clean. Silverfish eat the starch and unfortunately, will devour the textile's fibers along with the starch. The appetite of moths is well known.

At best, cleaning most Arts and Crafts textiles is a risky endeavor and is best left to a professional conservator. Typical cleaning instructions from the period stress that pieces are to be washed individually by hand, and that the first washing of an embroidery is risky. With each washing the risk lessens. This is because of the possibility of loose dye migrating to other parts of the piece. With each washing, there is less loose dye to contend with, hence running is less of

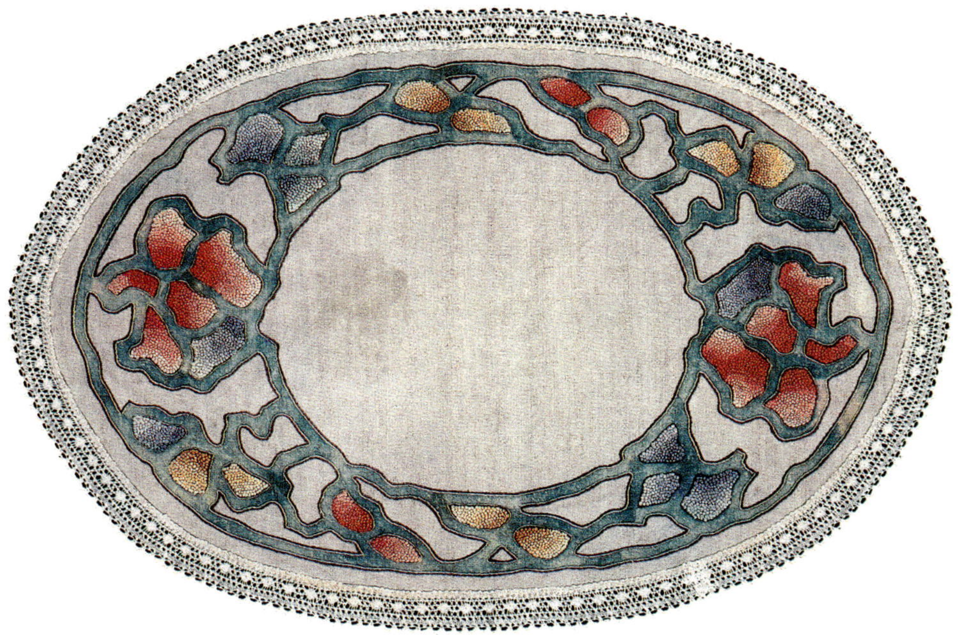

◀
Oblong table cloth. c. 1910. Cotton embroidery on linen, 23½ × 34½" (60 × 88 cm). Collection Timothy Hansen and Dianne Ayres
In an attempt to remove the stain in the center field, the piece was dry cleaned. The stain did not come out, but a significant amount of blue stencil paint was dissolved from the areas between the embroidery. Originally the blue stenciling was uniform.

a problem. Period instructions also stress working quickly, and that it is acceptable to rub soiled areas between the hands, but that a general rubbing should be avoided.

When drying, never hang the piece up, as the loose dye is likely to run down and soil the linen. Never fold the piece over onto itself, as loose dye might transfer to another part of the linen. The method recommended for drying is to put the embroidery between two dry towels and roll it up, then squeeze or gently pound it. This way the dry towels can absorb the moisture, which will help prevent running.

Since many collectors iron pieces, it is important that the risks involved are understood. First, the embroidery floss should be dry before ironing because wet embroidery hit with a hot iron can produce steam, which drives loose dye into other unwanted parts of the piece. Steam will also injure silk. *Home Needlework* for April 1906 outlined a timeless process:

> *Ironing.*—Lay the piece face down upon an ironing board well covered with several pieces of material. Spread a clean white cloth over the embroidery and iron lightly the whole surface, being careful not to press too heavily upon the embroidered portions. A hot iron placed upon embroideries the silk in which is wet will produce a steam that will injure the same. Do not

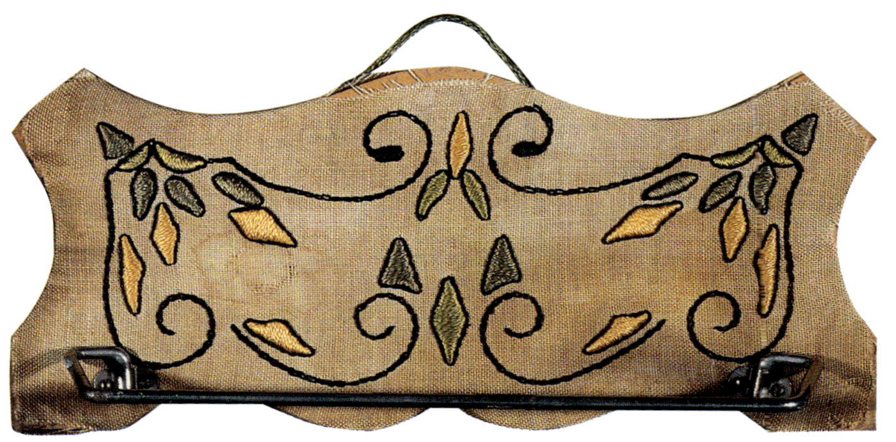

◀
Tie rack kit. c. 1907. Linen over cardboard on wood, 11½ × 5" (29 × 13 cm). Collection Tommy and Beth Ann McPherson
The acidity of the board has caused the linen to deteriorate. This is particularly severe where the linen was held in close contact to the board, as seen at the edges.

> press hard at first, but work rapidly. Should the center have become too dry, use a dampened cloth to run the iron over, as this method will leave the linen sufficiently damp for pressing. It also leaves the linen fresh and holds the natural stiffening of the same.[1]

Dry cleaning is not recommended, as it is a harsh process. The chemicals may dissolve stenciled areas, cause dyes to migrate, and/or permanently set stains.

Textile collectors are guided by the responsibility of preserving the items in their charge. To this end, they take the steps necessary to preserve items and strive to take no steps that are not reversible. Pieces of fabric that come in contact with cardboard are subject to deterioration because of the acidity in the board. A conservator should be consulted to reduce the acidity and stop further deterioration. Silk can also be treated to increase its life. A piece with mold should be kept separate so as not to contaminate the rest of the collection. A conservator should be consulted to correct the problem.

By cleaning a period piece only when necessary for its preservation and not for cosmetic reasons, and by taking those steps necessary to slow or stop deterioration, the collector plays an important role in preserving America's textile heritage. ❖

Notes

Chapter 1

1. Florence Montgomery. *Textiles in America 1650–1870* (1991), xi.
2. The term derives from the title of a poem by Robert Louis Stevenson that depicts ultimate simplicity: "A Naked House, a naked moor, / . . . Such is the house I live in, / Bleak without and bare within." See Gwendolyn Wright, *Moralism and the Model Home: Domestic Architecture and Cultural Conflict in Chicago, 1873–1913* (1980), 141. *The House Beautiful*, by Clarence Cook, was published in 1878. A taste manual, the book represents the views of one of America's first important art critics on the subject of home decoration. The book emphasizes personalizing the home, filling it with what suits one's needs. These concepts reached large audiences and laid the groundwork for Arts and Crafts reformers.
3. Montgomery, xi.
4. Much has been published on British Arts and Crafts textiles, most notably: Jude Burkhauser, ed. *Glasgow Girls: Women in Art and Design 1880–1920* (Edinburgh: Canongate, 1990); Anthea Callen, *Women Artists of the Arts and Crafts Movement 1870–1914* (New York: Pantheon, 1979); and Fiona MacFarlane and Elizabeth Arthur, *Glasgow School of Art Embroidery 1894–1920* (Glasgow: Glasgow Museums and Art Galleries, 1980); in addition to other sources listed in the bibliography.
5. Irene Sargent, "A Recent Arts and Crafts Exhibition," *The Craftsman* 4, no. 2. (May 1903).
6. Eileen Boris, *Art and Labor* (1986), 115.
7. Candace Wheeler, "The Philosophy of Beauty Applied to Home Interiors," *Household Art* (1892): 14.
8. Boris, *Art and Labor*, 116.
9. Wheeler, *The Development of Embroidery in America* (1921), 107–21.
10. Boris, *Art and Labor*, 115.
11. James Jordan, *Southern Arts and Crafts* (1996), 73.
12. Boris, *Art and Labor*, 124.
13. "A Russian Peasant Industry," *The Craftsman* 4 (July 1903): 291–94.
14. Annual Report of the Society of Arts and Crafts (1910), 116.
15. Janet Kardon, ed., *The Ideal Home 1900–1920: The History of Twentieth-Century American Craft* (1994), 106.
16. Boris, *Art and Labor*, 117.
17. Ibid., 116.
18. Mary E. Allen, "A Village Remembered," *The Ladies' Home Journal* (Oct. 1901): 32.
19. Boris, *Art and Labor*, 118.
20. Frederic Allen Whiting, "Deerfield, Summer, 1908," Whiting Papers, Archives of American Art.
21. Nicola J. Shilliam, "Boston and the Society of Arts and Crafts: Textiles," in Marilee Boyd Meyer, ed., *Inspiring Reform: Boston's Arts and Crafts Movement* (1997), 102.
22. Boris, *Art and Labor*, 137.
23. Meyer, ed., *Inspiring Reform*, 104–13.
24. Native-American motifs shown by Mrs. Albee at the Society of Arts and Crafts, Boston.
25. A Native-American product.
26. Quoted in Ann Wallace, *Arts and Crafts Textiles* (1999), 49.
27. Jordan, *Southern Arts and Crafts*, 79.
28. Ibid., 115.
29. Ibid., 37.
30. Ibid., 21.
31. Ibid., 80.
32. Kardon, ed., *The Ideal Home*, 105.
33. Ibid., 104.

Chapter 2

1. The authors would like to acknowledge Suzanne Flynt's assistance and her on-going research of this topic.
2. Catalogue of the loan exhibition of the Ithaca branch of the New York Society of Decorative Art, opened Tuesday evening, Dec. 9, 1879.
3. Charles G. Leland, *Drawing and Designing* (1889).
4. Edward Hulme, *Plant-Works—Their Natural Growth and Ornamental Treatment* (1874).
5. Several texts concerning the abstraction of ornament, in addition to Leland and Hulme, were enormously popular. *Plant, Form and Design* was available in the United States. It went through multiple editions, and more than eighteen thousand copies were printed by 1910. W. Midgely and A. E. V. Lilley, *A Book of Studies in Plant Form with Some Suggestions for Their Application to Design* (1910).
6. Theodore M. Dillaway, *Decoration of the School and Home* (1916), 205.
7. Denman Waldo Ross, *A Theory of Pure Design, Harmony, Balance and Rhythm* (1907), v–vi.
8. E. A. Batchelder, *The Principles of Design* (1918), preface.
9. *Plant Analysis* (1905), 22.
10. Ibid., 15.

Chapter 3

1. Alexis de Tocqueville, *Democracy in America*.
2. *The Modern Priscilla* (Nov. 1911 and Feb. 1914), cover pages.
3. *The Craftsman*, July 1905.
4. "Exhibitions of Artistic Work of the Readers of *Harper's Bazaar* Was Viewed by Thousands," *Harper's Bazaar* (July 1912): 408–09.
5. Edith Merrill Kettell, "Crafts in Public Schools," *Applied Arts Book* I (Jan.1902): 18.
6. "Art Needlework in Newcomb College," *The Craftsman* 5, no. 3 (Dec. 1903): 282–85.
7. Jordan, *Southern Arts and Crafts*, 36.
8. Providence Arts & Crafts Exhibit, 1902.
9. Jordan, *Southern Arts and Crafts*, 76.
10. Jane Kessler, "If I Can: Influential Women and the Southern Craft Revival," in Jordan, *Southern Arts and Crafts*, 38.
11. Ibid., 22.
12. Quote from Jane E. Starnes, "Mary Crovatt Hambridge: Art and Nature," in Jordan, *Southern Arts and Crafts*, 55.
13. Ibid., 56.
14. Ibid., 57. Quoted from a letter, Mary Crovatt Hambridge to Hall Clovis, July 4, 1956.

15. Ibid., 58.
16. Kardon, ed., *The Ideal Home,* 106.
17. Boris, *Art and Labor,* 115.
18. Kardon, ed., *The Ideal Home,* 106.
19. Gustav Stickley, "Thoughts Occasioned by an Anniversary: A Plea for a Democratic Art," *The Craftsman* 7 (Oct. 1904): 53.
20. Craftsman advertising department, *The Craftsman* (Nov. 1913).
21. Anon., "Some Craftsman Designs for Door Curtains," *The Craftsman* 4, no. 5. (Aug. 1903): 387.
22. Gustav Stickley business papers. The Winterthur Library, Joseph Downs Collection of Manuscripts and Printed Ephemera. At this time it has not been demonstrated that any men worked in the department.
23. O. B. E. Stevens, *The Belding-Corticelli Story* (1951).
24. Date given is the year the book was offered, the copyright being the year before. The illustrations shown were chosen from those that were published in color, which the company presumably wished to highlight.
25. For an explanation of the term *mission* as used in the period, see Herbert E. Binstead, *The Furniture Styles* (Chicago: Trade Periodical Company, 1909), 169.
26. While termed a *floss*, the plies were not to be separated, as can be done with today's embroidery floss. Cotton embroidery thread used through the Arts and Crafts era was of the type that is now known as "perle" cotton. Stranded cotton embroidery threads did not come into wide use until the mid-1920s.
27. Kardon, ed., *The Ideal Home,* 100.
28. Belding Brothers & Co., *Needle and Hook, 1899–1900,* 1.

Chapter 4

1. Andrew Jackson Downing, *Victorian Cottage Residences* (1842; rpt. 1981), 15.
2. Wheeler, *Principles of Home Decoration* (1903), 3.
3. Ibid., 142–43.
4. Charlotte Perkins Gilman, *The Home, Its Work and Its Influence* (1903), 158.
5. Ibid., 152–53.
6. Stickley, *Chips from the Workshop of Gustav Stickley* (1901).
7. Stickley, *Catalog of Craftsman Furniture,* 5.
8. Stickley, *Craftsman Homes* (1909), 165.
9. Alice M. Kellogg, *Home Furnishing, Practical and Artistic* (1905), v.
10. The first appearance of Mission furniture was not in California. This is a common misconception stemming from nomenclature regarding the relationship between the simple, traditional furniture seen in the missions of the Southwest and the clean, rectilinear furniture produced by Gustav Stickley and other designers between 1900 and 1920. Stickley steadfastly refused to allow his furniture to be termed *mission* in an effort to counter the problem, calling his own lines "Craftsman." Nonetheless, in part due to the persistent popular use of the term in the press, the term *mission furniture* survives today.
11. Mabel Tuke Priestman, *Art and Economy in Home Decoration* (1908), 18.
12. Ibid., 15–16.
13. Helen Binkerd Young, in Brown, *Home Building and Decoration* (1912), 33–34.
14. Hazel H. Adler, *The New Interior* (1916), 25.
15. Charles F. Warner, *Work and Play Books: Home Decoration* (1911, reprinted 1916), 45–46.
16. "Our Home Department: Washable Wall-Covering," *The Craftsman* (Mar. 1906).
17. Wheeler, "The Philosophy of Beauty Applied to Home Interiors," *Household Art* (1892), 14.
18. "House in Decatur, Ill., Built After Craftsman Plans by a Member of the Home Builders' Club," *The Craftsman* (Feb. 1906).
19. Katherine Sanger Brinley, "A Revival of Needlecraft: Some Fresh Suggestions for Ornamenting Bedroom Draperies," *The Craftsman* (Oct. 1909).
20. Stickley, *Craftsman Homes,* 196.
21. Lillie Hamilton French, *Homes and Their Decoration* (1903), 274.
22. Margaret Greenleaf, "Window Draperies of Simple Materials for Country and Suburban Homes of Moderate Cost—Methods and Costs," in Henry H. Saylor, ed., *Distinctive Homes of Moderate Cost* (1911), 96.
23. Priestman, *Art and Economy in Home Decoration,* 105.
24. Halbert White, "Curtains and Draperies," in Henry Collins Brown and Clara Brown Lyman, eds., *Home Building and Decoration* (1912), 65.
25. George Leland Hunter, *Home Furnishing* (1913), 147.
26. Ruby Ross Goodnow, *The Honest House* (1921), 194–95.
27. Priestman, *Art and Economy in Home Decoration,* 108–09.
28. *Craftsman Fabrics and Needlework* (1908), 8–9.
29. Hint submitted by E. B. for the December 1910 "Hints for Needleworkers" a regular column in *The Modern Priscilla.* Some "hints" were of more dubious value, such as: "In washing for the first time a piece of needlework which has become badly soiled in working, grease with a little clean, pure lard and let it lay over night. In the morning wash in clean warm suds, rinse, starch, Art and Labor and iron while quite damp. This will thoroughly remove all of the dirt without rubbing. —O. J. M."
30. Goodnow, *The Honest House,* 192.
31. Ibid., 194–95.
32. White, "Curtains and Draperies," in Brown, *Home Building and Decoration,* 71.
33. Priestman, *Art and Economy in Home Decoration,* 117.
34. Ibid., 126–27.
35. White, "Curtains and Draperies," in Brown, *Home Building and Decoration,* 71.
36. Ibid., 68.
37. Sherwin-Williams Company, *Your Home and Its Decoration* (1910), 19.
38. White, "Curtains and Draperies," in Brown, *Home Building and Decoration,* 67.

39. Hunter, *Home Furnishing,* 151–52.
40. Ibid., 153. Arras cloth is identified in various sources as being a combination of linen and jute (Craftsman Workshops); linen and cotton (Priestman, *Art and Economy in Home Decoration)* or linen and wool (Kelly, "Bungalow Furnishings and Fitments," *The House Beautiful* [June 1914]: 24; this source also describes a linen-jute blend fabric).
41. Ibid., 149.
42. Priestman, *Art and Economy in Home Decoration,* 108.
43. White, "Curtains and Draperies," in Brown, *Home Building and Decoration,* 68.
44. Anon., "Home Department," *The Craftsman* (Mar. 1905): 137.
45. *Home Needlework* (Oct. 1909): 359.
46. Adler, *The New Interior,* 87.
47. Priestman, *Art and Economy in Home Decoration,* 13–14.
48. "Couch Pillows of Artistic Design," *Home Needlework* (Feb. 1910): 10.
49. Priestman, *Art and Economy in Home Decoration,* 95–96.
50. Stickley, *Craftsman Homes,* 125.
51. Ibid., 196.
52. Ibid., 196.
53. Ibid., 137.
54. Stickley, *Craftsman Houses: A Book for Homemakers* (1913), 43.
55. Margaret Pendleton. "The January Linen Counter," *The House Beautiful* (Jan. 1912): 41.
56. *Corticelli Home Needlework* 7, no. 1 (first quarter, 1905): 45–47.
57. "The Bedroom and Its Individuality," *The Craftsman* (Feb. 1906).
58. Ibid.
59. "Our Home Department," *The Craftsman* (Dec. 1905).
60. "Two Eleven-Room Craftsman Houses of Brick and Stucco, with Unusually Practical and Homelike Features," *The Craftsman* (Feb. 1913): 81.
61. Ibid.
62. Harriet Avery Gill, "The Charm of A Bedroom," *The House Beautiful* (Jan. 1912): 63.
63. Kellogg, *Home Furnishing, Practical and Artistic,* 95–99.
64. "A Child's Bedroom," *The Craftsman* (July 1903).
65. "Your Own Home: Number Seven: The Modern Nursery," *The Craftsman* (June 1915).
66. Wheeler, *Principles of Home Decoration,* 182–83.

Chapter 5

1. Mary Schenck Woolman and Ellen Beers McGowan, *Textiles* (1913), 256.
2. *Craftsman Fabrics and Needlework,* 14–24.
3. Charlotte M. Gibbs, *Household Textiles* (1914), 106–07.
4. Cheney Silks, *The Story of Silk*, 65.
5. Gibbs, *Household Textiles,* 20.
6. H. E. Verran Company, *The Hand Embroidered Way,* 4th ed. (1915).
7. Richardson Silk Company, *Art Needlework Catalog, 1911–1912,* 89.
8. Newcomb College, Arts & Crafts Sales Exhibition, 66.
9. "A Lesson in Darning Filet Net Illustrated with Original Craftsman Designs," *The Craftsman* 23, no. 3 (Dec. 1912): 104–07.
10. Clara L. Kellogg. "Practical Embroidery Work," *Interior Decoration* (Feb. 1907): 20.
11. Bessie Berry Grabowskii, "Biedermair Embroidery" *Home Needlework* 8, no. 4 (Oct. 1906): 322.
12. Marie Koch, "Two Novel Embroideries—Shelksting and Delsbo," *Home Needlework* 8, no. 4 (Oct. 1906): 356.
13. Kellogg, "Practical Embroidery Work," 19.
14. Brinley, "A Revival of Needlecraft: Some Fresh Suggestions for Ornamenting Bedroom Draperies," *The Craftsman* 17, no. 1 (Oct. 1909): 94.
15. "Some Craftsman Designs for Door Draperies," *The Craftsman* 4, no. 5 (Aug. 1903): 76.
16. Anon. "Peasant Embroidery, as Applied to Curtains," *The Delineator* 68 (Nov. 1906): 832.
17. Priestman, *Art and Economy in Home Decoration,* 153.
18. Priestman, "Linen Appliqué," *Home Needlework* 8, no. 5 (Dec. 1906): 418.
19. *The Good Housekeeping Home Handicraft Book,* 1.
20. Priestman, "The Easily Acquired Art of Stenciling," *Women's Home Companion* (May 1906): 54.
21. Ibid., 55.
22. Reviews of Priestman's books in *The Craftsman* note her as a skilled craftsperson and decorator as well, but her various publications provide little information on her own work.
23. See Anna Duane, "Some Pretty Curtains and How to Make Them," *Home Needlework* 11, no. 1 (Feb. 1909): 47–48; and Elma S. Ritter, "Stencil Work," *The Modern Priscilla* (Sept. 1913): 9.
24. Priestman, "The Easily Acquired Art of Stenciling," 54.
25. Priestman, *Art and Economy in Home Decoration,* 168.
26. Ethelyn J. Morris,"Christmas Stenciling," *The Modern Priscilla* (Dec. 1911): 11.
27. Priestman, *Art and Economy in Home Decoration,* 177.
28. Ibid., 172–73.
29. Thomas H. Cooper, "The New Block-Printing," *The House Beautiful* (Aug. 1910): 91–92; Warner, *Home Decoration,* 99–108; and *The Good Housekeeping Manual of Home Handicraft,* 95–101.
30. Priestman, *Art and Economy in Home Decoration,* 122.
31. Priestman, *Handicrafts in the Home,* 73–78.
32. See Priestman,"The Revival of a Primitive Form of Batik," *The Craftsman* 11, no. 5 (Mar. 1907): 131–37; and Gardner Teall, "The National Arts Club of New York: Its Position as a Factor in the Encouragement of the Fine Arts, and Why it is Worthwhile," *The Craftsman* 15, no. 5 (Feb. 1909): 93–102.
33. Tie-dye, or tied batik, varies from batik in that instead of wax, the resist is achieved by gathering areas of the fabric

and tying them tightly with string. This results in a somewhat circular undyed area, which, when arranged in a pattern, can form a larger design.

34. Amy Mali Hicks, "Batik, Its Making and Its Use," *House & Garden* (Nov. 1913): 289.

35. Pieter Mijer, *Batiks and How to Make Them* (1921), vi.

36. For illustrations of Bush-Brown's batiks see Shilliam, "Boston and the Society of Arts and Crafts: Textiles," in Meyer, ed., *Inspiring Reform,* 101–15; and Gillian Moss, "Textiles of the American Arts and Crafts Movement," in Linda Parry, *William Morris and the Arts & Crafts Movement* (1989), 21–22.

37. The series of eight articles was published in *The Craftsman* from June 1908 through September 1909 and later were consolidated into a book; see Charles E. Pellew, *Dyes and Dyeing* (1918).

38. Shilliam, "From Bohemian to Bourgeois: American Batik in the Early Twentieth Century," in *Contact, Crossover, Continuity* (1994), 253–63.

39. Anna Nott Shook, *The Book of Weaving* (1928), 3–4.

40. Harriet Joor, "An Artist of the Loom," *The House Beautiful* 26 (June 1909): 44.

41. According to Rosalind Webster Perry in "Marie Webster, Quilt Designer," *A Joy Forever, Marie Webster's Quilt Patterns*, 17, the author was actually Elizabeth's older sister, Isabelle, or "Bessie," who collected the information during her missionary work in the Appalachian Mountains.

42. Ibid. *The Ladies' Home Journal* published "Kentucky Mountain Patchwork Quilts" in July 1909 and "The Kentucky Mountain Quilt" in February 1912, both by Elizabeth Daingerfield.

43. For more information on Marie Webster, see Niloo Imami-Paydar, "Marie Webster: A Retrospective," in *American Quilt Renaissance: Three Women Who Influenced Quiltmaking in the Early 20th Century* (1997); Rosalind Webster Perry and Mary Frolli, *A Joy Forever: Marie Webster's Quilt Patterns* (1992); and a biography by Rosalind Webster Perry in the new edition of Marie D. Webster, *Quilts: Their Story and How to Make Them* (1990).

44. Constance Goddard Du Bois, "The Indian Woman as a Craftsman," *The Craftsman* 6, no. 4 (July 1904): 73.

45. Katherine Lord, "The Greenwich Handicraft School," *The Craftsman* 13, no. 6. (Mar. 1908): 106.

46. See Lord, "How to Make Irish Laces at Home," *The Craftsman* 18, no. 4 (July 1910): 83–87; and "A Lesson in Making Filet Lace," *The Craftsman* 17, no. 2 (Nov. 1909): 97–103.

47. Adler, *The New Interior,* 14–15.

48. Mary Schoeser and Celia Rufey, *English and American Textiles* (1989), 160.

Chapter 6

1. Quoted in Ken Montague, "The Aesthetics of Hygiene: Aesthetic Dress, Modernity, and the Body as Sign," *Journal of Design History* 7, no. 2 (1994).

2. "Godwin and the Costume Department Antique Embroideries," in Alison Adburgham, *Liberty's: A Biography of a Shop* (1975), 54.

3. *The Queen* (Jan. 3, 1880).

4. *The Queen* (Jan. 10, 1880); article by Lili.

5. "Pre-Raphaelite Dress," *The Queen* (Feb. 9, 1878).

6. Wallace, *Arts and Crafts Textiles,* 75.

7. Helen Kinne and Anna Cooley, *Shelter and Clothing* (1916), 301.

8. Ibid., 303.

9. Norah Waugh, *The Cut of Women's Clothes* (1968), 228.

10. Ibid., 294–95.

11. Kinne and Cooley, *Shelter and Clothing,* 305.

12. Valerie D. Mendes,"Women's Dress Since 1900," *Four Hundred Years of Fashion* (1996), 78.

13. Ibid., 78–79.

14. Edward Bok, *The Americanization of Edward Bok* (1924), 327.

15. James Playsted Wood, *Magazines in the United States* (1949), 104–20.

16. Bok, *The Americanization of Edward Bok,* 327–28.

17. Stickley, *The Craftsman* (May 1907).

18. Kinne and Cooley, *Shelter and Clothing,* 299.

19.Valerie Cummings, *Gloves* (1982), 76.

20. Julius M. Price, *Dame Fashion Paris–London (1786–1912)* (1913), 175.

21. Stickley, "Dress and Its Relation to Life," *The Craftsman* (Nov. 1906): 269–70.

Chapter 7

1. *Home Needlework* 8, no. 2 (April 1906): 159.

Bibliography

Act of Dressmaking. Butterick Publishing Company. 1927.

Adler, Hazel H. *The New Interior, Modern Decoration for the Modern Home*. New York: The Century Company, 1916.

Archer, Effie Archer. *The Library of Work and Play, Needlecraft*. Garden City, New York: Doubleday, Page & Company, 1911.

Art Needlework. Newark: Joseph Doyle & Co.

Audsley, G. A. *Color Harmony in Dress*. New York: Robert M. McBride & Co., 1916.

Bailey, Henry Turner, ed. "Our Wonder World, A Library of Knowledge." *Amateur Handicraft*. Volume 7. 1914. Reprint, Chicago, Boston: Geo. L. Shuman & Co., 1926.

Baker, Walter Davis, and Ida Strawn Baker. *Batik and Other Pattern Dyeing*. Chicago: Atkinson, Mentzer & Company, 1920.

Batchelder, E. A. *Design in Theory and Practice*. New York: The Macmillan Company, 1912.

_____. *The Principles of Design*. Chicago: The Inland Printer Company. 1918.

Baynes, Ken and Kate. "Edwardian Summer." *The Shoe Show*. New York: American Crafts Council, 1979.

The Blue Book Textile Directory of the United States and Canada 1911–1912. New York: Davison Publishing Co., 1911.

Bok, Edward. *The Americanization of Edward Bok*. New York: Charles Scribner's Sons, 1924.

Boris, Eileen. *Art and Labor: Ruskin, Morris, and the Craftsman Ideal*. Philadelphia: Temple University Press, 1986.

Bragg, Jean Moore, ed. *Newcomb College, Arts & Crafts Sales Exhibition*. New Orleans, LA: Jean Moore Bragg, 1998.

Brown, Henry Collins, and Clara Brown Lyman, eds. *Home Building and Decoration*. Garden City, NY: Doubleday, Page & Co., 1912.

Capey, Reco. *The Printing of Textiles*. New York: John Wiley & Sons, 1930.

Catalogue of the loan exhibition of the Ithaca Branch of the New York Society of Decorative Arts, 1879.

Craftsman Fabrics and Needlework. New York: Craftsman Workshops. Reprint, Razmataz Press, 1989.

Cummings, Valerie. "The Growth of Informality, 1900–1980." In *Gloves*. London: Batsford Books, 1982.

De Osma, Guillermo. *Fortuny: The Life and Work of Mariano Fortuny*. New York: Rizzoli, 1994.

Desmond, H. W. *Building a Home, a Book of Fundamental Advice for the Layman about How to Build*. New York: The Baker and Taylor Company, 1908.

de Tocqueville, Alexis. *Democracy in America*. New York: Oxford University Press, 1947.

De Wolfe, Elsie. *The House in Good Taste*. New York: The Century Company, 1914.

Dillaway, Theodore M. *Decoration of the School and Home*. Springfield, MA: Milton Bradley Company, 1916.

Dow, Arthur Wesley. *Composition*. Garden City, NY: Doubleday, Page & Company, 1919.

_____. *Theory and Practice of Teaching Art*. New York: Teachers College, Columbia University, 1912.

Downing, Andrew Jackson. *Victorian Cottage Residences*. 1842. Reprint, New York: Dover Publications, 1981.

Dresser, Christopher. *Principles of Decorative Design*. London, Paris, and New York: Cassell, Petter & Galpin, 1873.

Dunwell, Steve. *The Run of the Mill: A Pictorial Narrative of the Expansion, Dominion, Decline and Enduring Impact of the New England Textile Industry*. Boston: David R. Godine, 1978.

Durant, Stuart. *Ornament*. Woodstock, NY: The Overlook Press, 1986.

Dvorine, Esrael. *Dvorine Color Perception Testing Charts*. Baltimore, MD: Waverly Press, Inc., 1944.

Elder-Duncan, J. H. *The House Beautiful and Useful, Being Practical Suggestions on Furnishing and Decoration*. New York, London, Toronto, and Melbourne: Cassell and Company, Ltd. 1911.

Ellsworth, Evelyn Peters. *Textiles and Costume Design*. San Francisco: Paul Elder and Company, 1917.

Embroideries and Their Stitches. New York: The Butterick Publishing Company, 1905.

Farnsworth, Eva Olney. *The Art and Ethics of Dress: As related to Efficiency and Economy*. San Francisco: Paul Elder & Company, 1915.

Foy, Jessica H., and Karal Ann Marling. *The Arts and the American Home*. Knoxville: University of Tennessee Press, 1994.

French, Lillie Hamilton. *Homes and Their Decoration*. New York: Dodd, Mead, and Company, 1903.

Gibbs, Charlotte M., A.M. *Household Textiles*. Boston: Whitcomb & Barrows, 1914.

Gilman, Charlotte Perkins. *The Home, Its Work and Its Influence*. New York: McClure, Phillips & Co., 1903.

The Good Housekeeping Home Handicraft Book. New York: The Phelps Publishing Co., 1908.

Goodnow, Ruby Ross. *The Honest House*. New York: The Century Company, 1914; reprinted 1921.

Gordon, Beverly. *Domestic American Textiles: A Bibliographic Sourcebook*. Pennsylvania: Center for the History of American Needlework, 1979.

_____. "Spinning Wheels, Samplers, and the Modern Priscilla: The Images and Paradoxes of Colonial Revival Needlework." *Winterthur Portfolio* 33, nos. 2/3 (summer/autumn 1998).

Green, Nancy E., and Jessie Poesch. *Arthur Wesley Dow and American Arts & Crafts*. New York: The American Federation of Arts, 1999.

Hall, Eliza Calvert. *A Book of Hand Woven Coverlets*. Boston: Little, Brown & Company, 1912.

Harrison, Constance C. *Woman's Handiwork in Modern Homes*. Charles Scribner's Sons, 1881.

Hulme, Edward. *Plant-Works—Their Natural Growth and Ornamental Treatment*. 1874.

Hunter, George Leland. *Home Furnishing.* New York: John Lane Company, 1913.

Imami-Paydar, Niloo. "Marie Webster: A Retrospective." In *American Quilt Renaissance: Three Women Who Influenced Quiltmaking in the Early Twentieth Century.* Tokyo: Kokusai Art, 1997.

Izor, Estelle Peel. *Costume Design and Home Planning.* New York, Chicago, Dallas: Mentzer, Bush and Company, 1916.

Jessup, Anne L. *The Sewing Book.* New York: The Butterick Publishing Company, 1913.

Jordan, James. *Southern Arts and Crafts.* Charlotte, NC: Mint Museum of Art, 1996.

Kaplan, Wendy. *"The Art That is Life": The Arts and Crafts Movement in America, 1875–1920.* Boston: Museum of Fine Arts, Boston, 1987.

Kardon, Janet. *The Ideal Home: The History of Twentieth-Century American Craft, 1900–1920.* New York: Abrams in association with the American Craft Museum, 1994.

Keeler, Charles. *The Simple Home.* Reprint, Santa Barbara, CA: Peregrine Smith, Inc., 1979.

Kelley, Charles Fabens, and William Luther Mowll. *A Text-Book of Design.* Boston: Houghton Mifflin Company, 1912.

Kellogg, Alice M. *Home Furnishing, Practical and Artistic.* New York: Frederick A. Stokes Company, 1905.

Kettell, Edith Merrill. "Crafts in Public Schools" In *Applied Arts Book I,* 1902.

Kinne, Helen, and Anna Cooley. *Shelter and Clothing.* New York: The Macmillan Company, 1916.

Kurella, Elizabeth. *The Complete Guide to Vintage Textiles.* Wisconsin: Krause Publications, 1999.

Lasdun, Susan. *Victorians at Home.* London: Weidenfeld & Nicholson, 1981.

Lawrence, Maude, and Caroline Sheldon. *The Use of the Plant in Decorative Design for High Schools.* Teacher's Edition. New York: Scott, Foresman and Company, 1912.

_____. *The Use of The Plant in Decorative Design for the Grades.* Teacher's Edition. New York: Scott, Foresman and Company, 1912.

Leland, Charles G. *Drawing and Designing.* Chicago & New York: Rand McNally & Co., 1889.

Lemos, Pedro J. *Applied Art.* Mountain View, CA: Pacific Press Publishing Association, 1920.

Lewis, Gertrude C. *First Lessons in Batik.* Chicago: The Prang Company, 1921.

Lynes, Russell. *The Tastemakers.* New York: Harper & Brothers, 1954.

MacArthur, Burke. *United Littles: The Story of the Needlework Guild of America.* New York: Van Rees Press, 1955.

MacIntosh, Eileen. *Sewing and Collecting Vintage Fashions.* Philadelphia and New York: Chilton Book Co., 1988.

McPherson, Tommy, and Beth Ann McPherson. *Arthur Wesley Dow and His Influence upon the Arts and Crafts Movement in America.* Berkeley, CA: The Arts and Crafts Press, 1999.

Mendes, Valerie D. "Women's Dress Since 1900." In Natalie Rothstein. *Four Hundred Years of Fashion.* London: Victoria and Albert Museum, 1996.

Meyer, Marilee Boyd, ed. *Inspiring Reform: Boston's Arts and Crafts Movement.* Wellesley, MA: Davis Museum and Cultural Center, in association with Harry N. Abrams, Inc., 1997.

Midgely, W., and A. E. V. Lilley. *A Book of Studies in Plant Form with Some Suggestions for Their Application to Design.* New York: Chas. Scribner's and Sons, 1910.

Mijer, Pieter. *Batiks and How to Make Them.* New York: Dodd, Mead and Company, 1921.

Montague, Ken. "The Aesthetics of Hygiene: Aesthetic Dress, Modernity, and the Body as Sign." *Journal of Design History* 7, no. 2 (1994).

Montgomery, Florence. *Textiles in America 1650–1870.* New York: W. W. Norton & Co., 1991.

Morris, May. *Decorative Needlework.* London: Joseph Hughes & Co., 1893.

Ormond, Suzanne, and Mary E. Irvine. *Louisiana's Art Nouveau: The Crafts of the Newcomb Style.* Gretna, LA: Pelican Publishing Group, 1976.

"Painting and Interior Decoration, History of Architecture." *I.C.S. Reference Library.* London: International Textbook Company, 1909.

Parry, Linda. *Textiles of the Arts and Crafts Movement.* New York: Thames and Hudson, 1988.

_____. *William Morris and the Arts and Crafts Movement.* New York: Portland House, 1989.

Parsons, B. S., Frank Alvah. *Interior Decoration: Its Principles and Practice.* Garden City, NY: Doubleday, Page & Company, 1916.

Pellew, Charles E. *Dyes and Dyeing.* New York: Robert M. McBride & Company, 1918.

Perry, Rosalind Webster, and Marty Frolli. *A Joy Forever: Marie Webster's Quilt Patterns.* Santa Barbara, CA: Practical Patchwork, 1992.

Picken, Mary Brooks. *Embroidery Stitches, Parts 1 and 2.* Scranton, PA: Women's Institute of Domestic Arts & Sciences 1921.

"Plant Analysis." In *I.C.S. Reference Library.* London: International Textbook Company, 1905.

Poesch, Jesse. *Newcomb Pottery.* Exton, PA: Schiffer Publishing Limited, 1984.

Price, Julius M. *Dame Fashion Paris–London (1786–1912).* New York: Charles Scribner's Sons, 1913.

Priestman, Mabel Tuke. *Art and Economy in Home Decoration.* New York: John Lane & Company, 1908.

_____. *Artistic Homes.* Chicago: A. C. McClurg & Co., 1910.

_____. *Handicrafts in the Home.* Chicago: A. C. McClurg & Co., 1910.

Reed, Cleota. "Gustav Stickley and Irene Sargent: United Crafts and *The Craftsman.*" *Syracuse University Library Associates Courier* 20 (1995).

Rhead, G. Woolliscroft. *Modern Practical Design*. London: B. T. Batsford, 1912.

The Room Beautiful. New York: Clifford & Lawton, 1915.

Rothstein, Natalie. *Four Hundred Years of Fashion*. London: Victoria & Albert Museum, 1996.

Ross, Denman Waldo, Ph.D. *A Theory of Pure Design, Harmony, Balance and Rhythm*. Boston and New York: Houghton Mifflin Company, 1907.

_____. *On Drawing and Painting*. Boston and New York: Houghton Mifflin Company, 1912.

Saylor, Henry H. *Bungalows*. New York: McBride, Winston & Company, 1911.

_____, ed. *Distinctive Homes of Moderate Cost*. Philadelphia: The John C. Winston Company, 1911.

Schoeser, Mary, and Celia Rufey. *English and American Textiles from 1790 to the Present*. New York: Thames and Hudson, 1989.

Seegmiller, Wilhelmina. *Primary Hand Work*. Boston: Atkinson, Mentzer & Grover, 1906.

Sell, Maud Ann, and Henry Blackman Sell. *Good Taste in Home Furnishing*. New York: John Lane Company, 1915.

The Sherwin-Williams Company Decorative Department. *Your Home and its Decoration*. New York, 1910.

Shilliam, Nicola J. "Boston and the Society of Arts & Crafts: Textiles." In Marilee Boyd Meyer, ed. *Inspiring Reform: Boston's Arts and Crafts Movement*. Wellesley, MA: Davis Museum and Cultural Center, in association with Harry N. Abrams, Inc., 1997.

_____. "From Bohemian to Bourgeois: American Batik in the Early Twentieth Century." In *Contact, Crossover, Continuity: Proceedings of the Fourth Biennial Symposium of the Textile Society of America, Inc.* Los Angeles: The Textile Society of America, Inc., 1994.

Shook, Anna Nott. *The Book of Weaving*. New York: The John Day Company, 1928.

Smith, Emory E. *The Golden Poppy*. San Francisco: The Murdock Press, 1901.

Sparrow, W. Shaw. *Hints on House Furnishing*. New York: John Lane Company, 1909.

Stevens, G. R. *The Belding-Corticelli Story*. Toronto: Belding-Corticelli Limited, 1951.

Stickley, Gustav. Business Papers. The Winterthur Library, Joseph Downs Collection of Manuscripts and Printed Ephemera.

_____. *Catalog of Craftsman Furniture*. New York: The Craftsman Publishing Company, 1910.

_____. *Chips from the Craftsman Workshops*. New York: The Craftsman Publishing Company, n.d.

_____. *Craftsman Homes*. New York: The Craftsman Publishing Company, 1909.

Todd, Mattie Phipps. *Hand-Loom Weaving*. New York: Rand McNally & Company, 1914.

Trapp, Kenneth R. *The Arts and Crafts Movement in California: Living the Good Life*. New York: Abbeville, 1993.

U.S. Department of Agriculture, Leaflets and Bulletins. "Removing Stains from Fabrics." Verdaa McLendon. June 1959.

Vanderpoel, Emily Noyes. *Color Problems*. New York: Longmans, Green & Co., 1903.

Vollmer, William A., ed. *A Book of Distinctive Interiors*. New York: McBride, Nast & Company, 1912.

Wallace, Ann. *Arts and Crafts Textiles*. Salt Lake City: Gibbs Smith, 1999.

Wallick, Ekin. *The Attractive Home*. Boston: The Carpenter-Morton Co., 1916.

_____. *Inexpensive Furnishings in Good Taste*. New York: Hearst's International Library Co., 1915.

Warner, Charles F., Sc.D., Prof. *Work and Play Books: Home Decoration*. Garden City, NY: Doubleday, Page & Company, 1911.

Waugh, Norah. *The Cut of Women's Clothes*. New York: Theatre Art Books, 1968.

Webster, Marie D. *Quilts: Their Story and How to Make Them*. New York: Doubleday, 1915; reprint, Santa Barbara, CA: Practical Patchwork, 1990 (includes biography of the author by Rosalind Webster Perry).

Wharton, Edith. *The Decoration of Houses*. New York: Charles Scribner's and Sons, 1897.

Wheeler, Candace. *The Development of Embroidery in America*. New York: Harper, 1921.

_____. *Household Art*. New York: Harper & Brothers Publishers, 1893.

_____. *Principles of Home Decoration*. New York: Doubleday, Page, & Company, 1903.

Whiting, Frederic Allen. "Deerfield, Summer, 1908." Whiting Papers, Archives of American Art, Washington, D.C.

Wilcox, R. Turner. *The Mode in Costume*. New York: Charles Scribner's Sons, 1958.

Wood, James Playsted. *Magazines in the United States*. New York: The Ronald Press Company, 1949.

Woolman, Mary Schenck, and Ellen Beers McGowan. *Textiles*. New York: The Macmillan Company, 1913.

Wright, Gwendolyn. *Moralism and the Model Home: Domestic Architecture and Cultural Conflict in Chicago, 1873–1913*. Chicago: University of Chicago Press, 1980.

Wright, Richardson, ed. *Inside the House of Good Taste*. New York: McBride, Nast & Co., 1915; reprinted 1918.

Periodicals

The following periodicals contain a number of articles of interest on American Arts and Crafts textiles, many of which are listed in the endnotes for the various chapters.

Annual Report of the Society of Arts & Crafts (1910)

Index

The Craftsman
The Delineator
The Embroidery Catalog, Pictorial Review
Good Housekeeping
Harper's Bazaar
Home Needlework Magazine
House & Garden
The House Beautiful
Interior Decoration
International Studio
The Ladies' Home Journal
The Modern Priscilla
The Queen
The School Arts Book
School Arts Magazine
Women's Home Companion

Catalogues and Other Company Literature

Belding Brothers & Company
Brainerd & Armstrong Co.
Brenlin Window Shades
Carlson Currier Company
Cheney Brothers
Colonial Drapery Fabrics
Joseph Doyle & Co.
Liberty's
Marshall Field & Co.
Orchard & Wilhelm Carpet Co.
Richardson Silk Company
Sherwin-Williams Company
Valley Supply Company
H. E. Verran Company

Page numbers in *italics* refer to picture captions.

Photograph Credits

Craftsman Farms Foundation: 98
Peter Frahm: 14, 16, 51, 52, 62, 63, 65 top, 71, 74, 75, 134, 137, 140, 145, 146, 149, 166, 167, 170, 190 bottom
Timothy Hansen: 11, 17, 31, 32, 34, 37, 38, 39, 40, 41, 42, 43, 44, 45, 46, 47, 48, 49, 50, 54, 55, 56, 57, 58, 60, 65 bottom, 68, 77, 81, 82, 83, 84, 85, 86, 88, 89, 90, 93, 94, 96, 104, 106, 107, 108, 110, 114, 115, 116, 117, 120, 122, 123, 124, 125, 126, 128, 133, 135, 139, 142, 143, 153, 154, 155, 156, 157, 158, 159, 160, 161, 163, 164, 168, 171, 172, 173, 174, 175, 177, 178, 179, 181, 185, 186, 187, 188, 189, 190 top left, 190 right, 191, 192, 193, 194, 195, 196, 198, 199, 200, 201, 202, 203, 204, 206, 208, 210, 211, 213, 214, 215, 216, 218, 219, 220, 222, 224, 226, 229, 234, 235, 236, 237
Erika Marin: 9, 78, 131, 180
Stephen Petegorsky: 18
Linda Svendsen: 73, 100, 102, 103, 111, 112, 118, 121, 127, 129, 232

Acknowledgments

The authors are privileged to have worked on this project together. For years, we have gathered all of the bits and pieces of information that each of us had tucked away for so long, and translated many years of friendships, research, and collecting into a survey of a topic that is dear to each of us. The authors have been particularly blessed to develop long-standing friendships and relationships with numerous collectors, dealers, and curators, without whom this book would not be possible. This book is the product of a community's interest in the topic; our friends and colleagues have generously provided dozens of turn-of-the-century magazines, catalogues, images, textiles, and artifacts for our study.

Numerous curators have shared their advice, expertise, museum photo collections, and enthusiasm with the authors. Richard Knotts of the Riordan Mansion State Park and Michael Freisinger, Museum Curator, Arizona State Parks, provided invaluable time and assistance to the authors and made the Riordan Mansion available for study and for photographs. Stephanie Gaskins, President of the Ipswich Historical Society, shared her time and arranged for several photographs of weaving, lace, and hooked rugs related to the Arts and Crafts movement in Ipswich. Suzanne Flynt, Curator of the Potumcuck Valley Memorial Association, provided invaluable insights regarding Deerfield Industries, and the authors are looking forward to the fruits of her research in ensuing years. Rita C. Pittman has done an enormous amount of research on Newcomb College textiles and we thank her for her help. Research on Marie Webster was facilitated by Niloo Paydar, Curator of Textiles, Indianapolis Museum of Fine Art, who provided access to their extensive collection; Rosalind Webster Perry; and Madonna Fowler of the Quilters Hall of Fame, Marie Webster House, Marion, Indiana.

Donald P. Hallmark, Director of Frank Lloyd Wright's Dana-Thomas House in Springfield, Illinois; Suzanne Baizerman, Imogene Gieling Curator of Crafts and Decorative Arts, Oakland Museum of California Art Department; Corina Corusi, Director, Glessner Mansion; Tammie Bennett, Registrar, San Diego Historical Society; Marianne Curling, former Curator, The Mark Twain House; and Dave Tomsky, Director of Public Relations at the Grove Park Inn, all assisted in providing images for the project.

Private collectors and friends who have shared their homes, collections, ideas, and enthusiasm with the authors include Ann and Andre Chaves, Phil Chun, Brian Coleman, Frank Ferguson, Tim Gleason, Stephen Gray, Robert Kaplan, Craig Kuhns, Caro MacPherson, Jim Messineo, Wanda and Richard Pettler, Paul Freeman, Jim Marrin, Don and Paula Nord, Bruce Smith and Yoshiko Yamamoto, MaryAnn and Steve Voorhees, Chris Walther, Allen Thomsen, and Mike Witt.

Our special thanks goes to Crab Tree Farm. The collections and interiors at Crab Tree Farm have provided the authors with both inspiration and information and can be seen throughout the book. We are grateful to Jo Hormuth and Dru Muskovin for their support throughout this project.

No art publication can succeed without spectacular photography. Many of the textiles could not have been successfully shared with you without the talent of photographers Tim Hansen, Linda Svendsen, Erika Marrin, Kate Cameron, and Peter Frahm.

We would especially like to thank our editor, Elisa Urbanelli, for her enthusiastic and never-ending support for this project; and Abrams for deciding to publish our book on this relatively unexplored and timely topic. ❖